T0301521

LIMITS TO STAKEHOLDER INFLUENCE

Limits to Stakeholder Influence

Why the Business Case Won't Save the World

Michael L. Barnett

*Rutgers Business School – Newark & New Brunswick,
Rutgers University, USA*

 Edward Elgar
PUBLISHING

Cheltenham, UK • Northampton, MA, USA

Published by
Edward Elgar Publishing Limited
The Lypiatts
15 Lansdown Road
Cheltenham
Glos GL50 2JA
UK

Edward Elgar Publishing, Inc.
William Pratt House
9 Dewey Court
Northampton
Massachusetts 01060
USA

A catalogue record for this book
is available from the British Library

Library of Congress Control Number: 2018958447

This book is available electronically in the **Elgar**online
Business subject collection
DOI 10.4337/9781788970693

ISBN 978 1 78897 068 6 (cased)
ISBN 978 1 78897 069 3 (eBook)

Contents

Acknowledgements

The editor and publishers wish to thank the authors and the following publishers who have kindly given permission for the use of copyright material.

Academy of Management for articles: Michael L. Barnett, 'Stakeholder Influence Capacity and the Variability of Financial Returns to Corporate Social Responsibility', *Academy of Management Review*, **32** (3), 2007, 794–816; Michael L. Barnett and Andrew A. King, 'Good Fences Make Good Neighbors: A Longitudinal Analysis of an Industry Self-Regulatory Institution', *Academy of Management Journal*, **51** (6), 2008, 1150–70.

Board of Trustees of the Leland Stanford Jr. University, with permission of Stanford University Press, for excerpt: Andrew A. King, Michael J. Lenox and Michael L. Barnett, 'Strategic Responses to the Reputation Commons Problem', in Andrew J. Hoffman and Marc J. Ventresca (eds), *Organizations, Policy, and the Natural Environment: Institutional and Strategic Perspectives*, Chapter 17, 2002, 393–406.

John Wiley & Sons for articles: Michael L. Barnett and Robert M. Salomon, 'Beyond Dichotomy: The Curvilinear Relationship between Social Responsibility and Financial Performance', *Strategic Management Journal*, **27** (11), 2006, 1101–22; Michael L. Barnett, 'Finding a Working Balance Between Competitive and Communal Strategies', *Journal of Management Studies*, **43** (8), 2006, 1753–73; Michael L. Barnett and Robert M. Salomon, 'Does it Pay to be *Really* Good? Addressing the Shape of the Relationship between Social and Financial Performance', *Strategic Management Journal*, **33**, 2012, 1304–20.

SAGE Publications for articles: Charles J. Fombrun, Naomi A. Gardberg and Michael L. Barnett, 'Opportunity Platforms and Safety Nets: Corporate Citizenship and Reputational Risk', *Business and Society Review*, **105** (1), 2000, 85–106; Michael L. Barnett, 'One Voice, But Whose Voice? Exploring What Drives Trade Association Activity', *Business & Society*, **52** (2), 2013, 213–44; Michael L. Barnett, 'Why Stakeholders Ignore Firm Misconduct: A Cognitive View', *Journal of Management*, **40** (3), 2014, 676–702; Michael L. Barnett and Sohvi Leih, 'Sorry to (Not) Burst Your Bubble: The Influence of Reputation Rankings on Perceptions of Firms', *Business & Society*, **57** (5), 2018, 962–78 (first published 2016, pp. 1–17); Michael L. Barnett, 'The Business Case for Corporate Social Responsibility: A Critique and an Indirect Path Forward', *Business & Society*, 2019 (first published 2016, pp. 1–24).

Every effort has been made to trace all the copyright holders but if any have been inadvertently overlooked the publishers will be pleased to make the necessary arrangement at the first opportunity.

[1]

The business case is a basket case: an introduction

Oh, I hear you: 'Barnett, what are you trying to pull here? Isn't this just a collection of reprints?' Sure, the bulk of the book consists of reprints. But if you'll allow me to explain, there's much more to it than that. And besides, there's merit in reprints.

In this book, I put forth a critical view of the business case for corporate social responsibility. Management scholars have claimed for decades that firms can 'do well by doing good' and firms have backed this claim. Unlike most things academic, the idea has caught fire beyond the ivory tower. Today it's hard to even imagine a firm declaring that society is none of its business. You don't tend to hear a CEO saying, 'Yes, we harpoon some whales and kick a puppy or two along the way, but come on, we have to make a buck somehow!' Firms instead spend their limited resources engaging in various good deeds and broadcasting how doing so benefits both society and their firms. For example, Target donates five percent of its profits to communities and proclaims prominently on its corporate website: 'We believe diversity and inclusivity make teams and Target better. And we'll live that belief as champions of a more inclusive society by creating a diverse and inclusive work environment, cultivating an inclusive guest experience, and fostering equality in society.'

That said, revealed corporate behaviors all too often fall short of the rhetoric of widespread corporate social responsibility. With the same ease that I can find a press release or annual report from just about any firm declaring that it is a paragon of social virtue, I can also uncover not just assertions but settlements and convictions for irresponsible and often illegal corporate behaviors that harm society. Look, whales really are being harpooned and puppies really are getting kicked in the pursuit of profit. Just watch a few Greenpeace or ASPCA videos (on an empty stomach). We people and our planet also suffer at the hands of ongoing corporate irresponsibility and misconduct, from bribery and bid rigging, to catastrophic climate change.

Despite decades of academic and practitioner support for the assertion that firms do best by bettering society, firms still do many bad things that cause substantial harm to society. Yet these misdeeds may have few consequences for the offending firms; in fact, firms that do bad things can still prosper. Chevron, De Beers, Exxon, Nestlé, Pfizer, and Volkswagen are a few amongst a too-long list of highly profitable firms that paid fines and settlements related to some truly horrible actions. Also troubling for the business case, firms that do good things may see little or no reward for their efforts; even the most socially responsible of firms remains vulnerable to bankruptcy.

Clearly the relationship between doing good and doing well is imperfect. My aim in this book is to shine a light on these imperfections, argue that they exist because there are limits to stakeholder influence, and offer insights on what to do in light of these limits if we really want business to be more responsible to and for society. How lucky is it, then, that I've been publishing studies in myriad academic journals on precisely this topic since the dawn of this millennium! To write a book that takes a critical view of the business case for corporate social responsibility, it is necessary to draw from these previously published studies. How best to do so? I suppose I could gently paraphrase my prior work until the cows come home (say, 5pm? When exactly do the cows get back to their places of residence?). But rather than test the boundaries of plagiarism, why not offer up the original source material? Unwisely sticking with the farm theme, why not get the details straight from the horse's mouth? Sure, some suggest that academic studies are to be found at the other end of the horse, but without question each article reprinted herein is an in-depth, (painfully) peer-reviewed, stand-alone case for some aspect of the argument I seek to make in this book. Why rephrase or relitigate each point when I can instead reproduce them?

If you're reading this, you probably have already seen or could easily gain access to most of the articles reprinted here. I'm saving you some hassle in that case. Here they are, all curated and cozy, in one place. But many haven't previously seen these articles and don't have ready access. Of more value, though, is that the articles in this book are organized and integrated to build a cohesive argument, rather than presented as independent pieces for readers to patch together on their own. In the remainder of this opening chapter, I will outline the overall argument and explain how each included reprint advances it.

This book also contains a concluding chapter filled with new material that makes a case for where we should go from here as scholars, practitioners, and society. That's right, this book is far more than old wine in a shiny new bottle, my dear reader! Though transparently self-serving to say so, I see this not as a book of reprints but as an original book with bonus supporting material. That makes it a bargain, even before I mention just how many ever-sharp Ginsu knives I'm willing to throw in to convince you to buy a copy or two today. Act now!

Clarifying the case
With the hard sell out of the way, let's get down to business on what this criticism of the business case is all about. The bottom line is that because the corporate bottom line is not firmly connected to corporate behavior, the business case does not motivate firms to consistently behave in socially responsible ways. And that's a shame, because the business case offers such an easy, win–win path to widespread corporate social responsibility; one in which there's no need for heavy-handed formal regulation. The argument is that if we just let the market have at it, firms will become more socially responsible as they doggedly pursue their own self-interest. After all, if they don't make nice, they know that they will suffer in the marketplace. Logically then, they will behave well. You may be familiar with Warren Buffett's famous quote: 'It takes 20 years to build a reputation and five minutes to ruin it. If you think about that, you'll do things differently.' Buffett has been one of the richest men in the world for more than 20 years based on investing in firms according to such logic, so this would seem to be sage business advice.

But how does the market actually enforce its discipline on firms? How is a firm's behavior linked to its financial performance? This is where stakeholders enter the picture. The market is not some soulless, shapeless monolith. It is composed of myriad sapient beings – stakeholders – who, by giving and rescinding their support, alter the standing of these firms. If a firm opens a daycare facility to ease the burden on working parents, it may be rewarded with increased loyalty from its current employees and improved recruitment yield from potential new employees. If a firm releases toxic pollutants into a stream, it may be punished by members of its community who block licenses for new facilities and by activists through protests and boycotts. The reputation and market value of the firm changes in accordance with changes in the favorability of the relationships the firm has with these and other stakeholders. I compare it to alchemy, a process by which a substance like lead magically transforms into gold. The stakeholder is the alchemical agent required for a firm's good acts to transform into something valuable to the firm; likewise, when a firm does something bad, it takes a stakeholder reaction to cause the firm to feel the pain of it.

Recognizing the role of stakeholders as the agents that make the business case work is an essential step forward. The next essential step is recognizing that stakeholders are fallible. Most of the time most stakeholders have no idea what is going on at most firms. Even were firms completely transparent, keeping track of everything exceeds anyone's bandwidth. Quick: what's going on right now at Walmart? K-mart? Motomart? Because stakeholders are fallible, the alchemical reaction required to turn corporate good into gold does not always complete; sometimes it fizzles or is inert, and sometimes it backfires. But when, and to what degree? That's what we are here to sort out. It cannot *always* pay to be good. If it did, then corporate social responsibility would be a money machine that enables enlightened firms to transform as much goodness as they can muster into as much profit as they can haul away. Money machines, like unicorns, Sasquatch, and ample on-campus parking, are of course mythical. To remain in the restrained realm of reality, where corns are multi, feet are mini, and parking spaces are scarce, we must explain how the process of transforming corporate good into gold really works, and clarify how it sometimes fails to work. Onward to the next section to see how these tasks are tackled in this book.

Building and bounding the case
Each of the reprints in this book sheds light on the mechanisms and limits of the business case. The reprints are organized into three sections. The first section introduces the business case by developing a conceptual model to explain how it pays to be good, then empirically demonstrates that financial returns indeed do accrue to good behavior. However, as first outlined in theory and then empirically validated, these returns vary based on a firm's history of responsibility, creating a curvilinear relationship between social and financial performance. The second section shifts analysis up a level to explain variation in the social performance of industries. A firm's performance, social and otherwise, is perceived relative to its peers. This interdependence can give rise to shared problems that require rival firms to work together, commonly through trade associations, though trade associations face difficulty in balancing the individual and shared interests of their member firms. The third section then turns to the implications of the dynamics discussed in the prior sections, arguing that stakeholders are often inattentive to firm behavior and rely on shortcuts to cope with their limited abilities, which only enlarges the void between how firms behave and how they are perceived, thereby bounding the business case.

The arc of the business case
In a special issue of *Business and Society Review* published in 2000, Charles Fombrun, Naomi Gardberg, and I (Chapter 2 in this volume) rang in the new millennium by explaining why firms spend their limited resources on 'doing good.' The question itself was far from novel even back then, but our take on it was new. We focused on the ways in which CSR (though corporate citizenship is the term we used) affects corporate reputation, rather than the common practice of looking at how it directly affects financial measures of 'doing well' such as stock

market valuation and annual accounting returns. Our contention, an underlying theme that I will return to in the final reprint included in this book, was that social performance affects financial performance indirectly, via its effects on reputational capital.

Reputational capital is built by engaging in CSR and functions as a 'safety net' that buffers firms from reputational losses in times of crisis. Firms with good CSR practices get the benefit of the doubt from their stakeholders and so tend to suffer smaller losses and have quicker recoveries when things go wrong, relative to firms that have not accrued reputational capital. The reputational capital built through CSR also serves as an 'opportunity platform' on which myriad profitable opportunities may be built. Applying a novel real options perspective to CSR, we explained how the supportive stakeholder relationships associated with reputational capital create growth options that allow 'good' firms favorable access to future opportunities, whereas firms without such accrued goodwill lack the option to strike these deals.

This paper added depth to the established model of how doing good relates to doing well by addressing the intervening process and noting the bi-directional benefits of CSR. Moreover, it enriched understanding of variation in stakeholder action. The literature had tended to treat stakeholders as a monolith, but different stakeholders reward and punish firms in different ways. In this paper, we addressed the varying promises and threats to the firm from its relationships with investors, employees, partners, customers, regulators, communities, media, and activists. For example, employees offer the promise of commitment but the threat of rogue behaviour, while the media offer the promise of favorable coverage alongside the threat of exposure.

Our argument 'that corporate citizenship is a strategic tool that companies can use to manage reputational risk from stakeholder groups' caught on in academia, as indicated by this paper's high citation count. It has also been used to underpin consultant and media reports that argue, in broad strokes, for the value of CSR. However, a paper that I co-authored with Rob Salomon and published in *Strategic Management Journal* in 2006 (Chapter 3 in this volume) has probably had more influence on one specific aspect of the business case, that of socially responsible investing (SRI). SRI entails making investment choices on the basis of social performance. In the early 2000s, there were about 160 mutual funds and about a trillion dollars of total assets being managed on the basis of SRI. Those figures have grown massively since. Examples of SRI funds include Eventide Gilead, which is a Christian-based fund that avoids businesses that profit from abortion in any way, and the Vanguard FTSE Social Index, which excludes firms that are involved in alcohol, tobacco, pornography, military sales, and nuclear power, as well as those that do not have at least one woman on the board of directors, do not have an equal opportunity policy in place, have been subject to human rights violations, or have negative environmental impact.

While doctoral students, Rob and I teamed up to write a short book on the idiocy of SRI for an upstart publisher that a senior faculty member had vouched for. The publisher didn't survive long enough to allow us to complete our short book (and the senior faculty member retired soon after), but we didn't want our work to go to waste, so we analysed the data we had gathered and found a surprising result. Consistent with many SRI critics that had dismissed SRI funds as a dumb idea because limiting investment choices restricts earnings potential, we expected to find that SRI funds financially underperform non-SRI funds. And we did find this. But we also found that SRI funds outperformed non-SRI funds. That is, we found support for both opposing positions. Huh?

   Finance and accounting scholars had long been comparing the financial performance of SRI funds to non-SRI funds and finding mixed results. There is a great deal of variation in the screening intensity of SRI funds, though, and this variation was largely being ignored. Some SRI funds screen out a great many potential investments on the basis of their social performance, while others have much more porous screening criteria, so much so that their holdings resemble non-SRI funds. We reasoned that previous studies had found mixed results because they had muddled this range of screening intensity. When we accounted for screening intensity, we found a curvilinear relationship: those firms that screened the least and those that screened the most had the best financial performance, while those that screened a moderate amount were 'stuck in the middle,' earning the lowest financial returns.

   Our findings suggested that it pays to be good, but also recognized that there are costs to being good; an important factor often overlooked in management scholarship on CSR. More intensely screening investments according to social performance criteria means ruling out more and more firms, industries, and sectors. As investment choices become more limited, a fund's ability to fully diversify becomes more constrained, causing it to bear unsystematic risk and thereby harming its risk-adjusted returns. This is why accounting and finance critics of SRI find it an inherently flawed approach to investing. However, while intense screening forces a smaller investment choice set, it may leave fund managers with a richer set of firms from which to make their investment choices. Screening more intensely can help SRI funds to eliminate risk-prone firms from their portfolios, thereby yielding a stronger and more stable set of stocks that earn higher risk-adjusted returns. Those funds that screen only moderately suffer the costs of loss of diversification but don't fully achieve the benefits of intense screening.

   Our study was at the portfolio level and so did not directly address the firm-level relationship between social and financial performance, though. To dig directly into firm-level dynamics, in 2007 I published a paper in *Academy of Management Review* (Chapter 4 in this volume) that developed the concept of stakeholder influence capacity (SIC). Think of SIC like this: someone who has always been a jerk to you for as long as you've known them is now walking up to you, smiling, saying flattering things, and handing you a fragrant bouquet of beautiful flowers and a huge box of fine chocolates. What's your reaction? You're probably skeptical, since it's out of character. Though they've gone to all this trouble, they are unlikely to gain your favor. In fact, you may suspect they're up to no good, so it could backfire.

   It's like this with firms, too. Stakeholders view CSR through the prism of history. Without a history of relevant CSR, a sudden good act, no matter how nice, is likely to be viewed with a healthy dose of skepticism by stakeholders. In contrast, a firm with a history of good deeds has the capacity to favorably influence its stakeholders with a similar act. Imagine that McDonald's has made a sizeable contribution to the American Heart Association, a non-profit organization that fights heart disease. Would you interpret this differently than Subway's equivalent contribution to the same organization? What if Fatburger or The Heart Attack Grill took on this same charitable cause? Because history matters to how acts of CSR are interpreted, even the same firm can provoke different stakeholder responses to the same act at different points in time. Imagine the difference in reactions if Union Carbide had donated $10 million to a hospital in Bhopal, India, prior to its deadly poison gas leak that killed thousands there in 1984, versus after.

Developing the concept of SIC and clarifying how it influences returns to CSR helped to push the literature past its decades-long quest to prove that it either does or does not pay to be good. Different firms receive different returns from different acts of CSR because they have different histories. Rather than continuing to battle, with increasingly complex data sets and methods, over whether or not it universally pays to be good, the conversation could instead shift to sorting out the contingencies that determine whether or not a specific act of CSR pays for a given firm at a particular point in time.

In a paper published in *Strategic Management Journal* in 2012 (Chapter 5 in this volume), Rob Salomon and I teamed up again (now as faculty members!), this time to empirically validate that a firm's history affects the degree to which it profits from CSR. We again compared contrasting perspectives on the relationship between social and financial performance and determined the net result by accounting for both the costs and benefits of CSR. However, this time we focused directly on firms, not funds. To become more and more socially responsible, a firm must allocate more and more of its limited resources toward CSR. Whether it be philanthropy, pollution abatement, employee benefits, community volunteering, or some other good act, doing more of it requires more resources, to include time, attention, and money. If CSR were costless, then there would be no need to debate its business merits. But it is costly, so as a firm engages in more CSR, its costs necessarily rise and, all else equal, its financial performance must decline.

Of course, all else is never equal. As a firm engages in more CSR, it improves its stakeholder relationships, which helps the firm to garner resources on more favorable terms, as well as safeguard its downside risk. What is the net result of these two opposing forces on the bottom line? Do the benefits fully negate the costs and thereby net insignificant or neutral returns from CSR? Or do the costs from CSR exceed accrued benefits, or vice versa? If SIC functions as previously advertised, then the net result should be … drumroll please … a curvilinear relationship. And indeed, that is what we found.

Those firms with a weak history of being good get little back from any CSR investments they might make because they lack SIC. For each dollar they invest in CSR, they should expect to lose nearly all of it because their good acts are not credible. More CSR thus means more losses for those firms with little SIC. This creates the downward portion of a U-shaped curve. However, as they continue to engage in acts of CSR, firms accrue SIC, so the amount they lose on each invested dollar declines, causing the U-shape to bottom out. Eventually, with enough of a record of ongoing CSR investment, the firm gains SIC ample to profit from further CSR. Thereafter, a dollar invested in CSR returns not a loss but a gain. More CSR thus means more profit, creating the upward-sloping side of the U-shape. In sum, it pays to be good, but only if you're good enough. If you aren't going to be *really* good, then staying relatively bad is more likely to maximize your financial returns because it limits the costs associated with engaging in CSR. What doesn't pay is to be a 'sorta nice guy' who suffers much of the cost of being nice yet does not go far enough to gain the offsetting benefits of being distinguished as a nice guy.

Overall, these four studies portray the business case as a moderated process with stakeholders at the center. Stakeholders determine which acts of CSR are rewarded, as well as which acts of irresponsibility are punished, and they are swayed in their assessments by firm history, which helps to explain variation in returns to CSR. However, firm history is not the only contingency to consider when mapping the contours of the business case. A stakeholder's perception of a particular firm at a particular point in time is shaped by the behaviors of similar other firms. For example, though you may know little about the activities of DTE Energy Company, you may be very familiar with activities at other firms in its industry such as those at Three Mile Island, Chernobyl, and Fukishima, and on that basis form a view of DTE. Stakeholders view a firm through the prism of not just its own history, but also that of its industry. I next shift the discussion to the industry level to view the business case from this vantage point.

Industry matters
Also around the turn of the millennium, I began working with Andy King and Mike Lenox, who were on the faculty at NYU at the time. Funded in part by an Environmental Protection Agency grant, their Business & Environment at Stern (BES) research group sought to explain how industry self-regulation (ISR) affects corporate environmental performance. I brought my expertise in corporate reputation to bear on this issue and together, as spelled out in the chapter we published in 2002 in the edited book, *Organizations, Policy, and the Natural Environment* (Chapter 6 in this volume), we developed strategic solutions to 'reputation commons problems' (RCP).

A commons is a shared space. As most anyone who has used a public bathroom can attest, a commons can be problematic to maintain. Economic logic dictates that overuse will occur, causing the commons to collapse unless some centralized authority arises to govern it or it is parceled out for private ownership. Examples of over-grazed public lands, over-fished public waterways, and over-felled public forests abound.

We pushed the concept beyond the realm of physical space in characterizing an industry's reputation as a commons. When stakeholders cannot or do not distinguish one firm's actions from those of similar others, reputation commons arise. Reputation commons need not be problematic; a firm can benefit from improvements to its industry's reputation that are brought about by the good behaviors of rival firms. A reputation commons becomes a problem, though, when stakeholders punish an industry broadly for the misconduct of one or a few firms within it. We reasoned that when such problems arise, firms seek solutions that lessen their exposure to these spillovers either by reducing the threat of stakeholder sanction or 'privatizing' the reputation commons. ISR initiatives are the organizational structures through which industries often try to implement these solutions. But do they work?

Drawing on my dissertation work, Andy King and I published a paper in *Academy of Management Journal* in 2008 (Chapter 7 in this volume) in which we empirically tested the functionality of ISR as a solution to RCPs. The chemical industry formed a sort of natural experiment for this. In late 1984, a Union Carbide facility in Bhopal, India, leaked toxic gas that killed thousands. Thereafter, the entire chemical industry suffered severe reputational damage and faced louder calls for much more extensive formal regulation each time more minor chemical spills and leaks occurred at any facility. It became increasingly difficult for firms to gain and retain licenses to operate their plants in many communities. To decrease the risk that another accident would cripple the industry as a whole, the industry's main trade association created an ISR initiative called Responsible Care (RC). We tested whether or not RC was able to mitigate this RCP.

Picture an RCP as ripples spreading across a pond after something disturbs the calm. If you're floating on that pond, a gentle ripple from a pebble is no problem. However, a major shock wave from a boulder being tossed in may sink you. To determine the effectiveness of the RC program, we compared the spread of disturbances before and after its implementation and found that RC was indeed effective in calming the waters of the chemical industry, turning future disturbances from shock waves back into gentle ripples. But how? Well, that's really the more interesting part of the paper. Our analysis suggests that it worked by building 'mental fences' in the minds of stakeholders that helped them to individualize firm behavior. When firms 'fence in' their own problems, they mitigate the collective risk that another firm's problem will spread beyond its borders and cause harm to rivals. We discussed how the stakeholder relationship management programs that were central to RC built and maintained these mental fences, helping firms to be judged on their own merits rather than tarred by the same brush as their rivals.

As the RC program demonstrated, rival firms can sometimes come together to resolve shared problems. However, maintaining this cooperation over time is difficult. Each firm faces a balancing act in allocating its limited resources to the industry's efforts while still furthering its individual interests. In a paper published in *Journal of Management Studies* in 2006 (Chapter 8 in this volume), I took on the problem of how firms find their working balance between competitive and what I termed communal strategy. Communal strategy refers to a given firm's contributions to efforts to manage the shared interests of their industry, as contrasted with competitive strategy by which a firm seeks to stand apart from its rivals. Put another way, through communal strategy firms seek to influence the 'industry effect,' and through competitive strategy they seek to influence the 'firm effect.' Both factors drive firm performance, but they compete for the firm's limited resources. I established a framework that explains how the dynamics of an organizational field can make industry effects 'matter' more or less to firm performance over time, thereby altering a firm's incentive to divert resources from competitive strategy and toward communal strategy. When they perceive industry effects to impinge on their reputation and financial performance, firms shift resources to communal strategy, at least for long enough to improve industry effects, but once the shared problem is resolved, the balance shifts back to competitive strategy.

Firms typically engage in communal strategy through the organizational structure of a trade association. There are thousands of trade associations representing the interests of almost every industry, from advertising to wine and everything in between. By coordinating the resources and uniting the voices of member firms, trade associations can have major impacts on governmental policy, social welfare, and of course industry performance. Yet we know little about them. The few management studies have focused primarily on population dynamics, noting the conditions under which trade associations tend to be founded, merge, or disband. However, there is a great deal of variation in the activity of trade associations. Some are virtually inert while others accrue massive resources and a great deal of internal and external influence. What explains this variation?

In a paper published in *Business & Society* in 2013 (Chapter 9 in this volume), I measured changes in trade association activity. Based on the balancing framework described previously, I expected to find that firms would shift resources to increase their investment in trade association activity during times of industry-wide trouble. But when I tested this assumption on a set of 148 major industry trade associations over time, I found that increases in trade association spending were not related to industry-wide downturns. Instead, decreases in the profitability of the four largest firms in their industries drove increases in the spending of trade associations. This suggests that the interests of large firms drive trade association agendas. Thus, it is necessary to attend to the balancing act between competitive and communal strategy even within communal organizations.

As the studies in this section collectively pointed out, to stakeholders trying to make sense of CSR and to firms trying to manage their relationships with these stakeholders, industry matters. The reputation of an industry is a sort of commons that is difficult to maintain, and if not collectively well-managed can lead stakeholders to punish many firms for the irresponsibility of one or a few firms. This reputational interdependence occurs because stakeholders are unable to parse and make sense of the myriad individual behaviors of voluminous individual firms. The next section digs more deeply into the nature and implications of stakeholder cognitive constraints.

Assessing the assessors

If you happen across someone from Star-Kist casually harpooning a whale or someone from Purina gleefully kicking a puppy, you may say something or even do something about it, to include altering your seafood and dogfood purchasing habits, and perhaps much more. But you'll never see much of what most firms do, especially the bad stuff. Firms obviously have incentive to hide the bad stuff rather than publicize it as they do their good acts. Even if they put it on a pedestal, though, or as is more likely, media outlets report on it, most stakeholders are unlikely to be aware of most of what most firms do.

Stakeholders can attend to only a small portion of what firms do. They're human. Nonetheless, much of the research on how stakeholders respond to firm misconduct starts from the premise that stakeholders are aware of specific acts. In a paper published in *Journal of Management* in 2014 (Chapter 10 in this volume), I challenge this assumption. I describe stakeholder action not as a singular decision point (*Do I punish this firm or not for what it did?*), but as the result of a probabilistic multi-stage cognitive process. Characteristics of individual stakeholders and the situations in which a given act occurs affect the likelihood that a stakeholder will first notice a particular act of misconduct, as well as how they make sense of it, before finally affecting whether and how they decide to respond. Stakeholders may not notice a given act, or if they notice it, they may give a firm the benefit of the doubt, or even if they do notice and deem it misconduct, they may choose to do nothing about it. This combination of steps explains why firms often fail to 'feel the pain' of stakeholder backlash in response to their bad acts. It's not just that stakeholders are often unwilling to take on the burden of punishing firms, but more so, that many bad acts are filtered out before stakeholders face this decision point.

As Sohvi Leih and I showed in a paper published in *Business & Society* in 2018 (Chapter 11 in this volume), cognitive constraints affect not only how stakeholders deal with firm misconduct but how they deal with firm behavior in general. Lacking the ability to directly observe what is going on at all firms at all times, stakeholders rely on intermediaries for information about firm behavior. Media outlets have been quick to capitalize on this need. Those of us in universities and business schools especially can attest that rankings of the qualities of various organizations abound nowadays from nearly every corner of the media world, from *Businessweek* to *US News & World Report*. These rankings have proven to be highly influential, guiding major decisions such as what to buy, where to attend college, where to work, and whom to deem *Sexiest Man Alive* in any given year (no, I'm not bitter; I'm holding my breath and toning my abs for 2027).

We sought to better understand how people use media rankings to assess firms, particularly in comparison to other information they may have about these firms. In an experimental study, we found, as expected, that rankings did shape what people thought about firms. But there is some nuance. This influence was strongest when the ranking was congruent with other information one had about the firm and this other information was negative. However, if one was already aware of negative information about a firm, seeing a favorable ranking had little influence on assessment. People are loathe to challenge their established beliefs, instead discounting or ignoring disconfirming information. Reputations can thus be sticky. It seems that Warren Buffett may have overstated the case for reputational fragility, as firms can rest on their laurels for a while before reputation catches up to reality. In consonance with Buffett's logic, though, this also suggests that it is harder to fix a damaged reputation than it is to maintain it.

Clearly the link between how a firm behaves and how its stakeholders relate to it is a loose one. But as I point out in a paper that is to be published in *Business & Society* in 2019 (Chapter 12 in this volume), the link between firm behavior and social welfare may be outright broken, and that's the link we are really concerned with. Over time, the literature has confused attending to stakeholders with attending to the needs of society. Sure, managing a firm to be responsive to the demands of its stakeholders is an important step forward from the days of firms focusing solely on shareholder issues. However, prioritizing the allocation of a firm's limited resources according to stakeholder power, as the business case prescribes, is unlikely to guide firms toward tackling many of society's pressing problems. CSR stands for corporate social responsibility, not critical stakeholder responsiveness. Those in society who struggle the most are least likely to have power adequate to garner priority from firms seeking to more efficiently allocate their scarce resources to keep their myriad stakeholders satisfied. Thus, as the business case guides firms to focus on actions that maintain and improve stakeholder relations, it seems to also be guiding firms away from involvement in many important social issues.

Closing the current case

Corporations have come a long way since child labor, labor camps, black lung, open pollution, and so on were commonplace. But they still have a long way to go, and the studies discussed above and reproduced in the pages to follow suggest that the business case for corporate social responsibility will not get us much farther. The disconnect or at least lag between a firm's actions and the response of its stakeholders is problematic for the business case. If its good acts don't seem to bring about stakeholder favor, then a firm may see no merit in doing more good things. Even worse, if its bad acts don't seem to bring about stakeholder disfavor, then a firm may see no reason to stop being bad. Sure, as the business case currently stands, lots of firms are still motivated to do lots of nice, responsible things like giving employees paid vacations and providing philanthropic support to their communities. But lots of firms continue to do lots of irresponsible things, and huge social problems like climate change and poverty remain and worsen.

Can we do better? The final chapter of this book sets the stage for future research on the business case for corporate social responsibility, calling for more research on the cognitive mechanisms that underpin the business case, outlining the need for government intervention to fill gaps where market solutions fail, and pushing extant theoretical perspectives into the digital age. Since I predicted earlier that it'll be 2027 before *People* magazine recognizes my superficial merits, and it may take longer for the Nobel committee to get around to rewarding my scholarly merits, I suppose I have no choice but to remain cautiously optimistic that together we will find a viable way forward in the coming years.

[2]

Business and Society Review **105:1** 85–106

Opportunity Platforms and Safety Nets: Corporate Citizenship and Reputational Risk

CHARLES J. FOMBRUN, NAOMI A. GARDBERG, AND MICHAEL L. BARNETT

W hy do managers regularly allocate corporate resources to 'doing good'? Doing good is costly, and the expenditures of public companies come under extensive scrutiny from investors and analysts. What justifies managers in allocating a company's scarce resources to these elective activities?

Recent discussions of 'corporate citizenship' propose a fusion of two arguments.[1] On one hand, a citizenship portfolio helps to integrate companies into the social fabric of local communities by strengthening the social bonds between the company, its employees, and the local community.[2] On the other hand, a citizenship portfolio helps a company build reputational capital, and so enhances its ability to negotiate more attractive contracts with suppliers and governments, to charge premium prices for its products, and to reduce its cost of capital.[3]

Both of these benefits are consistent with a view of corporate citizenship as a strategic tool that managers can use to cope with the *bi-directional risk* that companies face. By doing good, managers generate *reputational gains* that improve a company's ability to attract resources, enhance its performance, and build competitive advantage.[4] Citizenship programs also mitigate the risk of *reputational losses* that can result from alienating key stakeholders.

Charles J. Fombrun, Naomi A. Gardberg, and Michael L. Barnett are at the New York University Stern School of Business. The authors wish to gratefully acknowledge the many helpful comments and suggestions of the editors of this special edition.

Thus, we argue that no simple correlation can be established between 'corporate social performance' (CSP) and 'corporate financial performance.'[5] The activities that generate CSP do not directly impact the company's financial performance, but instead affect the bottom line via its stock of 'reputational capital'—the financial value of its intangible assets.[6]

Recent statements by senior executives of several prominent companies[7] describe five complementary motivations for pursuing citizenship activities:

- Build community ties and maintain a license to operate

  Chris Marsden, former Coordinator, British Petroleum: *The benefits to BP come in many different forms but they can all be categorized as reputation enhancement (including what we call license to operate), staff benefits in terms of morale and personal development, and creating a healthy economy in which our business can prosper.*[8]

- Increase morale and attachment of current employees

  Walter Haas, Jr., Chairman, Levi-Strauss: *I believe that if you can create an environment that your people identify with, that is responsive to their sense of values, justice, fairness, ethics, compassion, and appreciation, they will help you be successful.*[9]

- Prepare and attract potential employees

  Arnold Langbo, Chairman, Kellogg Company: *More than ever, the success of business is directly related to the success of societies, families and communities in preparing a competent workforce. We consider it good business to view corporate philanthropy not only as charity but as a wise and strategic investment in our future.*[10]

- Develop potential customers

  Sir Allen Sheppard, Chairman, Grand Met: *The long term continued success of our business depends on the existence of prosperous consumers to buy those products. Our involvement in the community is genuinely business driven, even if measuring the returns is not that easy.*[11]

- Enact an environment where the company can prosper

  Charles Fettig, Senior Director of Marketing, Merck: *We're a very successful company because we make a lot of money and we do a lot of good things. There's not a direct return on it, and I*

FOMBRUN, GARDBERG, AND BARNETT   87

*don't know that there will be any. Maybe this will help govern-
ments accept our products, but no one really knows. But it does
make us a company worth dealing with. . . .*[12]

In these statements, executives describe a relationship between
company and society captured well in terms of reputation and reci-
procity, social integration and economic performance. Executives
justify corporate citizenship as *investments* in community or society rather than as expenses—even if they concede that measuring
the returns from those investments is seldom attempted.

We suggest that corporate citizenship programs can be designed
to help companies address reputational threats and opportunities
—to achieve reputational gains while mitigating reputational losses.
To that end, in the pages that follow, we introduce the concept of
reputational risk, examine how corporate citizenship modifies
reputational risk, and support the integration of citizenship with
other managerial activities.

REPUTATION AND RISK

A corporate reputation is a cognitive representation of a company's
actions and results that crystallizes the firm's ability to deliver
valued outcomes to its stakeholders.[13] When these expected outcomes are not delivered, the damage to the company's reputation
manifests itself in impoverished revenues, decreased ability to
attract financial capital, and reduced appeal to current and potential employees. These negative outcomes translate into lessened
economic returns and shareholder value. The fluctuating value of
the company's reputation has been termed *reputational capital* and
calculated as the market value of the company in excess of its liqui-
dation value and its intellectual capital. It constitutes the *residual
value of the company's intangible assets over and above its stock of
patents and know-how.*[14]

A company's reputational capital is therefore the value of the
company that is 'at risk' in everyday interaction with stakeholders.
Reputational capital fluctuates in the equity markets as stakeholders convey or withdraw support from the company.
Reputational capital is created when managers convince employees
to work hard, customers to buy the company's products or services,
and investors to purchase its stock. It grows when managers induce

analysts and reporters to praise the company and recommend its shares. It is destroyed when stakeholders withdraw their support because they lose confidence in the company's managers, its products, prospects, or jobs.

Research suggests that managers view risk principally in terms of the *potential for loss*. Focusing solely on potential losses, however, ignores the *potential for gains* from risk. We therefore define **reputational risk** as *the range of possible gains and losses in reputational capital for a given firm.*[15] Thus, we examine here how corporate citizenship helps manage both the upside and downside components of reputational risk. Since reputational capital depends on stakeholder support, each stakeholder group is a source of reputational risk to be managed. A key task for executives is to manage the risks that come from the company's dependency on those stakeholder groups.[16]

Consider giant retailer Wal-Mart. Investors applaud its profitability; employees cherish its family-like culture; and customers welcome its quality at a low price ethic. However, communities and the media often deplore the arrival of a new Wal-Mart store. To counter negative sentiments and build reputational capital, Wal-Mart has developed an extensive portfolio of citizenship activities that targets its key stakeholders. These initiatives seem to be effective, as evidenced by Wal-Mart's tremendous levels of capital. Between 1990 and 1993, the company's reputational and intellectual capital averaged $51 billion, some 3.5 times that of rival Sears Roebuck, and equivalent to 90% of all other retailers combined.[17]

Figure 1 suggests that corporate citizenship is an integral part of a cycle through which companies generate reputational capital, manage reputational risk and enhance performance. Companies invest in citizenship activities that generate reputational capital. In turn, stocks of reputational capital serve a twofold purpose. On one hand, reputational capital builds a platform from which future opportunities may spring. On the other hand, reputational capital safeguards the existing assets of the firm, serving as a buffer against loss. As we suggest in a later part of the article, achieving consistency across programs and throughout the cycle is crucial to fully managing reputational risk. In the next two sections, we examine the reputational risk management cycle in more detail by unraveling the role that corporate citizenship plays in maximizing reputational gains and minimizing reputational losses.

FIGURE 1. The Reputational Risk Management Cycle

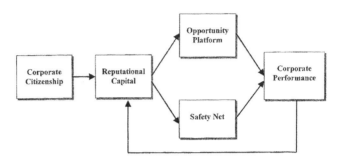

BUILDING AN OPPORTUNITY PLATFORM THROUGH CORPORATE CITIZENSHIP

Effective citizenship programs heighten stakeholder support that savvy firms then utilize to enact new opportunities. J. P. Morgan serves as a case in point. In the early 1990s, Morgan's portfolio of citizenship activities included community development programs, charitable grants, volunteering, and donations. These programs contributed to the large stock of reputational capital the company enjoyed, particularly in its New York home base. In 1991, when several large non-profit organizations in New York City needed an underwriter, they turned to J. P. Morgan. The bank underwrote a $20 million financing package for the National Audubon Society in New York City, as well as another $54 million for the renovation of Manhattan's Guggenheim Museum. In short order, Morgan realized the potential to capitalize on an untapped source of synergy between its line activities and its citizenship activities. To do so, the bank created a not-for-profit group to market its asset and liability management services to nonprofit agencies and assist philanthropists in structuring trusts and foundations. The group quickly became a large profit center for the bank.[18]

Citizenship programs like those of Morgan create the potential for gains by increasing the *real options*[19] available to a company. The premise is simple: Sustained corporate citizenship creates reputational capital and so provides a platform from which other opportunities may spring. The supportive social relationships that a company builds through its citizenship programs today put it in a more favorable position to take advantage of opportunities that emerge tomorrow. In contrast, companies that fail to invest in corporate citizenship today may lack the relationships and reputational capital that they need to exploit emerging opportunities tomorrow.

In this way, Morgan's citizenship programs can be viewed as platform investments from which new paths for growth arise.[20] These platform investments derive value not from direct income creation, but from indirectly creating potential for future gains. On the upside, therefore, corporate citizenship programs are comparable to R&D and training: They are platform investments whose value partly lies in unlocking future growth opportunities for companies.

Furthermore, citizenship programs are boundary-spanning activities that sensitize employees to environmental conditions and help companies adapt to changing circumstances.[21] 'Hands on' corporate volunteerism and community development typically expose employees directly to the diverse needs and perspectives of multiple constituencies, thereby fostering increased awareness and understanding of stakeholders and their expectations. Some companies treat community involvement as a 'leadership laboratory.'[22] Through 'action learning', managers develop "a broader repertoire of cultural, relational, and self-leadership competencies."[23] Through community involvement, employees learn valuable information about the environment that enhances the company's adaptability. In turn, personal understanding increases corporate opportunities for profit making, and makes it more likely the company can capitalize on those opportunities.

Figure 2 suggests that citizenship programs increase a company's potential for gain by increasing support from the company's eight stakeholder groups, which then leads to cooperation in the execution of corporate initiatives designed to achieve strategic objectives. Each stakeholder group offers a specific promise of support that fosters the growth of reputational capital.

FOMBRUN, GARDBERG, AND BARNETT   91

TABLE 2. Managing the Upside of Reputational Risk

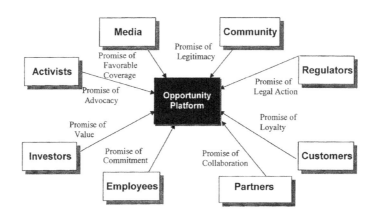

From Employees: The Promise of Commitment

Employees have the highest potential impact on a company's reputational capital. The quality of their work influences the quality of the products and services offered to customers. When they interact with customers, colleagues, neighbors, and friends, they convey the merits of the company they work for, and so help to diffuse more or less favorable word-of-mouth about the company. Most employees approve of citizenship programs, even if only a small proportion of them participate.[24] Companies benefit from resulting increases in both participant and non-participant motivation, teamwork, morale, and commitment, thereby decreasing hiring and training costs, and increasing the company's appeal to new recruits.[25] For example, to generate employee support, Wal-Mart provides employee health benefits that are often superior to those provided by local businesses and also offers part-time income to local senior citizens.[26]

From Customers: The Promise of Loyalty

The principal promise from customers is loyalty that generates repeat purchases and recommendations. Citizenship programs act much like advertising in promoting an attractive image of the company. A growing body of evidence suggests that some customer segments favor the products and services of companies that demonstrate corporate citizenship, and willingly pay a premium price for the products of these companies. Johnson & Johnson, which is renowned for its attentiveness to customer needs in a quality-sensitive yet highly competitive industry, benefits from intense customer loyalty. As one customer in a recent survey noted, "There's this comfortability, familiarity level. When I'm faced with 45 products on the drug store shelf, I'd gravitate to theirs."[27]

From Investors: The Promise of Value

Investors enhance reputational capital when they speak favorably of a company, purchase shares, and instigate an upward spiral in the company's market value. Companies that 'do good' can create positive word-of-mouth, increased share purchases, and ultimately higher market value. A staggering $1.4 billion of investment dollars has moved into mutual fund portfolios that include only companies screened for their social responsibility.[28] Citizenship may even help to lower the cost of capital and so enhance economic returns by inducing favorable recommendations from buy-side analysts.[29] Ben & Jerry's is the seminal example of a corporation gaining investment dollars by 'doing right' in the community. Many of Ben & Jerry's investors prefer social responsibility over high returns. Though returns are often below industry average, Ben & Jerry's is still able to obtain adequate capital.[30]

From Partners: The Promise of Collaboration

Citizenship programs can create opportunities for partnerships to develop as well as enhance the trust between existing partners by increasing familiarity and social integration. Corporate volunteer programs, for instance, often bring together employees of potential partners. These encounters heighten collaboration and are often said to have indirect benefits for the alliance. Good corporate citizens are also more likely to attract high-caliber partners. Dealers and suppliers expect fewer disruptions in the supply chain from disgruntled customers or employees; joint venture partners are less concerned about stakeholder threats. For instance, J. P. Morgan's employees, through off-site citizenship interactions, developed a network of potential business clients that proved useful in developing investment opportunities. Its school liaison program evolved into community development and investment opportunities in New York City's Harlem.[31]

From Regulators: The Promise of Favorable Regulation

Anecdotal evidence suggests that legislators and regulators will react more favorably to companies that 'do good.' Legislators are elected by local constituents, and insofar as those voters speak favorably of a company, they reduce the likelihood of the company being reviled and made prey for regulators. Moreover, regulators themselves are community members and are more likely to grant the benefit of the doubt to strong corporate citizens. Firms with strong regulatory relations may be able to shape zoning laws in their favor, reduce stringent regulations, and otherwise create favorable conditions for business.

Firms expanding globally often employ citizenship programs to overcome nationalistic barriers and enhance perceived legitimacy.[32] Through corporate citizenship activities, firms ingratiate themselves with the local community and with local regulators. In countries with restrictive practices for foreign companies, those firms with active citizenship portfolios can increase opportunities to expand into and within profitable markets.

From Activists: The Promise of Advocacy

Purchases of many consumer products and services can be substantially swayed by the endorsements of activist groups. In a highly competitive marketplace, the added advantage of an activist group's seal of approval may directly translate into improved sales. The recent consumer emphasis on recycled goods led to premiums for those products that carried the recycling seal. Honors bestowed upon select firms for safety, pollution prevention, philanthropy, equal employment opportunity, and so forth, make the company more visible to consumers and provide a way to distinguish themselves from the pack. The Council on Economic Priorities, for example, publishes a best-selling book *Shopping for a Better World*[33] that identifies the corporate parents behind many popular brands to better inform consumers which products to buy and which to avoid.

From the Community: The Promise of Legitimacy

Although most companies perceive local communities as passive stakeholders, occasionally some communities mobilize and act. Local communities may act to attract new investments or protect local companies that share their values and interests. Companies that participate in local communities benefit from community protection when threatened by insurgent groups of stakeholders. In early 1999, when the Coca-Cola company was slapped with a race-bias suit by a group of disgruntled employees, the company received support from black community leaders who pointed to the company's strong record of sustained citizenship in favor of black colleges.[34] The resulting publicity stands to enhance the visibility of Coca-Cola's citizenship programs and thereby generate favorable regard for the company.

From the Media: The Promise of Favorable Coverage

The media magnify a company's actions for other stakeholders, and so influence how they come to regard a company. The media also seek out attention-getting stories. To do so they selectively filter from a company's initiatives those more likely to draw readers and viewers, potentially creating or destroying corporate reputations. Insofar as citizenship programs are unexpected and often involve interactions between wealthy companies and less privileged sectors of local communities, they are likely to attract the attention of reporters and generate favorable publicity for the company. Johnson & Johnson's extraordinary handling of the Tylenol tampering crises in 1982 and 1986 garnered such positive press coverage that its market share and stock price rapidly recovered.[35] This positive media coverage continues today.

FOMBRUN, GARDBERG, AND BARNETT   95

BUILDING A SAFETY NET THROUGH CORPORATE CITIZENSHIP

Companies must also manage the downside risk associated with potential loss of reputational capital. Figure 3 suggests that the downside of a company's reputational risk is rooted in threats from its eight stakeholder groups. Citizenship initiatives help companies buffer themselves against the downside risk of reputational loss by mitigating these threats.

From Employees: The Threat of Rogue Behavior

The principal downside risk from employees is the threat of rogue behavior. Rogue behavior refers to actions that are in the employees' self-interest but are inconsistent with corporate policies and are not in the long-term best interests of the company. At a minimum these actions can create negative publicity; at a maximum they can bring the company to its knees. Companies victimized by rogue employees abound, none more visibly perhaps than in the financial services industry, where small infractions of rules by zealous employees virtually bankrupted such well-regarded institutions as Barings Brothers and Salomon Brothers.

FIGURE 3. Managing the Downside of Reputational Risk

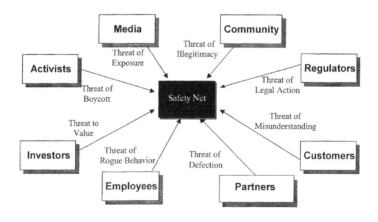

Key factors that determine a company's vulnerability to rogue behavior are its corporate culture and its associated control systems. Strong cultures that emphasize internalization of corporate objectives and teamwork are less likely to experience rogue behavior because they produce close alignment between individual self-interest and the collective good. Similarly, companies with extensive monitoring systems, intensive recruitment practices, formalized training, and team-based compensation systems are less likely to experience rogue behavior than companies that glorify individual 'stars.'[36]

In addition, citizenship activities can help companies defend their reputational capital by strengthening the bonds between employees and hence the corporate culture. Volunteerism and community projects also foster altruism and dampen individualism, thereby reducing the potential for purely self-interested behavior that heightens reputational risk.[37]

From Customers: The Threat of Misunderstanding

The principal threat to reputational capital that comes from customers is the threat of misunderstanding. The more complex, important, and costly the products that customers buy from a company, the more likely customers are to depend on the company for guidance in how to use those products, and so the more vulnerable the company is to possible misunderstanding by those customers.

Consider pharmaceutical companies. Their prescription products are often complex, important, and expensive to their customers. To reduce the reputational risk from customers, pharmaceutical companies try hard to clarify the appropriate applications for their products by performing extensive testing, passing regulatory hurdles, and releasing detailed guidelines that describe side effects and interaction effects involved in their use. In so doing, they demonstrate their concern for customers. Pharmaceutical companies often rely on citizenship initiatives to reinforce their reputations as companies that care for the well-being of their customers. Product donations have been particularly effective acts of generosity for pharmaceutical companies: Merck's donation of Mectizan to people infected with 'river blindness' who could not afford to buy the drug reinforced the company's reputation as a concerned partner in the promotion of human health.[38] With such citizenship programs, managers signal their concern for customers, convey favorable images of their companies, and reduce the chance that customers will misuse or misunderstand their products and services.

From Investors: The Threat to Value

Investors threaten reputational capital when they speak badly of a company, call in loans, and sell off their shares, thereby sparking a downward spiral in the company's market value. Investors assess value based on two criteria: the company's past performance, and its future prospects for growth. The higher and less volatile the company's past profitability has been, the greater its value. The greater the estimates of future cash flows generated from the company's core business, the more favorably investors assess the company's future prospects.

Managers routinely reduce the potential for loss of reputational capital by maintaining 'transparency' in their interactions with investors and analysts. Extensive disclosure, openness, and frequent contact with analysts and the media induce favorable perceptions of a company's quality and so enhance valuations.[39] Citizenship programs can help reduce the threat to value from investors by increasing the visibility and transparency of the company to investors. Companies that involve themselves in community activities become 'neighbors of choice'[40] and stand to benefit from enhanced assessments of their future prospects by activist institutional investors.

For example, during the introduction of its Pentium computer chip, Intel learned of a flaw that it considered insignificant. The company ignored criticism and denied the importance of the flaw. The public disagreed causing an uproar that threatened the firm's future prospects and reduced its stock price. Intel's inappropriate initial response tarnished its reputation—decreasing its reputational capital. However, within weeks Intel altered its strategy by creating a dialogue with the public and investors that renewed confidence that the company would do the right thing to resolve this situation and act appropriately in the future.[41]

From Partners: The Threat of Defection

When partners defect, they threaten the company's performance and reputation by ending crucial flows of products, services and resources. For example, Delta Airlines ended a strategic
alliance with Korean Airlines (KAL) when the latter was cited for
safety violations. Delta's defection reduced KAL's access to the
valuable U.S. market.[42]

Reputation also spills over from one partner to the other.[43] Use of
child labor by Asian subcontractors, for instance, has tarnished the
reputation of sporting goods manufacturers Nike and Adidas. Companies often try to reduce that risk by nurturing local responsibility,
sharing business risk, and investing in local citizenship initiatives.
They can also enlist support from another stakeholder group. Wil-
liams-Sonoma (WS), the mail order company, is a case in point. WS
relies on its Memphis neighbor Federal Express (FedEx) to ship all of
its customer orders. In 1998, when a pilot strike threatened FedEx,
WS worked closely with the shipper to develop alternate means of
transporting products. During media interviews, WS became an
advocate by proclaiming its confidence in FedEx's ability to handle
the potential crisis. WS thus assisted FedEx in defusing the situation and restoring other stakeholders' confidence.[44]

From Regulators: The Threat of Legal Action

Regulators threaten a company's reputational capital by setting
reporting requirements, and by initiating investigations and legal
action. Vulnerability is greater in highly regulated industries and in
industries that provide vital, dangerous, or life-threatening products
or services. Nonetheless, firms in every industry in the U.S. have
some degree of threat from regulation, stemming from enactment of
the 1991 Federal Sentencing Guidelines for Organizations.[45]

Under these guidelines, organizations convicted of certain criminal activities can be fined up to $290 million. The definition of crime
is quite broad, allowing organizations to be held responsible for the
criminal acts of rogue employees, even when such behavior is in
direct violation of company policy. A firm's best defense to such
charges is imposition of effective compliance programs that impart
to employees the importance of ethical corporate behavior.[46]

FOMBRUN, GARDBERG, AND BARNETT   99

Corporate citizenship activities help to relay such information,
aiding in building a corporate atmosphere that not only mitigates
the risk of rogue behavior, but also lessens the risk of conviction
and the imposition of heavy penalties if and when such behavior
does occur.

From Activists: The Threat of Boycott

Activists threaten a company's reputational capital by calling
attention to corporate policies that they deem socially irresponsible.
They do so principally through press releases, marches, and
boycotts that are intended to draw media attention and public support. Activists instigate their actions to depress corporate revenues,
and thereby bring pressure to bear on the company to change
its policies. In the early 1990s, a reported 18 percent of Americans
participated in boycotts.[47] Many observers believe that activist boycotts will increasingly affect American companies as consumers
refuse to buy a branded product or class of products to achieve
some social outcome.[48]

Companies are more vulnerable to activists: (1) when their products and services can potentially harm the environment or human
health; and, (2) when their actions can be perceived as damaging
social values. Recent examples include Disney and Phillip Morris.
Disney's granting of domestic partner benefits to gay couples has
enraged conservative activists, bringing undesired controversy to
this traditional epitome of family values.[49] Actions against Phillip
Morris' cigarette lines have spilled over into boycotts of unrelated
product lines within the product portfolio such as Kraft foods.[50]

Research shows that boycotted companies experience significant
decreases in market value in the 60-day period following boycott
announcements.[51] Negative information about one product from
a multi-product company also proves contagious in inducing negative perceptions of other brands from the same company.[52]

Companies generally counter the threat of boycotts by building
relationships with activist groups, and encouraging an open dialogue about contentious issues. Citizenship programs can help
reduce corporate vulnerability to boycotts by promoting favorable
images of the company through its involvement in social programs.

From the Community: The Threat of Illegitimacy

Public opinion plays an important role in setting standards of acceptable corporate behavior.[53] When communities mobilize and act, it is generally because they perceive a company to be undermining the welfare of the community—failing to live up to community expectations or challenging local values. Four factors contribute to a company's vulnerability to illegitimacy: social distance, unattractiveness, deviance, and uniqueness.

Social distance refers to the difference between a company's beliefs and those of the local community. Attractiveness describes a company's emotional and economic appeal to community residents. Deviance refers to behavior that is inconsistent with prevailing community norms. New and unique companies are those that have no track record of dependability, and so are poorly understood. Socially distant, unattractive or deviant firms often find themselves victims of not-in-my-back-yard (NIMBY) campaigns.

Wal-Mart is a case in point. In recent years, the giant retailer with operations in all 50 states has found domestic expansion in the U.S. increasingly difficult as local grassroots groups from Vermont and Massachusetts to Georgia and Colorado protest new stores due to its reputation for hollowing out small towns. Community opponents claim that Wal-Mart displaces small, locally owned enterprises, destroys the character of Main Street by replacing quaint store fronts with generic boxes, creates traffic and environmental problems, and diminishes the quality of life in local communities. They describe the company's expansion as "corporate colonialism . . . organizations from one place going into distant places and strip mining them culturally and economically."[54]

Companies can reduce their vulnerability to threats of illegitimacy by reducing the social distance and perceived deviance of their values and activities from those of the local community. Citizenship programs can help companies do so and thereby dampen community protests and fend off threats to the legitimacy of their operations. Economic assistance, volunteerism, grants for local schools, and investments in much-needed community infrastructure are some of the ways Wal-Mart has invoked support for its operations. The company initiates many of these programs even in advance of opening a store in a host community. In a recent survey of corporate reputations in America, Wal-Mart ranked sixth

overall and fourth in social responsibility.[55] Clearly these citizenship initiatives help to reduce perceptions of the company as a
predator and thereby reduce the company's vulnerability to loss of
community support.

From the Media: The Threat of Exposure

A company's reputational capital is vulnerable to media exposure
about its activities. The level of vulnerability to media exposure is
influenced by four factors: (1) The company's uniqueness; (2) the
quality of its interactions with the media; (3) its earnings volatility;
and, (4) its advertising visibility.[56] Media exposure increases when
a company develops and promotes new and unique product or
service offerings. Frequent interaction with reporters increases
familiarity with the company and enhances the probability that the
company will be featured. Unusually high returns and volatility
draw media attention. Finally, a company with a large advertising
presence is more likely to be targeted by reporters than less visible
companies. Hence, the more newsworthy a company and the more
it draws attention to itself the more media coverage it receives.

Royal Dutch/Shell was heavily impacted by media magnifica-
tion of activist boycotts and community protests. News shots of
an ugly platform buzzed by Greenpeace helicopters conveying
determined volunteers were instrumental in giving the activists
a media victory against a company that was portrayed as huge,
powerful, and uncaring.[57]

Companies reduce the threat of exposure from the media by
nurturing their media relationships. Some avoid media exposure
altogether—an introvert position that shelters the company in
the short term, but exposes the company to increased risk when a
crisis develops. At that point, reporters starved for information
indulge in a feeding frenzy about the 'unknown' company they
seek to expose, and often do far more damage to the company's
reputational capital than was warranted.

Citizenship programs can help reduce a company's vulnerability
to exposure by increasing the familiarity of the media with the
company, its employees, and activities. Corporate affiliation with
philanthropic and charitable organizations such as Habitat for
Humanity or the American Cancer Society provides the media with
positive corporate images to broadcast. Familiarity also reduces

the potential for misrepresentation and increases the likelihood that the company will be given the benefit of the doubt when discrepant information comes to the fore.

CONCLUSION

In this paper, we have argued that corporate citizenship is a strategic tool that companies can use to manage reputational risk from stakeholder groups. Citizenship initiatives facilitate execution of corporate strategies and enrich opportunities while buffering firms from loss of reputational capital, all of which enhances performance. To reap these benefits, care must be taken in designing and implementing citizenship activities.

Efforts at quickly building an image as an upstanding corporate citizen generally fail. The time to build a stock of reputational capital is before a firm is struck by a crisis. Reputations form over time as observers interpret the patterns of corporate actions and, once formed, are resistant to change even in the face of discrepant information. Knee-jerk responses lack believability and may be seen as self-serving, leading to a loss of reputation instead of the intended gain.[58]

A consistent and sustained message requires continuous investment in and commitment to citizenship activities, despite the difficulty in directly quantifying the gains. This 'difficult to quantify' aspect of corporate citizenship makes it a hard sell to many firms. Without numbers, many firms may not see the link between citizenship and profitability, and thus may underinvest in citizenship. Were firms to view citizenship through the real options lens, they might overcome these myopic tendencies. We have presented a strong framework in which to consider the bi-directional nature of risk as it relates to corporate citizenship. Investments in corporate citizenship build a hedge against downside risk while creating a platform from which future opportunities for gain may spring. By considering upside potential along with protection from loss, firms may more easily justify investments in corporate citizenship programs.

We therefore encourage a deeper investigation of the complex relationship between citizenship activities, reputational risk, and the process through which companies build reputational capital

FOMBRUN, GARDBERG, AND BARNETT   103

and competitive advantage. Future research should examine not only how companies use corporate citizenship to manage reputational risk, but how they link citizenship initiatives to complementary reputation management activities such as advertising, public relations, and related communications functions.

NOTES

1. Noel M. Tichy, Andrew R. McGill, and Linda St. Clair, *Corporate Global Citizenship: Doing Business in the Public Eye* (San Francisco: The New Lexington Press, 1997).

2. Amitai Etzioni, *The Moral Dimension* (New York: Free Press, 1988).

3. Charles J. Fombrun, *Reputation: Realizing Value from the Corporate Image* (Boston, MA: Harvard Business School Press, 1996).

4. Charles J. Fombrun and Violina Rindova, "Fanning the Flames: Corporate Reputations as Social Constructions of Performance," in *The Social Construction of Industries and Markets*, eds. Joseph Porac and Mark Ventresca (NY: Oxford University Press, 1999).

5. Ronald M. Roman, Sefa Hayibor, and Bradley R. Agle, "The Relationship between Social and Financial Performance," *Business and Society* 38 (1999), 109–125.

6. Fombrun, 1996.

7. Positions listed are those held at the time of quotation.

8. Chris Marsden, "Competitiveness and Corporate Responsibility," *Alli@nce* 1:2 (1997), 63–71.

9. Stratford Sherman, "Levis: As Ye Sew, So Shall Ye Reap," *Fortune* 135:9 (1997), 104.

10. Morse, "Survey of International Youth (2): Soft Philanthropists Under Fire—The IYF Is Seeking Caring Companies," *Financial Times*, 2 February 1996, 2.

11. Tucker, "Survey of the World's Young People (5): Mere Survival Is Not Enough—The International Youth Foundation," *Financial Times*, 12 February 1994, 8.

12. Jane E. Dutton and Michael G. Pratt, "Merck & Co., Inc." in *Corporate Global Citizenship: Doing Business in the Public Eye*, eds. Noel M. Tichy, Andy R. McGill, and Linda St. Clair (San Francisco, CA: The New Lexington Press, 1997, 150–167).

BUSINESS AND SOCIETY REVIEW

13. Charles J. Fombrun and Mark Shanley, "What's in a Name? Reputation-building and Corporate Strategy," *Academy of Management Journal* 33 (1990), 233–258.

14. Fombrun, 1996.

15. James G. March and Zur Shapira, "Managerial Perspectives on Risk and Risk Taking," *Management Science* 33 (1987), 1404–1418.

16. Jeffrey Pfeffer and Gerald R. Salancik, *The External Control of Organizations: A Resource Dependence Perspective* (New York: Harper & Row, 1978).

17. Fombrun, 1996.

18. Fombrun, 1996.

19. Stewart C. Myers, "Determinants of Corporate Borrowing," *Journal of Financial Economics* 5:2 (1977), 147–175.

20. Bruce Kogut and Nalin Kulatilaka, "Options Thinking and Platform Investments: Investing in Opportunity," *California Management Review* 36:2 (1994), 52–71.

21. Daniel Katz and Robert L. Kahn, *The Social Psychology of Organizations* (New York: Wiley, 1966).

22. Shari Caudron, "Volunteerism Efforts Offer Low-cost Training Options," *Personnel Journal* (June 1994), 8–44. Joel Makower, *Beyond the Bottom Line: Putting Social Responsibility to Work for Your Business and the World* (New York: Simon & Schuster, 1995).

23. Caroline A. Bartel, Richard Saavedra, and Linn Van Dyne, "Learning to Lead with a Conscience through Community Involvement" (1999). Manuscript submitted for publication.

24. Fombrun, 1996.

25. Daniel B. Turban and Daniel W. Greening, "Corporate Social Performance and Organizational Attractiveness to Prospective Employees," *Academy of Management Journal* 40:3 (1996), 658–672.

26. Kristin Storey, "Wal-Mart Greeters Put on a Happy Face and Beat Retirement," *Detroit News*, 15 April 1996, C6.

27. Ronald Alsop, "The Best Corporate Reputations in America: Johnson & Johnson (Think Babies!) Turns Up Tops," *Wall Street Journal*, 23 September 1999, B6.

28. Joanne Legomsky, "Socially Aware Funds Grow; Investors Enjoy Righteous Returns," *Times-Picayune*, 24 January 1999, F1.

29. Fombrun, 1996.

30. R. Rigby, "Tutti Frutti," *Management Today* (February 1998), 54–56.

31. Fombrun, 1996.

32. Charles J. Fombrun and Naomi A. Gardberg, "Corporate Global Citizenship: Mitigating the Liability of Foreignness." Unpublished manuscript, New York University (1999).

33. Benjamin Hollister, Rosalyn Will, and Alice T. Martin, *Shopping for a Better World* (New York: Council on Economic Priorities, 1994).

34. Nikhil Deogun, "A Race-Bias Suit Tests Coke," *Wall Street Journal*, 18 May 1999, B1.

35. Fombrun, 1996.

36. Edgar H. Schein, *Organizational Culture and Leadership* (San Francisco: Jossey-Bass Publishers, 1997. Deborah Vidaver-Cohen, "Creating and Maintaining Ethical Work Climates: Anomie in the Workplace and Implications for Managing Change," *Business Ethics Quarterly* 3:4 (1993), 343–358.

37. Linn Van Dyne, Jill W. Graham, and Richard M. Dienesch, "Organizational Citizenship Behavior: Construct Redefinition, Measurement and Validation," *Academy of Management Journal* 37 (1994), 765–802.

38. Dutton and Pratt, 1997.

39. Vernon J. Richardson, "The Effect of Firm Disclosure Policy on Firm Reputation." Unpublished manuscript, University of Illinois at Urbana-Champaign (1999).

40. Edmund M. Burke, *Corporate Community Relations: The Principle of the Neighbor of Choice* (Westport, CT: Quorum, 1999).

41. Fombrun, 1996.

42. Andy Pasztor, Anna W. Mathews, and Martha Brannigan, "Delta Suspends Code-Sharing With Korean Air," *Wall Street Journal*, 19 April 1999, A3.

43. Bernard L. Simonin and Julie A. Ruth, "Is a Company Known by the Company it Keeps? Assessing the Spillover Effects of Brand Alliances on Consumer Brand Attitudes," *Journal of Marketing Research* 35 (February 1998), 30–42.

44. William Margaritis, Corporate Vice-President, Worldwide Communications and Investor Relations, FedEx. Presentation during the *3rd International Conference on Corporate Reputation, Image and Competitiveness* (January 1999).

45. United States Sentencing Commission, *Federal Sentencing Guidelines Manual* (St. Paul, MN: West Publishing, 1994).

46. R. Romrell, "Why Companies Should Be Concerned About Corporate Compliance," *Business Credit* (March 1997).

47. A. Miller, "Do Boycotts Work?" *Newsweek*, 6 July 1992, 58–61.

48. Betsy D. Gelb, "More Boycotts Ahead? Some Implications," *Business Horizons* (March–April 1995), 70–76.

49. Report from Reputation Institute, *The Best Reputations in America* (1999).

50. Reputation Institute, 1999.

51. Stephen W. Pruitt and Monroe Friedman, "Determining the Effectiveness of Consumer Boycotts: A Stock Price Analysis of their Impact on Corporate Targets," *Journal of Consumer Policy* (December 1986), 375–387.

52. Marc G. Weinberger, "Products as Targets of Negative Information: Some Recent Findings," *European Journal of Marketing* 3/4 (1986), 110–186.

53. John W. Meyer and Brian Rowan, "Institutionalized Organizations: Formal Structure as Myth and Ceremony," *American Journal of Sociology* 83 (1977), 340–363.

54. Bob Ortega, "Ban the Bargains: Aging Activists Turn, Turn, Turn Attention to Wal-Mart Protests," *Wall Street Journal*, 11 October 1994, A1.

55. Ronald Alsop, "The Best Corporate Reputations in America: Just as in Politics, Trust, Reliability Pay Off Over Time," *Wall Street Journal*, 23 September 1999, B1.

56. Fombrun and Shanley, 1990.

57. Suzanne Moore, "Mooreover: Sea Changes in Political Talk," *The Guardian*, 22 June 1995, T5. See Mirvis' article on Shell transformation in this volume.

58. Fombrun and Gardberg, 1999.

Strategic Management Journal
Strat. Mgmt. J., **27**: 1101–1122 (2006)
Published online 13 September 2006 in Wiley InterScience (www.interscience.wiley.com) DOI: 10.1002/smj.557
Received 21 November 2003; Final revision received 3 March 2006

BEYOND DICHOTOMY: THE CURVILINEAR RELATIONSHIP BETWEEN SOCIAL RESPONSIBILITY AND FINANCIAL PERFORMANCE

MICHAEL L. BARNETT[1]* and ROBERT M. SALOMON[2]
[1] *College of Business Administration, University of South Florida, Tampa, Florida, U.S.A.*
[2] *Stern School of Business, New York University, New York, New York, U.S.A.*

A central and contentious debate in many literatures concerns the relationship between financial and social performance. We advance this debate by measuring the financial–social performance link within mutual funds that practice socially responsible investing (SRI). SRI fund managers have an array of social screening strategies from which to choose. Prior studies have not addressed this heterogeneity within SRI funds. Combining modern portfolio and stakeholder theories, we hypothesize that the financial loss borne by an SRI fund due to poor diversification is offset as social screening intensifies because better-managed and more stable firms are selected into its portfolio. We find support for this hypothesis through an empirical test on a panel of 61 SRI funds from 1972 to 2000. The results show that as the number of social screens used by an SRI fund increases, financial returns decline at first, but then rebound as the number of screens reaches a maximum. That is, we find a curvilinear relationship, suggesting that two long-competing viewpoints may be complementary. Furthermore, we find that financial performance varies with the types of social screens used. Community relations screening increased financial performance, but environmental and labor relations screening decreased financial performance. Based on our results, we suggest that literatures addressing the link between financial and social performance move toward in-depth examination of the merits of different social screening strategies, and away from the continuing debate on the financial merits of either being socially responsible or not. Copyright © 2006 John Wiley & Sons, Ltd.

Are financial and social performance negatively or positively associated? Extant theoretical and empirical research has supported both contradictory positions (Margolis and Walsh, 2003; Orlitzky, Schmidt, and Rynes, 2003; Rowley and Berman, 2000; Mahon and Griffin, 1999; Roman, Hayibor, and Agle, 1999; Griffin and Mahon, 1997; Ullmann, 1985). In this paper, we reconcile these divergent views through an empirical

Keywords: stakeholder theory; modern portfolio theory; corporate social responsibility; socially responsible investing
* Correspondence to: Michael L. Barnett, College of Business Administration, University of South Florida, 4202 E. Fowler Ave., BSN 3527, Tampa, FL 33620-5500, U.S.A.
E-mail: mbarnett@coba.usf.edu

study of socially responsible investing (SRI). SRI is the practice of choosing financial investments on the basis of social responsibility criteria. By some accounts more than $1 trillion, or about 10 percent of all U.S. assets under management, including about 160 mutual funds, can be categorized as SRI (Glassman, 1999; Hutton, D'Antonio, and Johnsen, 1998; LaRose, 1998).

Many scholars have compared the financial performance of SRI funds to those of funds that do not screen their holdings based on social criteria (Statman, 2000; Guerard, 1997; Sauer, 1997; Kurtz and DiBartolomeo, 1996; Diltz, 1995; Hamilton, Jo, and Statman, 1993; Luck and Pilotte, 1993; Teper, 1992; Mueller, 1991; Rudd, 1979). As with the broader debate on the link between financial and

1102   *M. L. Barnett and R. M. Salomon*

social performance, the results of SRI and non-SRI fund performance comparisons have been mixed. Many studies have shown that SRI funds can perform as well as (e.g., Guerard, 1997; Diltz, 1995; Hamilton *et al.*, 1993), and even better than (e.g., Statman, 2000; DiBartolomeo and Kurtz, 1999; Luck and Pilotte, 1993) unscreened funds. But other studies have shown that SRI funds perform worse than unscreened funds (Geczy, Stambaugh, and Levin, 2003; Teper, 1992; Rudd, 1979). Moreover, SRI critics have suggested that the strong financial performance of some SRI funds in recent years may be the result of a decrease in the stringency of their social screening criteria (Glassman, 1999; Goetz, 1997).[1] That is, they contend that SRI funds lowered their social performance in order to raise their financial performance. Thus, the stronger financial performance of SRI funds in recent years could actually serve as further evidence that financial and social performance are negatively, not positively, related. Indeed, SRI funds vary greatly in the type and intensity of social screens applied to their investments. Prior empirical studies have not addressed this heterogeneity, and so have confounded a range of social responsibility practices.

In order to advance this long-standing and contentious debate, rather than again comparing socially screened to unscreened mutual funds, we address differences *within* SRI funds. In this paper, we measure how variation in the intensity and type of social screening employed by SRI funds affects their financial performance. We first review the debate over the link between financial and social performance. We then develop a set of hypotheses, grounded in modern portfolio theory (Campbell *et al.*, 2001; Fama, 1971; Markowitz, 1952; Sharpe, 1964) and stakeholder theory (Freeman, 1984; Donaldson and Preston, 1995; Jones, 1995), that predict how variation in both the intensity and type of social screening influences risk-adjusted financial performance. We test these hypotheses on a panel of 61 SRI funds. We find that the relationship between financial and social performance is neither strictly negative nor strictly positive. Rather, it is curvilinear, with the strongest financial returns to low and high levels of social responsibility, and significantly lower financial returns to

moderate levels of social responsibility. In addition, we find that some types of social responsibility are linked to higher financial performance than others. We conclude by discussing the implications of these findings for the future of research on the link between social and financial performance.

THE LINK BETWEEN SOCIAL AND FINANCIAL PERFORMANCE

The nature of the relationship between the socially beneficial behaviors of a corporation and its financial performance has long been debated, yet it remains unresolved (Margolis and Walsh, 2003). One group of scholars has argued, simply, that social responsibility detracts from a firm's financial performance (Friedman, 1970; McWilliams and Siegel, 1997; Jensen, 2002). Any discretionary expenditures on social betterment unnecessarily raise a firm's costs, thereby putting it at an economic disadvantage in a competitive market. In contrast, another group of scholars has argued that the better a firm's social performance, the better it can attract resources (Cochran and Wood, 1984; Waddock and Graves, 1997), obtain quality employees (Greening and Turban, 2000; Turban and Greening, 1996), market its products and services (Fombrun, 1996; Moskowitz, 1972), and even create unforeseen opportunities (Fombrun, Gardberg, and Barnett, 2000). Thus, social responsibility is a source of competitive advantage (Porter, 1991; Porter and van der Linde, 1995). Empirical tests of these opposing positions have long produced mixed results, and so have not resolved this debate (Ullmann, 1985; Griffin and Mahon, 1997; Margolis and Walsh, 2003; McWilliams and Siegel, 2000; Wood and Jones, 1995).

In this paper, we test the relationship between social and financial performance within mutual funds. Mutual funds seek to maximize performance across a portfolio of firms, not within a single firm. As with the firm-level debate, the basic issue concerns whether the costs of social responsibility are offset or exceeded by financial returns over some period of time. However, mutual funds are also concerned with diversification (Sharpe, 1964; Black, Jensen, and Scholes, 1972; Campbell *et al.*, 2001; Geczy *et al.*, 2003).[2] If a mutual fund

---

[1] Refer to Figure 3 for consideration of this argument.

[2] Throughout this paper, we use diversification to mean efforts of a mutual fund to invest in a broad set of firms so as to create a

Strat. Mgmt. J., **27**: 1101–1122 (2006)
DOI: 10.1002/smj

implements strict social performance criteria that exclude firms, industries, or sectors from its portfolio, that mutual fund may be unable to adequately diversify. Without ample diversification, the fund will be exposed to additional risk for a given level of return and so by definition will incur a loss in risk-adjusted financial returns. SRI proponents argue, though, that while there may be less potential breadth in an SRI fund's portfolio, those firms that are chosen for the portfolio are substantively better managed than the average firm and so tend to generate equal or higher financial returns, even on a risk-adjusted basis. The remainder of this section reviews these opposing views on the link between social and financial performance and develops a set of hypotheses that predict the financial outcomes of variability in intensity and type of social screens.

The financial costs of social responsibility

Critics of corporate social responsibility point out that it is costly and administratively burdensome for a firm to engage in socially responsible practices such as doling out corporate philanthropy, providing employee day care, granting paid parental leave, and reducing environmental impact. These additional costs and administrative burdens directly detract from the bottom line and so can put socially responsible firms at a competitive disadvantage relative to rivals who do not engage in such practices (Friedman, 1970; McWilliams and Siegel, 1997; Jensen, 2002). Through a process termed 'screening,' SRI funds restrict their investments to those firms that engage in these costly and burdensome social practices:

> Screening describes the inclusion or exclusion of corporate securities in investment portfolios based on social or environmental criteria. Socially concerned investors generally seek to own profitable companies with respectable employee relations, strong records of community involvement, excellent environmental impact policies and practices, respect for human rights around the world, and safe and useful products. Conversely, they often avoid investments in those firms that fall short in these areas. (Social Investment Forum, 2002)

As a result, SRI funds intentionally select firms that are likely to have above-average operating

portfolio of investments that eliminate unsystematic, or specific, risk.

costs and so, all else equal, below-average financial performance. Thus, as one SRI critic bluntly concluded, 'Socially conscious investing is a dumb idea, yielding sub-par returns, and screaming with contradictions' (Rothchild, 1996: 197).

Moreover, screening may involve the exclusion of not merely certain firms, but entire industries and even economic sectors from the portfolios of SRI funds. For example, the tobacco industry is commonly screened out of SRI funds, and the entire defense sector is excluded from many SRI funds (Social Investment Forum, 2002). The exclusion of firms, industries, and economic sectors has significant implications for the financial performance of an investment portfolio, regardless of its social orientation. According to modern portfolio theory, an investment portfolio bears two types of risk: systematic and unsystematic, or 'specific,' risk (Markowitz, 1952; Sharpe, 1964; Fama, 1971). Systematic risk is the risk inherent in the volatility of the entire capital market, while specific risk is associated with the volatility of an individual security. Investors may assemble portfolios in such a way that the specific risk carried by any individual security within the portfolio is offset by the specific risk carried by another. This is referred to as diversification. Efficient capital markets reward investors for bearing systematic risk, but because diversification is possible, investors are not rewarded for bearing specific risk. That is, when a fund carries specific risk, it fails to reach the efficient frontier, wherein the risk/return trade-off is optimized. Because they exclude certain firms, industries, and sectors, SRI funds thus tend to bear a substantial degree of specific risk (Kurtz and DiBartolomeo, 1996; DiBartolomeo and Kurtz, 1999), and so should experience decreased risk-adjusted returns.

However, a mutual fund can achieve diversification ample to effectively eliminate most specific risk even if it does not select the entire universe of securities. The traditional 'rule of thumb' in the finance literature is that a fund can closely approximate a well-diversified portfolio with as few as 20 or 30 randomly selected stocks (Fisher and Lorie, 1970; Bloomfield, Leftwich, and Long, 1977). More recently, due to increasing volatility in the stock market, researchers have concluded that the minimum number of randomly selected stocks necessary to closely approximate a well-diversified portfolio is at least 50 (Campbell *et al.*, 2001), and some have estimated this figure to be as high as 200 (Statman, 1987). Regardless, one need not hold the entire universe of stocks to be sufficiently diversified. However, the subset selected for the portfolio needs to be randomly chosen for this rule of thumb to hold, and even then, some specific risk remains. For example, Campbell *et al.* (2001) found that a random portfolio of 50 securities still bore a 5 percent excess standard deviation relative to the market portfolio.

SRI portfolios, as with the holdings of many other mutual funds, are not randomly chosen. They are intentionally selected based on a set of screening criteria. Thus, one can expect SRI funds, even those with large and relatively diverse holdings, to bear specific risk (Kurtz, 1997). For example, the Domini Social Index (DSI), which serves as the benchmark portfolio for socially responsible investing and is the SRI fund most often criticized for having broad holdings (Glassman, 1999; Goetz, 1997), holds some 400 non-randomly selected stocks. Measures of both its beta and standard deviation of returns have shown that it is riskier than the S&P 500 (Statman, 2000). Other researchers have also found that there are financial costs associated with the lack of diversification of SRI funds. Teper (1992) estimated that funds that chose their portfolios based on social criteria bore a one percent loss in returns relative to diversified funds. Rudd (1979) measured the returns to portfolios that screened out firms with holdings in South Africa and found that they suffered a 4 percent loss in returns. More recently, Geczy *et al.* (2003) found a range of losses to risk-adjusted return, from just a few basis points per month, to more than 1500 basis points per month. Thus, a substantial body of both theoretical and empirical research in modern portfolio theory indicates that SRI funds are bound to suffer a financial loss of some magnitude due to inadequate diversification.

The financial benefits of social responsibility

Despite the financial logic of modern portfolio theory, many researchers have found that SRI funds yield returns that equal or exceed those of mutual funds that operate without the constraints of social responsibility. For example, Diltz (1995), Guerard (1997), and Hamilton *et al.* (1993) all found that there were no significant differences between the risk-adjusted returns of portfolios composed of socially responsible firms and portfolios selected

without social screening. The DSI, outperformed the S&P 500 index from its inception in May 1990 through March 1999, earning a total of 470 percent as compared to 389 percent for the S&P 500 (DiBartolomeo and Kurtz, 1999). Even on a risk-adjusted basis, the DSI's financial performance exceeded that of the unscreened S&P 500 (Luck and Pilotte, 1993; Statman, 2000).

How can SRI funds possibly earn equal or higher risk-adjusted returns than unconstrained funds? Though modern portfolio theory rightfully assesses the costs to limiting investment choices through social screening, it does not account for the benefits that social screening may bring. Portfolio theory assesses only the ability of a given stock to push a portfolio toward or away from the efficient frontier, wherein risk-adjusted return is maximized (Markowitz, 1952). However, it takes no account of any variation in the ability of a firm upon which a stock's value is based to create value. Rather, under the assumption of perfectly efficient markets, each stock is treated as homogeneous in all but its volatility relative to the market.[3]

SRI proponents counter that, while SRI portfolio managers are constrained from choosing amongst the entire universe of stocks, the pool of stocks from which they do choose is superior to that of the overall market and therein more likely to provide favorable financial returns over time. Firms are embedded in a social environment (Granovetter, 1985; Scott, 1981). In order to maintain legitimacy and effectively attract resources, firms must build favorable relations with those groups that compose this environment. Strong social performance is an indicator that a firm possesses superior management talent (Alexander and Bucholtz, 1978; Bowman and Haire, 1975) that understands how to improve internal and external relationships through socially responsible activities (Moskowitz, 1972). Thus, SRI proponents argue that because social relationships matter to financial

---

[3] We recognize that some form of market failure is central to a strategy literature in which firms can achieve above-average returns (see Barney, 1991; Dierickx and Cool, 1991; Wernerfelt, 1984; Williamson, 1975, 1985). This presents an obvious dilemma relative to an efficient markets hypothesis (EMH), the resolution of which is outside the scope of this paper. There remains considerable debate in the finance literature as to whether, and in what form, the EMH holds. In fact, this has been one of most researched topics in the field of finance (see Fama, 1991, for a review). The interested reader is encouraged to consult this literature for more on this debate.

performance, social responsibility is not merely a cost, but a wise investment.

This basic rationale is supported by stakeholder theory, which suggests that the better a firm manages its relationships with the myriad groups that have some interest, or 'stake,' in the firm, the better its financial performance over time (Donaldson and Preston, 1995; Freeman, 1984). For example, a firm with a favorable work environment can decrease its hiring costs and increase its employee retention rate, decrease community opposition and legal costs when opening a new factory, and more easily lobby for tax breaks from local governments (Freeman, 1984; Waddock and Graves, 1997). A favorable social agenda builds valuable goodwill that can buffer a firm from unforeseen problems and even provide valuable new opportunities not available to less socially responsible firms (Fombrun *et al.*, 2000). All in all, effective stakeholder management can create competitive advantage. Empirical results bear this out. Graves and Waddock's (2000) study of 'built to last' companies suggested that the investments in stakeholder relations made by these firms led to their above-average financial performance over an 8-year window, as measured by return on equity, return on assets, and return on sales. Hillman and Keim's (2001) study of the market value added of 308 firms within the S&P 500 found that effective stakeholder management was significantly correlated with, and preceded improved financial performance. Thus, even though SRI funds must draw from a limited pool of firms, they draw from a richer pool—one that is more likely to contain well-run, stable firms that outperform the broader market over the long run. The competitive advantage these individual firms possess aggregate into superior financial returns at the portfolio level.

Variable financial returns to social responsibility

Many studies have been published supporting a negative relationship, and many studies have been published supporting a positive relationship. Which is it? If one sums up this conflicting empirical work, it appears that the relationship is positive on the whole: 'A simple compilation of the findings suggests there is a positive association, and certainly very little evidence of a negative association, between a company's social performance and its financial performance' (Margolis

and Walsh, 2003: 277). Orlitzky *et al.* (2003) recently conducted a meta-analysis that led to a similar conclusion: the prior literature, in aggregate, indicates that social and financial performance are positively related. However, as Margolis and Walsh (2003: 278) caution, such a conclusion is illusory. A compilation of findings cannot produce a definitive conclusion given the limitations of the underlying studies. As many reviews of this body of literature note, these studies are imperfect in a variety of ways (see Wood and Jones, 1995; Griffin and Mahon, 1997; Rowley and Berman, 2000). Thus, Margolis and Walsh (2003: 278) argue that '[t]he CSP-CFP empirical literature reinforces, rather than relieves the tension surrounding corporate responses to social misery.' Overall, despite all the attention to the topic, the nature of the relationship remains contested.

Further fueling the debate, some critics of SRI studies have argued that the strong financial performance of some SRI funds could be an indication that the relationship between social responsibility and financial performance is actually negative. When SRI funds were first introduced, they were 'the butt of Wall Street jokes' (Glassman, 1999: 4) because their financial returns were often quite poor. These critics suggest that many SRI funds have become strong financial performers only because their 'once-strict screening criteria have turned porous' (Goetz, 1997: 43). That is, the improved financial performance of SRI funds is a result of gradually minimizing social performance standards for those firms to be included in their portfolios. SRI funds have 'opened the door to less-than-angelic companies whose high returns have helped SRI gain the upper hand in the longstanding performance debate' (Goetz, 1997: 43). Therefore, social performance must indeed be sacrificed to gain financial returns.

This argument points to the need to account for heterogeneity in the standards of social responsibility employed by SRI funds. The standard approach in research on SRI funds is to contrast the financial performance of a set of screened funds with that of a set of unscreened funds or the overall market (e.g., Guerard, 1997; Hamilton *et al.*, 1993). This approach confounds a range of screening practices within SRI funds. Because some SRI funds have more stringent social screening standards than others, the SRI literature must examine variances *within* screened funds to better determine the underlying nature of the relationship between

Strat. Mgmt. J., **27**: 1101–1122 (2006)
DOI: 10.1002/smj

financial and social performance. The uncertainty of extant empirical results, despite decades of study, may be a function of treating social responsibility as a dichotomous variable.

If the heterogeneity in the intensity of social screens applied by SRI funds is accounted for, the combination of modern portfolio and stakeholder theories points toward neither a strictly positive nor negative relationship, but a curvilinear relationship between social and financial performance. Based on the efficient market assumption that underlies modern portfolio theory, consider the entire universe of stocks to have a uniform distribution of returns. Those stocks in the center of the distribution earn the market return, while those in the left tail earn less, and those in the right tail earn above-average returns. A fund manager taking random draws from this universe can expect to assemble a portfolio that will earn the market return, so long as the resulting portfolio is diversified. If the stocks picked do not sum to a diversified portfolio, the fund carries unsystematic risk and so can expect to have a risk-adjusted return that underperforms the market. Since social screening systematically constrains the ability to diversify, an SRI fund is thus expected to underperform the market.

However, a fund manager using social screens may have better odds of avoiding stocks in the left tail of the distribution and picking stocks in the right tail. Based on stakeholder theory, we expect that firms engaging in socially responsible practices are more likely to achieve superior long-run performance (Freeman, 1984; Jones, 1995; Wicks, Berman and Jones, 1999). Thus, socially responsible firms are more likely to be in the right tail of the distribution. In contrast, firms

with poor stakeholder relations are more risky and susceptible to crises (Cornell and Shapiro, 1987; Fombrun *et al.*, 2000), and so more likely to be in the left tail of the distribution. As a result of using social screens that exclude firms with poor stakeholder relations and funnel in firms with good stakeholder relations, SRI fund managers become more likely to select firms that will achieve above-average returns, and less likely to select firms that will earn below-average returns.[4] Figure 1 illustrates this relationship.

The combination of modern portfolio theory and stakeholder theory, as well as a long history of mixed empirical findings, then suggests that the relationship between social and financial performance may be curvilinear, not strictly monotonic. SRI funds that have relatively weak social responsibility standards will be able to choose from a larger universe of potential investments, thereby increasing their odds of achieving ample diversification and hence improving risk-adjusted financial performance. As an SRI fund's social standards increase, its pool of investment opportunities shrinks, and so it will have a decreased likelihood of establishing a well-diversified portfolio. However, this negative effect is offset as the stringency of social screening intensifies. Those funds that greatly restrict potential investments benefit from improved selection of investment targets

---

[4] This argument does not address skill differences across fund managers. Rather, it is premised on averages; given that the pool of firms from which SRI fund managers select is richer, better returns are more likely, regardless of individual fund manager characteristics. Nonetheless, it seems reasonable to conclude, and some have argued, that the actions inherent in screening can provide useful information to fund managers about a target firm's relationships with its stakeholders (e.g., Lowry, 1991).

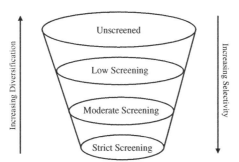

Figure 1. The effects of social screening on the universe of stock choices

(Lowry, 1991). Though an SRI fund may bear more and more specific risk by choosing from an increasingly smaller pool of stocks, the pool from which it does choose becomes richer. As a fund manager dips into this increasingly rich pool, he/she is more likely to pick a stock that will provide above-average financial returns. SRI funds that are 'stuck in the middle' may bear all the costs of either pure strategy without gaining any of the benefits. That is, an SRI fund with a moderate level of social screening may bear specific risk yet not consistently exclude underperforming firms or consistently select those firms with above-average financial performance. Thus, we hypothesize:

> *Hypothesis 1: The relationship between the intensity of social screening and financial performance for SRI funds is curvilinear (U-shaped).*

The financial returns to different types of social responsibility

SRI funds vary not only in the intensity of their social screening, but also in the types of social screens they employ. SRI fund investors can choose from a variety of funds tailored to a specific social issue or group of social issues. For example, the Aquinas line of SRI funds pursue investment in only those firms that they deem to amply reflect Catholic religious values, and the Sierra Club mutual funds invest in only those firms that they believe have acceptable environmental performance. Whereas previous studies, in comparing SRI to non-SRI funds, have largely ignored the rich heterogeneity within SRI funds, we expect to find significant financial performance differences not only across varying levels of screening intensity, but also across the varying types of social screens that SRI funds use.

As Jones (1995: 430) noted: 'Certain types of corporate social performance are manifestations of attempts to establish trusting, cooperative firm/stakeholder relationships and should be positively linked to a company's financial performance.' However, engaging in the socially responsible behaviors that build these relationships is costly. For example, firms that dole out corporate philanthropy, provide day care centers and paid parental leave, or engage in other such socially responsible behaviors incur significant expenses. Faced with a large set of often-conflicting demands

from a broad set of stakeholders and a limited budget, firms must decide where to allocate their resources. Which investments in stakeholder relationship building are likely to generate the greatest financial returns?

Instrumental stakeholder theory provides a theoretical basis for predicting the varying financial implications of differing types of social performance. It points out that some stakeholder relationships are more instrumental to a firm's success than others. The more a firm relies on a particular stakeholder group, the more that firm stands to gain by investing in the creation and maintenance of trusting relations with that group (Preston and Post, 1975; Waddock and Graves, 1997; Wicks *et al.*, 1999). Employees, in particular, are instrumental to a firm's financial performance. Employees constitute the 'front line' of the firm, and are responsible for transforming the firm's inputs into outputs. As we have moved further and further away from the industrial age and begun to rely more and more on the knowledge and creativity of employees to create value, labor relations have become increasingly important (Florida, 2002). Positive labor relations can facilitate increased productivity, decreased turnover, and decreased strife (Freeman, 1984). For example, during a period when most major airlines suffered one or more strikes, Southwest Airlines, a firm with much-heralded labor relations, avoided such disruptions and maintained profitability. Several studies have shown that the better a firm's labor relations, the better its financial performance (Berman *et al.*, 1999; Greening and Turban, 2000; Jones and Murrell, 2001; Turban and Greening, 1996; Waddock and Graves, 1997; Wright *et al.*, 1995). Thus, we hypothesize the following:

> *Hypothesis 2: SRI funds that select firms for their portfolios based on labor relations screening criteria will earn higher financial returns than those that do not.*

Firms must physically locate their operations within the boundaries of specific communities. Poor relations with these host communities can create a variety of costly problems. For example, poor community relations can increase the difficulty and cost of expansion and thereby limit a firm's growth. A firm with poor community relations may face 'not-in-my-back-yard' (NIMBY) protests when attempting to open new plants. Such protests decrease the ability of a firm to obtain essential building and zoning permits from local governments and force the firm to bear significant litigation expenses (Dear, 1992; Sellers, 1993). On the other hand, favorable community relations bring a number of benefits. Favorable community relations can not only decrease the likelihood and intensity of NIMBY protests, but can also decrease the likelihood of attacks by shareholder activists (Rehbein, Waddock, and Graves, 2004: 239). Moreover, favorable community relations increase the likelihood of successful bargaining with local government officials for favorable taxation and regulation (Waddock and Graves, 1997). More generally, 'Companies that treat local communities well reap many returns, including better schools, fewer local restrictions, and a better infrastructure to support the firm. In the long term, these decrease corporate operating costs' (Waddock and Smith, 2000: 79). This better infrastructure includes access to more highly skilled employees (Greening and Turban, 2000). A variety of empirical studies have indeed found that a firm's efforts to improve relations with their host communities through activities such as philanthropy and support of employee volunteering can lead to improved financial performance (Hillman and Keim, 2001; Preston and O'Bannon, 1997; Simpson and Kohers, 2002; Waddock and Graves 2000). Therefore, we expect the following:

Hypothesis 3: SRI funds that select firms for their portfolios based on community relations screening criteria will earn higher financial returns than those that do not.

Finally, responsible environmental practices have become critical to a firm's relationships with a variety of stakeholder groups. Over the last few decades, stakeholders have increased their expectations about the degree to which firms should assume responsibility for protection of the natural environment (Hoffman, 1997, 1999). Today, firms with poor environmental performance risk consumer disfavor, protest by activist groups, negative media coverage, and general degradation of their reputation (Fombrun *et al.*, 2000; King and Lenox, 2000). Poor environmental practices can also place firms at increased risk for serious industrial accidents that may result in large regulatory fines, costly lawsuits, and even the shutdown of operations (Perrow, 1984; Rees, 1994). However,

it can be quite costly for a firm to substantially improve its environmental performance. Do the benefits outweigh the costs? A growing body of literature indicates that it does, indeed, 'pay to be green.' Studies have shown that strong environmental performance is associated with increased operational efficiency, improved learning and innovation, decreased insurance costs, improved relationships with stakeholders, differentiation of products and services, and other such benefits that, individually and in combination, can more than offset the costs of implementing environmental improvements (Hart and Ahuja, 1996; King and Lenox, 2002; Klassen and McLaughlin, 1996; Klassen and Whybark, 1999; Konar and Cohen, 2001; Russo and Fouts, 1997; Porter and van der Linde, 1995). We therefore hypothesize:

Hypothesis 4: SRI funds that select firms for their portfolios based on environmental screening criteria will earn higher financial returns than those that do not.

METHODOLOGY

The data we employ come from several sources. Our initial sample consisted of the socially responsible mutual funds tracked by the Social Investment Forum. The Social Investment Forum is a national non-profit organization that encourages and promotes the growth of socially responsible investing. Data from this source provide information about the social screening strategies (number and type of social screens used) of 67 socially responsible funds.[5] After identifying our initial sample of 67 socially responsible mutual funds, we used CRSP data to track each fund's financial performance. We compiled monthly financial performance data from 1972 to 2000, which encompass the entire substantive existence of SRI funds. We supplemented this data with mutual fund information from Weisenberger and ICDI. Weisenberger

---

[5] Although screening data were only available from 1997 on, in the results presented herein, we use performance data from as far back as was available to get as complete a picture as possible. We acknowledge that the inherent assumption in using such data is that the screening strategy of the mutual fund did not change prior to 1997. To check the implications of this assumption, we performed two sensitivity analyses. First, we limited the sample to those funds that were founded in 1997 or later. Second, we eliminated the data for all funds prior to 1997 to check for potential biases. In both cases, the quantitative and qualitative results were consistent with those shown.

Strat. Mgmt. J., **27**: 1101–1122 (2006)
DOI: 10.1002/smj

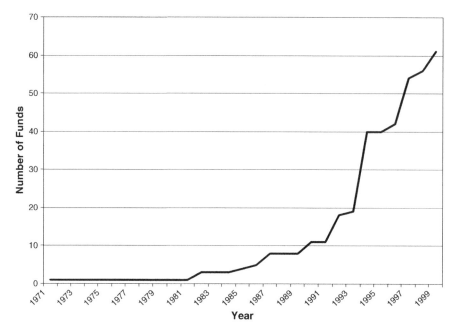

Figure 2.   Population of SRI funds

and ICDI are mutual fund tracking services that provide a standard directory of information on mutual funds and their holdings such as mutual fund total assets and general investment strategy (e.g., growth, income, capital appreciation).

The resultant sample from these sources is an unbalanced panel of 61 funds and 4,821 fund-month observations. The total available sample could have reached 22,512 fund-month observations (67 funds × 28 years × 12 months of performance data). However, six funds failed to report their social screening strategies to the Social Investment Forum. Most data were lost, though, because SRI boomed only in recent years. Only one fund, the PAX World Fund, existed at the beginning of the sample (1972). No other fund entered the sample until 1982. As illustrated in Figure 2, most SRI funds did not exist prior to 1996, with a 218 percent growth in the number of funds since then. Fortunately, none of the funds in our sample exited during the event window, therein eliminating concern of a survival bias that has plagued other studies of this type (see Elton, Gruber and Blake, 1996b).

Dependent variable

We test for the effects of social screening on financial performance. Thus, our dependent variable is the risk-adjusted financial performance of a given SRI fund in a given month. *Risk-adjusted performance* (RAP) is defined as the average monthly return, measured as the percentage change in a fund's market value from the beginning to the end of a given month, adjusted by the fund's specific beta (see Sharpe, 1964). For details on how we used the CAPM model to calculate RAP, refer to the Appendix.

Independent variables

Previous research has taken a largely dichotomous approach to categorizing SRI funds: either a fund screens for social responsibility, or it does not. Most empirical work then compares the performance of SRI funds to non-SRI funds. However, SRI funds are not homogeneous. Some have more stringent social screening standards than others. Gains to highly diversified but weakly screened SRI funds may have offset performance losses in

Strat. Mgmt. J., **27**: 1101–1122 (2006)
DOI: 10.1002/smj

1110   *M. L. Barnett and R. M. Salomon*

less intensively screened SRI funds. Then again, intensively screened SRI funds may have selected a stronger portfolio, thereby subsidizing the poor choices of the weakly screened funds. Thus, lumping all SRI funds into a single category may have contributed to the largely contradictory findings of prior research. Moreover, such studies shed no light on the argument of SRI opponents that 'the key to the recent success of many SR[I] funds could be that they own what conventional funds own' (Glassman, 1999: 4). To advance the debate, we examine the performance implications of varying the stringency of screening strategies used by different SRI funds.

The Social Investment Forum lists 12 types of screens that SRI funds may use to filter firms from their investment portfolios. Potential screening criteria include excluding firms based upon their affiliation with the following 12 industries or issues: alcohol, tobacco, gambling, defense/weapons, animal testing, product/service quality, environment, human rights, labor relations, employment equality, community investment, and community relations. We refer to an SRI fund's choice of number of screens to apply to its investment portfolio as its *screening intensity*. Screening intensity varies from 1 to 12. If a fund's screening intensity is given a value of 12, this indicates that the fund employs all 12 of the above-listed screens, whereas a value of 1 indicates that the fund uses only 1 of the 12 available screens.[6] Each SRI fund determines how many and which of these screens it wishes to use. For example, the Ariel Socially Responsible Fund uses only two screens (tobacco and nuclear power) while the Calvert Social Equity Fund uses all twelve screens to select its investment portfolio.

The number of screens employed by the fund proxies for the extent of diversification of the

fund. As illustrated in Figure 1, the greater a fund's screening intensity, the smaller its universe of potential investment targets. In contrast, lesser screening intensity implies a larger universe from which a fund manager might select, and so a closer resemblance to a broadly diversified portfolio. Thus, a large value for screening intensity indicates an increasing tendency toward a narrower SRI portfolio, while a small value for screening intensity reflects a more diversified SRI portfolio.[7]

In order to test Hypotheses 2, 3, and 4, we must tease out the variance in performance associated with employment, community, and environmental screens. To do this, we created a dichotomous variable for each of the screening strategies related to workforce, community, and environmental issues. For instance, in order to test Hypothesis 4, we assigned a value of 1 to the variable *environment* if a fund screened out firms based on environmental performance, zero otherwise. We similarly defined two variables related to workforce issues in order to test Hypothesis 2: *labor relations* and *equal employment*. Finally, as a test of Hypothesis 3, if a fund screened out firms based on what it deemed as a poor community record, then the variables *community investment* and *community services*, respectively, received a value of 1, zero otherwise. Table 1 provides general definitions of how each of the above screens is employed by the various socially responsible mutual funds.

Control variables

Because our dependent variable captures the financial performance of a fund, we must control for

---

[6] In sensitivity analyses we dropped those funds that reported extreme screening intensity values (e.g., fewer than 3 and greater than 10 screens) to test for outliers or influential points. Results remained qualitatively unchanged.

[7] The inherent assumption in using such an additive screening intensity variable is that any one screen is the same as another inasmuch as it decreases the opportunity for diversification. We acknowledge that this is a coarse proxy, as each screen may not contribute equally to the ability of a mutual fund manager to diversify. We therefore checked the robustness of the results by using different weightings of the screening intensity variable. Results were largely consistent with those presented herein.

Table 1.   Definitions of social screens

Type of social screen	Firms affected by screen
1. Environment	Excludes firms with a record of poor environmental performance
2. Labor relations	Excludes firms with a record of poor labor relations practices
3. Employment/equality	Excludes firms that violate norms of equal employment and diversity at work
4. Community investment	Excludes firms that do not invest in and/or develop economically depressed communities
5. Community relations	Excludes firms that have a poor record of accountability to local community stakeholders

Strat. Mgmt. J., **27**: 1101–1122 (2006)
DOI: 10.1002/smj

factors that could systematically affect financial performance. We therefore include variables previously identified as likely to influence the financial performance of mutual funds, while controlling for unobservables using a combination of fixed and random effects. We discuss the details of the econometric specification in the subsequent section.

A fund's age is a potential factor in its financial performance. Older funds may have different cost structures from new or young funds. Moreover, the collective experience of a particular fund accumulates over time, and that learning may be a valuable asset in choosing and managing its portfolio (Argote, 1999). We control for any age effects with the variable *fund age*, a count of the number of months since the fund's inception.

Larger funds may outperform smaller funds because of economies of scale in fund management. For instance, larger funds may spread costs of information gathering, investor solicitation and communication, and other fund management expenses across a greater asset base. On the other hand, larger funds may face liabilities of size. As they seek ways in which to invest cash, they may find it increasingly difficult to uncover bargains. Moreover, when larger funds make sizable market purchases, the size of the trades may move the market, making it difficult for these funds to purchase undervalued stocks without the act of purchase raising the value of the stock. Therefore, larger funds may be constrained to make smaller purchases than desired, spread across a larger number of stocks than desired. In order to control for any potential size effect, we include a measure of overall fund assets (measured in millions of U.S. dollars). We label this variable *total assets*.

Global economic cycles and the risks (or potential rewards), over and above those inherent in the underlying U.S. market, may affect financial performance. Thus, funds with holdings only in the United States may perform differently from funds with international holdings. In order to control for performance differentials across funds with national and international holdings, we include the dummy variable *global fund*. This variable takes the value of 1 for funds with international holdings, zero otherwise.[8]

---

[8] In sensitivity analyses we eliminated those funds with international holdings. Results were largely consistent with those presented herein.

Even after adjusting for a fund's risk profile, there may still remain some difference in the risk-adjusted performance between bond funds and stock funds. Bonds may be a better investment vehicle than stocks, or vice versa. We therefore include two control measures to capture the effects of pursuing different general investment strategies (see Elton, Gruber, and Blake, 1996a). ICDI gathers information on the percentage of total assets each fund invests in stocks vs. bonds. We label these measures as *percent stock* and *percent bonds*, respectively.

Finally, we include yearly dummy variables to control for any residual macro-economic factors that affect all funds similarly and to control for the potential for simultaneity bias and residual serial correlation of the error (Greene, 2000).

Statistical methods

In selecting an appropriate multivariate statistical method, we begin with an ordinary least squares (OLS) specification. As shown in Equation 1, we first specify a fund's risk-adjusted performance (RAP_{it}) as a linear function of the vector X of independent variables for fund i at time t that we wish to examine and can measure, in addition to an error term, which we label u_{it}:

$$RAP_{it} = X_{it}\beta + u_{it} \qquad (1)$$

Given the panel data structure, with several observations per fund, the possibility arises that u_{it} in Equation 1 will not be independent across time (Greene, 2000). Thus, any systematic effect on risk-adjusted performance that is not included in X will be captured in the error term. Previous research has identified many macro-economic factors associated with performance, including government policy or systemic shocks that influence industries and sectors. Should we be unable to identify and measure all of these effects, there exists the potential for a systematic component to be embedded in u_{it}. This systematic component will lead to correlated errors across observations, which violates an assumption of OLS (Kmenta, 1997; Kennedy, 1998).

Conceptually, we can decompose u_{it} into a vector of systematic (fixed) effects, which we label Z_t, plus a truly random error component, which we label e_{it}. In this case, Z_t represents the yearly dummy variables. After we extract Z_t from u_{it}, we can more confidently assume that e_{it} is i.i.d. normal with zero mean. Equation 2 represents this decomposition of u_{it}:

$$RAP_{it} = X_{it}\beta + Z_t + e_{it} \qquad (2)$$

Finally, because there are several observations for each mutual fund, the possibility still exists that e_{it} in Equation 2 will not be independent within a common fund. This would occur, for instance, if some funds performed, on a risk-adjusted basis, differently from others over time owing to systematically better fund management, or owing to each fund's idiosyncratic application of particular screens. In theory, either a fund fixed- or random-effects model may be used to correct for this (Greene, 2000). However, in our data, some funds exhibit very little variance in total assets and screening strategies across time. Under this condition, and because we have few observations per fund on average, a random-effects model is preferred (Kennedy, 1998). We therefore arrive at our final econometric specification as listed below in Equation 3:

$$RAP_{it} = X_{it}\beta + Z_t + F_i + v_{it} \qquad (3)$$

In this case, F_i represents the individual mutual fund disturbance. The efficient estimator employed is generalized least squares, and nested models can be compared by the chi-square test.

In summary, we include a fixed year effect and a random fund effect to control for characteristics not directly measured by our other variables but that might correlate with risk-adjusted mutual fund performance. The advantage of the fixed- and random-effects specifications are that they control for unobserved heterogeneity without having to precisely specify the source of that heterogeneity. Therefore, they provide robust estimates that eliminate bias in statistical results. The disadvantage, however, is that we cannot precisely isolate or identify every individual factor that influences the dependent variable. Because our goal is to control for and not investigate or test these effects, we accept this trade-off.

RESULTS

Table 2 presents descriptive statistics and product moment correlations for the variables we used to test the hypotheses. For the most part, the descriptive statistics and correlations are as expected. The

Table 2.   Descriptive statistics and product moment correlations

	1.	2.	3.	4.	5.	6.	7.	8.	9.	10.	11.	12.
1. RAP	1											
2. Screening intensity	−0.001	1										
3. Fund age	0.019	0.066	1									
4. Total assets	0.025	0.035	0.604	1								
5. Percent stocks	0.072	−0.039	0.000	0.113	1							
6. Percent bonds	−0.107	−0.082	0.118	0.019	−0.630	1						
7. Global fund	−0.033	0.134	−0.127	−0.027	0.199	−0.153	1					
8. Labor relations	−0.019	0.588	−0.163	0.065	0.050	0.048	0.238	1				
9. Equal employment	−0.019	0.609	0.151	0.074	−0.046	−0.157	0.167	0.201	1			
10. Community investment	−0.018	0.442	0.195	−0.104	−0.211	0.092	0.054	0.039	0.409	1		
11. Community relations	−0.002	0.735	−0.216	−0.075	0.030	−0.066	0.133	0.612	0.570	0.316	1	
12. Environment	−0.044	0.405	0.045	−0.016	−0.016	0.070	0.124	0.260	0.235	−0.067	0.214	1
Mean	0.13	7.79	68.38	93.00	67.30	16.02	0.07	0.46	0.73	0.50	0.47	0.83
S.D.	0.03	3.02	58.62	173.20	37.51	29.11	0.26	0.49	0.44	0.50	0.50	0.37
Minimum	−3.02	1	1	0.19	0	0	0	0	0	0	0	0
Maximum	3.08	12	354	1483.92	106.7	100	1	1	1	1	1	1

Strat. Mgmt. J., **27**: 1101–1122 (2006)
DOI: 10.1002/smj

average fund held about 67 percent of its portfolio in equity and 16 percent in bonds, thus explaining the relatively low fund beta.[9] The greater the percentage of assets allocated to stocks, the greater the mutual fund financial performance. Likewise, the more a mutual fund invested in bonds, the lower the risk-adjusted performance of the fund.

Table 2 suggests that many of the screens tend to be used in conjunction with others. For instance, mutual funds that screened on the basis of community relations also tended to screen out firms with poor labor relations ($\rho = 0.612$). It is also interesting to note the relative popularity of particular types of social screens. Whereas many SRI funds screened out firms based on their environmental performance (83%) and equal employment records (73%), less than half of SRI funds concerned themselves with labor relations (46%) or community relations (47%). This presents some econometric challenges. The main concern is that such high correlations may infuse multicollinearity into the regression. Given this concern, we performed various sensitivity analyses to ensure the robustness of the results. First, we added each type of social screening strategy separately into the regressions; the results were largely consistent across specifications. Second, we entered the independent variables in different orders. The results did not change substantively. Finally, we explored the variance inflation contribution of each of the independent variables. All were well within the acceptable range (Kennedy, 1998; Belsley, Kuh, and Welsch, 1980). As a result, interpretations of the findings do not change.

Figure 3 presents two graphs that display (a) average monthly RAP and (b) average screening intensity for all funds in the study over time. Figure 3(a) illustrates that there was a dip in performance in the early 1990s, and then the financial performance of SRI funds tended to increase over time. As discussed previously, some have argued that this increase in performance has come at the expense of a decrease in the stringency of social screening (Glassman, 1999; Goetz, 1997).

Figure 3(b) provides modest support for this position, as it shows that average screening intensity has declined over time, though most of the decline occurred in the early 1990s, with only small declines from the late 1990s until the end of the study in 2000. Of course, these graphs do not control for intervening factors that have the potential to influence the relationship between RAP and screening intensity. We address these additional influences in the analyses below.

In Table 3 we present results of regression models testing the first hypothesis. While we included fixed year effects in the empirical specification, we did not report them here. Briefly though, the results suggested that while mutual fund performance was best in 1997 and 1998 in raw terms, the funds in this sample assumed more risk during those years, which raised their risk profile and actually decreased their risk-adjusted performance. Consistent with the correlation tables, funds with a greater percentage of equity investments achieved the best overall risk-adjusted performance, while funds that invested heavily in bonds were the worst overall performers in our sample. However, we should point out that the economic impact of such findings is negligible. For example, the marginal effects in Model 1 indicate that a 10 percent increase in stock holdings amounts to about a 0.06 percent increase in risk-adjusted performance per month, or about 0.72 percent per year. Not surprisingly, global mutual funds performed consistently worse than funds with a purely domestic investment orientation. This result may be due to the additional risk involved with investing in foreign locations (Hymer, 1976) over and above the risk imposed by the domestic market.

In Model 1, we posit risk-adjusted performance to be a linear function of screening intensity. In this specification we test whether including more social screens is positively or negatively related to fund financial performance. A negative relationship would support those who contend that social screening has a detrimental affect on financial performance by limiting a fund's ability to diversify, while a positive relationship would support the stakeholder argument that well-screened socially responsible funds outperform more broadly diversified funds because they are able to select from a better subset of firms. Interestingly, we find no linear association between the number of screens and fund performance.

---

[9] The maximum percentage of equity reached 106.7 percent in this sample. This suggests that a fund borrowed to invest more than its total assets in stocks. Mutual funds are generally restricted from leveraging assets by the Investment Company Act of 1940; however, at times, they may borrow to invest more than their total assets. This is not a common practice. In our sample, only two of the funds were ever levered (invested greater than 100% of their assets) at any point in time. When we eliminated these levered funds from the analysis, the results did not change.

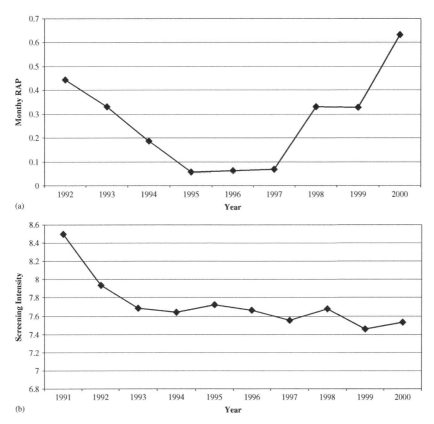

Figure 3.   Fund performance and screening intensity over time. (a) Average monthly RAP (all funds). (b) Average screening intensity (all funds)

Model 2 adds a squared screening intensity term. Because the models are nested, we can directly compare the χ^2 statistic across the two to determine which dominates. The $\chi^2_{(1)}$ increase of 7.12 from Model 1 to Model 2 is significant at the $p < 0.01$ level, suggesting that Model 2 better fits the data. Consistent with our expectations, we find a negative and significant coefficient for screening intensity and a positive and significant coefficient for its quadratic. This result implies a curvilinear, non-monotonic relationship between screening intensity and fund performance, thus supporting Hypothesis 1. Risk-adjusted performance declines at first as screening intensity increases, reaching a minimum at 7 screens, but then increases continuously until it reaches the

maximum social screening intensity of 12 screens. We note that even at the maximum of 12 screens, however, performance does not recover to reach the levels achieved by those funds with 1 screen. In fact, the results suggest that we should expect funds with 12 screens to suffer performance decrements of about 0.2 percent per month (about 2.4% per year) vs. more broadly diversified funds. We therefore cannot conclude that screening comes without costs. Figure 4 depicts this relationship graphically.

In Table 4 we explore the variance across the screening strategies of interest. Not surprisingly, we find that some screening strategies significantly influence mutual fund performance. However, some of the relationships are not as hypothesized.

Strat. Mgmt. J., **27**: 1101–1122 (2006)
DOI: 10.1002/smj

Table 3.   Regression results for screening intensity

	Model 1 (RAP)	Model 2 (RAP)
Constant	0.533**	1.090***
	(1.84)	(2.56)
Screening intensity	−0.005	−0.202**
	(−0.22)	(−1.78)
Screening intensity^2		0.014**
		(1.77)
Fund age	0.001	0.001
	(0.87)	(0.88)
Total assets	0.000	0.000
	(0.33)	(0.46)
Percent stocks	0.006***	0.006***
	(2.35)	(2.53)
Percent bonds	−0.009***	−0.009***
	(−2.69)	(−2.68)
Global fund	−0.609**	−0.698***
	(−2.19)	(−2.46)
Mutual fund effects	Included	Included
No. of observations	4821	4821
No. of mutual funds	61	61
$\chi^2_{(d.f.)}$	94.23***	101.35***
	(16)	(17)

* *p*-value < 0.10; ** *p*-value < 0.05; *** *p*-value < 0.01 (one-tailed tests)

Although there is no significant relationship between labor relations screening strategies and risk-adjusted performance, mutual funds that actively screened out firms based on their equal employment records suffered performance decrements compared to the baseline fund. The latter result, as shown in Model 1, runs counter

Table 4.   Regression results for screen types

	Model 1 (RAP)	Model 2 (RAP)	Model 3 (RAP)
Constant	0.605***	0.711***	0.950***
	(2.59)	(2.98)	(3.58)
Labor relations	0.110	−0.152	−0.099
	(0.68)	(−0.77)	(−0.51)
Equal employment	−0.287*	−0.571***	−0.471**
	(−1.61)	(−2.50)	(−2.07)
Community investment		−0.091	−0.138
		(−0.54)	(−0.84)
Community relations		0.550**	0.535**
		(2.20)	(2.22)
Environment			−0.381**
			(−1.91)
Fund age	0.002	0.002*	0.002*
	(1.01)	(1.44)	(1.35)
Total assets	0.000	0.000	0.000
	(0.17)	(0.15)	(0.36)
Percent stocks	0.004**	0.004**	0.004**
	(1.92)	(1.72)	(1.81)
Percent bonds	−0.011***	−0.011***	−0.010***
	(−3.39)	(−3.42)	(−3.24)
Global fund	−0.570**	−0.430*	−0.396*
	(−2.03)	(−1.51)	(−1.44)
Mutual fund effects	Included	Included	Included
No. of observations	4821	4821	4821
No. of mutual funds	61	61	61
$\chi^2_{(d.f.)}$	100.57***	110.63***	134.24***
	(16)	(18)	(19)

* *p*-value < 0.10; ** *p*-value < 0.05; *** *p*-value < 0.01 (one-tailed tests)

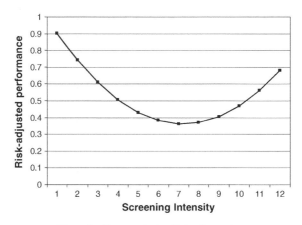

Figure 4.   Non-monotonic effects of screening

Strat. Mgmt. J., **27**: 1101–1122 (2006)
DOI: 10.1002/smj

to Hypothesis 2. Funds that excluded firms that violated norms of equal employment actually suffered a financial penalty of about 0.29 percent per month. This result implies at the firm level that the costs of implementing such programs may outweigh their benefits, and/or that the diversification penalty incurred by mutual funds that use such screens exceed financial gains.

Model 2 adds our proxies for community screening strategies. Although there was no systematic relationship between the screening of those firms that invested in their local community (community investment) and performance, mutual funds that included firms that fostered positive relationships with their local community (community relations) performed better. Therefore, Hypothesis 3 receives some support. This implies, consistent with instrumental stakeholder theory, that firms that foster positive relationships within their communities are financially rewarded.

Finally, contrary to Hypothesis 4, screening on the basis of environmental criteria was negatively related with risk-adjusted financial performance. All else equal, SRI funds that culled environmentally poor performers out of their holdings performed about 0.38 percent worse per month than the baseline SRI fund. The costs of implementing environmentally sound policies appear to outweigh their potential benefits, and they do not compensate mutual funds for the loss in diversification that they impose. These findings stand in contrast to a growing body of literature that suggests that firms that perform better on environmental criteria will experience better overall financial performance (Dowell, Hart, and Yeung, 2000; Porter and van der Linde, 1995; Russo and Fouts, 1997).

Sensitivity analyses

In order to assess the robustness and sensitivity of the results, we tested several variants of the models presented herein.[10] First, because equity returns are sensitive to the time frame of study, the time window used may impact the findings. Although we include time dummies to control for bias that may be induced from pooling data across time, we reran the results using various time windows. Regardless of the time frame selected, the results did not change. In some instances the results were

slightly weaker in statistical significance given a reduction in sample size, but the marginal effects, and so inferences, do not change.

Second, because we are using data both pooled across time, and within funds across time, there is the potential for residual serial correlation of the error. In order to assess whether our results were biased by serial correlation, we ran two specific tests. We pooled the data by year and tested whether AR(1) processes were at work after controlling for year effects. The Durbin–Watson statistic did not suggest that serial correlation of the AR(1) type was present in any of the models. We then arranged the data by fund-year and assessed the within-fund correlations of the residuals over time. We found a within-fund average correlation of around 0.007 across all models; further, none of the individual fund correlations was greater than 0.30 or less than −0.30. We therefore conclude that, after controlling for fund and year effects, the results are not biased by serial correlation.

Third, the inherent assumption underlying our screening intensity measure is that any one screen is the same as another inasmuch as it decreases the opportunity for diversification and increases the opportunity for selectivity. However, some of the screens represent 'positive' screens in that they select certain firms into the portfolio (e.g., environment, labor relations, community relations) while some screens are negative screens in that they eliminate entire industries and sectors from a portfolio. To the extent that negative screens impose more diversification costs upon a fund and positive screens disproportionately increase a fund's selectivity, we might plausibly expect a negative performance effect for 'negative' screens and a positive performance effect for 'positive' screens. In order to test for this possibility, we grouped screens into negative or positive and reran the results presented in Model 1 of Table 3 using counts of positive and negative screens instead of screening intensity. Both variables were economically and statistically insignificant, suggesting that positive and negative screens contribute to both decreased diversification and increased selectivity.

Fourth, we sought to verify that the results presented in Table 4 are not just an artifact of the screening intensity data. If the results are driven by low screening intensity funds employing all of the screens that appear positive and significant, mid-range intensity funds employing all of the screens with negative and significant coefficients,

---

[10] We thank the anonymous reviewers for motivating and suggesting several of the sensitivity analyses.

Copyright © 2006 John Wiley & Sons, Ltd.

Strat. Mgmt. J., **27**: 1101–1122 (2006)
DOI: 10.1002/smj

and high screening intensity funds employing all of those with neutral coefficients, we could be mistakenly attributing our results to differences in screen usage though the results are actually driven by variation in the degree of diversification. In order to assess this possibility, we split the sample into low (1–4 screens in use), medium (5–8 screens in use), and high (9–12 screens in use) screening intensity subsets to conduct a more nuanced analysis of the screen usage patterns of the funds. We found no patterns to suggest that low intensity funds were disproportionately using community relations screens or that medium intensity funds were disproportionately favoring equal opportunity and environmental screens. We therefore conclude that we are capturing variance that is unique to the individual screen in question.

Fifth, there is some disagreement among financial economists as to which asset-pricing model is most accurate (for a review see Fama and French, 1992, 1996; Kothari, Shanken, and Sloan, 1995). Some support the CAPM advanced by Sharpe (1964) and Lintner (1965), while others advocate more elaborate models such as the 3-factor model proposed by Fama and French (1993) or the 4-factor model proposed by Carhart (1997). Although we use CAPM to calculate our measure of risk-adjusted performance (RAP) in this study, those who believe in a Fama and French 3-factor or Carhart 4-factor world might suggest that using CAPM will bias our results because betas alone do not adequately explain average return. We therefore reran our results using RAP calculated from the Fama and French (1993) 3-factor model and then the Carhart (1997) 4-factor model. In the case of the Fama and French (1993) 3-factor model, results were similar in statistical significance but slightly weaker in magnitude. Using the Carhart (1997) 4-factor model, results were both statistically and economically stronger than those reported in this paper. Because CAPM is the standard asset-pricing model applied in strategy research, we report CAPM results herein.

Finally, asset-pricing models generally do not incorporate a bond term in addition to other market factors to explain returns. Fama and French (1993) found that using a bond term explains little variation in the return of funds comprised mostly of stocks. Because bond holdings comprise only 16 percent of the total invested assets of the funds in our sample, the funds are likely representative of the type of portfolios that Fama and French (1993)

described. Following prior literature, therefore, we do not include a bond term to help quantify RAP in our CAPM equation. Instead, we incorporate percentage bonds as a control variable in our regression models. To determine whether the absence of a bond term introduces any bias, we reran our analyses excluding the 11 funds in our sample that hold bonds at any given point in time. This left a set of 50 pure equity funds and 3026 fund-month observations. The results did not change.[11]

DISCUSSION

If we assume that investors are rewarded only for bearing systematic risk and all firms are homogenous in all but their risk premium, as modern portfolio theory contends, then SRI can only harm financial performance. However, as stakeholder theory argues, some firms may be consistently better financial performers than others because of their socially oriented characteristics. The fundamental market logic of SRI is that social screening can help in selecting these firms. Our findings support both portfolio and stakeholder theories to varying degrees. It appears that even though social screening forces a narrowing of investment choices, if adequately implemented, social screening can lead to an increase in financial returns. That is, the financial performance of those limited firms chosen through intensive social screening offsets costs from loss of portfolio diversification to some degree.

These trade-offs help explain how two long competing viewpoints in the SRI literature may actually be complementary. Funds that employ many social screens may effectively eliminate underperforming firms from their portfolio in order to improve financial performance. On the other hand, SRI funds that employ few social screens improve financial performance through benefits received from increased diversification.[12] Those

---

[11] All results discussed in this section are available from the authors upon request.

[12] It could be argued that since mutual funds are required to perform active analysis of social performance, one would expect operating costs (and the funds' associated expense ratios) to be higher as screening intensity increases. Increased costs reduce performance, and would propose an alternative interpretation of the negative portion of our curvilinear effect, potentially calling our diversification inferences into question. However, returns compiled by CRSP and used in our analyses do not factor in expense ratios. This allows us to specifically isolate the effects

Strat. Mgmt. J., **27**: 1101–1122 (2006)
DOI: 10.1002/smj

funds that are 'stuck in the middle' may not be able to either effectively diversify away unsystematic risk, or eliminate enough underperforming firms from their portfolios to improve financial performance.

The results of our analyses of different types of social screens prove more vexing. We found support for Hypothesis 3 that, indeed, funds that screened on the basis of community relations had relatively stronger financial performance. Thus, our findings concur with those of others who have shown that the costs incurred by a firm to improve its relations with its local communities are more than offset by financial gains (Hillman and Keim, 2001; Simpson and Kohers, 2002; Waddock and Graves, 2000). However, our findings ran counter to Hypotheses 2 and 4.[13] These results suggest that the financial costs of increasing equal employment opportunity and diversity, as well as environmental performance to levels adequate to pass the screening standards of SRI funds (above and beyond what is mandated by law) may outweigh their financial benefits. Considering recent findings suggesting that it 'pays to be green' (e.g., Klassen and Whybark, 1999; Konar and Cohen, 2001; Russo and Fouts, 1997; Porter and van der Linde, 1995), our result concerning environmental screening seems particularly difficult to reconcile.

There are several possible reasons why we found that it did not pay to screen out firms with better labor relations or to 'screen for green.' First, our measures of CSP are admittedly coarse. For example, the environmental performance measure cannot distinguish between proactive and reactive environmental initiatives. King and Lenox (2002) found that waste prevention, not 'end of pipe' cleanup drives financial gains. If the SRI funds in this sample disproportionately include firms that

engage in reactive environmental initiatives, the findings could thus be skewed. Ultimately, finer-grained measures may be needed to adequately tease out such variance in performance.

Second, in our study, we used market measures of financial performance. Orlitzky *et al.* (2003: 403) concluded that 'CSP [Corporate Social Performance] appears to be more highly correlated with accounting-based measures of CFP [Corporate Financial Performance] than with market-based indicators ....' A fruitful area of future research on the nature of the relationship between social and financial performance therefore might be to relate how differences in research measures and methods might contribute to different empirical findings. Prior studies have used a variety of measures, to include both market-based indicators (e.g., Klassen and McLaughlin, 1996; Shane and Spicer, 1983; Belkaoui, 1976) and accounting-based measures (e.g., King and Lenox, 2002; Russo and Fouts, 1997; Hart and Ahuja, 1996). A recent study by DellaVigna and Pollet (2005) suggests that investors rarely attend to information that extends beyond a 5-year horizon and therefore do not accurately price for the long-term. For SRI funds, this implies that the market might not accurately value social initiatives with extended payback periods.

Finally, as with any study of financial performance, our analysis is retrospective and so must be interpreted with caution. By necessity, we analyzed the appropriateness of screening strategies based upon the historical performance of mutual funds. Some of the financial benefits of certain social screens may not be discernible until farther in the future. For example, though we found that screening out firms with poor environmental records actually harmed an SRI fund's performance, a firm's up-front investment in environmental improvements may pay off in future years. Since the majority of the funds in our study were less than 5 years old, our study may have missed these gains. The market's preference for certain types of social screens may also change over time. For example, the market may at first be slow to reward firms for particular social actions, then provide increasing financial incentives as the issue becomes salient and popular, only to later simply expect firms to take such actions without financial reward. For all of these reasons, we are hesitant to draw strong conclusions from our findings on labor and environmental screening.

---

of diversification so as to ensure that they are not confounded with the effects of screening costs on mutual fund performance—thereby reducing the plausibility of such an alternative. Moreover, in sensitivity analyses conducted using expense ratios, we did not find any relationship between screening intensity and expense ratios, and our results did not change.

[13] It is important to note that the negative results for the labor relations and environmental screens do not invalidate the stakeholder theory arguments used to justify the positive portion of the curvilinear relationship suggested (and found) in Hypothesis 1. Rather, these negative results only imply that the loss of diversification associated with adopting either of these two particular screens *in isolation* outweighed any gains. In contrast, the financial gains from superior stakeholder relations possessed by firms with positive community relations added more to the RAP of SRI funds than the associated decrease in diversification necessary to select such firms took away from their RAP.

Strat. Mgmt. J., **27**: 1101–1122 (2006)
DOI: 10.1002/smj

Implications

The aforementioned caveats notwithstanding, our study has several important implications for both practitioners and scholars. First, it implies that fund managers need to more carefully consider the effects their chosen screening strategies are likely to have on the performance of their funds. The choice is not as simple as either being an SRI fund or not, but rather, just how socially responsible to be. The prescription is that managers should either wholeheartedly commit to broadly screening socially irresponsible firms from their funds, or exclude very few firms such that they do not interfere with their ability to diversify. Additionally, SRI fund managers must be aware of which types of social screens are rewarded at any particular point in time.

For scholars, this result suggests that both camps can peacefully coexist. Those who base their arguments on the financial logic of modern portfolio theory and those who support instrumental stakeholder theory may not be at odds. Funds that use few screens gain the benefits of diversification, and those that filter stocks and limit their universe of investments do not handicap their portfolio as much as some contend. The real danger lies in not committing to one strategy or the other—in being 'stuck in the middle.' Failure to control for screening intensity amongst SRI funds may explain, in part, the mixed findings that have allowed this debate to rage on for so long.

In conclusion, we have uncovered findings that appear to bring together long-divided factions in the broad literature on the link between financial and social performance. Given our findings, further research that moves beyond the dichotomy inherent in prior studies seems well warranted. We encourage others to improve upon our contribution by looking at improved data sets with more fine-grained measures.

REFERENCES

Alexander G, Bucholtz R. 1978. Corporate social responsibility and stock market performance. *Academy of Management Journal* **21**: 479–486.

Argote L. 1999. *Organizational Learning: Creating, Retaining and Transferring Knowledge*. Kluwer: Boston, MA.

Barney J. 1991. Firm resource and sustained competitive advantage. *Journal of Management* **17**: 99–120.

Belkaoui A. 1976. The impact of the disclosure of the environmental effects of organizational behavior on the market. *Financial Management* **5**: 26–31.

Belsley DA, Kuh E, Welsch RE. 1980. *Regression Diagnostics: Identifying Influential Data and Sources of Collinearity*. Wiley: New York.

Berman SL, Wicks AC, Kotha S, Jones TM. 1999. Does stakeholder orientation matter? The relationship between stakeholder management models and firm financial performance. *Academy of Management Journal* **42**(5): 488–506.

Black F, Jensen M, Scholes M. 1972. The capital asset pricing model: Some empirical tests. In *Studies in the Theory of Capital Markets*, Jensen M (ed). Praeger: New York; 79–121.

Bloomfield T, Leftwich R, Long J Jr. 1977. Portfolio strategies and performance. *Journal of Financial Economics* **5**: 201–218.

Bowman E, Haire M. 1975. A strategic posture towards CSR. *California Management Review* **18**(2): 49–58.

Campbell J, Lettau M, Malkiel B, Xu Y. 2001. Have individual stocks become more volatile? An empirical exploration of idiosyncratic risk. *Journal of Finance* **56**(1): 1–43.

Carhart M. 1997. On persistence in mutual fund performance. *Journal of Finance* **52**: 57–82.

Cochran PL, Wood RA. 1984. Corporate social responsibility and financial performance. *Academy of Management Journal* **27**(1): 42–56.

Cornell B, Shapiro AC. 1987. Corporate stakeholders and corporate finance. *Financial Management* **16**(1): 5–14.

Dear M. 1992. Understanding and overcoming the NIMBY syndrome. *Journal of the American Planning Association* **58**(3): 288–300.

DellaVigna S, Pollet JM. 2005. Attention, demographics, and the stock market. NBER working paper #11211.

DiBartolomeo D, Kurtz L. 1999. Managing risk exposures of socially screened portfolios. Northfield Information Services working paper.

Dierickx I, Cool K. 1991. Asset stock accumulation and sustainability of competitive advantage. *Management Science* **35**(12): 1504–1511.

Diltz JD. 1995. The private cost of socially responsible investing. *Applied Financial Economics* **5**: 69–77.

Donaldson T, Preston LE. 1995. The stakeholder theory of the corporation: concepts, evidence, and implications. *Academy of Management Review* **20**(1): 65–91.

Dowell G, Hart S, Yeung B. 2000. Do corporate global environmental standards create or destroy market value? *Management Science* **46**: 1059–1074.

Elton E, Gruber MJ, Blake CR. 1996a. The persistence of risk-adjusted mutual fund performance. *Journal of Business* **69**(2): 133–157.

Elton E, Gruber MJ, Blake CR. 1996b. Survivorship bias and mutual fund performance. *Review of Financial Studies* **9**(4): 1097–1120.

Fama EF. 1971. Risk, return, and equilibrium. *Journal of Political Economy* **79**(1): 30–55.

Fama EF. 1991. Efficient markets: II. *Journal of Finance* **46**: 1575–1617.

1120   *M. L. Barnett and R. M. Salomon*

Fama EF, French KR. 1992. The cross-section of expected stock returns. *Journal of Finance* **47**: 427–465.

Fama EF, French KR. 1993. Common risk factors in the returns on stocks and bonds. *Journal of Financial Economics* **33**: 3–56.

Fama EF, French KR. 1996. The CAPM is wanted dead or alive. *Journal of Finance* **51**: 1947–1958.

Fisher L, Lorie JH. 1970. Some studies of the variability of returns on investments in common stocks. *Journal of Business* **43**(2): 99–134.

Florida R. 2002. *The Rise of the Creative Class*. Basic Books: New York.

Fombrun CJ. 1996. *Reputation: Realizing Value from the Corporate Image*. Harvard Business School Press: Boston, MA.

Fombrun CJ, Gardberg NA, Barnett ML. 2000. Opportunity platforms and safety nets: corporate citizenship and reputational risk. *Business and Society Review* **105**(1): 85–106.

Freeman RE. 1984. *Strategic Management: A Stakeholder Approach*. Pitman: Boston, MA.

Friedman M. 1970. The social responsibility of business is to increase its profits. *New York Times Magazine* 13 September: 122–126.

Geczy C, Stambaugh R, Levin D. 2003. Investing in socially responsible mutual funds. Wharton School of Business working paper.

Glassman JK. 1999. Letting your conscience be your investment guide. *Houston Chronicle* 8 February: 4.

Goetz T. 1997. Dealing with the devil. *Village Voice* 19 August: 43–44.

Granovetter M. 1985. Economic action and social structure: the problem of embeddedness. *American Journal of Sociology* **91**(3): 481–510.

Graves S, Waddock S. 2000. Beyond built to last ... stakeholder relations in 'built-to-last' companies. *Business and Society Review* **105**(4): 393–418.

Greene WH. 2000. *Econometric Analysis*. Macmillan: New York.

Greening DW, Turban DB. 2000. Corporate social performance as a competitive advantage in attracting a quality workforce. *Business and Society* **39**(3): 254–280.

Griffin JJ, Mahon JF. 1997. The corporate social performance and corporate financial performance debate: twenty-five years of incomparable research. *Business and Society* **36**(1): 5–31.

Guerard JB Jr. 1997. Is there a cost to being socially responsible in investing? *Journal of Investing* **6**(2): 11–18.

Hamilton S, Jo H, Statman M. 1993. Doing well while doing good? The investment performance of socially responsible mutual funds. *Financial Analysts Journal*, November–December: 62–66.

Hart S, Ahuja G. 1996. Does it pay to be green? An empirical examination of the relationship between emissions reduction and firm performance. *Business Strategy and the Environment* **5**: 30–37.

Hillman A, Keim G. 2001. Shareholder value, stakeholder management, and social issues: what's the bottom line? *Strategic Management Journal* **22**(2): 125–139.

Hoffman A. 1997. *From Heresy to Dogma: An Institutional History of Corporate Environmentalism*. New Lexington Press: San Francisco, CA.

Hoffman A. 1999. Institutional evolution and change: environmentalism and the U.S. chemical industry. *Academy of Management Journal* **42**: 351–371.

Hutton RB, D'Antonio L, Johnsen T. 1998. Socially responsible investing: growing issues and new opportunities. *Business and Society* **37**(3): 281–305.

Hymer SH. 1976. *The International Operations of National Firms: A Study of Direct Foreign Investment*. MIT Press: Cambridge, MA.

Jensen M. 2002. Value maximization, stakeholder theory, and the corporate objective function. *Business Ethics Quarterly* **12**: 235–256.

Jones R, Murrell A. 2001. Signaling positive corporate social performance: an event study of family-friendly firms. *Business and Society* **40**(1): 59–78.

Jones T. 1995. Instrumental stakeholder theory: a synthesis of ethics and economics. *Academy of Management Review* **20**(2): 404–437.

Kennedy P. 1998. *A Guide to Econometrics*. MIT Press: Cambridge, MA.

King A, Lenox M. 2000. Industry self-regulation without sanctions: the chemical industry's Responsible Care program. *Academy of Management Journal* **43**(4): 698–716.

King A, Lenox M. 2002. Exploring the locus of profitable pollution reduction. *Management Science* **48**(2): 289–299.

Klassen R, McLaughlin C. 1996. The impact of environmental management on firm performance. *Management Science* **42**(8): 1199–1214.

Klassen R, Whybark D. 1999. The impact of environmental technologies on manufacturing performance. *Academy of Management Journal* **42**(6): 599–615.

Kmenta J. 1997. *Elements of Econometrics*. Macmillan: New York.

Konar S, Cohen M. 2001. Does the market value environmental performance? *Review of Economics and Statistics* **83**(2): 281–289.

Kothari SP, Shanken J, Sloan RG. 1995. Another look at the cross-section of expected stock returns. *Journal of Finance* **50**: 185–224.

Kurtz L. 1997. No effect, or no *net* effect? Studies on socially responsible investing. *Journal of Investing* **6**(4): 37–49.

Kurtz L, DiBartolomeo D. 1996. Socially screened portfolios: an attribution analysis of relative performance. *Journal of Investing* **5**(3): 35–41.

LaRose JA. 1998. More than profits: selected resources in socially responsible investing. *Reference and User Services Quarterly* **38**(1): 33–40.

Lintner J. 1965. The valuation of risk assets and the selection of risky investments in stock portfolios and capital budgets. *Review of Economics and Statistics* **47**: 13–37.

Lowry R. 1991. *Good Money: A Guide to Profitable Investing in the '90's*. W. W. Norton: New York.

Strat. Mgmt. J., **27**: 1101–1122 (2006)
DOI: 10.1002/smj

Luck C, Pilotte N. 1993. Domini Social Index performance. *Journal of Investing* **2**: 60–62.

Mahon JF, Griffin JJ. 1999. Painting a portrait. *Business and Society* **38**(1): 126–133.

Margolis J, Walsh J. 2003. Misery loves company: rethinking social initiatives by business. *Administrative Science Quarterly* **48**: 268–305.

Markowitz H. 1952. Portfolio selection. *Journal of Finance* **7**(1): 77–91.

McWilliams A, Siegel D. 1997. The role of money managers in assessing corporate social responsibility research. *Journal of Investing* **6**(4): 98–107.

McWilliams A, Siegel D. 2000. Corporate social responsibility and financial performance: correlation or misspecification? *Strategic Management Journal* **21**(5): 603–609.

Moskowitz M. 1972. Choosing socially responsible stocks. *Business and Society Review* **10**: 71–75.

Mueller S. 1991. The opportunity cost of discipleship: ethical mutual funds and their returns. *Sociological Analysis* **52**: 111–124.

Orlitzky M, Schmidt F, Rynes S. 2003. Corporate social and financial performance: a meta-analysis. *Organization Studies* **24**: 403–441.

Perrow C. 1984. *Normal Accidents: Living with High-Risk Technologies*. Basic Books: New York.

Porter M. 1991. Towards a dynamic theory of strategy. *Strategic Management Journal*, Winter Special Issue **12**: 95–117.

Porter M, van der Linde C. 1995. Green and competitive. *Harvard Business Review* **73**(5): 121–134.

Preston LE, O'Bannon D. 1997. The corporate social–financial performance relationship. *Business and Society* **36**(4): 419–429.

Preston LE, Post JE. 1975. *Private Management and Public Policy: The Principle of Public Responsibility*. Prentice-Hall: Englewood Cliffs, NJ.

Rees J. 1994. *Hostages of Each Other: The Transformation of Nuclear Safety Since Three Mile Island*. University of Chicago Press: Chicago, IL.

Rehbein K, Waddock S, Graves S. 2004. Understanding shareholder activism: which corporations are targeted? *Business and Society* **43**(3): 239–267.

Roman RM, Hayibor S, Agle BR. 1999. The relationship between financial and social performance: repainting a portrait. *Business and Society* **38**(1): 109–125.

Rothchild J. 1996. Why I invest with sinners. *Fortune* 13 May: 197.

Rowley T, Berman S. 2000. A brand new brand of corporate social performance. *Business and Society* **39**(4): 397–418.

Rudd A. 1979. Divestment of South African equities: how risky? *Journal of Portfolio Management* **5**(3): 5.

Russo M, Fouts P. 1997. A resource-based perspective on corporate environmental performance and profitability. *Academy of Management Journal* **40**: 534–559.

Sauer D. 1997. The impact of social-responsibility screens on investment performance: evidence from the Domini 400 Social Index and Domini Equity mutual funds. *Review of Financial Economics* **6**(2): 137–149.

Scott R. 1981. *Organizations: Rational, Natural, and Open Systems*. Prentice-Hall: Englewood Cliffs, NJ.

Sellers M. 1993. NIMBY: a case study in conflict politics. *Public Administration Quarterly* **16**(4): 460–477.

Shane P, Spicer B. 1983. Market responses to environmental information produced outside the firm. *Accounting Review* **58**: 521–538.

Sharpe WF. 1964. Capital asset prices: a theory of market equilibrium under conditions of risk. *Journal of Finance* **19**: 425–442.

Simpson WG, Kohers T. 2002. The link between corporate social and financial performance: evidence from the banking industry. *Journal of Business Ethics* **35**: 97–109.

Social Investment Forum. 2002. http://www.socialinvest.org/Areas/SRIGuide/Screening.htm [15 January 2002].

Statman M. 1987. How many stocks make a diversified portfolio? *Journal of Financial and Quantitative Analysis* **22**(3): 353–363.

Statman M. 2000. Socially responsible mutual funds. *Financial Analysts Journal* May/June: 30–39.

Teper J. 1992. Evaluating the cost of socially responsible investing. In *The Social Investment Almanac* (1st edn), Kinder P (ed.). Henry Holt: New York; 340–349.

Turban DB, Greening DW. 1996. Corporate social performance and organizational attractiveness to prospective employees. *Academy of Management Journal* **40**(3): 658–672.

Ullmann A. 1985. Data in search of a theory: a critical examination of the relationship among social performance, social disclosure, and economic performance. *Academy of Management Review* **10**: 450–477.

Waddock SA, Graves SB. 1997. The corporate social performance–financial performance link. *Strategic Management Journal* **18**(4): 303–319.

Waddock SA, Graves SB. 2000. Performance characteristics of social and traditional investments. *Journal of Investing* **9**(2): 27–38.

Waddock SA, Smith N. 2000. Corporate responsibility audits: doing well by doing good. *Sloan Management Review* **41**(2): 75–83.

Wernerfelt B. 1984. A resource-based view of the firm. *Strategic Management Journal* **5**(2): 171–180.

Wicks AC, Berman SL, Jones TM. 1999. The structure of optimal trust: moral and strategic implications. *Academy of Management Review* **24**(1): 99–116.

Williamson OE. 1975. *Markets and Hierarchies: Analysis and Antitrust Implications*. Free Press: New York.

Williamson OE. 1985. *The Economic Institutions of Capitalism*. Free Press: New York.

Wood D, Jones R. 1995. Stakeholder mismatching: a theoretical problem in empirical research on corporate social performance. *International Journal of Organizational Analysis* **3**: 229–267.

Wright P, Ferris S, Hiller J, Kroll M. 1995. Competitiveness through management of diversity: effects on stock price valuation. *Academy of Management Journal* **38**(1): 272–287.

APPENDIX: CALCULATION OF RISK-ADJUSTED PERFORMANCE (RAP)

A fund's expected return is a linear function of the market return. A market index represents the market return (in our case, the S&P 500), and the coefficient beta represents the linear relationship of the fund's return to the market return. As is conventional in CAPM (see Sharpe, 1964), this study computes beta on the basis of monthly returns. Specifically:

$$R_{it} - R_{ft} = a_i + B_i{}^* \ (R_{mt} - R_{ft}) + e_{it} \qquad (4)$$

where R_{it} represents the return on fund i in month t, a_i is Jensen's alpha, R_{mt} represents the return

on the market portfolio for month t, R_{ft} reflects the risk-free rate of return (e.g., the 30-day T-bill rate), B_i captures the fixed beta of fund i, and e_{it} represents random error.

The risk-adjusted return of the fund is the difference between the risk premium of that fund and the fund's expected return, given its beta and the market's risk premium. The risk-adjusted performance (RAP) then for fund i in month t, RAP_{it}, is:

$$RAP_{it} = (R_{it} - R_{ft}) - B_i{}^* \ (R_{mt} - R_{ft}) \qquad (5)$$

In essence, RAP_{it}, from Equation 5, captures the fund's return over and above what is expected based upon its beta.[14]

---

[14] When we model RAP as the dependent variable, we are parameterizing the error term and Jensen's alpha to uncover residual systematic noise in a fund's performance. We found similar results when we parameterized the standard CAPM equation.

[4]

© Academy of Management Review
2007, Vol. 32, No. 3, 794–816.

STAKEHOLDER INFLUENCE CAPACITY AND THE VARIABILITY OF FINANCIAL RETURNS TO CORPORATE SOCIAL RESPONSIBILITY

MICHAEL L. BARNETT
University of South Florida

I argue that research on the business case for corporate social responsibility must account for the path-dependent nature of firm-stakeholder relations, and I develop the construct of stakeholder influence capacity to fill this void. This construct helps explain why the effects of corporate social responsibility on corporate financial performance vary across firms and time. I develop a set of propositions to aid future research on the contingencies that produce variable financial returns to investment in corporate social responsibility.

John Hyde, a retiree in Placerville, Calif., says it's hard to believe Philip Morris is "a good guy just because it donates water to flood victims, or helps the hungry" (Alsop, 2002: 1).

There is a lot of skepticism out there when a company like McDonald's starts to talk about salads, because people know McDonald's is not especially concerned about the health of America (Rich Polt, consultant, quoted in Dressel, 2003: 1).

I guess it depends if it's [the firm's participation in an act of corporate social responsibility] part of the total picture and [if] they really go out of their way. Like with Kroger, it isn't a one-time shot, they're always doing stuff for Egleston [Children's Hospital], or they've got the big barrels out there for the people to bring cans for the homeless or something at Thanksgiving and Christmas. It just seems more a way of business for them, continuously, so in that case, that's fine. . . . But if somebody's doing it just for the publicity, then that would not make me think better of them (survey respondent quoted in Webb & Mohr, 1998: 235).

Should public corporations serve as agents of progressive social change? For example, should Levi Strauss fund a campaign to end racism? Should Ford contribute to finding a cure for AIDS? If so, how much should these corporations contribute to these social causes? Because there are ethical considerations inherent in answering these questions, reasonable people can and do disagree. Some argue that because corporations draw resources from society, they have a moral obligation to give back to society, whereas others counter that corporations are inefficient and inappropriate agents of social change, and any voluntary contributions to social causes are misappropriations of shareholders' funds (Friedman, 1970).

Given the intractability of this ongoing ethical debate, many researchers have turned to examination of the "business case" for corporate social responsibility (CSR). A large and ever-growing body of literature has investigated whether the financial benefits to the corporation can meet or exceed the costs of its contributions to social welfare (for recent reviews, see Margolis & Walsh, 2003, and Orlitzky, Schmidt, & Rynes, 2003). If so, CSR can be justified as a wise investment; if not, CSR can be condemned as an agency problem. The result is that after more than thirty years of research, we cannot clearly conclude whether a one-dollar investment in social initiatives returns more or less than one dollar in benefit to the shareholder.

The lingering murkiness of the business case has been attributed to a variety of shortcomings present in the research of scholars approaching the topic from myriad (a)theoretical angles (Griffin & Mahon, 1997; Ullmann, 1985). Yet even as the rigor of CSR studies has increased to address these shortcomings, the link between CSR and financial performance has become only murkier. Margolis and Walsh recently described this body of research as "self-perpetuating: each successive study promises a definitive conclusion, while also revealing the inevitable inadequacies of empirically tackling the question"

I thank John Jermier, Rob Salomon, Sandra Waddock, Tim Fort, and the anonymous reviewers for advice on assorted aspects of this manuscript. I also thank the College of Business Administration at the University of South Florida for summer financial support.

794

(2003: 278). As a result, it "reinforces, rather than relieves, the tension surrounding corporate responses to social misery" (Margolis & Walsh, 2003: 278). Thus, the seemingly tractable business case for CSR remains just as debatable as the associated ethical dilemma.

The continuing chaos surrounding the business case should not come as a surprise. The unique and dynamic characteristics of firms and their environments preclude stability in financial returns to CSR across firms and time, so we should not expect to empirically discern a consistent financial benefit—essentially, a universal rate of return—to a generic corporation for some given unit of social investment. Consider McDonald's and Subway restaurants. Although they are both in the same industry and so face similar competitive conditions, were each to contribute $1 million to efforts to curb obesity, it is unlikely they would experience identical financial returns. In fact, their returns could differ radically, with one achieving a positive return and the other experiencing losses. Even within the same firm, identical levels of CSR investment over different time periods are likely to lead to different financial returns, such as before and after lawsuits, intense media scrutiny, or other external shocks (cf. Alsop, 2002; Hoffman, 1997). Thus, efforts to universally legitimize or condemn the business case are "theoretically untenable" (Rowley & Berman, 2000: 406).

Researchers have often overlooked the many contingencies that cause variability in returns to CSR, perhaps in their zeal to legitimize or discredit the business case (Rowley & Berman, 2000; Ullmann, 1985). As a result, the business case has been neither made nor discredited, despite extensive research (Margolis & Walsh, 2003). My goal for this paper is to help reorient CSR research away from the long-fought battle for replicable empirical findings of the financial returns to CSR in general and toward a quest for deeper understanding of the underlying drivers of whether and when particular firms may earn positive financial returns from CSR—in short, to make the business case firm specific, not universal. In furtherance of this goal, I present a conceptual framework that illustrates how firms generate financial returns from acts of CSR. Building on the stakeholder theory argument that firms can benefit financially from attending to the concerns of their stakeholders (Freeman, 1984), I discuss how these financial benefits vary

as a result of *stakeholder influence capacity*, a construct that captures variation across and within firms in their ability to use CSR to profitably improve relationships.

I next present an overview of the business case for CSR. I then distinguish CSR from several related and sometimes confounded concepts. Thereafter, I introduce the construct of stakeholder influence capacity, embed it within a conceptual framework, and elaborate the bounds of this framework through a set of propositions. The paper concludes with an extended discussion of the implications of stakeholder influence capacity for the future of CSR research and practice.

THE BUSINESS CASE FOR CSR

CSR is often described as any discretionary corporate activity intended to further social welfare. For example, Target reported that it donates more than $2 million each week to the arts, education, and social services in the communities in which its stores operate. The presence of discretion is key. Many corporate activities that further social welfare are mandated by law, such as equal employment opportunity and medical leave. But why, in the face of often-fierce competition, do for-profit firms voluntarily allocate additional limited resources to social welfare as an "almost universal practice" (Dressel, 2003: 1)? Certainly, these resources could be put to better use in improving the efficiency of the firm, or could be returned to shareholders.

This is the core of the argument against CSR. Critics of CSR contend that expending limited resources on social issues necessarily decreases the competitive position of a firm by unnecessarily increasing its costs. Furthermore, even if a firm has slack resources but no favorable investment opportunities, and even if the costs of CSR are not ample enough to put the firm at a competitive disadvantage, the firm should still refrain from CSR. Devoting corporate resources to social welfare is tantamount to an involuntary redistribution of wealth, from shareholders, as rightful owners of the corporation, to others in society who have no rightful claim. Thus, CSR, although almost universally practiced, is considered by some to be an agency loss; managers pursue CSR for personal gain, not shareholder benefit (Friedman, 1970).

McWilliams and Siegel's definition of CSR, though they argue for a neutral relationship between CSR and financial performance, exemplifies the agency loss perspective: "We define CSR as actions that appear to further some social good, *beyond the interests of the firm* and that which is required by law" (2001: 117; emphasis added). Simply put, critics contend that CSR is not in the firm's interests and so should not be countenanced.

CSR proponents counter that when one takes a more enlightened view of how firms achieve competitive advantage, one can see that CSR is, in fact, in firms' best interests. Stakeholder theory (Freeman, 1984), the cornerstone of the business case for CSR, highlights the importance of a firm's relationships with a broad set of individuals and organizations, beyond just shareholders. Instrumental stakeholder theory (Jones, 1995) further clarifies how CSR contributes to the bottom line via its favorable influence on the firm's relationships with important stakeholders. The importance of stakeholders can be determined by their relative power, legitimacy, and urgency (Mitchell, Agle, & Wood, 1997). The overall logic is that CSR (e.g., philanthropy) increases the trustworthiness of a firm and so strengthens relationships with important stakeholders (e.g., increases employee satisfaction), which decreases transaction costs and so leads to financial gain (e.g., decreased employee turnover, more eager talent pool, union avoidance). CSR can differentiate a firm's products (Porter, 1991), reduce its operating costs (King & Lenox, 2000), and serve as a platform for future opportunities, as well as a buffer from disruptive events (Fombrun, Gardberg, & Barnett, 2000). Thus, from this angle, one can view CSR as an investment, perhaps with sizable financial returns, in addition to or despite any benefits that might accrue to society. In short, CSR supporters argue that there is ample private incentive for improving social welfare.

So, does CSR build or destroy corporate wealth? Over the last three decades, many researchers have taken on the task of empirically testing the business case. According to Orlitzky et al. (2003), fifty-two quantitative studies have been published on this topic. Margolis and Walsh (2003) put this figure at 127. For more than two decades, researchers have also taken on the task of reviewing these many studies and bemoaning the mixed findings. Margolis and

Walsh (2003) tallied thirteen reviews since 1978. In one of the earlier instances, Ullmann (1985) described this body of research as "data in search of a theory." A dozen years later, Griffin and Mahon (1997) entitled their review "Twenty-Five Years of Incomparable Research." Roman, Hayibor, and Agle (1999) "repainted the portrait" they ascribed to Griffin and Mahon's (1997) critical study to recast it as more supportive of the business case, but Mahon and Griffin (1999) immediately repainted that repaint so as to return the portrait to its original critical state. Most recently, Orlistky et al. (2003) performed a meta-analysis of the population of quantitative studies to date and found support for the business case. Margolis and Walsh (2003: 278), however, argued that any conclusion that the business case is now established because more empirical studies have been published in support of it than against it is "illusory."

The question remains without a definitive answer. The mixed findings have been attributed to a variety of shortcomings: "a lack in theory, inappropriate definition of key terms, and deficiencies in the empirical data bases currently available" (Ullmann, 1985: 540); stakeholder mismatching (Wood & Jones, 1995); "conceptual, operationalization, and methodological differences in the definitions of social and financial performance" (Griffin & Mahon, 1997: 6); failure to control for risk, industry affiliation, and asset age (Cochran & Wood, 1984); and failure to control for investment in R&D (McWilliams & Siegel, 2000). Many of these shortcomings have been repeated in subsequent studies, but many have also been corrected as they have been brought to light.

CSR studies have improved over time, offering stronger theoretical rationales, more relevant operationalizations, and more and better controls for previously omitted variables. Yet the improved rigor has only produced rigor mortis. Mahon and Griffin have argued that twenty-five years of research has not produced a solution but, rather, isolated islands of partial insight about an unseen larger picture, akin to "the fable of the five blind Indian men" (1999: 126). As Rowley and Berman put it, "Researchers have combined various mishmashes of uncorrelated variables, which render correlation and ordinary least squares regression results indiscernible" (2000: 405). Margolis and Walsh (2003) concur that, even after thirty years of research, with scholars increasing the depth and breadth of their databases, differences in perspective have only cumulated, not dissipated, thereby further obscuring the big picture.

Rowley and Berman (2000) further argue that efforts to universally prove the business case are doomed to failure, no matter how ingenious the theory, crystal clear the terminology, or rigorous the data and methodology. They contend that the thirty-year quest "represents an attempt to legitimize the researcher and the business and society field, rather than build understanding" (2000: 401). Theory and empirics that suggest a universally favorable rate of return to CSR validate the business case and so help to legitimize the business and society field. Yet it is clear that CSR cannot universally produce favorable returns for all firms all the time, so favorable findings will never be replicable across all data sets. Returns to CSR are contingent, not universal (Ullmann, 1985). Although some studies have begun to empirically tease apart these contingencies (Barnett & Salomon, 2006; McWilliams & Siegel, 2000; Orlitzky et al., 2003), Rowley and Berman (2000) argue that the results of such studies are not interpretable because the theoretical underpinnings to explain which contingencies are relevant have not yet been established. Therefore, researchers should attempt to develop theory that explains heterogeneity in financial returns to CSR. In the remainder of this paper I heed this call.

THE BOUNDARIES OF CSR

CSR research has often been criticized for running fast and loose with its concepts (Griffin & Mahon, 1997; Ullmann, 1985). In this section I define CSR and demarcate its boundaries by distinguishing it from related concepts.

Distinguishing CSR from Corporate Social Performance

This study explores the business case for CSR by examining how acts of CSR influence corporate financial performance (CFP). In contrast, most studies of the business case have examined the relationship between corporate social performance (CSP) and CFP. For example, recent comprehensive reviews, both critical (Griffin & Mahon, 1997; Margolis & Walsh, 2003; Rowley & Berman, 2000) and supportive (Orlitzky et

al., 2003) of the business case, all refer to CSP studies. Although "CSR" and "CSP" are often used interchangeably, there is an important distinction. CSP may be described as a snapshot of a firm's overall social performance at a particular point in time—a summary of the firm's aggregate social posture. For example, Wood's commonly cited definition of CSP is "a business organization's configuration of principles of social responsibility, processes of social responsiveness, and policies, programs, and observable outcomes as they relate to the firm's social relationships" (1991: 693). Many researchers have attempted to gauge a firm's CSP at a point in time and, more rarely, over time, through such measures as reputation rankings and stakeholder surveys, and then correlate these proxies for CSP to CFP (Margolis & Walsh, 2003).

Although certainly of interest, this body of research does not directly aid managers in making decisions about devoting limited resources to socially responsible actions in the face of competing demands. Rather, CSP–CFP studies address the financial benefits of having achieved a certain socially responsible posture at a particular point in time. Either a firm has achieved this posture, and so might expect these benefits (or harms), or a firm has not achieved this posture, and so should not expect them. Often unexplained and untested are the costs and benefits of gaining this posture—the incremental steps toward attainment of a certain strategic CSP posture, or the value of discrete or less directed socially oriented activities undertaken as a firm "muddles" (Lindblom, 1959) its way through its strategy.

Firms are not imbued with a certain CSP state. There is no "market for CSP" wherein such a state can be purchased. Rather, firms make investments that, over time, aggregate into certain CSP postures. These investments are CSR. For example, Ben & Jerry's created a favorable CSP posture through the CSR activities of its Ben & Jerry's Foundation and its involvement in a variety of specific campaigns, such as "One Sweet Whirled" and "Rock the Vote." Was each of these activities a wise corporate investment? That is the question of interest in this paper, so CSR is used.[1]

---

[1] Nonetheless, CSP and CSR are both important factors in predicting the marginal returns to social investment oppor-

Distinguishing CSR from Other Corporate Resource Allocations

Recent scandals have channeled a great deal of attention toward acts of CSR, but these constitute only a subset of the many activities in which corporations engage. Arguably, all law-abiding and profit-maximizing corporate activities have a social component because they help to improve the economic conditions that support society. As Friedman put it, "There is one and only one social responsibility of business—to use its resources and engage in activities to increase its profits so long as it stays within the rules of the game" (1970: 126). Yet such a broad conception of CSR only confounds the study of the business case. In terms of social responsibility, is the construction of a new plant, with an attendant increase in employment, akin to the establishment of a company day care center or a donation to a local charity? Relatively few scholars have interpreted CSR as broadly as Friedman (1970), but CSR scholars have made generous use of the concept. Where do the appropriate boundaries lie?

Within the boundaries of CSR. There are two characteristics that distinguish acts of CSR from other corporate investments: *social welfare orientation* and *stakeholder relationship orientation*. The most obvious and distinctive characteristic of an act of CSR is its focus on increasing social welfare. Whereas other corporate investments, at least from a normative perspective, are focused on improving the wealth of the owners of the corporation, CSR activities involve efforts to improve social welfare. Research on the business case seeks a link to profitability, but any financial gains from CSR activities (e.g., corporate philanthropy) are necessarily by-products of these direct contributions to social welfare. It is this aspect of CSR that makes it so controversial.

Stakeholder relationship orientation is an essential yet often implicit characteristic of the business case for CSR. The business case tries to move beyond the contentious ethical debate by claiming that CSR, even if focused on improving social welfare, also increases CFP and so

can be considered an investment. In order to increase CFP, an act of CSR must ultimately increase a firm's revenues or decrease its costs.

Unfortunately, the mechanisms by which CSR can do this are not always clear. Many early studies did not offer a theoretical framework to demonstrate this and were therefore dismissed as atheoretical (Ullmann, 1985). The advent of a stakeholder perspective (Freeman, 1984) helped dampen these criticisms but did not silence them because its vague boundaries frustrated the development of a viable stakeholder theory of the firm (Donaldson & Preston, 1995). Instrumental stakeholder theory (Jones, 1995) brought stronger theoretical underpinnings to the business case, primarily by linking it to transaction cost economics (Williamson, 1975):

> Certain types of corporate social performance are manifestations of attempts to establish trusting, cooperative firm/stakeholder relationships and should be positively linked to a company's financial performance. . . . firms that contract with their stakeholders on the basis of mutual trust and cooperation will have a competitive advantage over firms that do not. . . . [This advantage stems from] reduced agency costs, transaction costs, and costs associated with team production. More specifically, monitoring costs, bonding costs, search costs, warranty costs, and residual losses will be reduced (Jones, 1995: 422, 430).

Others have augmented stakeholder theory with aspects of resource dependence theory (Pfeffer & Salancik, 1978) so as to clarify "who and what really counts" (Mitchell et al., 1997) in regard to stakeholder relationships, and resource-based theory (Barney, 1991; Penrose, 1959; Wernerfelt, 1984) to elicit how favorable stakeholder relationships produce not only cost savings but also increased revenues (Russo & Fouts, 1997).

There is now a substantive theoretical framework to explain how CSR produces increases in CFP. The basic premise is that CSR improves CFP by improving a firm's relationships with relevant stakeholder groups. As these relationships improve and trust builds, transaction costs decline and certain risks decline or are eliminated. For example, certain types of CSR may lead to more trusting labor relations, which can increase employee retention rates and so decrease labor costs (Greening & Turban, 2000). On the revenue side, improved stakeholder relationships can bring in new customers and new investment opportunities and can enable a firm

---

tunities. The core premise of this paper is that the financial returns to CSR depend on a firm's history. Measures of CSP can proxy for a firm's history. See the discussion section for more detail.

to charge premium prices (Fombrun et al., 2000; Porter, 1991; Porter & van der Linde, 1995).

The key point is that CSR improves CFP by first improving relationships with key stakeholders. This indirect relationship between CSR and CFP inherent in the business case is distinct from corporate investments that have a direct impact on CFP, as well as those that indirectly impact CFP through channels other than stakeholder relationship building and the advancement of social welfare. The nature of CSR and the relevance of both characteristics— social welfare orientation and stakeholder relationship orientation—become more apparent when contrasted with those corporate activities that do not meet these criteria, as discussed next.

Outside the boundaries of CSR. Much that is often lumped in with CSR actually falls outside its bounds, as illustrated in Figure 1. Let us first examine the upper left quadrant of Figure 1, "Agency loss." Some types of social spending are not intended to directly or even indirectly increase CFP. They may be acts of pure corporate altruism or pet projects of management. A substantial donation to a small charity headed by the spouse of the CEO or an anonymous donation to any charity would fall into this category. These allocations may improve managers' welfare by increasing their self-image, social standing, or career prospects. However, if these allocations are not instrumental to im-

FIGURE 1
Types of Corporate Resource Allocations

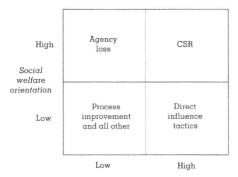

proving the corporation's relations with important stakeholders, than any near- or even long-term increase in CFP is unlikely; it is neither countenanced nor accounted for.

Resource allocations without concern for shareholder value maximization were what disturbed Friedman (1970). One cannot argue that the benefits to the corporation from such activities outweigh their costs, because the benefits accrue to management or to society, not to shareholders. These are straightforward agency losses (Jensen & Meckling, 1976). Because there is no question about their effect on CFP, these types of resource allocations are not of interest to the business case. Therefore, corporate resource allocations that aid social welfare but are not instrumental in improving key stakeholder relationships (and thereby increasing CFP) should be at the center of the ethical debate over the role of the corporation in society, but they should not be confounded with the business case for CSR.

"Direct influence tactics," as listed in the lower right corner of Figure 1, are also distinct from CSR. This category includes political lobbying and campaign donations, the establishment of contractual relationships, and other means of directly influencing or "capturing" regulators, legislators, nongovernmental organizations (NGOs), and other stakeholders who can affect the discretion and performance of a firm. Firms have long allocated significant resources to lobbying and political campaigns in order to curry favor with those who control legislative and regulatory agendas (de Figueiredo, 2002; Hillman, Keim, & Schuler, 2004). "Green alliances" and other forms of cooperation between firms and NGOs have become increasingly common (Stafford & Hartman, 1996). These cooperative relationships can include the payment of fees and royalties to NGOs in exchange for their endorsement of a firm's products and services (Hartman & Stafford, 1997). Such direct influence tactics are focused on improving relationships with important stakeholders, but they are not necessarily focused on improving social welfare. In fact, corporate efforts to capture regulators and legislators and co-opt activist NGOs can be instrumental in *reducing* a firm's contributions to social welfare (Baron, 1995; Baysinger, 1984; Pfeffer & Salancik, 1978; Stigler, 1971).

Direct influence tactics can best be distinguished from CSR activities by noting to whom the benefits accrue. The benefits of direct influence tactics—contributions, royalties, licensing fees—accrue directly to the stakeholders the firm seeks to influence; the benefits of CSR do not. The business case for CSR implies that as stakeholders observe a firm's socially responsible behaviors, they will deem the firm a more favorable party with which to conduct their own transactions. For example, Turban and Greening (1997) found that firms with favorable social performance records were more attractive to potential employees, and Brown and Dacin (1997) found that such firms were also more attractive to customers.

Trust arises and relationships improve as stakeholders observe a firm's CSR activities, not as a consequence of a firm's use of direct influence tactics to capture their favor. Direct influence tactics, or perceptions of attempts at direct influence, can actually reduce trust (cf. O'Sullivan, 1997; Varadarajan & Menon, 1988) or simply make trust less relevant by substituting financial payouts and direct contractual ties (cf. Oliver, 1990). Direct influence tactics are of no less interest or importance to understanding CFP than is CSR (Shaffer, Quasney & Grimm, 2000), but in seeking to clarify the business case for CSR, it is essential to factor out those activities that affect CFP through other mechanisms.

Shown in the lower left corner of Figure 1, more commonly confounded with CSR are process improvement efforts such as energy conservation, waste reduction, and pollution abatement (Hart, 1995; Klassen & Whybark, 1999). Social welfare gains can certainly arise from corporate efforts to improve processes and so lessen waste and harm to the natural environment. However, the link sought between the investment and the financial return is direct, and thus again distinct from the indirect mechanism of the business case (cf. Windsor, 2001). That is, the gains to CFP are sought through cost savings achieved from improving the efficiency of operations (King & Lenox, 2002), not from improvements in stakeholder relations. Therefore, such process improvement efforts merit categorization with other standard corporate investments in improving operational efficiency.

Complex investments and hidden motives. Figure 1 and the above discussion provide a useful conceptual distinction to help sort out the myriad activities often confounded with CSR, but many corporate investments do not fit neatly within one box. A single investment can focus on both social welfare and stakeholder relationships yet can also entail aspects of direct influence, process improvement, and even agency loss. For example, one might classify a $1 million donation by a large financial institution to a preschool as a clear example of CSR, concluding that the financial institution wished to demonstrate a commitment to education to its customers and the community in which it operates. However, if one of the financial institution's co-CEOs spent the $1 million in order to directly influence one of its analysts, using the donation to get the analyst's child placed into this prestigious preschool so that the analyst would upgrade a stock, so that the CEO of the firm whose stock rating improved, a member of the financial institution's board of directors, would then vote to oust the financial institution's other co-CEO (Gasparino, 2005), then one might also classify this $1 million investment as a direct influence tactic (direct payment to improve relations with an important stakeholder, the analyst) and as an agency loss (a clear misappropriation of shareholder funds, for management gain). Less salacious but also complex could be a company's decision to invest $1 million in office and plant design technologies that reduce energy consumption. Although previously described as a process improvement effort, advertising and public relations arms of the firm may tout the environmental benefits of such actions in hopes of improving relationships with stakeholders (CSR). The $1 million project could also include funding for a partnership with an energy conservation NGO that had been pressuring the firm and so could function as a means of co-opting that group (direct influence tactic), or it could be an inflated contract awarded to a relative of the CEO (agency loss).

Examples such as these illustrate that classification can be tricky, but the complex nature of some investments makes classification particularly important. Complex investments confound the relationship between CSR and CFP. If agency losses are confounded with CSR, findings may be biased toward a negative relationship and so toward refutation of the business case. However, confounding CSR with direct influence tactics and especially process improvement gains may bias findings toward a positive relationship and so toward support for the business case. It is therefore beneficial to parse out the CSR portion of complex investments. For example, the $1 million investment in energy conservation previously mentioned could be disaggregated into process improvement and CSR components. To measure the net financial benefits that accrued to CSR, the costs of the process improvement expenditures could be separated from any resources expended to internally and externally publicize this program, and the efficiency gains could be culled from the total financial gains from this investment, netting the financial gains attributable to improved stakeholder relations. Such parsing can be subjective, but no more so than commonly accepted practices involved in accounting for intangibles (Lev, 2001).

Another tool is real options analysis (Barnett, 2003, 2005; Bowman & Hurry, 1993; Kogut & Kulatilaka, 2001; McGrath, 1997). Fombrun et al. (2000) have suggested that firms view investments in social responsibility as "opportunity platforms" that generate future opportunities, or real options (cf. Kogut & Kulatilaka, 1994). From this perspective, the $1 million energy conservation project would be treated as a platform investment, and the additional opportunities it produces to enhance stakeholder relations would be valued as real options. A variety of techniques exist to place a separate financial value on these real options (Copeland & Antikarov, 2003; Trigeorgis, 1996).

A further complication is determination of motives. Particularly regarding social responsibility, firms may disguise the motives behind an action or even misrepresent them (Beder, 1997; Greer & Bruno, 1996; Laufer, 2003). This is not problematic for managerial decision making, since managers are aware of their own motives and can therefore make informed cost-benefit projections about even the most Machiavellian of acts. However, it does present a serious challenge to observers, such as researchers. In the discussion section I suggest research methods to cope with this issue.

As described above, then, CSR may be more narrowly defined as a discretionary allocation of corporate resources to improving social welfare that serves as means of enhancing relationships with key stakeholders. Research on the business case for CSR extends the link to CFP, seeking to measure financial outcomes and so determine whether there is ample private incentive for firms to engage in these publicly beneficial activities. An effort to ultimately enhance CFP by demonstrating social responsibility to important stakeholders is much different from an effort to enhance CFP by squeezing more efficiency and effectiveness out of processes and machinery or by directly capturing key stakeholders. Once these other types of resource allocations are cleared from our view of the business case, the mechanisms of true interest become more visible and subject to scrutiny.

EXPLAINING HETEROGENEITY IN THE FINANCIAL RETURNS TO CSR

The theoretical framework underlying the business case proposes that CSR improves key stakeholder relationships, which decreases costs and increases income and so increases CFP. However, an extensive amount of empirical testing has failed to conclusively support the business case. Does this mean that the theory is flawed? As argued below, I assert that the basic theoretical underpinnings of the business case are correct, but a key construct that moderates the transformation of CSR into improved stakeholder relationships is missing. This section outlines this key construct and embeds it within a conceptual framework that better explains the relationship between CSR and CFP.

CSR has a variable effect on CFP. Equal investments by different firms, or even the same firm at different points in time, do not return equal amounts of financial gain, as implied by thirty years of inconsistent findings. How can this variability be explained? Over the past several decades scholars have added myriad control variables to their studies to capture variation, but they have done so in an ad hoc fashion, leaving critics to contend that the end result is nothing more than a "mishmash" (Rowley & Berman, 2000: 405) of variables. We now understand the effects of isolated pieces of the overall puzzle, ceteris paribus, but the dots remain unconnected through any theoretical framework that adequately explains the contingent nature of the business case (Mahon & Griffin, 1999; Margolis & Walsh, 2003).

McWilliams and Siegel (2001) made one notable attempt at connecting the dots. They constructed a supply and demand model of CSR that explained how size, level of diversification, R&D, advertising, government sales, consumer income, labor market conditions, and stage in

802   *Academy of Management Review*   July

the industry life cycle influenced the level of CSR output by a given firm. Their "theory of the firm perspective" assumed, however, "that each firm makes optimal choices, which means that each produces at a profit-maximizing level of output" (McWilliams & Siegel, 2001: 125). Under this logic, since CSR is an "almost universal practice" (Dressel, 2003: 1), it must also be an almost universally wise investment. Support for the business case is an assumption of the model, since each firm makes only optimal choices—if CSR did not maximize profit, then firms would not engage in it. Thus, while offering an economic rationale for why firms supply CSR (because there is profitable demand for its supply), such a model fails to explain why or even acknowledge that some firms might earn negative financial returns from CSR activities.

In their call for theoretical development of a contingent approach to the business case, Rowley and Berman (2000: 410) outlined a model of heterogeneity in financial returns to CSR that proposed "some of the dimensions" that drive stakeholders to action. The conceptual framework I develop in this section builds on the insights of Rowley and Berman (2000) regarding the importance of stakeholder action in making the business case. However, it was McWilliams and Siegel's (2000) call for the use of R&D measures in CSR studies that sparked the development of the key construct in this framework. McWilliams and Siegel (2000) argued that previous CSR studies were misspecified because they failed to control for R&D, a known predictor of CFP.

The use of R&D as a predictor of CFP elicits an interesting comparison with research on the link between organizational learning and innovation. One of the fundamental issues in the literature on innovation concerns why so many firms invest in basic R&D even though the fruits of such efforts are public goods. The prevailing logic for several decades was that basic R&D was primarily the province of well-diversified firms, since such firms are able to capture a larger share of these otherwise public benefits (Nelson, 1959). However, Cohen and Levinthal's (1990) introduction of the "absorptive capacity" construct, which they defined as "the ability of a firm to recognize the value of new, external information, assimilate it, and apply it to commercial ends" (1992: 128), shifted innovation research away from a quest to elucidate the

structural conditions that produce spending on basic research and toward a quest to gain a deeper understanding of how basic research can serve as a form of organizational learning that mediates and moderates financial returns to R&D. Although costly R&D activities can increase social welfare by generating public knowledge, absorptive capacity helped explain how such activities can also benefit the sponsoring firm and, moreover, how these benefits vary across firms and time. In effect, the construct of absorptive capacity solidified what could be called "the business case for basic R&D" by demonstrating the contingent link between R&D and CFP.

As Lane, Koka, and Pathak declared, "Absorptive capacity is one of the most important constructs to emerge in organizational research over the past decades" (2002: M1). It clarified the cumulative and path-dependent nature of learning, arguing that the stronger the base in learning, the greater the payoff to future investments in learning: "Prior knowledge permits the assimilation and exploitation of new knowledge.... Accumulating absorptive capacity in one period will permit its more efficient accumulation in the next" (Cohen & Levinthal, 1990: 135–136). Without absorptive capacity, new knowledge has no context, no way to associate and embed. It is analogous to soil; its presence is required for a seed to grow, and the richer the soil, the greater the growth. An extensive body of theoretical and empirical research now attests that some firms have more absorptive capacity than others and so are able to transform a given unit of investment in learning into greater financial gains than others (Zahra & George, 2002). Therefore, the business case for basic R&D is contingent (on absorptive capacity), not universal.

The relationship between CSR and CFP is, in many ways, like that between learning and innovation as addressed in the absorptive capacity literature. One of the fundamental issues in the CSR literature is to explain why so many firms devote resources to CSR given that the benefits are public and the costs private. The long-standing assumption of the business case (normative and agency issues aside) has been that those firms that can capture more of the private benefits of CSR will invest more in it. Therefore, researchers have sought to clarify the structural conditions under which firms might receive private gains from CSR. We now have insight regarding why firms supply CSR (McWilliams & Siegel, 2001). However, we still have no theoretical framework to explain heterogeneous returns to CSR (Rowley & Berman, 2000).

To fill this void, I introduce the construct of *stakeholder influence capacity (SIC): the ability of a firm to identify, act on, and profit from opportunities to improve stakeholder relationships through CSR.* Similar to the way that the ability of a firm to notice, assimilate, and exploit new knowledge depends on its prior knowledge, the ability of a firm to notice and profitably exploit opportunities to improve stakeholder relations through CSR depends on its prior stakeholder relationships. The basic premise is that stakeholders draw from their prior knowledge of a firm when they assess the implications of new information generated by that firm's CSR activities. In short, the actions of a firm and the responses by its stakeholders in regard to CSR are path dependent such that different firms obtain different results from CSR, depending on their unique histories. SIC is an umbrella construct that accounts for those factors that forge this history and so influence how stakeholders react to new CSR initiatives, as well as limit the range of CSR initiatives a firm will pursue.

If a firm's CSR activity is to alter its relationship with a stakeholder, that stakeholder must notice, interpret, and act on the information conveyed by the CSR activity. The SIC construct augments interest-based (Frooman, 1999) and identity-based (Rowley & Moldoveanu, 2003) views of stakeholder action by pointing out that the likelihood a stakeholder will notice a firm's CSR act, the way a stakeholder will interpret a noticed act of CSR, and a stakeholder's reaction to that interpretation are all influenced by the history of the focal firm. The path-dependent nature of stakeholder relations means that a given investment in CSR may provoke different stakeholder reactions and yield different financial results for different firms at different points in time. Moreover, a firm's history affects the degree to which it will be presented with CSR investment opportunities, be cognizant of their presence, and be willing and able to exploit them. Therefore, similar to Cohen and Levinthal's argument that "lack of investment in an area of expertise early on may foreclose the future development of a technical capability in that area" (1990: 128), the SIC construct points out that lack of investment in stakeholder rela-

tionship building can limit the scope of future profitable CSR opportunities.

Figure 2 places SIC within a conceptual framework illustrating the business case for CSR.[2] In the remainder of this section I discuss the mechanisms of this framework.

CSR Flows Build SIC Stocks

The core of Figure 2 illustrates the mediated relationship that defines CSR. CSR does not directly contribute to CFP but, instead, affects CFP through its influence on stakeholder relations. As previously discussed, corporate activities that directly affect CFP or that indirectly affect CFP in ways other than through stakeholder relationship building are not CSR. In addition to its effects on stakeholder relations, an act of CSR produces a substantial by-product—it contributes to a firm's SIC. Dierickx and Cool (1989) pointed out that many strategically valuable assets such as trust and reputation cannot be bought on "strategic factor markets" (Barney, 1986) but must be built over time instead through a series of investments. These discrete investments are the "flows" that contribute to the attainment of a certain asset "stock" at a particular point in time. Accordingly, CSR flows forge SIC stocks.

But what constitutes an SIC stock? SIC is a multidimensional, firm-level construct composed of the dynamic relationships a firm has with its myriad stakeholders. Each stakeholder has his or her own fluid relationship with a firm. When these individual relationships are aggregated at some point in time, they form an intangible asset that a firm possesses—its SIC stock. That is, although SIC is revealed in the dynamic relationships between a firm and its myriad stakeholders, it can be treated in the aggregate as a firm-level intangible resource; a firm possesses a certain stock of SIC.

Other common constructs are conceptualized in a similar fashion. For example, absorptive capacity is considered a firm-level intangible

---

[2] Figure 2 is not a complete model of the business case for CSR. Rather, it is a framework that illustrates the effects of a discrete act of CSR, as discussed in Propositions 1 through 5. Stated differently, the box containing "Corporate social responsibility" refers to a discrete act of CSR, and the remainder of the figure illustrates the effects that this discrete act has on the status of the other variables.

FIGURE 2
A Conceptual Framework Underlying the Business Case for CSR

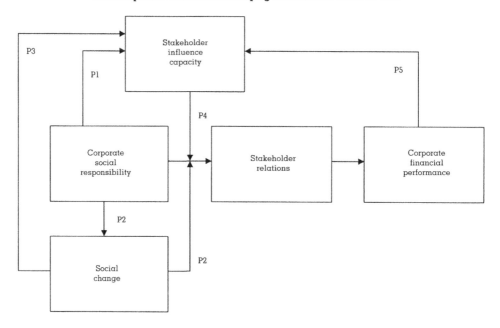

resource (Cohen & Levinthal, 1990), yet its stock is a function of the knowledge present in the minds of individuals and the ability of those individuals to interrelate with other sources of knowledge (Lane & Lubatkin, 1998). Another example is corporate reputation, "a collective representation of a company's past actions and future prospects that describes how key resource providers interpret a company's initiatives and assess its ability to deliver valued outcomes" (Fombrun, 2001: 293). Each "key resource provider" has his or her own unique "image" of a firm, but these images can be aggregated into a collective representation. This collective representation, corporate reputation, is treated as a firm-level intangible asset (Fombrun, 1996). Creating an aggregate firm-level intangible asset is perhaps the only pragmatic means of dealing with a construct of this nature (Wartick, 2002: 375). However, an aggregate measure can mask variation that may be relevant to the relationship of interest. Such criticism has been leveled against absorptive capacity (Lane & Lubatkin,

1998) and corporate reputation (Wartick, 2002). The merits and methods of disaggregating SIC are addressed in the discussion section.

As addressed earlier, the construct of SIC was inspired by research on absorptive capacity, but it shares a close affiliation with corporate reputation, given that both concern how a firm's history affects current perceptions and thereby influences behavior toward that firm. However, SIC and corporate reputation differ in significant ways. The dominant component in measures of corporate reputation is financial, not social, performance (Brown & Perry, 1994). Moreover, as Fombrun's (2001) definition states, corporate reputation entails an assessment of the firm's ability to deliver valued outcomes. These valued outcomes tend to depend on the self-interests of each of the key resource providers who assess the firm.

Brown and Dacin made a parallel distinction in subdividing consumer opinions about a firm into two distinct dimensions: "Corporate ability associations are those associations related to the company's expertise in producing and delivering its outputs. Corporate social responsibility associations reflect the organization's status and activities with respect to its perceived societal obligations" (1997: 68). Thus, corporate reputation is instrumental to answering the question "Given how this firm has performed (mostly financially) in the past (summed up by its corporate reputation), is it likely to deliver value to me in the future?" In contrast, SIC is more an overall assessment of "the soul of a business" (Chappell, 1993) wherein observers ascribe character to the firm (Sen & Bhattacharya, 2001) that helps them to answer the question "Given how this firm has behaved (mostly socially) in the past (summed up by its SIC), can I trust it in the future?"

Nevertheless, corporate reputation is an ill-defined construct that has been broadly conceptualized and whose definition continues to evolve (Barnett, Jermier, & Lafferty, 2006; Wartick, 2002). Popular measures of corporate reputation have weighted financial performance heavily, leading researchers to conclude that corporate reputation ratings such as *Fortune*'s Most Admired Corporations result from, rather than predict, CFP (Brown & Perry, 1994). However, more recent approaches have suggested more focus on stakeholder relationships, beyond just shareholders (Mahon, 2002). Thus, the argument that corporate reputation focuses on financial performance to the detriment of concern for a firm's relationships with other stakeholders is increasingly a strawman. It is entirely possible that corporate reputation could be enlarged so as to effectively encompass the domain herein ascribed to SIC. However, such a possibility makes development of the SIC construct no less important. Whether SIC is treated as an independent construct or as part of an enlarged conceptualization of corporate reputation, its distinctive nature needs to be clearly specified.

To summarize, charitable donations, support of social causes, and other CSR acts are a means of improving stakeholder relations. As firms engage in CSR acts to improve stakeholder relations, a record of social performance incidentally accrues, forging a firm's SIC stock—much as R&D investments, although intended to further innovation, incidentally contribute to a firm's absorptive capacity (Cohen & Levinthal, 1990).

Proposition 1: A firm's current stock of SIC is positively related to its prior CSR activity.

Flows to SIC from acts of CSR are generally incidental—a by-product of the firm's intentions to improve stakeholder favor—but firms may make direct investments in SIC. Such investments do not return near-term increases in stakeholder favor, but a firm might directly invest in SIC in order to build the necessary platform to create future CSR opportunities (Fombrun et al., 2000). Such SIC-building investments include hiring personnel and establishing organizational structures that facilitate timely recognition and execution of emergent CSR opportunities. Corporate owners must be vigilant, however, to maintain discipline in allowing management to cast activities into this vague role, lest agency losses arise (cf. Adner & Levinthal, 2004).

Effects of Social Change on SIC

If an act of CSR is characterized by its focus on social welfare, an obvious and relevant question is "Does CSR improve social welfare?" Oddly enough, this question is seldom asked or answered.[3] Studies of the business case typically do not measure the actual social benefits created by CSR, and there is seldom any accountability (Margolis & Walsh, 2003). Given the role of SIC in the business case for CSR, however, it can be in a firm's interest to provide evidence of the gains to social welfare brought about by its CSR efforts.

A firm's SIC is an aggregate representation of how stakeholders perceive the character or "soul" of that firm, and acts of CSR shape these perceptions over time. However, as the opening quotes of this paper anecdotally evidence, acts of CSR are often met with pessimism. Webb and Mohr categorized more than 20 percent of consumers as "skeptics" whose views are typified by responses such as "You show me something that shows exactly what people give and where it goes to and have someone to do this study that

---

[3] The literature on the natural environment is the primary exception to this rule, often seeking to distinguish discretionary corporate acts that improve the natural environment from mere "greenwashing" (e.g., Greer & Bruno, 1996; Laufer, 2003).

has nothing to do with that business and then I will listen to it. Otherwise, I just . . . I don't believe it at all" (1998: 234). Currall and Epstein claimed, "Because trust tends to be a very evidentiary decision, most of us behave as if we are from the 'Show Me' state of Missouri; we wish to see the evidence that someone is trustworthy" (2003: 195). Thus, in the absence of evidence, many stakeholders discount or ignore a firm's CSR acts.

This, in effect, implicit discount rate for acts of CSR can be diminished or overcome if firms provide evidence that their CSR efforts have produced social change. The stronger the evidence, the smaller the discount rate will be, and so the stronger the effects of the CSR act will be on both stakeholder relations and SIC. This effect can be negative, however, for firms that make their CSR processes and outcomes more transparent but fail to produce ample results—that is, transparency is double edged. Firms that claim to engage in acts of CSR but fall short of their rhetoric can face lawsuits claiming deceptive advertising, as Nike recently faced in regard to its allegedly false claims of eliminating child labor in its subcontracted manufacturing facilities. The more transparent a firm's CSR acts, the easier it is for activists to find evidence of their ineffectiveness and either file lawsuits or bring forth other public challenges to the trustworthiness of the firm.

Yet despite considerable evidence that many firms' CSR efforts are largely symbolic and sometimes even fraudulent (e.g., greenwashing; Beder, 1997; Greer & Bruno, 1996; Laufer, 2003), most stakeholders are willing to accept CSR acts at face value (Webb & Mohr, 1998). However, those firms that engage in symbolic-only acts of CSR are taking a risk. Trust is an asset that is built slowly but destroyed quickly (Currall & Epstein, 2003). If it is revealed that a CSR activity was insincere or fraudulent, any trust gained from the CSR act will be lost, and the firm's stakeholder relations may be seriously degraded.

Many recent examples of insincere and outright fraudulent corporate activity underscore the risk inherent in pursuing symbolism over substance. For example, The Body Shop, long hailed as "the Mother Theresa of capitalism" (Entine, 2002), suffered a staggering loss of image, and profits thereafter, following a report that many of its products were not manufactured

in the socially responsible manner advertised (Entine, 1994). Thus, firms that engage in symbolic CSR increase their risk and so effectively decrease their risk-adjusted returns to CSR. Despite the frequent effectiveness of symbolic adoption (Westphal & Zajac, 1994), when risk is factored in, the following proposition holds.

> *Proposition 2: The effects of an act of CSR on stakeholder relations and SIC are amplified in the presence of evidence of its effects on social welfare.*

As dubious corporate behaviors come to light, public trust in business declines. Some dubious corporate behaviors are sufficient to produce a shock that destroys public trust and brings about government regulation. For example, recent accounting scandals quickly led to the implementation of the Sarbanes-Oxley Act of 2002, which placed additional burdens on firms. Others have more gradual effects. Expectations of corporate environmentalism shifted "from heresy to dogma" (Hoffman, 1997) over several decades as evidence of industrial harm to the natural environmental mounted. These shifts in formal and informal expectations of the social obligations of business can occur across entire economies, as with Sarbanes-Oxley, or can be isolated to specific sectors or industries, as with the petrochemical sector in Hoffman's (1997) study.

These changes in societal expectations are not entirely exogenous—firms and industries influence the social standards by which they are judged. When a firm increases its CSR activities, its rivals feel pressure to increase theirs as well, since, all else being equal, most consumers prefer to buy from the most socially responsible firm (Mohr, Webb, & Harris, 2001). Firms also influence societal expectations through direct influence tactics. McWilliams, Van Fleet, and Cory (2002) have outlined the ways in which firms use "political strategy" to lobby for new laws that increase social obligations in certain industries so as to place their less capable rivals at a competitive disadvantage. Accidental behaviors, such as Union Carbide's disaster in Bhopal, India, and the Alaskan oil spill of the Exxon Valdez, can also lead to change in the formal and informal societal expectations facing those firms responsible for the acts, as well as their rivals (King, Lenox, & Barnett, 2002).

When expectations of CSR increase, the value of the status quo necessarily declines. In stock and flow terms, increasing societal expectations about CSR enlarge the "hole" in the "bathtub" that holds the stock of SIC, therein requiring additional flows of CSR to maintain a constant level (Dierickx & Cool, 1989: 1506). Overall, this points to a "Red Queen" effect (Barnett & Hansen, 1996) in CSR, whereby stationary firms lose ground because of increasingly stringent societal expectations. However, firms can also take part in collective efforts, through trade associations, to forestall and decrease the formal and informal social burdens placed on their industries (King & Lenox, 2000; Miles, 1982; Rees, 1994, 1997). When effective, these collective efforts increase firms' SIC.

> *Proposition 3: As societal expectations of a firm's social obligations increase (decrease), all else being equal, that firm's SIC will decrease (increase).*

SIC As Moderator

As individuals, we are limited in our ability to process the unlimited stimuli that surround us (Simon, 1955). To cope, we reduce complex situations to simplified cognitive representations, take action based on heuristics, and develop routines (Cyert & March, 1963; Nelson & Winter, 1982; Tversky & Kahneman, 1986). These simplifications allow us to lessen cognitive loads, but they also restrict our search for new information. We interpret and assess information according to existing cognitive representations, and we often overlook disconfirming evidence (Dutton & Dukerich, 1991; Weick, 1995). As a result, our cognitive representations are hard to change once established.

Such is the case with SIC. Stakeholders are boundedly rational and therefore rely on a simplified cognitive representation to proxy for a complex reality. Each stakeholder's reaction to an act of CSR by a firm is conditioned on his or her cognitive representation of the character of that firm. These cognitive representations affect which CSR actions stakeholders notice and how they make sense of those actions. Each stakeholder has his or her own unique and subjective representation. One stakeholder may view, say, Wal-Mart favorably because of its contributions to local charities, another may have an enduring

unfavorable view of Wal-Mart because of its questionable labor practices, and yet another stakeholder may have a consistently mixed view because of the conflicting facets of Wal-Mart's social efforts.

SIC acts as an aggregate gauge of these cognitive representations, or "perceptual filters" (Starbuck & Milliken, 1988), through which new information about the firm's CSR practices flows to stakeholders. Firms with poor SIC may have their CSR efforts overlooked or, if noticed, met with skepticism, or they may even experience degradation in stakeholder relations in response to CSR. People are loath to update their prior convictions even in the face of disconfirming evidence (Staw, 1981). They are unlikely to notice activities that they consider out of character with the actor. If they do notice such activities, they may react with cynicism, discounting them as self-serving. Therefore, their trust in the firm is unlikely to increase, and could even decrease, as they come to believe that the firm will do anything to appear socially responsible (Varadarajan & Menon, 1988; Webb & Mohr, 1998).

A variety of studies have suggested that stakeholder beliefs about the character of a firm affect how stakeholders notice, interpret, and react to new information about that firm. Brown and Dacin (1997) determined that consumer evaluations of new product offerings were contingent on their beliefs about the social responsibility of the firm; if the consumer believed the firm was socially responsible, his or her assessment of its new product was more favorable, but if the consumer believed the firm was not socially responsible, his or her assessment was unfavorable. Sen and Bhattacharya (2001) connected stakeholder perceptions of the social posture of a firm to purchase intentions, finding that CSR can actually reduce purchase intentions for consumers with unfavorable opinions of a firm's social posture. Linxwiler, Shover, and Clelland found that "when regulatory personnel perceive clients to be responsive to regulatory demands, their enforcement responses are more likely to demonstrate forbearance. The net result is leniency" (1983: 434). Thus, a firm's perceived character can even affect formal relationships.

> *Proposition 4: SIC moderates the effect of an act of CSR on stakeholder relations.*

The Paradox of Performance

The business case for CSR has been characterized as searching for an answer to the question "Can you 'do well while doing good?'" (Hamilton, Jo, & Statman, 1993). Although the answer remains in dispute, many studies have shown the reverse to hold—that strong CFP (i.e., doing well) is associated with increased CSR (i.e., doing good; see Margolis & Walsh, 2003, for a summary). But how are acts of CSR received when they come from a firm with strong CFP? Anecdotal evidence suggests that if a firm does particularly well (CFP), its efforts at doing good (CSR) may be perceived negatively. For example, Microsoft has a strong record of philanthropy, but because of its yet stronger record of profitability, some expect even more philanthropy, making it a "no-win situation," as Alsop exemplified with a quote from a stakeholder: "I also think they donate far less than they could given Bill Gates's billions" (2002: 2). Whereas a donation of $1 million from a small firm might trigger a favorable stakeholder response, the same donation from a large and highly profitable firm such as Microsoft might engender little attention or even pessimism.

SIC provides an explanation for why doing well may decrease the financial benefits of doing good. Doing too well can lead stakeholders to perceive that a firm is not doing enough good. Excessive CFP indicates that a firm is extracting more from society than it is returning and can suggest that profits have risen because the firm has exploited some of its stakeholders in order to favor shareholders and upper management. This can indicate untrustworthiness to stakeholders looking to establish or maintain relations with the firm. As a result, increases in CFP can lead to decreases in SIC.[4] This lower stock of SIC dampens the value of future acts of CSR. Overall, more profitable firms are expected to do more good but get less financial reward in return.

> *Proposition 5: Excessive CFP decreases SIC.*

This suggests a self-regulating cycle that places upper bounds on CSR contributions. Many studies have suggested a virtuous cycle without limits: "Financially successful companies spend more [on CSR] because they can afford it, but CSP also helps them become a bit more successful" (Orlitzky et al., 2003: 424).[5] But if CSR has a universally favorable rate of return, why would a firm ever stop investing in CSR? While not completely explaining the upper bounds of CSR investments, the negative effect of CFP on SIC highlights one way in which gains to CSR eventually extinguish themselves. This mechanism also helps to explain the findings of Seifert, Morris, and Bartkus that there is "a positive relationship between available resources and giving to charity, but neither a significant positive nor a significant negative relationship between giving to charity and financial returns" (2003: 208).

DISCUSSION

Consider your reaction were Union Carbide to announce a $10 million donation to community hospitals in Bhopal, India, or were Exxon to announce a $10 million donation to improve wildlife habitats along the Alaskan coast. Now consider your reaction were Ben & Jerry's to do either of the above. The simple premise of this paper is that your reactions would differ because of your prior beliefs about the characteristics of each of the donating firms. The path-dependent nature of firm-stakeholder relations helps to explain why the financial returns to CSR differ across firms and time, and serves as the cornerstone of a contingent framework for the business case, offered to supplant a long-standing quest for a universal business case for CSR.

The precise payoff for a particular CSR act for a particular firm at a particular point in time is not particularly predictable, however. There are many factors to consider. In this paper I focused on the role that a firm's unique history plays in eventually transforming an act of CSR into CFP. I did not distinguish between types of CSR, but

---

[4] This again distinguishes SIC from corporate reputation. Increases in CFP have consistently been linked to increases in common measures of corporate reputation, demonstrating corporate reputation's emphasis on CFP (Brown & Perry, 1994).

[5] Generally, this virtuous cycle is said to exist between CSP and CFP, not CSR and CFP. Bearing in mind confusion and lack of distinction between CSR and CSP in prior literature (as previously discussed), the same logic holds for CSR.

worked instead from the standpoint that a firm's history influences this relationship regardless of the type of CSR. However, the nature of the CSR investment itself is also bound to have an influence. Most tests of the business case have made only a binary distinction regarding a firm's overall social posture—a firm is considered to be socially responsible or not. The few studies that have disaggregated social responsibility have found variance in financial returns.

For example, Berman, Wicks, Kotha, and Jones (1999) found that the state of a firm's employee relationships and product safety/quality were positively related to CFP, but a firm's community relations and support of diversity and the natural environment were unrelated to CFP. Barnett and Salomon (2006) found a positive relationship between the financial performance of mutual funds and their decision to exclude firms with poor community relations, but a negative relationship when these funds excluded firms with poor labor relations or poor environmental performance. But as with most prior studies, these scholars measured CSP stocks, not CSR acts. Berman et al. (1999: 501) parsed the commonly used KLD database into subcategories, each representing a different "stakeholder posture." Barnett and Salomon (2006) divided the universe of socially responsible mutual funds by twelve measures of social responsibility, each of which assessed whether firms within a mutual fund's portfolio possessed a particular stock of social responsibility.

Not surprisingly, in light of the extant emphasis on forging a CSP–CFP link, there is no well-established means of categorizing acts of CSR. It is beyond the scope of this paper to fully develop a CSR classification system, and so this substantial task is left to future research. However, the framework developed here does suggest several viable directions. As previously discussed, the implicit logic behind CSR is to engage in explicitly selfless acts in order to exude general trustworthiness and so enhance relationships with important stakeholders. Such an approach is distinct from direct influence tactics, whereby corporate resource allocations are intended to directly influence specific stakeholders (see Figure 1). Nevertheless, it is possible that a corporate resource allocation could be intended to curry favor with particular stakeholders—perhaps those with the highest levels of power, legitimacy, and urgency (Mitchell et

al., 1997)—yet fall short of classification as a direct influence tactic. For example, a firm might make a highly visible and substantial donation to a national charity with the intent of improving relations with government officials in the specific community in which it seeks favorable zoning permits. This would not be a direct influence tactic, as previously defined, since the beneficiaries of the resource allocation are not the parties the firm intends to influence. Yet the intent to direct the act toward a specific set of stakeholders makes this something more than pure CSR.[6]

Insight into the intent behind specific acts of CSR could elicit contingencies of relevance to the business case. Of course, intent can be difficult to determine—it can be hidden from observers and even be disguised within the hierarchy of the firm itself, given agency issues. Fortunately, a variety of primary methods, such as observation, interviews, and surveys of top management, and secondary methods, such as content analyses of reports by the firm and about the firm, court documents, and top management speeches, are available to aid in discerning intent. Many of these methods are laborious, and none will perfectly reveal intent when firms and their managers wish to hide it. Arguably, though, most widely accepted methods of assessing firm behavior and performance suffer this same problem (e.g., formal certified accounting figures, as revealed by numerous scandals). Nonetheless, to the degree that intent can be discerned, important contingencies may be revealed.

One possibility, suggested by the above discussion, is that firms may intend some acts of CSR to be more "applied" than others. Analogous to the distinction between forms of R&D, some types of CSR may be "basic"—intended as a broad indicator of the trustworthiness of a firm—whereas others may be applied—intended to curry favor with a particular set of stakeholders. In terms of the framework presented in this paper, basic SIC would contribute more to building SIC stock than to immediately improving stakeholder favor, whereas applied SIC would achieve more immediate gains to

---

[6] Figure 1 actually represents a continuum, wherein acts vary from low to high on the dimensions of interest. The polar ends of each dimension are pure forms that may never be fully realized in practice.

810   *Academy of Management Review*   July

stakeholder favor, with a relatively small addition to SIC stocks. Such insight could help with the "stakeholder mismatch" problem (Wood & Jones, 1995) by clarifying which types of CSR are most likely to be discerned in which CFP measures. Applied CSR acts would be more likely to result in near-term gains and so lend themselves to empirical tests with stock price as the CFP measure, such as event studies. Basic CSR acts would be less likely to have a short-term impact and so would be more amenable to tests with accounting measures of CFP as the dependent variable, such as lagged multivariate regression.

Given the challenges of discerning intent, as well as the potential disparity between intent and outcome, researchers seeking to identify relevant categories of CSR may be more likely to succeed by focusing on the outcomes of CSR. The KLD database provides a good opportunity for such research. This database includes an annual rating, on a five-point Likert-type scale, of the state of a firm's relationship with several groups of stakeholders. Researchers could relate firms' varying KLD profiles to the flows of CSR activity that produced them, both cross-sectionally and longitudinally. For example, how do the prior CSR flows of a firm that scored a -2 on employee relations, a -1 on local community relations, and a $+2$ on product safety/quality compare with the CSR flows of a firm that scored $+2$, $+1$, -2, respectively?

Data on acts of CSR, or CSR flows, are publicly available by definition, since private acts are herein categorized as agency losses, not CSR. Factor or cluster analysis could help determine the types of CSR associated with changes in particular stakeholder relationships. For example, if a firm is more interested in improving employee relations than community relations, in which types of CSR should it engage? The revealed categories could help firms better target intended audiences without resorting to direct influence tactics, which have some negative properties as previously discussed. Thus, clear insight into the differing types of applied CSR and their effectiveness could significantly benefit management practice.

Studies of this nature could also illuminate the severity of the trade-off problem inherent in CSR. A firm's myriad stakeholders have myriad interests. In seeking to improve relationships with one set of stakeholders through a visible

act of applied CSR, a firm may worsen its relationships with other stakeholders. For example, in the past, Microsoft established a policy of providing benefits to the same-sex partners of its employees and openly advocating legislative action to more broadly increase gay and lesbian rights. Arguably, this policy improved Microsoft's relationships with its employees and gay and lesbian organizations, and possibly provided a more basic CSR benefit by softening Microsoft's often-harsh image with other stakeholder groups. Recently, because of its support for a Washington State antidiscrimination bill, Microsoft was threatened with a boycott led by a conservative pastor. In response, Microsoft ended its support of this bill. As a result, Microsoft avoided the threatened boycott but harmed its relations with employees and gay and lesbian organizations. A few weeks later, Microsoft reversed its reversed position and again supported this and other such bills.

Examples such as this demonstrate the trade-off problem and suggest that an act of CSR could even produce a net loss in aggregate SIC and stakeholder relations. Thus, further study of the severity of these trade-off problems is clearly warranted. Given the many stakeholder interests that a firm must balance, study of these trade-offs will necessarily be complex. Even within themselves, stakeholders have differing interests. For example, a single stakeholder may have multiple roles relative to a given firm, such as employee (works for the firm), investor (owns firm stock), community member (lives in the city in which the firm is located), and social activist (member of a civic group, church, or NGO). Researchers may rely on qualitative methods such as interviews and surveys to gauge changes in a firm's relationships with various stakeholder groups. Admittedly, it is often not feasible to obtain such data for all of a firm's stakeholders. As a standard proxy for an aggregate market reaction to a particular CSR event, researchers may employ event study methods (McWilliams & Siegel, 1997).

Timing may also be a relevant contingency. Researchers have noted a variety of ways that firms can financially benefit from instituting processes that reduce pollution and other harms to the natural environment (Hart, 1995; King & Lenox, 2002; Klassen & Whybark, 1999; Russo & Fouts, 1997). Many such process improvement efforts have minimal or no time component—

even late movers can improve financial performance by cutting waste. However, early movers can gain greater benefit in some instances; in particular, there are

> avenues for 'early mover' advantages whereby the firm can capitalize on an enviropreneurial opportunity before it is shared with or adopted by competitors (Porter & van der Linde, 1995). Enviropreneurial initiatives that lead to complex eco-efficiencies, patented technologies and products that are difficult for competitors to imitate could provide firms more sustainable competitive advantages (Stafford, Polonsky, & Hartman, 2000: 133).

The framework presented here provides perspective, beyond the ability of first movers to forge enduring barriers around new technologies, on why early mover advantages may exist for some types of socially responsible behavior. Proposition 3 suggests that as a particular type of CSR becomes common, societal expectations increase.[7] Firms that do not meet the increased expectations suffer a decline in SIC. Given that SIC moderates the gains from an act of CSR, the later a firm waits to engage in that particular CSR act, the less it will benefit. Therefore, CSR acts may have life cycles that produce early mover incentives. A CSR life cycle could help explain prior discrepant findings, owing to variation in sample windows, and so CSR studies should control for timing effects. To better specify CSR life cycles, future research should examine variation in the outcomes of specific types of CSR over time. As we further untangle CSR from process improvement,[8] timing may take on additional importance in the study of the business case.

This paper is based on the notion that accounting for a firm's SIC, herein treated as a

firm-level intangible asset, will increase the precision of studies of the business case. We currently have many proxies for SIC. In particular, measures of CSP, as snapshots of the state of a firm's stakeholder relations at a point in time, are proxies for the overall state of a firm's relationships with those stakeholders it wishes to influence. CSP alone has not resolved the business case, but because it represents a firm's stock of SIC, CSP can play an important role in future studies of the contingent nature of the business case. In a contingent framework, CSP becomes a measure of the given state as we advance beyond CSP to a new, more fruitful question for both research and practice: *Given a firm's SIC, which CSR acts are profitable?*

CSP has many well-established measures, such as the KLD database (see Margolis & Walsh, 2003, for a summary). Many of these are firm-level measures. Such summary measures are convenient for reporting, but they can mask important variations in a firm's relations with its myriad stakeholders. To cope with this issue, some CSP measures have been disaggregated into component relationships. However, CSP generally has been disaggregated into component parts without the guidance of a commonly accepted or even explicit theoretical rationale. Sharfman found that combinations of the subcategories of the KLD measure correlate with other common CSP measures, but noted that "there is no discernible theory underlying the choice of variables" that populate these subcategories (1996: 288).

Given the focus of the business case, relevant theory must provide guidance in discerning which of the relationships inherent in the aggregate concept have independent influence on CFP. Measures of corporate reputation, considering their emphasis on financial performance, might offer insight here. Indeed, some scholars have performed empirical tests with corporate reputation serving as a measure of CSP—commonly, *Fortune*'s ranking of Most Admired Corporations (McGuire, Sundgren, & Schneeweis, 1988; Sharfman, 1996). More recently, a special issue of *Business and Society* debated "whether reputation is a relevant and useful construct to integrate more explicitly into theories of business and society relationships" (Logsdon & Wood, 2002: 365). The conclusion was that, as with other measures of CSP, there is no

---

[7] Empirical testing of Proposition 3 necessitates a measure of change in societal expectations. Possible measures include changes in the number and magnitude of lawsuits, proxy fights, protests, media coverage, and congressional discussion concerning specific topics (cf. Hoffman, 1997). One might also take a reverse perspective and measure changes in the amount of a firm's or industry's attention to certain matters, as disclosed by coverage in their trade journals, under the assumption that firms increase attention to matters that are of increasing importance (Hoffman & Ocasio, 2001).

[8] As previously discussed, process improvement efforts are distinct from CSR (see Figure 1), but they may involve a CSR component. This component may be analyzed separately from the costs and benefits of process improvement.

theoretical basis for the ways in which corporate reputation has been parsed (Wartick, 2002).

An adequate theoretical framework must distinguish not only the component relationships inherent in a firm's overall social posture but also the relative importance of each component. Again, this presents a problem, "since theoretical work in stakeholder management and social issues participation has yet to identify a ranking of importance for the various stakeholder groups and issues" (Hillman & Keim, 2001: 131). As with the business case in general, the factors determining "who and what really counts" (Mitchell et al., 1997) and how much they count may be too firm specific to enable the development of useful universal categories. Regardless, it is beyond the scope of this paper to offer a well-developed categorization and weighting scheme of SIC's component parts and so this, too, is left as fertile ground for future research.

Path dependence has implications not only for how stakeholders notice and react to CSR but also for how firms notice and react to CSR opportunities. Employees in firms with a history of CSR may come to have CSR enmeshed in their identities (Dutton & Dukerich, 1991) and are more likely to be cognizant of new CSR opportunities. Because of adjusting aspiration levels (March & Simon, 1958), CSR-oriented firms are more likely to engage in CSR acts once opportunities are noticed. Cohen and Levinthal's discussion of absorptive capacity explains this self-reinforcing behavior:

> If the firm engages in little innovative activity, and is therefore relatively insensitive to the opportunities in the external environment, it will have a low aspiration level with regard to exploitation of new technology, which in turn implies that it will continue to devote little effort to innovation. This creates a self-reinforcing cycle. Likewise, if an organization has a high aspiration level, influenced by externally generated technical opportunities, it will conduct more innovative activity and thereby increase its awareness of outside opportunities. Consequently, its aspiration level will remain high (1990: 137–138).

Similarly, firms with weak (strong) histories of CSR are less (more) likely to notice and seek new CSR opportunities. This notion that cognition is a key determinant of CSR activity adds realism to McWilliams and Siegel's (2001) economic model of CSR supply and demand to help explain enduring nonoptimal supplies of CSR by some firms. McWilliams and Siegel (2001)

assumed that supply and demand for CSR always matched (or equilibrium was quickly reestablished). However, the SIC construct explains why firms vary in the degree to which they notice and act on demand for CSR. A firm must first notice and desire to act on any demand for CSR before supplying it, and its history affects the degree to which the firm will do this. If a firm has weak SIC, it may consistently undersupply CSR.

The normative implications of this paper are limited only to the business case—whether or not certain firms,[9] in certain situations, should invest in certain kinds of CSR in order to improve CFP. If we assume that stockholders are the sole owners of a firm, I argue a firm should not engage in an act of CSR that is unlikely to offer a compensating increase in stakeholder favor or stakeholder influence capacity. Given their histories, some firms should engage in little or no CSR at certain points in time because poor SIC prevents CSR from transforming into stakeholder favor. In fact, it can create stakeholder discontent and so will be money poorly spent. Future research must continue to uncover the contingencies that determine the benefits of CSR so as to allow managers to determine whether particular acts of CSR are wise investments for their firms.

CONCLUSION

Whether corporations are "owned" by their shareholders or by society and whether they have any obligations beyond becoming increasingly efficient at shareholder wealth production are topics that have long been fiercely debated. This debate recently intensified following many well-publicized instances of dubious corporate behavior. It shows no signs of resolution and will surely remain a contentious topic for the foreseeable future. This paper offers no resolution to this debate. As long as we desire capitalism with a safety net, this is a dialectic tension that our society must continuously manage, not resolve.

However, this paper has shed light on the business case for CSR. As others have surmised,

---

[9] The framework applies only to public corporations, not private firms. Private firms do not face the same agency issues that are integral to the definition of CSR and the framework presented here.

"Managers should treat decisions regarding CSR precisely as they treat all investment decisions" (McWilliams & Siegel, 2001: 125). The difficulty, however, is that the payoffs have been unclear because researchers have struggled for several decades to demonstrate a universal rate of return in a situation that clearly calls for a contingent perspective (Rowley & Berman, 2000; Ullmann, 1985). A contingent perspective argues that although all CSR activities are not profit maximizing, some may be, and so the careful use of CSR can fulfill management's fiduciary responsibilities. The SIC construct and the conceptual framework developed in this paper bring us closer to specifying a contingent model of the business case for CSR.

In many ways the struggle to make the business case for CSR resembles the struggle to show the financial merit of investments in a variety of intangible assets. Accounting and financial methods have developed over the years to justify many of the "gut feelings" of managers as they invest in projects that have no immediate financial return, such as R&D and advertising. Given that CSR is an almost universal practice, either we have a long-standing agency problem that boards of directors and the mechanisms of the free market have almost universally been unable to correct, or we have yet to amply demonstrate the financial merits of CSR. Here I advocate the latter and call for increased attention to a contingency perspective that affirms the payoffs to some forms of CSR for some firms at some points in time. CSR cannot financially please all of the corporations all of the time, but it can please some of the corporations some of the time. Researchers should try to figure out which ones and when.

REFERENCES

Adner, R., & Levinthal, D. 2004. What is not a real option: Considering boundaries for the application of real options to business strategy. *Academy of Management Review,* 29: 74–85.

Alsop, R. 2002. Perils of corporate philanthropy. *Wall Street Journal,* January 16: 1–2.

Barnett, M. 2003. Falling off the fence? A realistic appraisal of a real options approach to corporate strategy. *Journal of Management Inquiry,* 12: 185–196.

Barnett, M. 2005. Paying attention to real options. *R&D Management,* 35: 61–72.

Barnett, M., & Salomon, R. 2006. Beyond dichotomy: The cur-
vilinear relationship between social responsibility and financial performance. *Strategic Management Journal,* 27: 1101–1122.

Barnett, M., Jermier, J., & Lafferty, B. 2006. Corporate reputation: The definitional landscape. *Corporate Reputation Review,* 9: 26–38.

Barnett, W., & Hansen, M. 1996. The Red Queen in organizational learning. *Strategic Management Journal,* 17: 139–157.

Barney, J. 1986. Strategic factor markets: Expectations, luck, and business strategy. *Management Science,* 32: 1231–1241.

Barney, J. 1991. Firm resources and sustained competitive advantage. *Journal of Management,* 17: 99–120.

Baron, D. 1995. The nonmarket strategy system. *Sloan Management Review,* 37(1): 73–86.

Baysinger, B. 1984. Domain maintenance as an objective of business political activity: An expanded typology. *Academy of Management Review,* 9: 248–258.

Beder, S. 1997. *Global spin: The corporate assault on environmentalism.* White River Junction, VT: Chelsea Green.

Berman, S., Wicks, A., Kotha, S., & Jones, T. 1999. Does stakeholder orientation matter? The relationship between stakeholder management models and firm financial performance. *Academy of Management Journal,* 42: 488–506.

Bowman, E. H., & Hurry, D. 1993. Strategy through the option lens: An integrated view of resource investments and the incremental-choice process. *Academy of Management Review,* 18: 760–782.

Brown, T., & Dacin, P. 1997. The company and the product: Corporate associations and consumer product responses. *Journal of Marketing,* 61: 68–84.

Brown, B., & Perry, S. 1994. Removing the financial performance halo from *Fortune's* "most admired" companies. *Academy of Management Journal,* 37: 1346–1359.

Chappell, T. 1993. *The soul of a business: Managing for profit and the common good.* Des Plaines, IL: Bantam Books.

Cochran, P., & Wood, R. 1984. Corporate social responsibility and financial performance. *Academy of Management Journal,* 27: 42–56.

Cohen, W., & Levinthal, D. 1990. Absorptive capacity: A new perspective on learning and innovation. *Administrative Science Quarterly,* 35: 128–152.

Copeland, T., & Antikarov, V. 2003. *Real options: A practitioner's guide.* New York: Texere.

Currall, S., & Epstein, M. 2003. The fragility of organizational trust: Lessons from the rise and fall of Enron. *Organizational Dynamics,* 32(2): 193–206.

Cyert, R., & March, J. 1963. *A behavioral theory of the firm.* Englewood Cliffs, NJ: Prentice-Hall.

de Figueiredo, J. 2002. Lobbying and information in politics. *Business and Politics,* 4: 125–129.

Dierickx, I., & Cool, K. 1989. Asset stock accumulation and sustainability of competitive advantage. *Management Science,* 35: 1504–1513.

Donaldson, T., & Preston, L. 1995. The stakeholder theory of the corporation: Concepts, evidence, and implications. *Academy of Management Review,* 20: 65–91.

Dressel, C. 2003. For effective CSR campaigns, sincerity starts at home. *PR News,* August 18: 1–3.

Dutton, J., & Dukerich, J., 1991. Keeping an eye on the mirror: Image and identity in organizational adaptation. *Academy of Management Journal,* 34: 517–554.

Entine, J. 1994. Shattered image: Is The Body Shop too good to be true? *Business Ethics,* 8(5): 23–28.

Entine, J. 2002. Body flop. *Toronto Globe and Mail's Report on Business Magazine,* May 31: 1– 9.

Fombrun, C. 1996. *Reputation: Realizing value from the corporate image.* Boston: Harvard Business School Press.

Fombrun, C. 2001. Corporate reputations as economic assets. In M. Hitt, R. Freeman, & J. Harrison (Eds.), *The Blackwell handbook of strategic management:* 289–312. Malden, MA: Blackwell.

Fombrun, C., Gardberg, N., & Barnett, M. 2000. Opportunity platforms and safety nets: Corporate citizenship and reputational risk. *Business and Society Review,* 105: 85–106.

Freeman, R. 1984. *Strategic management: A stakeholder perspective.* Boston: Pitman.

Friedman, M. 1970. The social responsibility of business is to increase its profits. *New York Times Magazine,* September 13: 122–126.

Frooman, J. 1999. Stakeholder influence strategies. *Academy of Management Review,* 24: 191–205.

Gasparino, C. 2005. *Blood on the street: The sensational inside story of how Wall Street analysts duped a generation of investors.* New York: Free Press.

Greening, D., & Turban, W. 2000. Corporate social performance as a competitive advantage in attracting a quality workforce. *Business and Society,* 39: 254–280.

Greer, J., & Bruno, K. 1996. *Greenwash: The reality behind corporate environmentalism.* New York: Apex Press.

Griffin, J., & Mahon, J. 1997. The corporate social performance and corporate financial performance debate: Twenty-five years of incomparable research. *Business and Society,* 36: 5–31.

Hamilton, S., Jo, H., & Statman, M. 1993. Doing well while doing good? The investment performance of socially responsible mutual funds. *Financial Analysts Journal,* 49(6): 62–66.

Hart, S. 1995. A natural resource-based view of the firm. *Academy of Management Review,* 20: 986–1014.

Hartman, C., & Stafford, E. 1997. Green alliances: Building new business with environmental groups. *Long Range Planning,* 30(2): 184–196.

Hillman, A., & Keim, G. 2001. Shareholder value, stakeholder management, and social/issues: What's the bottom line? *Strategic Management Journal,* 22: 125–139.

Hillman, A., Keim, G., & Schuler, D. 2004. Corporate political activity: A review and research agenda. *Journal of Management,* 30: 837–857.

Hoffman, A. 1997. *From heresy to dogma: An institutional history of corporate environmentalism.* San Francisco: New Lexington Press.

Hoffman, A., & Ocasio, W. 2001. Not all events are attended equally: Toward a middle-range theory of industry attention to external events. *Organization Science,* 12: 414–434.

Jensen, M., & Meckling, W. 1976. Theory of the firm: Managerial behavior, agency costs, and ownership structure. *Journal of Financial Economics,* 3: 305–360.

Jones, T. 1995. Instrumental stakeholder theory: A synthesis of ethics and economics. *Academy of Management Review,* 20: 404–437.

King, A., & Lenox, M. 2000. Industry self-regulation without sanctions: The chemical industry's Responsible Care program. *Academy of Management Journal,* 43: 698–716.

King, A., & Lenox, M. 2002. Exploring the locus of profitable pollution reduction. *Management Science,* 48: 289–299.

King, A., Lenox, M., & Barnett, M. 2002. Strategic responses to the reputation commons problem. In A. Hoffman & M. Ventresca (Eds.), *Organizations, policy, and the natural environment: Institutional and strategic perspectives:* 393–406. Stanford, CA: Stanford University Press.

Klassen, R., & Whybark, D. 1999. The impact of environmental technologies on manufacturing performance. *Academy of Management Journal,* 42: 599–616.

Kogut, B., & Kulatilaka, N. 1994. Options thinking and platform investments: Investing in opportunity. *California Management Review,* 36(2): 52–71.

Kogut, B., & Kulatilaka, N. 2001. Capabilities as real options. *Organization Science,* 12: 744–758.

Lane, P., Koka, B., & Pathak, S. 2002. A thematic analysis and critical assessment of absorptive capacity research. *Academy of Management Best Paper Proceedings,* BPS: M1–M6.

Lane, P., & Lubatkin, M. 1998. Relative absorptive capacity and interorganizational learning. *Strategic Management Journal,* 19: 461–477.

Laufer, W. 2003. Social accountability and corporate greenwashing. *Journal of Business Ethics,* 43: 253–261.

Lev, B. 2001. *Intangibles: Management, measurement and reporting.* Washington, DC: Brookings Institution Press.

Lindblom, C. 1959. The science of "muddling through." *Public Administration Review,* 19(2): 79–88.

Linxwiler, J., Shover, N., & Clelland, D. 1983. The organization and impact of discretion in a regulatory bureaucracy. *Social Problems,* 30: 425–436.

Logsdon, J., & Wood, D. 2002. Reputation as an emerging construct in the business and society field: An introduction. *Business and Society,* 41: 365–370.

Mahon, J. 2002. Corporate reputation: A research agenda using strategy and stakeholder literature. *Business and Society,* 41: 415–445.

Mahon, J., & Griffin, J. 1999. *Painting a portrait. Business and Society,* 38: 126–133.

March, J., & Simon, H. 1958. *Organizations.* New York: Wiley.

Margolis, J., & Walsh, J. 2003. Misery loves companies: Rethinking social initiatives by business. *Administrative Science Quarterly,* 48: 268–305.

McGrath, R. G. 1997. A real options logic for initiating technology positioning investments. *Academy of Management Review,* 22: 974–996.

McGuire, J., Sundgren, A., & Schneeweis, T. 1988. Corporate social responsibility and firm financial performance. *Academy of Management Journal,* 31: 854–872.

McWilliams, A., & Siegel, D. 1997. Event studies in management research: Theoretical and empirical issues. *Academy of Management Journal,* 40: 626–657.

McWilliams, A., & Siegel, D. 2000. Corporate social responsibility and financial performance: Correlation or misspecification? *Strategic Management Journal,* 21: 603–609.

McWilliams, A., & Siegel, D. 2001. Corporate social responsibility: A theory of the firm perspective. *Academy of Management Review,* 26: 117–127.

McWilliams, A., Van Fleet, D., & Cory, K. 2002. Raising rivals' costs through political strategy: An extension of resource-based theory. *Journal of Management Studies,* 39: 707–723.

Miles, R. H. 1982. *Coffin nails and corporate strategies.* Englewood Cliffs, NJ: Prentice-Hall.

Mitchell, R., Agle, B., & Wood, D. 1997. Toward a theory of stakeholder identification and salience: Defining the principle of who and what really counts. *Academy of Management Review,* 22: 853–886.

Mohr, L., Webb, D., & Harris, K. 2001. Do consumers expect companies to be socially responsible? The impact of corporate social responsibility on buying behavior. *Journal of Consumer Affairs,* 35: 45–72.

Nelson, R. 1959. The simple economics of basic research. *Journal of Political Economy,* 67: 297–306.

Nelson, R., & Winter, S. 1982. *An evolutionary theory of economic change.* Cambridge, MA: Harvard University Press.

Oliver, C. 1990. Determinants of interorganizational relationships: Integration and future directions. *Academy of Management Review,* 15: 241–265.

Orlitzky, M., Schmidt, F., & Rynes, S. 2003. Corporate social and financial performance: A meta-analysis. *Organization Studies,* 24: 403–441.

O'Sullivan, T. 1997. Why charity schemes need a delicate touch. *Marketing Week,* November 20: 22.

Penrose, E. 1959. *The theory of the growth of the firm.* Oxford: Oxford University Press.

Pfeffer, J., & Salancik, G. 1978. *The external control of organizations.* New York: Harper & Row.

Porter, M. 1991. Towards a dynamic theory of strategy. *Strategic Management Journal,* 12: 95–118.

Porter, M., & van der Linde, C. 1995. Green and competitive: Ending the stalemate. *Harvard Business Review,* 73(5): 121–134.

Rees, J. 1994. *Hostages of each other: The transformation of nuclear safety since Three Mile Island.* Chicago: University of Chicago Press.

Rees, J. 1997. The development of communitarian regulation in the chemical industry. *Law and Policy,* 19: 477–528.

Roman, R., Hayibor, S., & Agle, B. 1999. The relationship between financial and social performance: Repainting a portrait. *Business and Society,* 38: 109–125.

Rowley, T., & Berman, S. 2000. A brand new brand of corporate social performance. *Business and Society,* 39: 397–418.

Rowley, T., & Moldoveanu, M. 2003. When will stakeholder groups act? An interest- and identity-based model of stakeholder group mobilization. *Academy of Management Review,* 28: 204–219.

Russo, M., & Fouts, P. 1997. A resource-based perspective on corporate environmental performance and profitability. *Academy of Management Journal,* 40: 534–559.

Seifert, B., Morris, S., & Bartkus, B. 2003. Comparing big givers and small givers: Financial correlates of corporate philanthropy. *Journal of Business Ethics,* 45: 195–211.

Sen, S., & Bhattacharya, C. 2001. Does doing good always lead to doing better? Consumer reactions to corporate social responsibility. *Journal of Marketing Research,* 38: 225–243.

Shaffer, B., Quasney, T., & Grimm, C. 2000. Firm level performance implications of nonmarket actions. *Business and Society,* 39: 126–143.

Sharfman, M. 1996. The construct validity of the Kinder, Lydenberg & Domini social performance ratings data. *Journal of Business Ethics,* 15: 287–296.

Simon, H. 1955. A behavioral model of rational choice. *Quarterly Journal of Economics,* 69: 99–118.

Stafford, E., & Hartman, C. 1996. Green alliances: Strategic relations between businesses and environmental groups. *Business Horizons,* 39(2): 50–59.

Stafford, E., Polonsky, M., Hartman, C. 2000. Environmental NGO–business collaboration and strategic bridging: A case analysis of the Greenpeace–Foron alliance. *Business Strategy and the Environment,* 9: 122–135.

Starbuck, W., & Milliken, F. 1988. Executive perceptual filters: What they notice and how they make sense. In D. Hambrick (Ed.), *The executive effect: Concepts and methods for studying top managers:* 35–65. Greenwich, CT: JAI Press.

Staw, B. 1981. The escalation of commitment to a course of action. *Academy of Management Review,* 6: 577–587.

Stigler, G. 1971. The economic theory of regulation. *Bell Journal of Economics,* 2: 3–21.

Trigeorgis, L. 1996. *Real options: Managerial flexibility and strategy in resource allocation.* Cambridge, MA: MIT Press.

Turban, D., & Greening, D. 1997. Corporate social performance and organizational attractiveness to prospective employees. *Academy of Management Journal,* 40: 658–672.

Tversky, A., & Kahneman, D. 1986. Rational choice and the framing of decisions. *Journal of Business,* 59: 251–275.

816   *Academy of Management Review*   July

Ullmann, A. 1985. Data in search of a theory: A critical examination of the relationship among social performance, social disclosure, and economic performance. *Academy of Management Review*, 10: 450–477.

Varadarajan, P., & Menon, A. 1988. Cause-related marketing: A coalignment of marketing strategy and corporate philanthropy. *Journal of Marketing*, 52: 58–74.

Wartick, S. 2002. Measuring corporate reputation: Definition and data. *Business and Society*, 41: 371–392.

Webb, D., & Mohr, L. 1998. A typology of consumer responses to cause-related marketing: From skeptics to socially concerned. *Journal of Public Policy and Marketing*, 17: 226–238.

Weick, K. 1995. *Sensemaking in organizations.* Thousand Oaks, SA: Sage.

Wernerfelt, B. 1984. A resource-based view of the firm. *Strategic Management Journal*, 5: 171–180.

Westphal, J., & Zajac, E. 1994. Substances and symbolism in CEOs' long-term incentive plans. *Administrative Science Quarterly*, 39: 367–390.

Williamson, O. 1975. *Markets and hierarchies.* New York: Free Press.

Windsor, D. 2001. Corporate social responsibility: A theory of the firm perspective—Some comments. *Academy of Management Review*, 26: 502–504.

Wood, D. 1991. Corporate social performance revisited. *Academy of Management Review*, 16: 691–718.

Wood, D., & Jones, R. 1995. Stakeholder mismatching: A theoretical problem in empirical research on corporate social performance. *International Journal of Organizational Analysis*, 3: 229–267.

Zahra, S., & George, G. 2002. Absorptive capacity: A review, reconceptualization, and extension. *Academy of Management Review*, 27: 185–203.

Michael L. Barnett (mbarnett@coba.usf.edu) is an assistant professor of strategic management at the University of South Florida. He received his Ph.D. in management and organizational behavior from New York University. In his research he tries to "enlighten" the notion of self-interest by investigating how, when, and if firms can use forecasting, real options, corporate social responsibility, industry self-regulation, trade associations, Zen teachings, and other such perspectives, techniques, and individual and collective forms of organizing to their long-term strategic advantage.

5

Strategic Management Journal
Strat. Mgmt. J., **33**: 1304–1320 (2012)
Published online EarlyView in Wiley Online Library (wileyonlinelibrary.com) DOI: 10.1002/smj.1980
Received 2 March 2010; Final revision received 21 March 2012

DOES IT PAY TO BE *REALLY* GOOD? ADDRESSING THE SHAPE OF THE RELATIONSHIP BETWEEN SOCIAL AND FINANCIAL PERFORMANCE

MICHAEL L. BARNETT[1] and ROBERT M. SALOMON[2]*
[1] *Saïd Business School, University of Oxford, U.K.*
[2] *Stern School of Business, New York University, New York, New York, U.S.A.*

Building on the theoretical argument that a firm's ability to profit from social responsibility depends upon its stakeholder influence capacity (SIC), we bring together contrasting literatures on the relationship between corporate social performance (CSP) and corporate financial performance (CFP) to hypothesize that the CSP-CFP relationship is U-shaped. Our results support this hypothesis. We find that firms with low CSP have higher CFP than firms with moderate CSP, but firms with high CSP have the highest CFP. This supports the theoretical argument that SIC underlies the ability to transform social responsibility into profit. Copyright © 2012 John Wiley & Sons, Ltd.

INTRODUCTION

Does it pay to be good? Or does the pursuit of societal betterment entail financial detriment? For decades, scholars have sought to determine whether corporate social performance (CSP) and corporate financial performance (CFP) are positively or negatively associated. According to Friedman's (1970) classic argument, the relationship ought to be negative. As firms voluntarily engage in more socially responsible activities, they incur more costs and thus have lower net financial performance. Freeman's (1984) stakeholder view, by contrast, underlies arguments that the relationship is positive. With increased social spending comes improved stakeholder relationships that reduce firms' transaction costs (Jones, 1995) and increase

market opportunities and pricing premiums (Fombrun, Gardberg, and Barnett, 2000), resulting in higher net financial performance. Dozens of studies have supported both opposing positions (for reviews, see Margolis and Walsh, 2003; Orlitzky, Schmidt, and Rynes, 2003) and so have thus far failed to resolve this debate.

In this paper, we do not aim to declare a victor in this long-standing debate. Rather, we demonstrate that despite their opposition, both positions might be correct over some range. That is, for some firms CSP and CFP are negatively associated, but for others they are positively associated. We argue that whether it pays to be good depends upon how well firms are able to capitalize on their social responsibility efforts. Barnett (2007) theorized that as firms engage in socially responsible practices, they accrue stakeholder influence capacity (SIC). Akin to the way in which absorptive capacity (Cohen and Levinthal, 1990), once adequately accrued, enables a firm to assimilate and exploit knowledge and thereby profit from its research investments, an adequate stock of SIC enables a firm to assimilate and exploit stakeholder favor and thereby profit

Keywords: corporate social performance; corporate financial performance; stakeholder influence capacity; stakeholder theory; business case
*Correspondence to: Robert M. Salomon, Stern School of Business, Department of Management and Organization, New York University, 44 West Fourth Street, KMC 7-59, New York, NY 10012, U.S.A. E-mail: rsalomon@stern.nyu.edu

from its social investments. In contrast, firms with inadequate SIC are unable to generate favorable returns on the investments they make in social responsibility and so the relationship is negative.

Based on the theoretical conceptualization of SIC, we therefore hypothesize that the relationship between CSP and CFP is not linearly positive or negative, but curvilinear. We test our hypothesized relationship on an unbalanced panel of 1,214 firms and 4,730 firm-year observations over the period of 1998 to 2006. Controlling for a variety of firm, industry, and year effects, we find support for a U-shaped relationship. In particular, we find that as a firm's overall net score across the 13 social performance criteria in the Kinder, Lydenberg, and Domini (KLD) ratings database increases, its return on assets and net income decline at first, reaching a low point at moderate levels of social performance, and increase thereafter. The U-shaped relationship is not symmetrical, however. Those firms with the highest net KLD scores had significantly higher return on assets and net income than did those firms with the lowest net KLD scores.

Overall, our results suggest that both critics and proponents of the business case for corporate social responsibility are right, to a degree. For some firms, it pays to be good, but for others, it does not. We conclude that future academic work would be well served to account for this curvilinear relationship, both theoretically and empirically. Moreover, future research could fruitfully explore additional contingencies in the relationship between CSP and CFP. For practitioners, our findings imply that firms should view CSP as a long-term investment in creating the capacity to influence stakeholders; though it may not pay to be good now, it may pay to be good later once adequate capacity is built. If a firm has little ability, or desire, to build such a capacity, then social responsibility appears to be a poor financial investment. However, if a firm is able to build such capacity, it may find that it really pays to be really good.

THEORETICAL BACKGROUND AND HYPOTHESIS

We are not the first to investigate whether it pays to be good. Over the last several decades, scholars have published hundreds of studies that have theorized and measured the financial returns

associated with corporate social performance. This body of work is so vast that it has produced more than a dozen published reviews (Margolis and Walsh, 2003). Rather than retread well-worn ground, herein we provide only a brief orientation to the literature. Thereafter, we develop our hypothesis that the relationship between CSP and CFP is U-shaped.

A brief orientation to the vast CSP-CFP literature

Milton Friedman is the traditional straw man in the CSP-CFP literature. Friedman (1970) saw CSP as an agency problem whereby managers were misallocating shareholder wealth to pursue a social mission of their choosing. He argued that firms ought to do no more than abide by the letter of the law, lest the additional costs associated with social spending place firms at a competitive disadvantage. Since managers' pursuits of their desired social missions degrade firms' ability to maximize shareholder wealth, CSP and CFP should thus be negatively related.

Despite his terse dismissal of CSP as 'hypocritical window-dressing,' 'fraud,' and worse, Friedman (1970) did nonetheless acknowledge that a firm's investment in social responsibility could 'make it easier to attract desirable employees, it may reduce the wage bill or lessen losses from pilferage and sabotage or have other worthwhile effects.' In noting that social responsibility can generate valuable goodwill for firms, he thus provided a basis for the counter-argument of stakeholder theorists that CSP and CFP are positively related.

Stakeholder theory, the origins of which are commonly credited to Freeman (1984), argues that the better a firm manages its relationships with the myriad groups that have some interest, or 'stake,' in the firm, the more successful it will be over time. In particular, instrumental stakeholder theory (Jones, 1995) views the firm as a nexus of contracts (Jensen and Meckling, 1976) and addresses the ability of a firm to increase its competitive advantage by minimizing the costs of contracting. A firm minimizes these costs by developing trusting relations with its various stakeholders (Wicks, Berman, and Jones, 1999). Engaging in socially responsible behaviors is one of the primary mechanisms through which a firm may foster and maintain trusting stakeholder relationships. As Jones

Strat. Mgmt. J., **33**: 1304–1320 (2012)
DOI: 10.1002/smj

(1995: 430) notes: '[c]ertain types of corporate social performance are manifestations of attempts to establish trusting, cooperative firm/stakeholder relationships and should be positively linked to a company's financial performance.' For example, firms with strong social performance have an easier time attracting desirable employees (Greening and Turban, 2000).

Hundreds of published empirical studies have tested the relationship between various types of CSP and CFP. Some have found a negative relationship (Vance, 1975; Wright and Ferris, 1997). Some have found a mixed relationship (Cochran and Wood, 1984; Hillman and Keim, 2001). Some have found no relationship of significance (McWilliams and Siegel, 2000; Patten, 1991). Many have found a positive relationship (Orlitzky *et al.*, 2003). Nonetheless, limitations in these myriad studies leave room for skepticism and confusion (Margolis and Walsh, 2003). This led Barnett (2007: 794) to surmise 'that after more than thirty years of research, we cannot clearly conclude whether a one-dollar investment in social initiatives returns more or less than one dollar in benefit to the shareholder.'

Stakeholder influence capacity: the case for a curve

Scholars have increasingly acknowledged that, despite all the effort devoted to doing so, trying to produce a universal answer to the question of whether or not it pays to be good might be futile. As Rowley and Berman (2000: 406) note, 'Only the most naïve (or blindly hopeful) among us will assume that poor (good) social behavior will always have negative (positive) financial implications.' But if a universal answer is 'untenable' (Rowley and Berman, 2000: 406), on what basis might we proffer a contingent answer to when social responsibility does and does not pay?

Barnett (2007) theorized that variance in financial returns to social responsibility is attributable to variance in firm capabilities. Building on the premise of instrumental stakeholder theory that the benefits to firms from social responsibility come through improved stakeholder relationships (Jones, 1995), Barnett (2007: 803) developed the concept of SIC, which he defined as 'the ability of a firm to identify, act on, and profit from opportunities to improve stakeholder relationships through CSR [corporate social responsibility].' Simply, SIC is a

formalization of the basic logic that stakeholders view some firms as more credible than others and reward firms for their acts of social responsibility accordingly.

Firms accrue SIC by consistently engaging in acts of social responsibility (Barnett, 2007). Firms with a weak history of social responsibility have little or no SIC and are not credible with stakeholders, as exemplified by the following stakeholder quote:

> *I guess it depends if it's [the firm's participation in (CSR)] part of the total picture and [if] they really go out of their way. Like with Kroger, it isn't a one-time shot, they're always doing stuff for Egleston [Children's Hospital], or they've got the big barrels out there for the people to bring cans for the homeless or something at Thanksgiving and Christmas. It just seems more a way of business for them, continuously, so in that case, that's fine... But if somebody's doing it just for the publicity, then that would not make me think better of them (survey respondent quoted in Webb and Mohr, 1998: 235).*

Because stakeholder response to their actions varies with SIC, firms with differing levels of SIC will receive different returns to social responsibility. For firms with high SIC, social responsibility can be a wise investment. The trusting stakeholder relationships these firms foster significantly decrease transaction costs and ease the firms' ability to contract with key stakeholders. Such actions are in consonance with the firm's character, so stakeholders are more likely to perceive them as credible. Stakeholders reward such firms accordingly, and so it pays to be good.

In contrast, firms with low SIC are less able to transform socially responsible activities into tangible returns because stakeholders are less likely to view their social pursuits as credible. Stakeholders perceive socially responsible actions on the part of such firms as self-serving or simply dismiss them as 'greenwashing,' as exemplified by this stakeholder quote:

> *John Hyde, a retiree in Placerville, Calif., says it's hard to believe Philip Morris is 'a good guy just because it donates water to flood victims, or helps the hungry' (Alsop, 2002: 1).*

Thus, for such firms, investment in social responsibility might not pay.

Strat. Mgmt. J., **33**: 1304–1320 (2012)
DOI: 10.1002/smj

Augmenting the variable returns explained by SIC with consideration of the costs of investing in social responsibility leads one to view the expected relationship between CSP and CFP as U-shaped. A negative CSP-CFP relationship, which forms the initial downward slope of the U, is explained by the inherent costs of CSP. A firm with weak CSP does not suffer the financial outlays of a firm that invests in additional employee benefits, pollution reduction, charity, community involvement, and other forms of social responsibility. Recognizing the costs inherent in social responsibility, Friedman (1970) decried such allocations as examples of agency loss. Of course, the costs of various social programs a firm might adopt vary, but regardless, taking on additional social programs is more costly than not. As a result, if all else is held equal, the higher a firm's social performance, the higher its costs, and thus, the lower its financial performance.

SIC, however, helps explain why the downward sloping line eventually switches direction. Despite the fact that spending on social performance is costly,[1] firms that have accrued adequate SIC through significant social performance may earn financial returns that offset and come to exceed the costs. Those firms with the highest SIC will get the most out of their social investments and so will have the highest financial performance. That is, firms with increasingly favorable SIC earn increasingly favorable returns on their social investments, much as firms replete with absorptive capacity earn more from their investments in knowledge (Cohen and Levinthal, 1990).

To better visualize the resulting U-shaped relationship, consider a universe of firms with a wide range of CSP. Because it is costly to be socially responsible, those firms with higher CSP have higher costs than do those firms with lower CSP. However, those firms that invest more of their resources into social performance accrue more SIC. For firms on the left side of the range (with low to moderate CSP), this SIC is likely inadequate to create gains that will offset the costs, and so the CSP-CFP relationship is negative over this

range. Firms on the right side of the range (with moderate to high CSP), however, possess adequate SIC and so have the capacity to transform social investment into financial returns. Though firms with higher CSP have higher costs, the additional social investments earn positive returns that more than offset the increased costs. In contrast, lacking adequate SIC to transform their social investment into financial returns, firms with low CSP earn negative returns on their CSP spending. Thus, as they spend more on CSP, they lose more, until the relationship neutralizes and turns positive as SIC accrues from the increased CSP spending. Overall, this means that prior to accruing adequate SIC, the curve slopes downward; CSP is an investment that offers negative returns. Thereafter, the curve evens out, and for those firms that accrue adequate SIC, the curve turns upward and CSP becomes an investment that offers positive returns.

Recent empirical studies provide some support for the existence of a U-shaped relationship between some types of CSP and CFP. Barnett and Salomon (2006) found that the financial returns of mutual funds that used socially responsible investment practices varied with the stringency of the social screening criteria. Those funds that screened the most intensely and so yielded portfolios with the highest overall social performance, and those that screened the least intensely and so yielded portfolios with the lowest overall social performance, did the best financially. Those funds with moderate screening intensity did the worst financially. However, both the theory and data used in Barnett and Salomon's (2006) study did not address the firm-level relationship between CSP and CFP.

In contrast, Brammer and Millington (2008) focused on the firm-level relationship between CSP and CFP and likewise found that the highest and lowest levels of CSP were associated with the highest levels of CFP. However, Brammer and Millington (2008) neither specifically hypothesized a U-shaped relationship nor explicitly tested for one. Instead, they inferred a curve from three performance groupings. Moreover, Brammer and Millington (2008) measured CSP on only a single dimension—corporate charitable giving. CSP is a comprehensive concept, consisting of a variety of socially responsible behaviors (Carroll, 1979). Thus, this narrow measure of CSP, while supportive of a curvilinear relationship, provides limited

---

[1] These costs need not be direct cash outlays, though often they are. The costs can be opportunity costs, such as use of managerial or employee time. Greenwashing or other symbolic acts of social responsibility are also costly to a firm, in terms of additional risk borne. Firms that engage in symbolic or fraudulent acts of social responsibility 'increase their risk and so effectively decrease their risk-adjusted returns' (Barnett, 2007: 806).

1308   *M. L. Barnett and R. M. Salomon*

insights about the broader relationship between CSP and CFP.

Taken together, recent theoretical and empirical advances strongly suggest an underlying U-shaped relationship between CSP and CFP. Nonetheless, to our knowledge, no study has yet to comprehensively test this relationship at the firm level. We therefore hypothesize:

> *Hypothesis: The relationship between corporate social performance and corporate financial performance is U-shaped.*

METHODOLOGY

The data we employ come from several sources. Our initial sample consisted of publicly traded firms tracked by Kinder, Lydenberg, and Domini (KLD). KLD is an independent agency with a long history of tracking, and rating, firms based on a number of corporate social responsibility dimensions. In fact, according to Deckop, Merriman, and Gupta (2006: p. 334), 'The KLD database is the largest multidimensional CSP database available to the public.' It is no surprise therefore that KLD ratings have been used extensively in academic research (e.g., Chatterji, Levine, and Toffel, 2009; Deckop, *et al.*, 2006; Harrison and Freeman, 1999; Waddock and Graves, 1997; Graves and Waddock, 1994).

KLD rates firms based on their environmental, social, and corporate governance performance. It began rating firms in 1991 with an initial sample of 650 firms, comprising largely S&P 500 firms. By 2001, the total number of firms tracked by KLD reached 1,100 as it expanded the sample to Russell 1000 firms. Beginning in 2003, the sample expanded to 3,100 firms by including firms from the Russell 3000 index. Our starting sample therefore represents an unbalanced panel of 3,100 firms from 1991–2006.

Given that the KLD sample included information on anywhere from 650 to 3,100 firms per year, the total usable sample could have reached a maximum of 21,100 firm-year observations ((650 firms × 10 years) + (1,100 firms × 2 years) + (3,100 firms × 4 years)). However, we were forced to drop observations prior to 1998 due to changes in reporting by KLD. Prior to 1998, KLD rated companies on only eight dimensions of social responsibility. Thereafter, the number was

increased to 13. This change in reporting resulted in the loss of 650 firms and 4,550 firm-year observations.[2]

We supplemented the KLD data with firm-level operational and performance data from COMPUSTAT. COMPUSTAT is a widely used database of fundamental and market data on over 30,000 publicly traded companies. It provides firm-specific balance sheet and cash flow data, and also supplemental firm and industry information. When we matched the COMPUSTAT data with the KLD data, we lost 1,236 firms due to missing data. This left a usable sample of 1,214 firms and 5,944 firm-year observations.

Finally, to control for within-firm dynamics, we incorporate a one-year lag of the dependent variable into our empirical specification (the specific method is described in detail below). The dynamics require at least two years of data for each firm. This restriction sacrifices 1,214 firm-year observations (one year's worth of observations for each firm). The final sample upon which we test our hypothesis is therefore an unbalanced panel of 1,214 firms and 4,730 firm-year observations from 1998–2006.

Dependent variable

We test for the effects of CSP on CFP. Thus, following Waddock and Graves (1997), our dependent variable is the *return on assets* (ROA) for a given firm in a given year.[3] ROA is defined as net income divided by total assets. We complement ROA with an unscaled measure of firm performance, *net income*. Net income is defined as the earnings (after interest, taxes, depreciation, and amortization) of a firm in a given year, expressed in millions of U.S. dollars. We include net income as a complement to ROA because

---

[2] In specifications not reported, we tested variants of the models using only those eight issues upon which firms had been rated throughout the entire 1991–2006 period. The results were qualitatively similar and stronger in economic magnitude to those presented herein.

[3] In this study, we employ ROA as a dependent variable not only because it is the standard in the corporate social responsibility literature, but also because it is a widely adopted measure of firm performance in the broader field of strategy (e.g., King and Zeithaml, 2001; McNamara, Luce, and Tompson, 2002; Wan and Hoskisson, 2003; Lavie, 2007; Derfus *et al.*, 2008; McNamara, Haleblian, and Dykes, 2008). However, as described later in the Sensitivity and Robustness section, we also tested models with market-based performance alternatives and found consistent results.

Strat. Mgmt. J., **33**: 1304–1320 (2012)
DOI: 10.1002/smj

scholars suggest that the use of ratio measures (such as ROA) as dependent variables in multivariate regression analysis may exaggerate relations of interest and confound the interpretation of results (see Wiseman, 2009). This is because the independent variables can influence the numerator, the denominator, or both, thereby complicating inference.

Using two distinct yet conceptually related performance measures provides several benefits. Assessing both measures mitigates some of the deficiencies inherent in selecting one measure to the exclusion of the other. Moreover, because each variable might reveal different aspects of performance, we can use variation in outcomes to inform our interpretation of the results. Although we expect the results to be consistent across measures, corroborating results further validate our findings.

Independent variables

KLD rates firms based on 13 individual social performance criteria. Seven of those are key stakeholder attributes (community, corporate governance, diversity, employee relations, environment, human rights, and product) for which firms receive scores based on both their strengths and weaknesses. The scores are based on an integer scale that ranges from $+1$ to -1, where -1 represents an area of weakness, $+1$ represents an area of strength, and 0 represents a neutral score. The remaining six relate to whether or not the firm participates in socially 'controversial' business activities (the production, sale, or service of alcohol, gambling, firearms, military, nuclear power, and/or tobacco). On these attributes, firms receive scores that reflect only whether the area represents one of weakness (i.e., where -1 represents an area of weakness and 0 represents a neutral score). Although the latter six attributes only capture areas of weakness, the scales used are comparable to those for the seven stakeholder attributes.

Following prior research, we aggregate the strengths and weaknesses ratings from KLD to create a net social performance score for each firm (e.g., Chatterji *et al.*, 2009; Johnson and Greening, 1999; Ruf *et al.*, 2001; Ruf, Muralidhar, and Paul, 1998; Waddock and Graves, 1997; Griffin and Mahon, 1997; Graves and Waddock, 1994). We label this measure the *net KLD score*. The net

KLD score is an assessment of a firm's overall level of social responsibility and so proxies for stakeholder influence capacity (Barnett, 2007). To achieve high net KLD scores, firms must have engaged in significant acts of social responsibility; the higher the score, the broader the scope of such behaviors—and these acts of social responsibility are the flows that accrue into a firm's stock of SIC. That is,

> *... measures of CSP, as snapshots of the state of a firm's stakeholder relations at a point in time, are proxies for the overall state of a firm's relationships with those stakeholders it wishes to influence (Barnett, 2007: 811)... As firms engage in CSR acts to improve stakeholder relations, a record of social performance... accrues, forging a firm's SIC stock... [Therefore], A firm's current stock of SIC is positively related to its prior CSR activity (Barnett, 2007: 805).*

The initial net KLD score measure varied from -12 to 15, with a mean of -0.43. However, because we have hypothesized a curvilinear relationship between social performance and financial performance, we need to compute a squared net KLD score. Unfortunately, testing for quadratics with a measure that can take negative as well as positive values distorts inference in multiple regression formats (Cohen *et al.*, 2002). We therefore follow the recommendation of Cohen *et al.* (2002) and perform a simple linear transformation of the net KLD score measure by adding 12 to each observation. Performing such a linear transformation meets the goal of creating a conceptually meaningful measure via a simple transformation that does not change the underlying functional form. Moreover, this linear transformation preserves within-measure ordinal relationships. That is, increasing values on the net KLD score index correspond to better social responsibility performance, where 0 now reflects the least socially responsible firm and 27 the most socially responsible firm (with a mean of 11.64).

Control variables

Because our dependent variable captures the financial performance of a firm, we control for factors that could systematically affect financial performance. We therefore include variables previously

Strat. Mgmt. J., **33**: 1304–1320 (2012)
DOI: 10.1002/smj

1310   *M. L. Barnett and R. M. Salomon*

identified as likely to influence the financial performance of firms, while controlling for unobservables using a combination of fixed (industry, firm, and year) effects. We discuss the details of the econometric specification in the subsequent section.

A firm's size is a potential factor in its financial performance. In order to control for any potential size effect, we include a measure of the number of firm employees (measured in thousands). We label this variable *size*. In addition to size, we control for the debt burden of the firm. We define *debt ratio* as the firm's long-term debt divided by total assets. Scholars point out that debt impacts the behavior of managers. On the one hand, debt imposes discipline upon managers and incentivizes them to make decisions that are in the best interest of the firm. On the other hand, because debt decreases managerial latitude, it can limit opportunities to explore new businesses, thereby negatively impacting profit. Finally, empirical research has shown that distinctive technological and marketing capabilities can be value creating for firms (e.g., Mahoney and Pandian, 1992). We therefore include a measure of research and development (R&D) and advertising intangibles. Following prior research (e.g., McWilliams and Siegel, 2000), we define *R&D intensity* as R&D expenditures divided by sales (expressed as a percentage) and *advertising intensity* as advertising expenditures divided by sales (expressed as a percentage).[4]

Statistical methods

In selecting an appropriate multivariate statistical method, we begin with an ordinary least squares (OLS) specification. As shown in Equation (1), we first specify a firm's performance (Perform$_{it}$) as a linear function of the vector X of independent variables for firm i at time t that we wish to examine and can measure, in addition to an error

term, which we label u$_{it}$.

$$Perform_{it} = \beta_0 + X_{it}\beta_1 + u_{it} \qquad (1)$$

Given the panel structure of our data with several observations per firm, the possibility arises that the errors (u$_{it}$) will be correlated within firms across time. Such serial correlation of residuals across observations within firms may lead to spurious regression results. We therefore turn to a dynamic longitudinal model to deal with serial correlation. We incorporate linear autoregressive dynamics with lags of the dependent variable as regressors to account for within-firm persistence in performance (see Greene, 2000). Specifically, we incorporate a one-year lag of the dependent variable, a within-firm AR(1) process, into every specification as follows:

$$Perform_{it} = \beta_0 + X_{it}\beta_1 + Perform_{it-1}\beta_2 + e_{it} \quad (2)$$

Although AR(1) dynamics go a long way in addressing within-firm serial correlation, the possibility still exists that e$_{it}$ in Equation (2) will not be independent across time (Greene, 2000). Any time-dependent effect on performance that is not included in X will be captured in the error term. Previous research has identified many macroeconomic factors associated with performance, including changes in government policy and systemic, macroeconomic shocks. Should we be unable to identify and measure all of these effects, there exists the potential for a systematic time component to be embedded in e$_{it}$. This systematic component will lead to correlated errors across observations over time, which violates OLS assumptions (Kmenta, 1997; Kennedy, 1998).

Conceptually, we can decompose e$_{it}$ into a vector of systematic (fixed) time effects, which we label Z$_t$, where Z$_t$ represents yearly dummy variables, and ν_{it}, an independent and identically distributed normal error term with zero mean. Equation (3) represents this decomposition of e$_{it}$.

$$Perform_{it} = \beta_0 + X_{it}\beta_1 + Perform_{it-1}\beta_2 + Z_t\beta_3 + \nu_{it} \qquad (3)$$

Finally, the possibility still exists that ν_{it} in Equation (3) will not be independent within firms or industries. This would occur, for instance, if some firms, or industries, perform systematically

---

[4] Because many firms in our sample did not report advertising expenditure to COMPUSTAT, we followed prevailing literature in assuming that unreported advertising expenditures were immaterial (e.g., Fee, Hadlock, and Pierce, 2009; Masulis, Wang, and Xie, 2009). We therefore assign zero values to those firm-year advertising observations that were missing. As an alternative, we replaced missing firm advertising intensity with its industry-specific mean level of advertising intensity. Irrespective of the approach, the results on the main independent variables of interest remain unchanged.

Strat. Mgmt. J., **33**: 1304–1320 (2012)
DOI: 10.1002/smj

Table 1.   Descriptive statistics and correlations

	1.	2.	3.	4.	5.	6.	7.	8.	9.
1. ROA	1								
2. Lag ROA	0.55	1							
3. Net income	0.35	0.12	1						
4. Lag Net Income	0.27	0.36	0.74	1					
5. Net KLD score	0.08	0.08	0.01	0.02	1				
6. Size	0.05	0.05	0.37	0.38	−0.07	1			
7. Debt ratio	−0.01	0.02	−0.03	−0.01	−0.05	0.03	1		
8. R&D intensity	−0.08	−0.07	−0.01	−0.01	0.00	−0.01	−0.01	1	
9. Advertising intensity	0.05	0.05	0.06	0.06	0.13	0.03	0.02	−0.01	1
Mean	0.03	0.03	343.04	356.56	11.64	21.76	0.05	1.63	0.13
Standard deviation	0.19	0.20	1800.12	1792.30	2.32	71.97	0.10	56.18	0.03
Minimum	−4.58	−4.58	−56121.90	−56121.90	0.00	0.00	0.00	0.00	0
Maximum	0.70	0.70	39500.00	36130.00	27.00	1900.00	2.06	3755.00	3.26

differently than others due to long-term, non-transient factors (e.g., not simply related to persistence in performance from one year to the next). In order to correct for this sort of unobserved heterogeneity, we incorporate firm/industry fixed effects into our specification (Greene, 2000). We present one representation of our final econometric specification (with firm fixed effects) in Equation (4):

$$\text{Perform}_{it} = \beta_0 + X_{it}\beta_1 + \text{Perform}_{it-1}\beta_2 + Z_t\beta_3$$
$$+ F_i\beta_4 + \varepsilon_{it} \qquad (4)$$

In this case, F_i represents the individual firm-specific disturbance. With a slight modification to the notation in Equation (4), we can incorporate North American Industry Classification System (NAICS) industry effects in lieu of firm effects.[5] The specification in Equation (4) is consistent with recommended estimation techniques for individual-specific variant and time invariant unobserved effects in panel data (Greene, 2000).

In summary, we include within-firm AR(1) dynamics, fixed year effects, and fixed firm/industry effects to control for characteristics that are not directly measured by our other variables

but that might correlate with firm performance. The advantage of this approach is it controls for unobserved heterogeneity without having to precisely specify the source of that heterogeneity. Therefore, the specifications provide robust estimates that eliminate bias in statistical results. The disadvantage, however, is that we cannot precisely isolate or identify each and every individual factor that influences the dependent variable. Because our goal is to control for and not investigate or test these effects, we accept this trade-off.

RESULTS

Table 1 presents descriptive statistics and product moment correlations for the variables we use to test the hypothesis. The average ROA for each of the firms in the sample is about three percent per annum. The average net income is about $343 million per year. Although the mean values for ROA and net income are consistent with expectations, the minimum value for ROA (−458 percent) and the minimum (−$56 billion) and maximum ($39.5 billion) values for net income seem exorbitant. Although at first glance the minimum/maximum performance values may appear out of line with the rest of the data, the other values that the firms in question report over time are very comparable to those values. Moreover, data checks revealed that they have been reported faithfully in COMPUSTAT. For example, the $56 billion net loss (and −458 percent ROA) was reported by JDS Uniphase in 2001. It was, up

---

[5] We note that we cannot include both firm and industry fixed effects in the same specification. This is because there is little variation in industry affiliation over time for firms in these data. Firms generally do not switch industries. Therefore, models with both firm and industry effects cannot be identified. However, because firm effects subsume industry effects (e.g., firm effects aggregated to the industry level capture industry effects), firm fixed effect specifications represent the most conservative test of the phenomenon.

to that point, the largest loss in corporate history.[6] Similarly, the $39.5 billion net income, which at the time represented the largest net income ever reported by any corporation, was recorded by Exxon Mobil in 2006. Nevertheless, to the extent that extreme values have the potential to bias our results, the within-firm dynamic and fixed effects approaches for panel data can aid in controlling for such effects.[7]

The descriptives demonstrate a substantial within-firm correlation between the prior year's ROA and the current year's ROA ($\rho = 0.55$) and the prior year's net income and the current year's net income ($\rho = 0.74$). This is indicative of a substantial persistence in firm performance over time. Not surprisingly, the correlations also indicate a substantial relationship between net income and ROA ($\rho = 0.35$). Firms with greater levels of net income generally have higher ROA.

The correlations between the independent variables and the dependent variables, and among the independent variables, are generally moderate in magnitude. Although the number of employees (size) is positive and significantly related to net income ($\rho = 0.37$), it is only weakly related to ROA ($\rho = 0.05$). This is because ROA eliminates much of the scale effect, since total assets (a correlate of firm size) is in the denominator.

Despite the moderate correlations among the variables, we examined influence tests to see if the results might be impacted in any way by multicolinearity. No independent variable had a variance inflation factor greater than 10, which is the generally accepted range for individual variables (Kennedy, 1998), and no model exceeded the conventional threshold of 30 (Belsley, Kuh, and Welsch, 1980). We therefore conclude that multicolinearity does not negatively impact the results presented herein.

With respect to the main independent variable of interest (net KLD score), its correlation with both dependent variables is positive, although stronger

for ROA ($\rho = 0.08$) than for net income ($\rho = 0.01$). We exercise caution, however, in drawing inferences from these relationships. First, the correlations are moderate in both statistical and economic magnitude. Second, the effect is linear. It does not explicitly test the quadratic relationship. Finally, it does not control for many other firm, industry, and time effects that we include in the multivariate analyses. Therefore, to better understand the nature of this relationship, we turn to the multivariate regression analyses.

In Table 2, we present results of regression models using the ROA dependent variable. In Model 1, we regress ROA on a base model of controls, including the within-firm AR(1) dynamics, but excluding fixed effects. Consistent with the correlation tables, we find a positive relationship between the prior year's ROA and current ROA. Model 1 also indicates that larger firms, and those that spend more on advertising, have higher ROA, while firms with larger debt burdens, and those that are more R&D intensive, have lower ROA.

Model 2 introduces our measure of social performance (net KLD score). Consistent with much of the social issues literature (e.g., Waddock and Graves, 1997), we find a positive and significant link between financial and social performance. That is, as firms become more socially responsible, their ROA increases. Although the results with the linear net KLD effect are upward sloping, Model 2 does not include the quadratic.

We introduce the quadratic in Model 3. The results support our hypothesis. The effect of corporate social responsibility (KLD net score) on financial performance is negative at first, but then positive. This indicates that the firms with the greatest ROA are those with the best social record *and* those with the worst social record. Firms in between risk getting 'stuck in the middle' (Porter, 1980: 41)—i.e., they neither benefit from the cost advantages of not engaging in discretionary expenditures over and above what is mandated by law, nor from the ability to use their social performance as a way to profitably improve stakeholder relations.

We subject our findings to stricter tests in Models 4, 5, and 6 by adding year fixed effects, industry (NAICS-6) fixed effects, and firm fixed effects. Although we included fixed effects (as noted at the bottom of each column), we do not report them here. Briefly though, the results suggest that firm performance was better in 2005 and 2006

---

[6] It has since been exceeded by AIG.

[7] That notwithstanding, in sensitivity analyses we dropped those firms that reported extreme values (e.g., greater than two standard deviations away from the mean). For example, since the mean for ROA is three percent (as described in Table 2) and the standard deviation is 19 percent, we dropped all observations for which ROA was greater than 41 percent and less than -35 percent. For net income, since the mean is $343M and the standard deviation is 1.8B, we dropped all observations with net income greater than $3.943B and less than $-$3.257B. In both cases, the results were similar to those reported herein.

Table 2.   Results with return on assets (ROA) as dependent variable

	Model 1 ROA	Model 2 ROA	Model 3 ROA	Model 4 ROA	Model 5 ROA	Model 6 ROA
Net KLD score		0.00***	−0.01**	−0.01**	−0.01**	−0.00
		(2.76)	(−1.89)	(−1.97)	(−1.73)	(−0.46)
Net KLD score^2			0.00***	0.00***	0.00***	0.00
			(2.50)	(2.60)	(2.60)	(1.08)
Lag ROA	0.43***	0.43***	0.43***	0.43***	0.38***	0.12***
	(44.29)	(43.98)	(43.96)	(43.79)	(37.46)	(9.40)
Size	0.00**	0.00**	0.00*	0.00*	0.00	−0.00
	(1.83)	(2.03)	(1.29)	(1.41)	(0.86)	(−1.07)
Debt ratio	−0.04**	−0.03**	−0.04**	−0.03**	−0.07***	−0.13***
	(−1.83)	(−1.68)	(−1.75)	(−1.74)	(−2.67)	(−3.44)
R&D intensity	−0.00***	−0.00***	−0.00***	−0.00***	−0.00***	0.00
	(−3.70)	(−3.71)	(−3.69)	(−3.72)	(−3.46)	(0.77)
Advertising intensity	0.12**	0.10*	0.09*	0.09*	−0.01	−0.03
	(1.86)	(1.48)	(1.46)	(1.48)	(−0.68)	(−0.13)
Constant	0.02***	−0.00	0.05**	0.07***	0.06**	0.04
	(10.23)	(−0.11)	(2.26)	(2.56)	(1.96)	(0.98)
Year effects	NO	NO	NO	FIXED	FIXED	FIXED
Industry effects	NO	NO	NO	NO	FIXED	NO
Firm effects	NO	NO	NO	NO	NO	FIXED
No. of observations	4730	4730	4730	4730	4730	4730
No. of firms	1214	1214	1214	1214	1214	1214
Adj./psuedo R-sq	0.301	0.302	0.304	0.312	0.310	0.167

* $p < .10$; ** $p < .05$; *** $p < .01$ (one-tailed tests).
z-statistics are in parentheses.

than in 2001, 2002, and 2003. Moreover, firms in service-based industries performed better (in terms of ROA) than those in manufacturing industries. This result is not surprising, as service firms generally have fewer total assets than manufacturing firms. Finally, the results for the firm fixed effects indicate that there is substantial firm-specific variation in performance in these data. That manifests in the adjusted R-square, as the explanatory power of the model (holding the firm effects aside) drops to 0.167.

Turning to our explanatory variables of interest, the quadratic effect remains robust to year and industry effects (from Models 4 and 5). However, the net KLD score result from Model 6, though directionally consistent, is not statistically different from zero. This likely has to do with the conservative nature of the fixed effect specification with firm dynamics, plus the limited variance in net KLD score within firms over time.[8] The conservative nature of the econometric approach including

the firm fixed effect with AR(1) firm dynamics is also evident in the substantial drop in economic magnitude of the lag ROA effect in Model 6 compared to that in the other models. Nevertheless, we acknowledge that, in light of the findings from Column 6, our results are not unequivocal and warrant caution with respect to interpretation. For greater insight, we turn to results with net income as the dependent variable.

Results regressing net income on the independent variables of interest, plus controls, are presented in Table 3. As with the results from Table 2, the results indicate that last year's net income is positively related to this year's net income. Likewise, larger firms, and those with greater advertising intensity, have greater net incomes, while firms with greater debt ratios have lower net income. The impact of R&D, while directionally consistent with that presented in Table 2, does not statistically differ from zero.

With respect to the independent variable of interest (net KLD score), we do not find evidence in Model 2 that social performance is significantly linearly related to net income, as was the case with ROA. Using net income as a dependent variable,

---

[8] In models including fixed effects with only the linear net KLD score measure (as in Model 2), we likewise find a statistically insignificant effect for net KLD score.

Strat. Mgmt. J., **33**: 1304–1320 (2012)
DOI: 10.1002/smj

1314   *M. L. Barnett and R. M. Salomon*

Table 3.   Results with net income as dependent variable

	Model 1 Net income	Model 2 Net income	Model 3 Net income	Model 4 Net income	Model 5 Net income	Model 6 Net income
Net KLD score		−1.18	−355.00***	−361.95***	−278.01***	−218.11***
		(−0.15)	(−9.18)	(−9.37)	(−5.88)	(−3.44)
Net KLD score²			14.55***	14.89***	12.53***	9.98***
			(9.33)	(9.56)	(6.69)	(3.98)
Lag net income	0.77***	0.77***	0.75***	0.75***	0.64***	0.22***
	(67.20)	(67.15)	(64.22)	(64.67)	(49.84)	(12.49)
Size	2.54***	2.54***	2.11***	2.15***	3.41***	5.91***
	(9.78)	(9.74)	(8.04)	(8.14)	(10.09)	(5.03)
Debt ratio	−544.61***	−546.17***	−605.63***	−578.57***	−291.13	−58.74
	(−2.69)	(−2.69)	(−3.01)	(−2.88)	(−1.18)	(−0.14)
R&D intensity	−0.07	−0.07	−0.04	−0.05	−0.17	−0.01
	(−0.23)	(−0.23)	(−0.14)	(−0.14)	(−0.55)	(−0.02)
Advertising intensity	881.87*	894.92*	889.51*	915.25*	1489.58**	−1672.90
	(1.37)	(1.38)	(1.38)	(1.43)	(1.69)	(−0.77)
Constant	96.77***	104.34	2193.57***	2263.01***	1571.66***	1151.77***
	(4.17)	(0.26)	(9.08)	(8.75)	(4.96)	(2.70)
Year effects	NO	NO	NO	FIXED	FIXED	FIXED
Industry effects	NO	NO	NO	NO	FIXED	NO
Firm effects	NO	NO	NO	NO	NO	FIXED
No. of observations	4730	4730	4730	4730	4730	4730
No. of firms	1214	1214	1214	1214	1214	1214
Adj./psuedo R-Sq	0.561	0.560	0.568	0.573	0.570	0.425

* $p < .10$; ** $p < .05$; *** $p < .01$ (one-tailed tests).
z-statistics are in parentheses.

we are unable to replicate the Waddock and Graves (1997) finding. This divergence in results across dependent variables is not altogether surprising and hints at a specific performance difference between service and manufacturing firms. Manufacturing firms generally have a much larger asset base than service firms, and they therefore generally have a lower ROA. Consistent with such an interpretation is the stylized fact that once we account for industry fixed effects (as in Model 5), we find a positive and significant effect for the linear net KLD score on net income, as for ROA.[9]

With respect to the quadratic effect introduced in Model 3, we find results that mirror those from Table 2. Namely, the impact of corporate social responsibility (net KLD score) on financial performance is U-shaped. As in Table 2, the results from Models 4 and 5 in Table 3 are robust to the inclusion of year and industry fixed effects. However, unlike in Table 2, the quadratic effect from Model 6 in Table 3 is robust to the inclusion of firm fixed effects. The evidence across

Models 3–6 in Table 3 corroborates our previous findings and confirms that firms with the best social records and the worst social records perform best. These results likewise favor our hypothesis.

Figures 1 and 2 graphically depict the nonmonotonic, curvilinear relationship between social and financial performance.[10] With respect to ROA (from Figure 1), performance declines at first as a firm's KLD rating increases, reaching a minimum at a net KLD score of 9, but then increases continuously until it reaches a maximum net KLD score of 27. For net income, presented in Figure 2, financial performance reaches a minimum around 12. We note that in both cases, the financial performance for the most socially responsible firms is greater in magnitude than for the least socially responsible firms. That is, financial performance is greater (in both cases) for firms with a net KLD score of 27 than for those firms with a net KLD score of

---

[9] These results are available from the authors upon request.

[10] We use the models with the most explanatory power to graph these relationships. For ROA, we base Figure 1 on Model 5 from Table 3. For net income, we use Model 4 from Table 4. The alternative models generate qualitatively similar results.

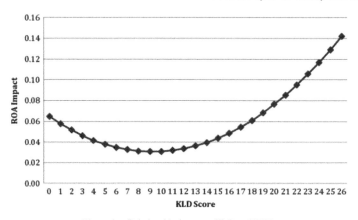

Figure 1.   Relationship between KLD and ROA

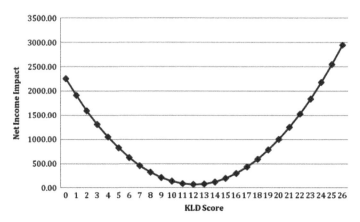

Figure 2.   Relationship between KLD and net income

0. Therefore, our results suggest that it is more financially beneficial to be maximally socially responsible than minimally socially responsible.

Sensitivity and robustness

To assess the sensitivity and robustness of the results, we tested several variants of the models presented herein.[11] First, although we theoretically advance and empirically substantiate a quadratic, U-shaped relationship between CSP and CFP,

there are myriad functional forms that could possibly describe the relationship between CSP and CFP. We therefore tested the robustness of our results to alternative functional forms. We ran models specifying a cubic function, a quartic function, and a fractional polynomial function. The findings supported none of these alternative functional forms, but rather, continued to support a U-shaped specification.

Second, although we follow the prevailing strategy and corporate social responsibility literatures in adopting ROA and net income as measures of firm performance, we checked the robustness of the results to market-based performance alternatives. Specifically, we tested models using two

---

[11] All results mentioned in this section are available from the authors upon request.

Strat. Mgmt. J., **33**: 1304–1320 (2012)
DOI: 10.1002/smj

alternative measures of performance: financial returns and market capitalization. Irrespective of the dependent variable used, we found U-shaped results consistent with those that we present herein.

Third, because KLD provides an imperfect proxy for corporate social performance (and SIC), we reran results using alternative net KLD scores. The inherent assumption in using an additive approach in calculating the net KLD score, as we have in this study, is that it treats any one KLD dimension the same as any other inasmuch as it impacts financial performance. However, each dimension may not equally impact financial performance. We therefore checked the robustness of the results by using different weightings of the social performance criteria as detailed by Ruf *et al.* (1998) and Waddock and Graves (1997). For example, we experimented with a KLD score whereby we weighted the dimensions by the underlying frequency with which firms receive positive and/or negative scores on each KLD dimension. The results were similar to those we present herein. In addition, because six of the KLD dimensions relate to whether the firm engages in 'controversial' areas of business activity, and those dimensions receive only negative scores, we reran results using a net KLD score based on the seven dimensions on which firms can receive both positive and negative scores. Not only does that create a measure that is wholly internally consistent (i.e., all KLD dimensions are measured in precisely the same way) but it also includes the subset of stakeholder attributes over which firms exercise the greatest discretion. Again, the results were consistent with those we present herein.

Finally, although we control for industry-specific effects in this study, we assessed the sensitivity of our results to industry effects at both greater levels of aggregation and disaggregation. For example, as an alternative to the six-digit NAICS industry fixed effects, we examined results using two- and three-digit NAICS industry effects. The results were entirely consistent with those we present in this study. In addition, we examined results using measures of market power based on firm market share, and overall industry measures of market power based on concentration ratios (CR) (both CR_4 and CR_8). The results for the KLD measures of interest are consistent with those reported herein, whether we control for market power using market share or concentration.

DISCUSSION

Social issues scholars have begun to back away from the long-pursued but fruitless quest to demonstrate that social responsibility is either always good or always bad. Some now seek to develop a contingent perspective that specifies the variables that determine not whether, but under what conditions it does or does not pay to be good (Rowley and Berman, 2000). In that vein we develop a contingent model that specifies a quadratic, U-shaped relationship between CSP and CFP. We hypothesized that though it is costly for firms to engage in socially responsible practices, there are benefits from improved stakeholder relations that can offset these costs. However, a firm's ability to capitalize on these potential benefits, and so profit from CSP, depends upon the firm's stock of SIC. For firms with weak social performance, and accordingly, inadequate SIC, the benefits do not arise, and so the costs produce a negative relationship between CSP and CFP. More investment in social issues, absent the ability to transform it into improved stakeholder relations, produces only more losses. However, as firms accrue SIC through increasing levels of social performance, they become better able to gain and profit from improved stakeholder relations, and so an inflection point in financial performance arises. Firms with the greatest social performance possess a superior capacity to transform social investment into positive financial returns, generating the upward slope in financial returns.

Consistent with our underlying theory, we indeed found a U-shaped relationship between CSP and CFP. We also discovered that firms with the highest CSP generally have the highest CFP. Thus, our findings support Barnett's (2007) theoretical argument that as firms engage in social responsibility, they amass stakeholder influence capacity that improves their ability to transform social investment into financial returns. The accrual of SIC causes the benefits of CSP to increase at a higher rate than the costs, producing an eventual upturn in the CSP-CFP relationship.[12]

---

[12] This begs the question: if extreme investments in SIC leads to increasing profitability, why not invest all of a firm's assets in building SIC? Barnett (2007: 808) explained how unusually high CFP increases stakeholder expectations of CSP and so dampens a firm's ability to produce SIC. Thus, firms have to spend more to create SIC, creating a 'self-regulating cycle that places upper bounds on CSR contributions.' For this reason, firms are likely

Strat. Mgmt. J., **33**: 1304–1320 (2012)
DOI: 10.1002/smj

Our findings add richness to Brammer and Millington's (2008: 1339) conjecture that the benefits of CSP, or lack thereof, come only in the extreme:

> *Those that give at an unexpectedly high rate differentiate themselves in the eyes of stakeholders and reap the benefits of this differentiation... Firms that give at an unexpectedly low rate conserve the financial resources they might have otherwise donated to charity.*

Indeed, we find a tipping point at which the total benefits of CSP outweigh the mounting costs (around a net KLD score of 12 for ROA and 9 for net income). But going beyond Brammer and Millington's (2008) findings, our study suggests that firms do not gain all the benefits only after exceeding this tipping point and none prior. Rather, our study suggests that there is variation in benefits across the range of CSP, such that as SIC accrues, it provides benefits that come to meet and then exceed the costs of being socially responsible. Much the same as the CSP-CFP relationship is neither purely positive nor negative, a firm is neither purely good nor bad. Consider Walmart, which provides low cost prescriptions, yet is frequently criticized for its labor practices; or Ben and Jerry's, which is renowned for its strong support of social and environmental issues yet produces a product that contributes to obesity. In this sense then, our study moves understanding of the CSP-CFP relationship beyond a linear, dichotomous world in which a firm is either socially responsible or not in the eyes of stakeholders, and into a world wherein a firm can accrue varying stocks of SIC that create a range of benefits.

Our findings complement a 'theory of the firm' perspective on corporate social responsibility. McWilliams and Siegel (2001) suggest that the CSP-CFP relationship is neutral because profit-maximizing firms will supply social responsibility at a level that meets demand. Some firms are more socially responsible than others because they face market conditions that demand more social responsibility. But all firms exhaust all profitable social investment opportunities by producing social responsibility at a level that equates to their

marginal costs, with the result being an overall neutral relationship. In contrast, we do not assume that firms are producing social responsibility at a level that equates to their marginal cost. Rather, we allow for the possibility that firms develop capabilities that allow some to better meet the market demand for social responsibility. If managers are aware that their firm has less capacity to influence its stakeholders through social performance than does its rivals, then they may make a rational strategic decision to be less socially responsible. Thus, different firms, at any given point in time, have different profit-maximizing levels of CSP due to their different stocks of SIC.

Also consonant with a theory of the firm perspective, our findings suggest that some firms are more efficient at supplying social responsibility than are others. Contrasting Figures 1 and 2, the gap between firms with the lowest and highest net KLD scores is greater for ROA than for net income. The fact that the upturn in ROA outpaces that of net income suggests that much of the benefit of high CSP comes from increased efficiency at the production of social responsibility rather than from increased ability to generate new customers or new markets, or to charge premium prices. This suggests that SIC operates not simply by increasing a firm's capacity to capture additional revenues by bringing in new customers and entering new markets but also by lowering operating costs through CSP. That is, the benefit of high CSP may primarily be the ability to better leverage existing assets rather than to convince skeptical consumers to pay, or buy, more. Future research should attempt to sort out the degree to which financial benefits from CSP come through decreased costs, perhaps from improved efficiency at providing social programs, rather than the ability to increase revenues.

There are some caveats to note with this study. First, we acknowledge that our KLD measure is an imperfect proxy for SIC in much the same way that R&D is an imperfect proxy for absorptive capacity. SIC, as originally conceptualized in Barnett (2007), is meant to be a dynamic, path-dependent construct; however, our measure captures relative differences in performance across firms at a given point in time. Although our econometric specification helps explain how within-firm deviations from a firm's mean CSP score affect CFP, our study does not explicitly examine how firms may alter their levels of SIC. Our research design does not

---

to stop investing in SIC when it no longer provides benefits, and we therefore do not observe firms overinvesting in SIC in our sample.

allow us to measure the ability of a low or moderate CSP firm to become a high CSP firm in time or to determine the most efficient way to make such a move, should it decide to do so. Future research would therefore be well served to reexamine our results using alternative proxies of SIC that better capture its underlying dynamic nature. We would also encourage future research to better exploit the extant KLD data to generate better proxies for SIC.

That notwithstanding, our results indicate that improving social performance is subject to a learning process. In order for some firms to increase their capacity to benefit from investments in social responsibility, they might have to endure a period of decreased financial performance. This is consistent with SIC as subject to learning effects whereby firms that commit to improving their SIC sacrifice performance in the near term in an effort to improve performance after they successfully build stakeholder relations.

For managers, this suggests that improving financial performance through social investments is not as simple as adopting certain practices in isolation. Rather, firms must make an earnest commitment to building stakeholder influence capacity over time before they can expect to see gains from such investments. Those who rely on measures of near-term financial returns to justify investment in any particular social action are likely to be disappointed. Rather, the returns may be intangible at first, in the form of increasing levels of SIC, with financial returns to follow thereafter. If firms, lacking evidence of immediate financial returns, abandon socially responsible practices, they may be abandoning a growing pool of SIC as well. Thus, managers ought to take heed of more intermediate measures of the returns to social responsibility—SIC—and seek ever improving ways to measure how a firm's socially responsible (and irresponsible) actions advance (or harm) its relationships with stakeholders, as it is SIC that facilitates (or hampers) the transformation of social responsibility into profit.

Second, although we believe that the quadratic, U-shaped relationship we propose is supported by recent advances in both the theoretical and empirical literatures, we acknowledge that we have not closed the book on the precise functional form of the relationship between CSP and CFP. Indeed, we would welcome additional research into the contingent nature of the relationship between CSP and CFP and, more specifically, the relationship

between CSP and SIC. In this respect, we hope that others will improve upon our contribution.

Finally, we note that our results were not robust to the firm fixed effects specification with ROA as the dependent variable (Model 6 from Table 2). Although we believe that this is largely a function of the conservative nature of our econometric specification (driven by temporal persistence in ROA coupled with the static nature of the fixed effects), we cannot be sure that this is the *de facto* explanation. We therefore acknowledge that one needs to exercise caution with respect to the inferences drawn from our results. Though our results overall are strongly suggestive, further corroboratory research is needed.

The aforementioned limitations notwithstanding, this study provides novel insight into the contingent relationship between CSP and CFP. It extends the burgeoning theoretical and empirical literature to demonstrate a U-shaped relationship between firm-level CSP and CFP, as shaped by a firm's stock of SIC. The relationship among CSP, SIC, and CFP is likely more complex than the available data allowed us to model herein, of course, and so we hope that this study will encourage future work that specifically examines how SIC mediates the relationship between social and financial performance. As such work progresses, we can move beyond the false 'Friedman vs. Freeman' debate (Freeman, 2008) and toward a clearer understanding of the contingent conditions under which it does, and does not, pay to be good.

REFERENCES

Alsop R. 2002. Perils of corporate philanthropy. *Wall Street Journal*, 16 January, 1–2.

Barnett ML. 2007. Stakeholder influence capacity and the variability of financial returns to corporate social responsibility. *Academy of Management Review* 32(3): 794–816.

Barnett ML, Salomon RM. 2006. Beyond dichotomy: the curvilinear relationship between social responsibility and financial performance. *Strategic Management Journal* 27(11): 1101–1122.

Belsley DA, Kuh E, Welsch RE. 1980. *Regression Diagnostics*. Wiley: New York.

Brammer S, Millington A. 2008. Does it pay to be different? An analysis of the relationship between corporate social and financial performance. *Strategic Management Journal* 29(12): 1325–1343.

Carroll A. 1979. A three-dimensional conceptual model of corporate performance. *Academy of Management Review* 4(4): 497–505.

Chatterji AK, Levine DI, Toffel MW. 2009. How well do social ratings actually measure corporate social responsibility? *Journal of Economics and Management Strategy* **18**(1): 125–169.

Cochran P, Wood R. 1984. Corporate social responsibility and financial performance. *Academy of Management Journal* **27**: 42–56.

Cohen P, Cohen J, West SG, Aiken LS. 2002. *Applied Multiple Regression/Correlation Analysis for the Behavioral Sciences*. Lawrence Erlbaum: Mahwah, NJ.

Cohen W, Levinthal D. 1990. Absorptive capacity: a new perspective on learning and innovation. *Administrative Science Quarterly* **35**: 128–152.

Deckop JR, Merriman KK, Gupta S. 2006. The effects of CEO pay structure on corporate social performance. *Journal of Management* **32**(3): 329–342.

Derfus PJ, Maggitti PG, Grimm CM, Smith KG. 2008. The red queen effect: competitive actions and firm performance. *Academy of Management Journal* **51**(1): 61–80.

Fee CE, Hadlock CD, Pierce JR. 2009. Investment, financing constraints, and internal capital markets: evidence from the advertising expenditures of multinational firms. *Review of Financial Studies* **22**: 2361–2392.

Fombrun CJ, Gardberg NA, Barnett ML. 2000. Opportunity platforms and safety nets: corporate citizenship and reputational risk. *Business and Society Review* **105**: 85–106.

Freeman R. 1984. *Strategic Management: A Stakeholder Perspective*. Pitman: Boston, MA.

Freeman R. 2008. Dialogue: toward superior stakeholder theory. *Business Ethics Quarterly* **18**(2): 153–190.

Friedman M. 1970. The social responsibility of business is to increase its profits. *New York Times Magazine*, 13 September, 122–126.

Graves SB, Waddock SA. 1994. Institutional owners and corporate social performance. *Academy of Management Journal* **37**(4): 1035–1046.

Greene WH. 2000. *Econometric Analysis*. Prentice-Hall: Upper Saddle River, NJ.

Greening D, Turban W. 2000. Corporate social performance as a competitive advantage in attracting a quality workforce. *Business and Society* **39**(3): 254–280.

Griffin JJ, Mahon JF. 1997. The corporate social performance and corporate financial performance debate: twenty-five years of incomparable research. *Business and Society* **36**(1): 5–31.

Harrison JS, Freeman RE. 1999. Stakeholders, social responsibility and performance: empirical evidence and theoretical perspectives. *Academy of Management Journal* **42**(5): 479–485.

Hillman AJ, Keim GD. 2001. Shareholder value, stakeholder management, and social issues: what's the bottom line? *Strategic Management Journal* **22**(2): 125–139.

Jensen M, Meckling W. 1976. Theory of the firm: managerial behavior, agency costs, and ownership structure. *Journal of Financial Economics* **3**: 305–360.

Johnson RA, Greening DW. 1999. The effects of corporate governance and institutional ownership types on corporate social performance. *Academy of Management Journal* **42**(5): 564–576.

Jones T. 1995. Instrumental stakeholder theory: a synthesis of ethics and economics. *Academy of Management Review* **20**(2): 404–437.

Kennedy P. 1998. *A Guide to Econometrics*. MIT Press: Cambridge, MA.

King AW, Zeithaml CP. 2001. Competencies and firm performance: examining the causal ambiguity paradox. *Strategic Management Journal* **22**(1): 75–99.

Kmenta J. 1997. *Elements of Econometrics*. MacMillan: New York.

Lavie D. 2007. Alliance portfolios and firm performance: a study of value creation and appropriation in the U.S. software industry. *Strategic Management Journal* **28**(12): 1187–1212.

Mahoney JT, Pandian JR. 1992. The resource-based view within the conversation of strategic management. *Strategic Management Journal* **13**(5): 363–380.

Margolis J, Walsh J. 2003. Misery loves company: rethinking social initiatives by business. *Administrative Science Quarterly* **48**: 268–305.

Masulis RW, Wang C, Xei F. 2009. Agency problems at dual-class companies. *Journal of Finance* **64**: 1697–1727.

McNamara GM, Haleblian J, Dykes BJ. 2008. The performance implications of participating in an acquisition wave: early mover advantages, bandwagon effects, and the moderating influence of industry characteristics and acquirer tactics. *Academy of Management Journal* **51**(1): 113–30.

McNamara GM, Luce RA, Tompson GH. 2002. Examining the effect of complexity in strategic group knowledge structures on firm performance. *Strategic Management Journal* **23**(2): 153–170.

McWilliams A, Siegel D. 2000. Corporate social responsibility and financial performance: correlation or misspecification? *Strategic Management Journal* **21**(5): 603–609.

McWilliams A, Siegel D. 2001. Corporate social responsibility: a theory of the firm perspective. *Academy of Management Review* **26**(1): 117–127.

Orlitzky M, Schmidt F, Rynes S. 2003. Corporate social and financial performance: a meta-analysis. *Organization Studies* **24**: 403–441.

Patten D. 1991. Exposure, legitimacy, and social disclosure. *Journal of Accounting and Public Policy* **10**: 297–308.

Porter M. 1980. *Competitive Strategy: Techniques for Analyzing Industries and Competitors*. Free Press: New York.

Rowley T, Berman S. 2000. A brand new brand of corporate social performance. *Business and Society* **39**(4): 397–418.

Ruf BM, Muralidhar K, Paul K. 1998. The development of a systematic, aggregate measure of corporate social performance. *Journal of Management* **24**(1): 119–133.

Ruf BM, Muralidhar K, Brown RM, Janney JJ, Paul K. 2001. An empirical investigation of the relationship

Strat. Mgmt. J., **33**: 1304–1320 (2012)
DOI: 10.1002/smj

between change in corporate social performance and financial performance: a stakeholder theory perspective. *Journal of Business Ethics* **32**: 143–156.

Vance S. 1975. Are socially responsible corporations good investment risks? *Management Review* **64**: 18–24.

Waddock SA, Graves SB. 1997. The corporate social performance-financial performance link. *Strategic Management Journal* **18**(4): 303–319.

Wan WP, Hoskisson RE. 2003. Home country environments, corporate diversification strategies, and firm performance. *Academy of Management Journal* **46**(1): 27–45.

Webb D, Mohr L. 1998. A typology of consumer responses to cause-related marketing: from skeptics to socially concerned. *Journal of Public Policy and Marketing* **17**: 226–238.

Wicks AC, Berman SL, Jones TM. 1999. The structure of optimal trust: moral and strategic implications. *Academy of Management Review* **24**(1): 99–116.

Wiseman RM. 2009. On the use and misuse of ratio variables in strategic management research. In *Research Methodology in Strategy in Management (Volume 5)*, Berg D, Ketchen D Jr, (eds). Emerald Ltd: Bingley, UK; 75–110.

Wright P, Ferris SP. 1997. Agency conflict and corporate strategy: the effect of divestment on corporate value. *Strategic Management Journal* **18**(1): 77–83.

6

17 STRATEGIC RESPONSES TO THE REPUTATION COMMONS PROBLEM

Andrew A. King, Michael J. Lenox, and Michael L. Barnett

Firms within an industry often find themselves "tarred by the same brush." When accidents occur, stakeholders often punish both the offending firm and the entire industry as well. For example, the Union Carbide accident in Bhopal, India, damaged public perception of the entire chemical industry (Rees, 1997). Similarly, the Exxon Valdez oil spill affected all members of the petroleum industry (Hoffman and Ocasio, 2001). Likewise, the Three Mile Island incident was caused by the missteps of a single firm at a single facility, but the reputation of the entire nuclear power industry was harmed (Rees, 1997). As these examples illustrate, a firm's reputation may be tied to other firms, and so reputation may be a common resource shared by all members of an industry.

As with many shared resources, an industry's reputation may be overexploited. A firm can benefit from the favorable reputation of an industry even as it takes individual actions that may harm this shared reputation. In other words, industry reputation can suffer from the "tragedy of the commons" often observed for natural resources such as fisheries and oil fields (Hardin, 1968). Collectively firms wish to maintain a positive reputation; privately they have incentives to overexploit that reputation. Thus firms must strategically manage the *reputation commons*.

In the following pages, we explore when a reputation commons is likely to occur and discuss how firms individually and collectively respond to the problems associated with it. We review traditional commons problems and discuss the special conditions under which reputation commons problems arise. In particular, we propose that when stakeholders cannot differentiate the individual performance of firms but can sanction them, a reputation commons is likely. Thereafter, we discuss strategies for resolving the reputation commons problem. We propose that firms can solve the reputation commons problem by reducing the sanctioning ability of stakeholders and by "privatizing" reputation.

THE REPUTATION COMMONS PROBLEM

As scholars have long observed, "rational, self-interested individuals will not act to achieve their common or group interest . . . unless there is coercion or some other special device to make individuals act in their common interest" (Olson, 1965: 2). As a result, when many individuals share a scarce resource, that resource is subject to "the tragedy of the commons" (Hardin, 1968). The tragedy ensues when the cost of overexploiting the common resource is distributed among all members of the group while the benefit accrues only to the exploiter. Each user tends to maximize personal welfare at the expense of collective welfare by extracting too much and returning too little. In such a "game," each player has a dominant strategy to deplete the commons (Dawes, 1980).

Although commons problems are pervasive and take many varied forms, scholars have tended to focus on only a narrow class often referred to as common pool resources (Ostrom, 1990; Ostrom, Gardner, and Walker, 1994). In a common pool resource (CPR) problem, firms directly affect a common resource and suffer directly from the depletion of this resource. For example, fishermen are directly harmed if they overfish a particular area. In contrast, many environmental problems relate to cases where users harm a common physical resource but are not directly affected by that resource's degradation. For example, a manufacturing facility may emit pollutants that damage a common resource (such as the atmosphere) yet be unaffected by or even profit from the damage they cause. The harm caused to the common resource is only passed to the polluter if stakeholders act to sanction the firm. For example, consumers may boycott the firm's products or suppliers may refuse to provide goods and services.

Traditionally, scholars have assumed that such stakeholder-mediated situations did not pose a commons problem (Pearce and Turner, 1989). Pollution, for example, is generally thought of as a pure externality—a by-product of one's action that has an impact on others. In the classic Coasian argument, one-to-one negotiation can efficiently resolve externality problems (Coase, 1960). For example, if one neighbor offends another by playing loud music, the offended neighbor may pay the other to reduce the noise. In doing so, the neighbors may maximize joint welfare.

However, such direct solutions to externalities require that the marginal impact of each polluter can be determined and affected parties can impose sanctions (or rewards). Determining the marginal impact of each polluting firm requires massive amounts of information. When such information is not available or is costly to acquire, stakeholders may simply identify a group of firms that may have harmed a resource and distribute the responsibility for any damage equally among them. For example, the U.S. Superfund legislation does not allocate the cost of cleaning up a hazardous waste dump in proportion to the contribution to the dump. Rather each and every contributor is held responsible for the full cost (Hoffman, 1997). In such cases, a unique type of commons problem exists. Because stakeholders do not differentiate between firms, all users (polluters) of a resource share a common threat of sanction. In essence, because stakeholders cannot distinguish the relative performance or effect of each user, all users share a common stakeholder assessment of their character. Consequently, the action of one firm affects the reputation of another.

In the presence of externalities where stakeholders do not differentiate among firms, we say that a *reputation commons* exists. A reputation commons becomes a *reputation commons problem* when stakeholders are able to act against firms. Consider, for example, the chemical industry. Union Carbide's accident in Bhopal, India, affected public support for every chemical company (Rees, 1997). This single accident damaged the financial performance of the entire industry. In this case, the chemical industry faced a reputation commons problem because stakeholders did not fully distinguish the relative quality or performance of each firm but could reward or sanction each firm. Not all industries suffer the common fate inherent in a reputation commons problem. In the following sections, we analyze when these two conditions may arise.

Ability to Differentiate

If stakeholders possess ample information on the relative performance of individual firms within an industry, then no reputation commons exists. Each firm's impact can be individually and distinctly measured, and stakeholders can directly influence each firm (Coase, 1960). Each firm possesses a unique reputation and can take unilateral action to effectively shape its reputation. In short, though reputation still remains a concern of the firm, it is not a *commons* problem.

However, in many instances stakeholders do not possess sufficient information to distinguish an individual firm's performance. At the extreme, stakeholders may not be able to distinguish which industry is responsible for damage to a resource. For example, a community may recognize that its river is polluted but may be unable to determine if this damage is caused by industrial activity or agriculture. More often, stakeholders can distinguish which industry is responsible but cannot differentiate the relative effect of individual firms. For example, environmental activists may note that dolphins are being killed in tuna nets without knowing the relative rate of dolphin fatalities for each tuna supplier.

When stakeholders know which industry is responsible for damage to a resource but cannot differentiate the relative effect of individual firms, they may collectively sanction *all* firms that they think might have damaged the resource. They may, for example, lobby for regulation that restricts access to important resources for the entire industry, or they may organize a boycott of the entire industry's products. In some cases, lacking the ability to distinguish among firms, stakeholders may choose to demonstrate their power by penalizing a single visible firm. This firm need not have below-average performance. Indeed, it may be chosen almost at random or simply because it is more vulnerable to stakeholder pressure. For example, Nike was attacked for its third-world labor practices, though many others in the athletic shoe industry employed similar practices (Lee and Bernstein, 2000). Along the same lines, Kathy Lee Gifford, the television personality, was singled out for attack because her Wal-Mart clothing line was manufactured in sweatshops (Greenhouse, 1997). However, many other popular clothing lines have similar practices.

This shared fate due to the inability of stakeholders to differentiate is the result of several factors. First, simply creating a worthwhile measure of impact is complicated. Consider the difficulties stakeholders face in determining the relative effect of firms in the chemical industry on cancer rates. Such firms manufacture or emit numerous chemicals. Some of these chemicals are toxic and some are not. Those that are vary greatly in their toxicity. In addition, how and where the firm releases each chemical also determines the probability that it will cause cancer. To determine the relative impact of each firm, a stakeholder would have to know about each chemical, its toxicity, the nature of its releases, and the state of the environment in which it was released. As demonstrated by recent tort cases, such a calculation can be both complicated and costly (Harr, 1996). Wealthier stakeholders may be better able to acquire the information and processing capabilities needed to perform such analysis. Indeed, in part for these reasons, scholars propose that firms choose to locate polluting facilities in less wealthy and less politically active areas (Lesbirel, 1998; McAvoy, 1998).

Determining the effect of firms' actions is even more difficult when those actions are combined. Physical resources may integrate the combined impact of firms over previous periods. As a result, the current inputs to the resource may not reflect the resource's condition. Physical systems can delay the effect of inputs, making it more difficult to infer the source of changes to the physical resource. Many simple resources, such as oceans and lakes, can have extremely complicated,

even chaotic, dynamic properties. As a result, stakeholders may have great difficulty in inferring each firm's influence on the common resource.

As the chemical industry example illustrates, the externalities of industrial action
are frequently unclear (Hironaka and Schofer, Chapter 9). Even with objective information, stakeholders may remain unable to properly differentiate firm-level
cause and effect, and thus a reputation commons may still exist. Commensuration
is a social process wherein unique entities (such as heterogeneous chemical manufacturers) are measured according to a common metric (Espeland and Stevens,
1998). Often simply knowing the absolute impact of each firm is insufficient.
Stakeholders must be able to determine the *relative* performance of each firm. To
do this they must consider how each firm's characteristics may affect its performance. It makes no sense, for example, to compare firms of widely different sizes.
It may also make no sense to compare firms that make even slightly different products, or that differ in the amount of the process they perform. Heterogeneity
among firms in an industry can make such performance appraisal more difficult.
Heterogeneity in reporting can also impede the analysis of firm performance. In
the absence of reporting standards, firms may release widely differing information
about their activities. Such nonstandardized reporting requires analysts to untangle each firm's effect out of a snarl of differing measures. In short, because
individual firm impact is difficult to parcel out in a complex world with limited information, stakeholders often judge all firms within an industry to be equally cul-
pable. This tarring by the same brush produces a reputation commons.

Ability to Sanction or Reward

Though firms may share a common reputation, it need not be a reputation commons *problem*. To become a reputation commons problem, stakeholders must
possess a credible threat to sanction or reward firms. The degree to which stakeholders can sanction or reward firms in an industry is determined by stakeholder
attributes, industry properties, and the institutional environment. Foremost are
the attributes of stakeholders. More numerous, distant, and heterogeneous stakeholders are less likely to coordinate their influence, and thus less likely to build into
a sufficiently powerful political force to sway firm actions. For example, Ford's recent introduction of the Excursion, the world's largest and most inefficient sports
utility vehicle, received only muted condemnation from stakeholders. The Excursion affects both the safety of fellow drivers and the state of the environment, but
consumer safety and environmental groups are very different and have little experience with coordinating joint action. Thus, despite dubbing it the "Ford Valdez,"

outraged but disparate stakeholder groups "proved no more worrisome to boat-towing Excursion owners than the Miatas they picked out of their grilles" (Ahrens, 2000: W14). Simply forming a common language and common measure to allow engagement presents a significant barrier. On the same day the Union of Concerned Scientists rated Ford as "one of the dirtiest auto companies on the planet," Calstart's Green Index rated Ford as the cleanest (O'Dell, 2000: G1).

Industry properties also may affect the degree to which stakeholders can reward or sanction firms. Concentrated industries may be able to use their market power to offset stakeholder action. Industries in the early stages of the value chain may be less vulnerable to boycotts or other manifestations of stakeholder pressure, as their products and services are less visible and thus less subject to scrutiny.

Institutional conditions strongly influence the degree to which stakeholders can sanction users of common resources. In some nations, stakeholders face the burden of proving the negligence of polluters. In other nations, stakeholders need only show that damage has occurred. Institutions also differ in the extent to which they require disclosure of business information (Delmas and Terlaak, Chapter 15). In the United States, the government requires firms to report toxic emissions, accidents, and the transfer of material waste. The U.S. government also collects and processes information on each industry. If stakeholders file suit against a company, they can access information about the company's production process. The litigious nature of U.S. society reduces informal social pressure against taking such legal action (Delmas and Terlaak, Chapter 15). Once legal precedents are established, stakeholders can routinize sanction procedures (Jennings, Martens, and Zandbergen, Chapter 3). These institutional conditions make it relatively easy for stakeholders to sanction firms in the United States.

STRATEGIC RESPONSES TO THE
REPUTATION COMMONS PROBLEMS

In general, scholars have proposed two main solutions to the commons problem: regulation and privatization. Some scholars argue that in many cases regulation by a central authority or "Leviathan" (Hobbes, [1668] 1960) is the only means of avoiding the tragedy of the commons (Hardin, 1968). It is difficult to make physical boundaries across common resources such as fisheries, underground water, oil fields, and the atmosphere. For example, due to the difficulty of portioning bodies of water, governments often issue limited fishing permits and enforce size and quantity limits on harvests. Of course, government regulation can be inefficient and burdensome, and so privatization remains the preferred solution to most com-

Table 17.1
Strategic Responses to the Reputation Commons Problem

Reducing the Threat of Stakeholder Sanction	*"Privatizing" the Reputation Commons*
Improve collective performance	Reveal individual performance
Manage stakeholder perceptions	Team with credible stakeholders
Lobby government	Make credible investments
Co-opt threatening stakeholders	Adopt standardized reporting
	Form an elite club

mons dilemmas. In the classic example of privatization, sheepherders who share a pasture erect fences to establish private property (Hardin, 1968). Today airwaves are auctioned and even air pollution has been divided into "pollution rights" and traded.

Unlike a physical resource that is privatized by physical barriers, a reputation commons may be privatized through differentiation. Privatizing such a resource requires firms to enact supporting institutional structures. Whereas building fences around parcels of land may subdivide a pasture, privatizing a reputation commons requires the building of "mental fences" in the minds of stakeholders to distinguish the reputation of individual or groups of firms.

As such, novel solutions are available for reputation commons problems that are not applicable to common pool resource problems. Given the sapient nature of stakeholders, firms can solve the reputations commons problem by "reasoning with the resource." For example, firms may placate stakeholders by improving the reputation of the entire industry. Firms may improve their collective performance or manage the perceptions of stakeholders. Alternatively, firms may "privatize" the reputation commons by actively differentiating themselves from others. Firms may ally with credible stakeholders, join standards for reporting, or form elite clubs of superior performers. Table 17.1 summarizes the strategies available to firms in coping with a reputation commons. We next consider each of these strategies in detail.

Reducing the Threat of Stakeholder Sanction

The most obvious strategy, yet perhaps most difficult to achieve, is for firms to reduce the threat of sanctions by collectively improving their performance and thus placating stakeholders. Firms may solve the reputation commons problem by actually reducing damage to the underlying physical commons of concern. To this end, firms may share information on best practices with each other to raise aggregate performance. Firms also may economize on improvement costs by collectively investing in research and development. Both of these solutions, though, suffer from the normal pitfalls of collective action. Some firms may try to free ride off the efforts of others by refusing to improve performance, reveal practices, or to invest in collective efforts.

To overcome free riding, firms have formed quasi-governmental bodies that create standards of conduct and penalize violations of these standards. Trade associations increasingly perform this function through the establishment of "codes of conduct." In one of the most publicized examples, the Chemical Manufacturers' Association established the Responsible Care program (Hoffman, 1997; King and Lenox, 2000). Firms agree to a set of principles and practices that purportedly minimize the environmental impact of chemical manufacturing. However, due to antitrust concerns, trade associations cannot force participation in codes of conduct. Thus such programs will likely still suffer from free riding, making it very difficult for them to improve the overall performance of the industry (King and Lenox, 2000).

Instead, firms may find it easier to manage perceptions rather than actually improve performance. To improve the overall reputation of the industry, firms may promote symbolic efforts to meet or exceed stakeholder demands (King and Baerwald, 1998). Trade associations often attempt to raise the image of the entire industry by coordinating public relations campaigns. For example, trade associations frequently purchase commercial media time to tout the improvements in quality of life due to plastics, the health benefits of milk, or the public service endeavors of tobacco companies.

In addition to managing perceptions, firms may erect institutional barriers that prevent stakeholders from sanctioning firms. Firms may form alliances with each other to form a more powerful political force. For example, members of the tobacco industry formed agreements for how to respond to stakeholder pressure to change cigarette legislation (Miles, 1982). Likewise, the American Medical Association provides a strong single political voice for medical doctors. In general, one of the primary activities of trade associations is lobbying government on their members' behalf.

Erecting institutional barriers need not be done collectively. Individual firms may attempt to prevent sanctions by forming alliances with important stakeholder groups. For example, companies may support local community action panels and even include representatives of these panels on their corporate boards. Once "co-opted," stakeholders may be less willing to impose sanctions (Pfeffer and Salancik, 1978; Selznick, 1949). For example, Shell Oil hired Sustainability Inc. to create a strategy for the company and a plan for measuring the company's social performance (Harrison, 1998). Similarly, Mitsubishi Motors formed an alliance with the Rainforest Action Network (RAN) to diffuse RAN's demonstrations about Mitsubishi's logging practices (Hayes, 1999).

"Privatizing" the Reputation Commons

Firms may engage in a number of strategies to privatize the reputation commons. Companies may take unilateral action to differentiate themselves from other companies. For example, they may provide information to stakeholders to differentiate their performance. Unfortunately, the complicated and subjective nature of environmental problems may encourage some firms simply to engage in empty propaganda. King and Baerwald (1998) argue that firms can manipulate the information that they reveal about their environmental impact to confuse or mislead stakeholders. Given this complexity and potential for misleading behavior, stakeholders may reject information provided by a firm unilaterally.

To add credibility to claims of superior performance, firms may choose to work with a reputable stakeholder. For example, McDonald's formed an alliance with the Environmental Defense Fund (EDF) to develop new packaging for its products. Although it was difficult to communicate the relative merits of the new packaging, EDF's participation lent credence to claims that the new design had lower environmental impact (Rayport and Lodge, 1990). However, the participation of an environmental organization may not always provide credibility. Stakeholders' interests may differ from those of the allied environmental organization, or stakeholders may fear that the organization has been "captured" by the cooperating company (Selznick, 1949). For example, following the EDF/McDonald's cooperative effort some stakeholders pointed out that the new design only provided superior performance in locations without established recycling programs. Others argued that better designs existed, but EDF sought to gain financial and reputation benefit from an amicable completion of the design effort (Rayport and Lodge, 1990).

In some cases firms may make a visible investment to demonstrate their superior quality. For example, a company might invest in waste treatment equipment to show commitment to a clean operation. Applied Energy Services (AES) invested in a tree farm in Guatemala to demonstrate to its stakeholders that it was serious about trying to be socially responsible (Shabecoff, 1988). These visible investments provide credible information to stakeholders only to the extent that superior companies adopt such actions and lower-quality companies do not. Unfortunately, determining if this is the case can be very complicated. To interpret the meaning of investments, stakeholders need rich information about costs and benefits of the action. For example, to determine the real meaning of the AES tree investment, stakeholders needed to know how much money was spent, the length of the contract, the effect of the trees, and what other companies had done.

Ironically, firms may simplify the information processing required to differentiate firms by banding together. For example, firms may agree to standards for reporting environmental impact that allow better comparison among themselves. Existing examples of standards of reporting differ substantially in their scope and fidelity. At one extreme, an industry may agree on simple labels to communicate basic information to stakeholders. For example, firms in the tuna industry created a simple label that informed the stakeholder whether or not the product was produced in a way that was "dolphin safe." At the other extreme, the Global Reporting Initiative (GRI) is creating worldwide standards for reporting the combined social and environmental effect of companies. The goal is to provide comprehensive and comparable information about companies' overall social performance.

Both types of reporting systems have their limitations. The "dolphin-safe" label does not provide information on damage to turtles and other endangered species. More complicated systems may provide more complete information but may provide so much information that it is too costly to process. For example, the Toxic Release Inventory in the United States takes more than a year to compile and still longer for analysts to interpret.

As an alternative, companies may band together to reveal information about industry subgroups. This can reduce the information processing costs for both firms and stakeholders. Interestingly, trade-association-sponsored codes of conduct have been used to distinguish the performance of members versus nonmembers. For example, by publicizing Responsible Care (RC) and providing reports about RC activities and the aggregate performance of firms in RC, the Chemical Manufacturers' Association helps to distinguish RC members from the rest of the industry. This does not differentiate individual members, but it may help elevate the reputation of member firms above that of nonmembers.

Of course, membership in such an elite subgroup must be carefully controlled. If membership elevates a firm's performance, all firms in the industry have an incentive to join. Indeed, the worst performing firms may gain the most from joining. If too many low-performing firms join, the aggregate performance of the subgroup may fall below that of the industry average. In anticipation of this problem, a successful industry subgroup must set entrance criteria that are sufficient to prevent adverse selection and moral hazard (King and Lenox, 2000).

CONCLUSION

Most research on commons problems investigates examples where users of a common resource are directly affected by the depletion of that resource. However, in many cases damage to a common resource does not automatically and directly affect the firms that cause the damage. Firms internalize the impact of the damage to the common resource only when individuals or groups that hold a stake in the common resource (that is, stakeholders) place pressure on these firms.

By recognizing that stakeholders act as a mitigating force between the actions of a firm and the consequences to the firm, we alter the commons paradigm considerably. Stakeholders must make sense of a firm's actions and assess sanctions in an environment where the impacts of industrial action are often unclear (Jennings, Martens, and Zandbergen, Chapter 3; Hironaka and Schofer, Chapter 9) and the common language necessary to make sense of outcomes is often lacking (Frank, Chapter 2; Levin and Espeland, Chapter 5). Under such conditions, stakeholders often cluster firms together when making assessments—imposing one common reputation on the group of firms.

When stakeholders can sanction firms but do not differentiate between the actions of individual firms, we say that a *reputation commons problem* exists. Because the "resource" in a reputation commons problem is the perceptions of mindful agents (the stakeholders), novel solutions are possible. Because stakeholders have the power of sanction and reward, managing the perceptions that form reputation is critical (Fombrun, 1996). Firms may attend to issues of symbolism and procedure as they engage in a dialogue with stakeholders in order to influence the perceptions that ultimately shape their reputation (Forbes and Jermier, Chapter 8; Lounsbury, Geraci, and Waismel-Manor, Chapter 14).

Information is the central and critical element of any solution to the reputation commons problem. Firms must communicate any improvements in individual and collective performance to stakeholders. To subdivide the common reputation, firms must help stakeholders to distinguish among firms with varying levels of performance. When it is costly to provide information to differentiate each firm's performance, groups of firms will form to privatize part of the common reputation. When both differentiation costs and economies of scale are minimal, firms may try to perfectly privatize the reputation commons by reporting information to stakeholders in a manner that allows stakeholders to distinguish each firm's performance.

It seems remarkable that information costs should create such problems in this emerging information age. But we must remember that raw data rarely has value and separate facts rarely provide understanding. To be useful, facts must be collected and organized so that they can be compared. Understanding the performance of firms in an industry requires that each firm disclose information about its own performance. When many strategic actors each hold a piece of a larger puzzle, we cannot assume that the full picture will be revealed. Instead, we must consider how each actor will use the possession of its piece to its best advantage. In some cases, the efforts of enough actors may prevent any part of the image from emerging. In other cases, a few clear regions of the puzzle may emerge. Finally, under just the right circumstances each actor may cooperate so that the entire puzzle can be solved.

REFERENCES

Ahrens, Frank. Oct. 1, 2000. "$88 a Fill-Up." *The Washington Post:* W14.

Coase, Ronald H. 1960. "The Problem of Social Cost." *Journal of Law and Economics,* 3:1–44.

Dawes, Robyn M. 1980. "Social Dilemmas." *Annual Review of Psychology,* 31: 169–193.

Espeland, Wendy N., and Mitchell L. Stevens. 1998. "Commensuration as a Social Process." *Annual Review of Sociology,* 24: 313–343.

Fombrun, Charles J. 1996. *Reputation: Realizing Value from the Corporate Image.* Boston: Harvard Business School Press.

Greenhouse, Steven. 1997. "Accord to Combat Sweatshop Labor Faces Obstacles." *New York Times,* April 13: 1.

Hardin, Garrett. 1968. "The Tragedy of the Commons." *Science,* 162: 1243–1248.

Harr, Jonathan. 1996. *A Civil Action.* New York: Vintage Books.

Harrison, Michael. 1998. "We Looked in the Mirror and We Didn't Like What We Saw." *The Independent,* April 22: 19.

Hayes, Randy. 1999. Speech given at Multi-Stakeholder Consultative Meeting to Identify the Key Elements of a Review of Voluntary Initiatives and Agreements. Toronto, Canada, March 12.

Hobbes, Thomas. [1668] 1960. *Leviathan.* Oxford: Basil Blackwell.

Hoffman, Andrew J. 1997. *From Heresy to Dogma: An Institutional History of Corporate Environmentalism.* San Francisco: New Lexington Press.

Hoffman, Andrew J., and William Ocasio. 2001. "Not All Events Are Attended Equally: Toward a Middle-Range Theory of Industry Attention to External Events." *Organization Science,* 12(4): 414–434.

King, Andrew, and Sara Baerwald. 1998. "Using the Court of Public Opinion to Encourage Better Business Decisions," in Ken Sexton, Alfred Marcus, K. William Easter, and Timothy D. Burkhardt, eds., *Better Environmental Decisions: Strategies for Governments, Businesses and Communities,* 309–330. Washington, DC: Island Press.

King, Andrew, and Michael Lenox. 2000. "Industry Self-Regulation Without Sanctions: The Chemical Industry's Responsible Care Program." *Academy of Management Journal,* 43: 698–716.

Lee, Louise, and Aaron Bernstein. 2000. "Who Says Student Protests Don't Matter?" *Business Week,* June 12: 94.

Lesbirel, S. Hayden. 1998. *NIMBY Politics in Japan: Energy Siting and the Management of Environmental Conflict.* Ithaca, NY: Cornell University Press.

McAvoy, Gregory E. 1998. "Partisan Probing and Democratic Decision-Making: Rethinking the NIMBY Syndrome." *Policy Studies Journal,* 26: 274–292.

Miles, Robert H. 1982. *Coffin Nails and Corporate Strategies.* Englewood Cliffs, NJ: Prentice-Hall.

O'Dell, John. 2000. "So Who's the Greenest of Them All?" *Los Angeles Times,* March 29: G1.

Olson, Mancur. 1965. *The Logic of Collective Action: Public Goods and the Theory of Groups.* Cambridge, MA: Harvard University Press.

Ostrom, Elinor. 1990. *Governing the Commons: The Evolution of Institutions for Collective Action.* Cambridge, UK: Cambridge University Press.

Ostrom, Elinor, Roy Gardner, and James Walker. 1994. *Rules, Games, and Common-Pool Resources.* Ann Arbor: University of Michigan Press.

Pearce, David W., and R. Kerry Turner. 1989. *Economics of Natural Resources and the Environment.* Baltimore: Johns Hopkins University Press.

Pfeffer, Jeffrey, and Gerald R. Salancik. 1978. *The External Control of Organizations: A Resource Dependence Perspective.* New York: Harper & Row.

Rayport, Jeffrey F., and George C. Lodge. 1990. "The Perils of Going 'Green.'" *St. Petersburg Times,* December 9: 7D.

Rees, Joseph. 1997. "Development of Communitarian Regulation in the Chemical Industry." *Law and Policy,* 19: 477–528.

Selznick, Phillip. 1949. *TVA and the Grass Roots.* Berkeley: University of California Press.

Shabecoff, Philip. 1988. "U.S. Utility Turns to Guatemala to Aid Air." *New York Times,* October 12: A14.

7

© *Academy of Management Journal*
2008, Vol. 51, No. 6, 1150–1170.

GOOD FENCES MAKE GOOD NEIGHBORS: A LONGITUDINAL ANALYSIS OF AN INDUSTRY SELF-REGULATORY INSTITUTION

MICHAEL L. BARNETT
University of South Florida

ANDREW A. KING
Dartmouth College

We extend theories of self-regulation of physical commons to analyze self-regulation of intangible commons in modern industry. We posit that when the action of one firm can cause "spillover" harm to others, firms share a type of commons. We theorize that the need to protect this commons can motivate the formation of a self-regulatory institution. Using data from the U.S. chemical industry, we find that spillover harm from industrial accidents increased after a major industry crisis and decreased following the formation of a new institution. Additionally, our findings suggest that the institution lessened spillovers from participants to the broader industry.

Interest in self-regulatory institutions, whereby firms in an industry create and voluntarily abide by a set of governing rules, has gone through a renaissance of late (cf. Prakash & Potoski, 2006). Scholars have investigated self-regulatory institutions in industries as diverse as chemicals (King & Lenox, 2000; Lenox, 2006), hospitality and recreation (Rivera & de Leon, 2004), nuclear power (Rees, 1994), and maritime shipping (Furger, 1997). Drawing from the work of Elinor Ostrom (1990) and Douglas North (1981), many of these scholars have argued that self-regulatory institutions arise to constrain individual actions that might harm an industry as a whole. Ostrom's (1990) work on community self-regulation has been particularly influential in framing recent research on industry self-regulation. She demonstrated that those who share in common pool resources like fisheries or forests can unite to create an institution that helps them avert the "tragedy of the commons" (Hardin, 1968), wherein individuals overuse and destroy commonly held resources.[1]

However, the theoretical and empirical foundations of this growing stream of research on industry self-regulation remain uncertain and contradictory. First, the common pool resource dilemmas that Ostrom considered are not apparent in many industries in which self-regulation has arisen. Research has yet to establish whether the same logic that Ostrom applied to the governance of shared physical resources can be extended to modern industries. Second, empirical studies of self-regulation have often fallen victim to what Granovetter (1985) dismissed as "bad functionalism"—the tendency to infer the function of an institution by assuming conditions it might serve to ameliorate rather than by actually observing conditions before and after the institution's creation. Third, research on some frequently studied institutions seems to provide contradictory evidence with respect to their functions. For several important self-regulatory institutions, scholars have failed to find any evidence that they limit the harmful practices of member firms, yet studies of these same institutions show that they provide a benefit to firms in their industries (King & Lenox, 2000; Lenox, 2006; Rivera & de Leon, 2004).

In this article, we address some of the deficiencies in previous research and so strengthen the theoretical and empirical foundation of the literature on self-regulatory institutions. First, we draw attention to a novel type of "commons problem" that exists in many industries. We argue that a firm's error can harm other firms in its industry and thus cause all firms in the industry to share a pooled risk. Second, we avoid bad functionalism by measuring this shared risk over a time period that spans both the emergence of our hypothesized

---

[1] The concept of the tragedy of the commons arose as a rebuttal to the common belief that the "invisible hand" of the market causes the pursuit of individual self-interest to aggregate into improved public welfare. In contrast, Hardin (1968), building on ideas advanced by Lloyd (1833), argued that because an individual's gains from increased consumption of a public good exceed the individual's costs (the individual captures all the gains, but the costs are shared by the members of the commons), individuals have a dominant incentive to overexploit unregulated public goods. As a result, "Ruin is the destination toward which all men rush, each pursuing his own best interest in a society that believes in the freedom of the commons. Freedom in a commons brings ruin to all" (Hardin, 1968: 1244).

commons problem and the formation of the self-regulatory institution. Finally, by more precisely identifying the mechanism by which the institution provides benefits to the industry, we provide insight on how inconsistencies in the existing literature may be resolved.

THEORY AND HYPOTHESES

Institutions are the "humanly devised constraints that structure political, economic and social interaction" (North, 1990: 97). North separated institutions into those that operate through formal constraints (e.g., rules, laws, and constitutions) and those that operate through informal constraints (e.g., norms of behavior, conventions, and self-imposed codes of conduct). Ingram and Clay (2000) refined North's typology by suggesting that institutions should be classified as (1) public or private and (2) centralized or decentralized. Public institutions are usually compulsory and are often run by the state. Private institutions—those run by organizations or individuals—are voluntary in nature, because actors can opt in or out. In the centralized form of these institutions, a central authority sets rules, incentives, and sanctions for noncompliance. For example, many private institutions (e.g., for-profit firms) have a principal that is ultimately in charge of internal procedures. Decentralized forms of these institutions lack a powerful central authority and thus rely on the action of numerous independent actors to encourage compliance with institutional rules. In many industrial settings, antitrust laws forbid centralized industry bodies from controlling and sanctioning member firm behaviors, and so industry self-regulation tends to take the form of a private and decentralized institution.

Until recently, many scholars dismissed the viability of self-regulatory institutions. Influential analyses by Olson (1965) and Hardin (1968) suggested that since participation is voluntary and free from enforcement by a central authority, each actor has an incentive to defect from agreements and that consequently, such institutions should never arise. As a result, absent government regulation or privatization, public goods should generally fall victim to the tragedy of the commons.

However, widespread skepticism about self-regulatory institutions began to change as a result of a series of investigations in the 1980s and 1990s (cf. Acheson, 1988; Berkes, 1989; Ostrom, 1990; Wade, 1988). Ostrom's work, in particular, changed perceptions of the potential for self-regulation. Through a series of comparative case studies, she demonstrated that individuals could, in fact, organize institutions to cope with overuse of commonly held resources such as fresh water aquifers, fisheries, and forests (Ostrom, 1990). When actors could negotiate, observe, and enforce compliance with common rules, she argued, self-regulatory institutions could protect commonly held resources, and the benefits provided by protection of these common resources could spur actors to create and participate in these institutions. In her own assessment, her work helped "shatter the convictions of many policy analysts that the only way to solve common pool resource problems is for external authorities to impose full private property rights or centralized regulation" (Ostrom, 1990: 182). Drawing on experimental and field research conducted by her workshop, she concluded that "individuals in all walks of life and all parts of the world voluntarily organize themselves so as to gain the benefits of trade, to provide mutual protection against risk, and to create and enforce rules that protect natural resources" (Ostrom, 2000: 138).

Although self-regulatory institutions have often been overlooked in the management literature, research on the topic is not without precedent (e.g., Gupta & Lad, 1983; Maitland, 1985). Yet it is only in recent years that growing awareness of research in other fields and increasing recognition of the importance of protecting common resources has caused management scholars to take a more active interest in self-regulatory institutions (Furman & Stern, 2006; Jiang & Bansal, 2003; King & Lenox, 2000). Most of these studies have focused on the determinants or consequences of participation in a self-regulatory institution. Few have explored the conditions both before and after an institution's formation. In their review, Ingram and Clay (2000) identified only one study in the management literature that analyzed antecedent and consequent conditions longitudinally, as is necessary to understand the relationship between the existence of a commons problem and self-regulation. In the identified study, Ingram and Inman (1996) showed that when faced with the threat of potential damage to a commonly valued resource, Niagara Falls, local hoteliers were able to form a self-regulatory institution that limited development and so protected the scenery of the Falls, thereby increasing the probability of survival of nearby hotels.

Ingram and Inman (1996) followed Ostrom (1990) in arguing that the need to protect a shared physical resource such as water or land can act as the catalyst for effective self-regulation. Yet many modern industries engage in self-regulation, even though few are challenged by dwindling stocks of a physical resource openly shared with rivals. For example, the Institute of Nuclear Power Operations did not arise in the face of overuse of shared stocks

Academy of Management Journal

of uranium in the nuclear power industry, nor did the Beer Institute Code arise in the face of threatened shortages of communal supplies of barley or hops in the brewing industry. What might explain the frequent presence of self-regulation in settings such as these?

One explanation, as we elaborate next, is that firms in an industry share an intangible commons that binds them to a shared fate. As with a physical commons, when the intangible commons is damaged, it can pose a serious threat to the success and survival of the firms that share it. We hypothesize that industry self-regulation in modern industries may function as a means of resolving this type of commons problem.

Industry Commons: A Shared Fate through Shared Sanctions

Firms are considered to be members of the same industry when the outputs they produce are closely substitutable. To produce closely substitutable outputs, firms in an industry tend to have similar characteristics and make use of similar processes. As a result, when new information is revealed about the characteristics of one firm, it reflects to some degree on all firms within its industry. Such interdependence can be favorable if, for example, one firm's success helps to legitimize an emerging industry and so eases all such firms' access to resources (cf. Hannan & Carroll, 1992), but it can also be problematic. Just as one firm's successes can "spill over" to other firms, so too can its problems. For example, recent news of contaminated spinach harmed the sale of all salad products—not just the products of those firms where the contamination was found (Galvin, 2007).

Tirole (1996) developed "a theory of collective reputations" to explain how the reputation of a group and those who compose the group, past and present, are intertwined. Building from the premise that a group's reputation is only as good as that of its members, Tirole (1996) argued that imperfect observability of individual behavior is the underlying cause of collective reputations. Because individual characteristics are observed with noise, a group cannot separate itself from the behaviors of its individual members, and these past behaviors of individuals within the group establish expectations that others hold of the entire group. As a result, "new members of an organization may suffer from an original sin of their elders long after the latter are gone" (Tirole, 1996: 1).

Whereas Tirole (1996) defined a group at the firm level, explaining how the behaviors of individuals within a firm culminate in a "collective" reputation

for the firm, management scholars have since applied similar logic in pushing collective reputation to the interfirm level, particularly to the industry level (Barnett & Hoffman, 2008). King, Lenox, and Barnett (2002) argued that firms in an industry share a "reputation commons." A firm's reputation is based on observers' judgments of the actions of that firm over time (Fombrun, 1996). If observers can judge the actions of a firm independently of the actions of its rivals, no commons exists, but when one firm's actions influence the judgments observers make of another firm or an industry as a whole, a commons arises. This reputation commons intertwines the fates of firms in an industry because all firms suffer when any firm engages in actions that damage the industry's shared reputation.

A shared reputation is just one mechanism that may cause firms in an industry to share a common fate. King et al. (2002) further noted the role of collective stakeholder sanctions or rewards. Firms may be grouped together because it is easier to administer a common policy over a number of firms. For example, U.S. water pollution regulation often follows categorical guidelines for each industry (Environmental Protection Agency [EPA], 1999). Such common policies also reduce the potential for regulatory corruption (Blackman & Boyd, 2002).

Regulators and other stakeholders also may impose common sanctions because they are unable to discriminate between high- and low-performer firms in an industry. For example, unable to ascertain which firms had contributed to toxic waste dumps, the U.S. government imposed a fee on all chemical producers to fund the Superfund cleanup effort. Nongovernmental stakeholders often have even greater difficulty evaluating the relative performance of firms, because such stakeholders usually lack the access and financial resources available to regulators. As a result, these stakeholders may advocate a general boycott of certain types of goods, or they may select individual firms arbitrarily for sanctioning, thereby putting all firms in the industry at risk (Spar & La Mure, 2003). For example, activist discontent with working conditions in the coffee, athletic shoe, and apparel industries led to high-profile protests and boycotts against individual firms in these industries (Starbucks, Nike, and Kathy Lee Gifford, respectively) that used suppliers with working conditions that were no worse than their rivals'—and were in some cases superior (Hornblower, 2000; Malkin, 1996). Although these sanctions were individually targeted, the arbitrariness with which firms were targeted for sanction created a risk that all firms in these industries shared.

Though it has not isolated the mechanisms that produce such effects, empirical research in financial economics has established that an error[2] attributable to a single firm can indeed have adverse financial consequences for an entire industry. Jarrell and Peltzman (1985) found that a drug recall by one pharmaceutical firm caused a portfolio of 50 rival firm stocks to drop by 1 percent. They found an even stronger industrywide effect in the automobile industry. When Ford or Chrysler initiated a recall, General Motors actually experienced a larger loss than the recalling firm. Hill and Schneeweis (1983) reported a loss in market value of a portfolio of all electrical utility stocks following the 1979 accident at the Three Mile Island nuclear plant. Mitchell (1989) concluded that the firms in the over-the-counter pharmaceutical industry lost $4.06 billion following the deadly Tylenol tampering incident. Accordingly, we hypothesize:

Hypothesis 1. An error at one firm harms other firms in the same industry.

Industry Commons as a Problem

An industry commons cannot be physically depleted in the same manner as a fishery, but it can become damaged in a way that significantly harms firms and even threatens the industry's ongoing legitimacy. For example, the crisis at Three Mile Island in 1979 sparked such deep and enduring public concern about nuclear safety that regulators have not since approved any new nuclear power plants in the United States. Major crises like this can be a catalyst for shifts in stakeholder perceptions of an industry (Hoffman & Ocasio, 2001; Meyer, 1982; Rees, 1997). Yu, Sengul, and Lester (2008) argued that crises alter stakeholders' mental classifications of firms. These mental classifications are simplistic and so can produce broad-brushed responses. As a result, a crisis stemming from the actions of one firm can cause stakeholders

to update their beliefs about the reliability and accountability of other firms in the same industry. Greenwood, Suddaby, and Hinings (2002) described a similar process in which "jolts" (Meyer, Brooks, & Goes, 1990) deinstitutionalize established industry practices and set in motion a process of "theorization" that determines how observers will view future industry practices.

Hoffman argued that stakeholder perceptions of an industry are based on metaphors. These perceptions can change "suddenly and unpredictably" (1999: 366) as significant events influence taken-for-granted assumptions and create new metaphors about the industry. These new metaphors influence the interpretation of future events, and they can cause even minor events to draw attention and raise the threat of greater sanctions across an industry. Consider the airline industry in the aftermath of the events of September 11, 2001. These events shifted how observers viewed the airline industry, causing many to assess airplanes not merely as a means of transportation, but also as a means of terrorism. Under this shifted mind-set, observers focused much more attention on airline activity and interpreted new events in light of their potential to be part of a terrorist plot. As a result, minor breaches of security that had previously gone unnoticed or unquestioned now drew media attention and engendered public calls for more stringent security protocols that raised costs and sometimes lowered demand for the entire industry.

Reports of executives in the petroleum and nuclear power industries validate the perspective that a major crisis can alter perceptions of an industry and, as a result, future problems within the industry carry the risk of more severe industrywide harm. As Hoffman (1997) recounted, following the Exxon Valdez oil spill in 1989, an Amoco executive noted that now his firm would "have to live with the sins of our brothers. We were doing fine until Exxon spilled all that oil. Then we were painted with the same brush as them" (Hoffman, 1997: 189). According to the founding chairman of the Institute of Nuclear Power Operations, in the aftermath of the Three Mile Island crisis, "It hit us that an event at a nuclear plant anywhere in our country . . . could and would affect each nuclear plant. . . . Each licensee is a hostage of each other licensee" (Rees, 1994: 2). Therefore, we hypothesize the following:

Hypothesis 2. A major crisis increases the degree to which an error at one firm harms other firms in the same industry.

---

[2] We use the term "error" to describe an event associated with a firm that carries adverse consequences. We later operationalize errors as industrial accidents. However, we do not use the terms "accident" or "mistake" because our theoretical framework deals with events that, though unintended and unplanned, may reveal intentional actions by managers and so reflect on the characteristics of the firm and, in particular, similar other firms. For example, an accident may reveal a managerial decision to underinvest in safety systems, and the discovery of child labor in a supplier's factories may reveal a managerial failure to adequately oversee suppliers.

Industry Self-Regulation as the Solution

How might an industry respond to a commons problem? Until recently, many scholars would have predicted there would be little response at all. Publications by Lloyd (1833/1968) and Hardin (1968) on the tragedy of the commons firmly established the dominant expectation that actors sharing a common resource cannot effectively self-govern their use of this resource. In the last few years, research on common pool resources has begun to change such expectations by suggesting that the risks from inefficient use of common resources can motivate members of a commons to create a self-regulatory institution (Ostrom, 1990). Yet it is also clear that forming a self-regulatory institution can be difficult. Competition, inertia, and the inherent cost of forming such an institution inhibit rival firms from coming together (Barnett, 2006).

Research has suggested that a sudden worsening of a commons problem, as described in the prior section, is often the catalyst that brings actors together to form a self-regulatory institution (Gunderson, Holling, & Light, 1995; Gunningham & Rees, 1997). For example, self-regulation in the Maine lobster industry arose after a collapse of the fishery caused the closure of important canneries (Acheson & Knight, 2000). Similarly, environmental emergencies in New Brunswick, the Everglades, and the Chesapeake Bay precipitated changes to governing institutions (Gunderson, Holling, & Light, 1995). Crises such as these can help actors overcome cognitive barriers and recognize the existence and importance of a commons (Weber, Kopelman, & Messick, 2004), and they can also change expectations of the value of taking action (Vasi & Macy, 2003).

Institutions created in response to a threat to a shared natural resource, scholars have argued, tend to reduce the shared threat (Acheson & Knight, 2000; Ostrom, 1990). This prediction matches a "functionalist" interpretation of institutions that suggests they arise to facilitate more efficient social exchange (cf. North, 1981; Williamson, 1985). However, evidence supporting the functionality of self-regulatory institutions remains largely lacking, in part because scholars often cannot access the information about conditions prior to the creation of the institution. As a result, many attempts at empirical validation have been soundly criticized as "bad functionalism." In an influential critique, Granovetter (1985) quoted Schotter's statement that many studies begin with a theory of the function of an institution and then infer "the evolutionary problem that must have existed for the institution as we see it to have developed" (Schotter [1981: 2], quoted in Granovetter, 1985: 489).

Herein, we advance a functional theory of self-regulatory institutions, but rather than inferring the problem that must have existed for such institutions to have arisen in modern industry, we use theory to hypothesize the creation of a particular type of problem: a major crisis exacerbates an industry commons, placing firms at heightened risk of harm from errors at other firms in the industry. To validate our functional theory, then, we next hypothesize that the institution formed in response to this crisis indeed functions to reduce the heightened commons problem.

Hypothesis 3. An industry self-regulatory institution created following a major crisis reduces the degree to which an error at one firm harms other firms in the same industry.

By specifying the existence of a particular commons problem and then testing whether or not an industry self-regulatory institution alleviated this problem, the prior set of hypotheses constitutes a proper test of a functional theory of self-regulation in modern industry. However, a thorough analysis of a self-regulatory institution should include a specification of the means through which it achieves its function. We next explore the institution's mechanisms.

Exploring the Mechanisms of Industry Self-Regulation

As we have theorized thus far, firms in an industry are subject to "spillover" harm from the errors of other firms, and an industry self-regulatory institution functions to lessen this harm. We have not yet specified how the institution might accomplish this objective. The literature on industry self-regulation suggests two possible mechanisms: the institution might forestall the threat of industrywide stakeholder sanctions (Stefanadis, 2003), or it might direct sanctions away from its members (Terlaak & King, 2006).

Forestalling sanctions to an industry. One way an institution might help firms forestall industrywide stakeholder sanctions would be by facilitating collective performance improvements relative to criteria of concern to stakeholders (Barrett, 2000; Dawson & Segerson, 2005). In doing so, the institution would impose costs on its members, but it would create greater value by reducing the risk of stakeholder action (e.g., government regulation). Although it is influential in setting research agendas, the general applicability of this model has been called into question by empirical evidence that participants in industry programs for environmental improvement do not have better performance than nonmembers, nor do they seem to improve more rapidly (Howard, Nash, & Ehrenfeld, 2000; King & Lenox, 2000; Rivera & de Leon, 2004).

Even if a self-regulatory institution failed to improve average industry performance, it might still reduce the threat of industrywide sanction by coordinating a unified "non-market strategy" among firms in the industry (Baron, 1995). For example, by acting together, firms might more efficiently and effectively lobby state regulators and so counter threats of increased regulation. Even if the target stakeholder is more diffuse than a state regulator (e.g., consumers or stakeholder groups), the institution might still aid in forestalling sanctions by assisting in the creation of a consistent message or by allowing firms to pool resources and so access economies of scale in communication (e.g., television advertisements).

Some mechanisms of forestalling stakeholder sanctions could differentially reduce the spillover harm from errors occurring at a member of an institution. One common case occurs when an institution facilitates the transfer of reassuring information following an error at a member firm. Research has demonstrated that open provision of information about an error such as an accident, spill, or drug-tampering incident can reduce the degree to which stakeholders sanction the focal firm (Shrivastava & Siomkos, 1989). Thus, when member firms do suffer errors, their coordinated efforts at communication could provide an efficient and effective means of reducing spillover harm.

A self-regulatory institution could also reduce spillover harm from the errors of member firms by coordinating communication before an error occurs. From the perspective of information economics, if a stakeholder already understands the propensity for an error, the occurrence of an error should provide no new information. From a psychological perspective, information provided in advance of an error may also influence how the error is interpreted by reducing the degree to which stakeholders view any observed error as informative about unobserved dangers, thus resulting in a soothing effect. Slovik and Weber (2002) reported that:

> The informativeness or signal potential of a mishap, and thus its potential social impact, appears to be systematically related to the perceived characteristics of the hazard. An accident that takes many lives may produce relatively little social disturbance (beyond that caused to the victims' families and friends) if it occurs as part of a familiar and well-understood system (e.g., a train wreck). However, a

small incident in an unfamiliar system (or one perceived as poorly understood), such as a nuclear waste repository or a recombinant DNA laboratory, may have immense social consequences if it is perceived as a harbinger of future and possibly catastrophic mishaps. (2002: 13)

Thus, an industry self-regulatory institution may fulfill its function of reducing spillover harm by disclosing key information about its member firms, so that future errors at these firms reveal little or no new information of relevance and so draw few or no industrywide stakeholder sanctions. Consistently with this notion, the first code of one influential self-regulatory institution, the chemical industry's Responsible Care Program, was focused on stakeholder outreach. It obliged managers of facilities of participating firms "to identify and respond to community concerns, [and] inform the community of risks associated with company operations" (Canadian Chemical Producers' Association [CCPA], 2007).

If a self-regulatory institution forestalls broad stakeholder sanctions by coordinating improvement, lobbying, or public relations for an industry, it should provide a general benefit to the industry as a whole.[3] However, if it forestalls industrywide sanctions by providing additional information about its members only, either before or after errors, spillover harm from members' errors should be reduced. Thus, we hypothesize the following:

Hypothesis 4. An industry self-regulatory institution decreases the degree to which an error at a member firm harms other firms in the same industry.

Diverting sanctions from members. In contrast to functioning as a means of forestalling industrywide sanctions, a self-regulatory institution might instead function as a type of "market signal" that directs sanctions away from members by helping stakeholders distinguish the superior but unobserved characteristics of member firms from those of nonmember firms.

As discussed earlier, stakeholders often cannot

---

[3] A prediction consistent with this method of industrywide stakeholder forestalling would be that the institution would reduce spillover harm evenly (to members and nonmembers), wherever an error occurs (at member or nonmember firms). We do not develop this prediction into a formal hypothesis because it requires a test of the null hypothesis of indistinguishable coefficient estimations for both variable pairs. Confirmation of Hypothesis 3 and disconfirmation of Hypotheses 4 and 5 would represent consistent but insufficient evidence of this institutional mechanism.

directly observe important attributes of a firm. For example, they may not be able to see the degree of accident preparedness in a particular petrochemical facility. Lacking such information, stakeholders may assume that all such firms tend to perform similarly. If participation in an institution acts as a market signal, it would credibly reveal to stakeholders information about desirable characteristics they could not otherwise observe. As a result, members of the institution should be less at risk of spillover harm than nonmembers, as only members are believed to possess these superior characteristics.

For an institution to allow firms to credibly signal their superior attributes, it must meet several restrictive conditions (Spence, 1973). First, there must be some way to keep firms with lower performance from joining the institution. This is commonly accomplished by setting rules for participation that make membership too costly for firms with inferior attributes. Second, high-performing firms must wish to participate. Stakeholders must be able to differentially reward participants, and the cost of participation must not exceed these benefits. Third, there must be a credible mechanism, usually a third-party auditor, for evaluating and certifying compliance with the institution's rules. Finally, there must be some way for stakeholders to sanction or reward individual firms (e.g., by boycotting or buying their products). Evidence supporting signaling theories has been found for institutions that seem to target buyers and suppliers, such as the International Organization for Standardization (ISO) management standards (Corbett, Montes-Sancho, & Kirsch, 2005).

Hypothesis 5. An industry self-regulatory institution decreases the degree to which an error at another firm in its industry harms a member firm.

RESEARCH SETTING AND METHODOLOGY

To test our hypotheses, we needed an industry that experiences frequent errors of varying significance, has suffered a major crisis, and has created a self-regulatory institution to recover from this major crisis. The U.S. chemical industry meets all of these requirements. Members of the industry suffer multiple errors each year, and these errors vary in significance. Most are small and involve the unplanned release of potentially toxic chemicals. More serious errors injure or kill employees or local citizens. Industry experts and industry members report that one error precipitated a major crisis for the industry. On December 3, 1984, methyl isocya-

nate leaked from a Union Carbide facility in Bhopal, India, and killed between 3,000 and 10,000 people. Many thousands more were injured (Shrivastava, 1987). It remains the most deadly industrial accident on record.

Anecdotal reports from managers in the chemical industry around the time of this event support the perspective on industry commons we have hypothesized. Numerous respondents reported that the incident at Bhopal created a crisis for the entire chemical industry by changing how observers viewed the risks of chemical manufacturing. Ronald Lang, then executive director of the Synthetic Organic Chemical Manufacturers Association, noted, "Bhopal focuses concern on something that had not been adequately addressed before—the possibility of catastrophe" (Gibson, 1985a: 21). Another industry leader described the post-Bhopal environment as "chemophobia" (Gunningham, 1995: 72).

Contemporaneous reports provide evidence that industry participants now had a greater sense of being part of a commons. Then-chairman of Union Carbide, Warren Anderson, remarked, "This is not a Carbide issue. This is an industry issue" (Gibson, 1985a: 21). Others noted that with such a close focus on the industry, further accidents at any chemical firm would have significant consequences for all chemical manufacturers (Gibson, 1985b). Industry managers also noted that one stakeholder in particular—insurance companies—formally implemented this increased perception of risk in a way that affected all firms in the industry, regardless of their individual characteristics: "Now the Bhopal tragedy has reinforced the new conservatism of insurance underwriters and, as one broker puts it, given them 'an excuse to say no.' . . . When they see any operations associated with chemicals—even chemical operations posing no hazard to the public—[underwriters] are ready to paint them with the same brush as Bhopal's" (Katzenberg, 1985: 30). Respondents also reported that the crisis drove industry members to create a prominent self-regulatory institution: The Responsible Care program of the American Chemistry Council (ACC).[4]

> "More than anything else," recalls [then] Union Carbide CEO Robert Kennedy, "it was Bhopal that finally put us on the path that would lead to Responsible Care." "Bhopal was the wake-up call," says [then] Dow Chemical vice president Dave Buzelli. "It brought home to everybody that we could have

---

[4] At the time of the events reported in this study, the American Chemistry Council was known as the Chemical Manufacturers Association.

the best performance in the world but if another company had an accident, all of us would be hurt, so we started to work together." (Rees, 1997: 485)

The first element of the program, Community Awareness and Emergency Response (CAER), appeared designed to reduce concern about accidents. Responsible Care encouraged firms to "open the doors and let the fresh air flow through" (Coombes, 1991) so that a skeptical public would be convinced that the dangers that Bhopal had brought to light were being rigorously dealt with and that there was no imminent danger. Responsible Care required extensive outreach efforts with local officials in communities where plants were located. As part of CAER, firms conducted thousands of plant tours. The ACC also spent millions on advertising campaigns to humanize the industry (Heller, 1991).

The potential of the program to actually change the operations of members has been questioned from its inception. Critics noted that the program did not include a mechanism for third-party certification of compliance with the rules and thus argued that it was unlikely to help stakeholders accurately determine those firms with higher performance (Ember, 1995). Others argued, however, that close connections within the industry could allow members to police adherence to the rules (Rees, 1997). As discussed earlier, empirical studies have suggested that member firms did not reduce their pollution any faster than nonparticipants but that the industry still benefited from the existence of the program (King & Lenox, 2000; Lenox, 2006).

Sample

Our sample included all firms in the Center for Research on Security Prices (CRSP) database that reported any operations in the chemical industry (SIC 2800–2899) in the Compustat business segment database between 1980 and 2000 or reported to the Environmental Protection Agency (EPA) that they operated a production facility in these sectors. We chose this time period to allow a nearly 5-year pretest window before the Bhopal crisis (1980–84), a 5-year interval between the Bhopal crisis and the creation of Responsible Care (1985–1989), and an 11-year posttest window after the creation of Responsible Care (1990–2000). We chose the sample to include all firms that reported any chemical operations, rather than only those with a primary denomination in the chemical industry, so as to include diversified firms with significant though nondominant chemical operations. Our final sample included 735 unique firms.

We obtained data about our sample firms from the CRSP database, the Compustat business sector database, and the EPA's Toxics Release Inventory (TRI). Reporting to the TRI began in 1987 and covers facilities with ten or more employees that produce, store, release, or transfer more than a threshold amount of any of more than 600 listed chemicals. We obtained data about errors by performing keyword searches of the major international and U.S. regional newspapers and wire databases within the Lexis-Nexis service. In some cases, we supplemented information from news articles with information from the Hoovers online database and Dialogweb.

Dependent Variable

Managers in the chemical industry consider industrial accidents to be serious errors (Greening & Johnson, 1997). Industry experts further claim that the Bhopal crisis changed the degree to which industrial accidents harmed the industry (Gibson, 1985b). Thus, we used industrial accidents at chemical plants as our measure of error.

To find industrial accidents, we performed keyword searches using terms such as "fire," "gas leak," "explosion," "chemical spill," "chemical release," and "chemical discharge." These are terms that top managers in the chemical industry associate with serious accidents (Greening & Johnson, 1997). Our search uncovered 359 possible accidents. As with any keyword search, however, we netted numerous inappropriate events, such as chlorine burns in swimming pools or ammonia spills on restaurant floors. We also found numerous accidents related to transportation (e.g., a tanker truck flipped and exploded into flames on a ramp to the Capital Beltway) and accidents related to petroleum transport and refining. We included accidents at refineries, since the petroleum and chemical industries are closely associated (i.e., petrochemicals; see Hoffman [1997]),[5] but we excluded leaks and spills from crude oil pumping or transport (e.g., the Exxon Valdez accident) because transportation is often subcontracted, and it is unclear if accidents in transport would reflect on the transporter, the producer, or the wholesaler/retailer. Incomplete reporting about key aspects of accidents further narrowed the sample. In total, we were able to qualify and determine the date, mag-

---

[5] In analyses not reported here, we created a dummy variable to indicate accidents that occurred at refineries (rather than at chemical plants) and found it to be insignificant in various analyses.

nitude, location, and responsible firm for 123 of the raw events.

Problems with the size of events or contemporaneous firm actions caused removal of an additional 31 accidents. Fifteen accidents resulted in neither an injury nor death. Our preliminary analysis showed that such accidents were too minor to affect the stock price of even the firms directly responsible for them, and so we excluded these events from our study of the spillover effects. At the opposite end of the scale, we removed the Bhopal event because of its extreme nature. Finally, events should not be confounded with endogenous actions that might bias coefficient estimates (McWilliams & Siegel, 1997). We excluded 15 events because other significant activities were mentioned in the newspaper accounts of them (e.g., leadership changes). The exclusions left us with 92 accidents.

To measure the degree to which these accidents "harmed" other firms in the industry, we evaluated the stock price movements of other firms with chemical operations following each accident. Market theory suggests that stock prices reflect the best assessment of future cash flows for firms. If investors think that an accident might decrease a firm's future cash flows, perhaps as a result of decreased demand resulting from increased stakeholder sanctions or increased costs resulting from increased government regulation, then that firm's stock price should fall.

Appendix A describes how we captured the harm of each accident with our dependent variable, cumulative abnormal return (CAR) on day 5. CAR is a measure of how much a stock's value deviates from its expected value over a particular period of time. Though our study focuses on the extent to which an accident at one firm causes harm to other firms, we first explored the effect of these accidents on CAR for the firms directly responsible for the events in order to validate that our search uncovered a set of accidents that might influence stock value. As Appendix B shows, in model 1, the stocks of the firms responsible for these 92 events lost an average of 1.01 percent of their expected values in the five days immediately following their accidents. If we use instead the point estimates from model 2, we find that an average accident (one that injured about 3.5 employees) caused about a 1.4 percent reduction in a firm's stock price. An accident that killed an employee caused an additional loss of 2.6 percent of market value. In model 3, we show how other variables influence the direct effect of an accident. For example, the positive coefficient for the variable "assets of perpetrator" shows that losses are greatly reduced for larger firms that experience accidents. We explain these

variables below and return to them for comparative analysis later in the article.

Independent Variables

We hypothesize that one firm's error can spill over to other firms within the same industry. Scholars commonly use the Standard Industrial Classification (SIC) code as the definition of an industry. Since we were examining spillovers from accidents in the chemical industry, we limited our set of firms to those that reported at least one segment in the 2800 SIC range, which encompasses chemicals. We also created a more refined measure of operations in the same industry by creating a binary variable, *same SIC*, that captures whether a firm owned a facility that was in the same four-digit SIC code as the one that had an accident.[6]

Our second hypothesis predicts that a major crisis will increase this spillover effect. As previously discussed, industry insiders assert that Bhopal caused a major crisis that affected all firms with chemical operations. To capture the changes caused by Bhopal, we created a dummy variable, *pre–Bhopal*, that captures the time period from the beginning of our sample through the end of 1984, when the Bhopal leak occurred. Events occurring in this period were coded 1, and those occurring later were coded 0.

Our third hypothesis predicts that industry self-regulation decreases this spillover effect. Aspects of the Responsible Care program began shortly after the Bhopal crisis, but no elements of the program were promulgated until late in 1989. Thus, to capture the *post–Responsible Care* period, we created a dummy variable coded 1 if after 1989 and 0 otherwise.

Finally, in order to explore the mechanisms of industry self-regulation, we had to distinguish Responsible Care participants from nonparticipants. To capture this effect, we measured membership in the parent association, the American Chemistry Council. We assigned this variable (*ACC member*) a value of 1 if the ACC listed the company as a member in a given

---

[6] We investigated whether a percentage measure would provide similar results or results with greater explanatory power. We found that a continuous specification provided no significant increase in explanatory power. It may be that spillover risk is not linearly related to the scale of a firm's operations in a given industry or that our continuous specification (the percentage of a firm's total employees employed in any of the firm's facilities that share the same four-digit SIC as the firm at fault) does not precisely measure relative scale across industries. Thus, we used the binary measure.

year, and 0 otherwise. From 1990 onward, participation in Responsible Care was a condition of membership in the ACC. We further separated out the unique attributes of the Responsible Care program by creating a dummy variable, *Responsible Care member*, that indicated ACC membership during a year when the Responsible Care program was in existence. We also sought to understand whether Responsible Care membership might have different effects, depending on the identity of the firm responsible for an accident. Thus, we created two variables, *perpetrator in ACC* and *perpetrator in Responsible Care*, that captured whether or not a firm that had an accident was a member of the American Chemistry Council or of the Responsible Care program.

Control Variables

Variation in the magnitude of an event should cause variation in the market's response, so we included two measures of each accident's severity. *Employee killed* was a binary variable assigned a value of 1 if an employee was killed in the accident. Only about 25 percent of the accidents in our study included a fatality, so the binary parameterization is appropriate and truncates little information. In contrast, we measured the number of employees injured (*employees injured*) using a continuous measure (log[number injured + 1]). We used the log parametric form to reduce the effect of outliers and to account for possible diminishing effects. Alternative parametric forms (binary and linear) for our measure of injuries reduce model fit but do not change the sign and significance of reported results.

The size of both a perpetrator (firm responsible for an accident) and a recipient firm (another firm in the industry that is subject to spillover) may influence the market response to accidents. Larger perpetrators often have better public relations and so may be able to

diffuse public reaction and response to their own accidents and to the accidents of others that might reflect on them. Moreover, larger firms tend to be more diversified, and so their overall stock price would suffer less from adverse events in any single industry. Finally, the size of a firm has been shown to influence the variability of its stock performance (Fama & French, 1992). We measured firm size as the log of total *assets* reported in Compustat for the year an accident occurred, and we further added *assets of perpetrator*, the log of the total assets of the firm where the accident occurred.

Table 1 provides descriptive statistics and correlations. We used several approaches to reduce the potential for unobserved firm differences or endogenous managerial choice to bias our coefficient estimates. We included fixed effects of different types to control for unobserved (but constant) differences in our sample (e.g., accident industry, spillover industry, and the year of the accident). To control for unobserved differences among the industries in which accidents occurred, we included fixed effects for all industries in which there was more than one accident. To control for unobserved firm-level differences, in some models we included fixed effects for a firm itself. These fixed effects account for constant attributes of any firm that might influence spillover effects. Endogenous choice processes might also bias our sample, particularly if they are based on changing firm characteristics not captured by our fixed effects. To help account for these, we also conducted a Heckman two-stage treatment model.

Analysis

Event study methodologies are commonly used to understand how stockholders interpret a single event (Blacconiere & Patten, 1994; Brown & Warner, 1980,

TABLE 1
Descriptive Statistics and Correlations for Spillover Analysis[a]

Variable	Mean	s.d.	1	2	3	4	5	6	7	8	9	10	11
1. CAR, day 5	0.14	9.80											
2. Pre-Bhopal	0.04	0.19	−.01										
3. Post–Responsible Care	0.79	0.41	.05	−.35									
4. Same SIC	0.44	0.50	−.05	−.06	.04								
5. Employee killed	0.27	0.45	−.03	.11	−.29	−.10							
6. Employees injured	1.44	1.17	−.05	.09	−.11	.08	.03						
7. Assets of perpetrator	9.52	1.43	.07	.05	.04	−.33	−.08	−.20					
8. Perpetrator in ACC	0.74	0.44	.01	.12	−.04	.13	−.01	−.15	.30				
9. Perpetrator in RC	0.57	0.50	.05	−.21	.59	.13	−.18	−.21	.30	.71			
10. ACC member	0.17	0.38	−.01	.09	−.11	.03	.04	.03	−.01	.01	−.06		
11. Responsible Care member	0.12	0.32	−.00	−.06	.16	.04	−.03	.00	−.001	.00	.10	.82	
12. Assets	4.87	2.36	.00	.04	.02	−.07	−.02	−.01	−.003	.01	.02	.52	.44

1985; Hamilton, 1995; Patten & Nance, 1998). McWilliams and Siegel (1997) criticized the use of this method when firms might be able to alter or time focal events so that they occur concurrently with other announcements. Accidents, however, are by their very nature unplanned and not amenable to strategic timing. Thus, such manipulation is not a concern in this study.

Our event study analysis allowed us to connect an accident with abnormal stock price movements. To understand the causes of variance within these movements, we used a linear regression:

$$CAR_{ij} = a + BX_{ij} + e_{ij} + v_p + u_J + v_i + \delta_t,$$

where CAR_{ij} is the cumulative abnormal return for firm i five days following event j and X_{ij} is a vector of independent variables for firm i at the time of event j. Clearly, we could not measure every possible factor that might influence the effect of an accident or the spillover from that accident to other firms. We used a series of fixed effects to try to reduce potential problems from unobserved heterogeneity. First, we attempted to account for unobservables in the industries in which the accidents occurred. We included a fixed effect (v_p) for all p industries in which we had more than a single accident (16 of 22 industries). These effects help to control for unobserved industry differences (e.g., the propensity to use subcontractors), which might affect the number or type of accidents. Second, we accounted for potential differences among industries that were affected by an accident (but not necessarily the industry in which it occurred) by including fixed effects for every two-digit SIC code (u_J). Alternatively, when we considered issues of variable spillover among firms and were interested in the effect of variables that were not collinear with firm identity, we included both firm (v_i) and year (δ_t) fixed effects.

Clearly, the decision to join the American Chemistry Council and participate in Responsible Care is endogenous to our analysis; that is, managers make decisions about participation conditional on the characteristics of their organization. To the extent that we capture the important firm characteristics through the inclusion of a direct measure or by the use of fixed effects, our coefficient estimate should be unbiased. However, these methods will fail to capture the effect of endogenous choice based on changing and unmeasured factors. To account for such factors and test the robustness of our analysis, we performed a two-stage Heckman treatment model.

The first stage consists of the model predicting participation in Responsible Care. We based the treatment selection function on a model of membership proposed by King and Lenox (2000), who found that participation in Responsible Care is influenced by a firm's relative emissions, the relative emissions of the industries in which it operates, the degree to which it is focused in chemicals, its size, and its reputation. Following their study, we used TRI data to estimate the median emissions for each industry (four-digit SIC) and create a weighted measure of this value (based on percentages of sales in this SIC) for each firm.[7] The log of this value became our measure of the degree to which a firm operated in sectors with many toxic chemicals (*industry emissions*). We measured the degree to which a firm operated in chemicals (*chemical focus*) by calculating the percentage of sales from chemical sectors (as estimated from Compustat data). We already had a measure of firm size (assets). Because of the limitation of the TRI, we could not estimate relative performance prior to 1987. We also could not develop contemporaneous measures of reputation for all of the firms in our sample. We provide descriptive statistics for these variables in Appendix C.

RESULTS

To explore the effect of spillovers from accidents, we evaluated the abnormal stock price movements of each firm in our sample (excluding the perpetrator) after each accident in our sample. To get a sense of the average scale of such spillovers, in Table 2 we first specify a simple model without fixed effects. In support of Hypothesis 1, model 1 shows that a firm that operated a facility in the same industry in which an accident occurred indeed experienced a negative spillover. We also found that accidents in which employees were killed or injured resulted in additional negative spillovers. Note that the effects are smaller than those to the focal firm (see Appendix B) but are still significant. Following an accident that injured an average number of employees (3.5), a chemical firm with operations in the same industry as that in which an accident occurred could expect to lose 0.15 percent of its stock price. After an accident that caused the death of an employee, the firm could expect to lose an additional 0.83 percent.

To explore whether the accident at Bhopal or the formation of Responsible Care influenced spillovers from accidents, we specified a new model (model 2) with the two dummy variables respec-

---

[7] For the years 1980–86, we estimated industry emissions on the basis of the 1987 TRI data.

TABLE 2
Spillover Effect of Accidents on Firms Not At Fault

Variable	Model 1	Model 2	Model 3	Model 4	Model 5	Model 6	Model 7	Model 8
Pre-Bhopal		0.75** (0.32)	1.01*** (0.33)	1.06*** (0.34)	1.16*** (0.34)	1.21*** (0.42)		
Post-Responsible Care		1.02*** (0.15)	0.92*** (0.17)	0.79*** (0.19)	0.27 (0.31)	0.18 (0.35)		
Accident in same SIC	−0.88*** (0.11)	−0.87*** (0.11)	−0.60*** (0.27)	−0.58** (0.27)	−0.60** (0.27)	−0.66** (0.32)	−0.57** (0.27)	−0.57** (0.27)
Employee killed	−0.83*** (0.13)	−0.59*** (0.13)	−0.38*** (0.14)	−0.37** (0.14)	−0.41*** (0.14)	−0.43*** (0.16)	−0.27* (0.16)	−0.27* (0.16)
Employee injured	−0.36*** (0.05)	−0.34*** (0.05)	−0.38*** (0.06)	−0.38*** (0.06)	−0.36*** (0.06)	−0.39*** (0.06)	−0.24*** (0.07)	−0.24*** (0.07)
Assets of perpetrator			0.37*** (0.05)	0.37*** (0.05)	0.33*** (0.06)	0.34*** (0.06)	0.23*** (0.06)	0.23*** (0.06)
Perpetrator in ACC					−0.81*** (0.31)	−0.97*** (0.36)	−1.16*** (0.32)	−1.16*** (0.32)
Perpetrator in Responsible Care					1.08*** (0.35)	1.25*** (0.41)	1.43*** (0.36)	1.49*** (0.37)
ACC member					0.21 (0.30)	0.04 (0.38)	0.00 (0.00)	0.00 (0.00)
Responsible Care member					−0.53 (0.33)	−0.59 (0.43)	−0.30 (0.36)	−0.40 (0.37)
Assets			0.01 (0.03)	−0.002 (0.10)	0.02 (0.03)	−0.03 (0.05)	0.02 (0.12)	0.01 (0.47)
Mills ratio						−0.20* (0.10)		
Responsible Care perpetrator → Responsible Care member								
Non-Responsible Care perpetrator → Responsible Care member								
Constant	1.28*** (0.11)	0.34* (0.18)						
n	30,751	30,751	30,751	30,751	30,751	26,139	30,751	30,751
R^2	0.01	0.01	0.01[a]	0.01[a]	0.01	0.01	0.02[a]	0.02[a]
Likelihood-ratio chi-square (comparison model)		44.59** (1)	161.63*** (2)		12.49* (3)			
Accident (four-digit)			Yes	Yes		Yes	Yes	Yes
Industry (two-digit)			Yes	Yes		Yes	Yes	Yes
Firm						Heckman	Yes	Yes
Year							Yes	Yes

[a] Within-R^2 (ω) reported for the fixed-effects analysis.

* $p < .05$

** $p < .01$

tively capturing the time period before the Bhopal accident and after the formation of Responsible Care. In support of Hypotheses 2 and 3, our results suggest that spillovers from accidents indeed increased after Bhopal and diminished after the formation of Responsible Care. In the intervening period, an average accident could be expected to reduce the stock price of other firms with operations in that industry by about 1.1 percent. We found that before Bhopal, this loss was only about 0.3 percent, and that after the creation of Responsible Care it was negligible. The increased spillovers after the Bhopal accident provide corroborating evidence for the observations of industry members. Speaking after the Bhopal accident, Dan Bishop, then Monsanto's director for environmental communication, remarked, "Every chemical incident becomes a national story now. A minor spill becomes front page stuff, and that tends to exaggerate the event and reinforce the public's concern" (Gibson, 1985b: 90).

In model 3, we included fixed effects and additional variables to account for unobserved differences among the industries in which the accidents occurred, as well as differences in the characteristics of the firms. In model 4, we conducted an alternative analysis in which we added a fixed effect for each firm. Because this would be collinear with a measure of industry, we removed the industry effects. In both models, we again find support for Hypotheses 1, 2, and 3. Accidents do cause spillover harm; this harm increased following a crisis in the industry; and it decreased after the formation of a self-regulatory institution.

We begin our exploration of the mechanism of Responsible Care with model 5. To explore whether Responsible Care provided a general benefit to the industry or only acted when one of its member firms was responsible for an accident (Hypothesis 4), we included additional interaction terms to capture spillovers from an accident at an ACC member firm in both time periods. In support of Hypothesis 4, we obtained a positive and significant coefficient for the variable identifying a perpetrator as a member of the program, indicating reduced harm to firms in our sample when an accident occurred at an ACC firm after the creation of the Responsible Care program. Interestingly, the inclusion of this variable also reduced the significance of the coefficient for our variable denoting the Responsible Care time period (post–Responsible Care). Thus, once we capture (through our inclusion of "perpetrator in Responsible Care" one hypothesized mechanism through which the program could have provided benefit, we no longer find significant evidence that the program provided

a general benefit to the industry through another mechanism.

Our argument that information disclosure may be the mechanism by which Responsible Care reduced spillover harm when one of its members experienced an accident is corroborated by the contemporaneous reports of industry experts. After touring the site of a chemical plant belonging to Exxon (a Responsible Care member) in his city, a city manager noted a change in how he viewed this plant:

> I don't harbor the fears that I had. I have learned about what they do. I hadn't realized the safety precautions, the amount of testing of final products, the monitoring of air and water that goes on. But I don't think this will eliminate all skepticism. It's ludicrous to think that industry is going to be safe all the time. But the fact that they have been open and honest is extremely important to me as city manager. (Heller, 1991: 82)

Others reported that when accidents inevitably did occur, Responsible Care coordinated a quick response. "Mutual assistance is on all Responsible Care practitioners' lips, with large firms helping out small firms an important dynamic" (Heller & Hunter, 1994: 31). Richard Doyle, vice president of Responsible Care, quoted in Begley (1994), described such efforts as operating out of a "war room":

> The emergency response effort in the war room also led to an upgrade in Chemtrec, recognized as the chemical emergency response center in the U.S. It was established in 1972 to provide timely information and connect emergency responders with industry experts on the chemicals they were dealing with. After Bhopal, CMA set about upgrading Chemtrec's operations and improving its mutual assistance activities. (Begley, 1994: 33)

We found no evidence to support Hypothesis 5, which states that an institution provides additional protection from spillover harm to its members. We tested this hypothesis by including a dummy variable for participation in the Responsible Care program. As shown in model 5, the coefficient for Responsible Care member is negative and insignificant, indicating that members received no more benefit than nonmembers. In the section below on robustness testing, we discuss an alternative test of this hypothesis, in which we separate spillover to Responsible Care members from accidents at (1) other members and (2) nonmembers. This analysis also failed to support Hypothesis 5.

Robustness Testing

To ensure the robustness of our analysis, we specified several alternative models. First, we accounted for endogenous choice processes based on unobserved fixed firm differences through the use of a Heckman correction technique. In model 6, we report the result for the second stage of a fully specified model. In the first stage of this specification we used a probit analysis to estimate the tendency of firms to participate in the ACC and Responsible Care in each year. The probit for the first stage (using 1990 as the example) is shown in Appendix C. The probit results are consistent with King and Lenox (2000) and suggest that ACC members tend to be in sectors with more toxic emissions and more focused on chemicals, and to have more assets. We controlled for the effect of endogenous decisions to participate in ACC and Responsible Care by including the Mills ratio obtained from the probit analysis as a variable in the second-stage regression. The Mills ratio represents the selection hazard for the treatment (participation in ACC/Responsible Care) occurring for a given firm in a given year. The coefficient estimations from model 6 provided confirmatory evidence of the robustness of our findings. Similarly, conducting an identical modification to models 1, 2, and 3 confirmed the findings already reported. To account for unobserved firm differences, we also ran all of the models (except those with Heckman corrections) using firm fixed effects and obtained consistent results.[8]

In model 7, we did not analyze the effect of time periods so as to allow the use of year fixed effects to account for any underlying macroeconomic changes that might distort our results. Once we included these year effects, we had to remove the time period dummy variables. As shown, an analysis with year fixed effects again suggests that Responsible Care provided a benefit to the industry by reducing the spillover effect of an accident at a firm participating in the Responsible Care program. Thus, we again confirmed our support for Hypothesis 4.

In model 8, we further explore our failure to find support for Hypothesis 5 by including a new operationalization of spillover effects to Responsible Care members. These two variables separate spillover harm to members from (1) accidents at another Responsible Care member firm and (2) accidents at a nonmember firm. The coefficients estimated for both variables were insignificant, and so we again found no support for Hypothesis 5.

---

[8] Interestingly, the coefficient estimate for the inverse Mills Ratio is consistently negative. This suggests that firms with unobserved attributes that tended to cause them to join RC also tended to experience greater spillover harm from accidents at other firms.

We conducted additional robustness testing to determine if our time period dummy variables (pre-Bhopal and post–Responsible Care) might be capturing some other temporal effect. First, we tested whether differences in the frequency of reporting might influence responses to accidents. To rule out this possibility, we specified models that included measures of the accident prior to the one under consideration. We included the days since the accident, whether an employee was killed, and whether an employee was injured. Models with additional variables confirmed the sign and significance of the reported results. We also explored whether we were simply capturing a wearing off of stakeholder concern as the Bhopal accident became a distant memory. We tested alternative models with a variable measuring linear and logged time since Bhopal in days. Coefficient estimates on both variables were not statistically significant. The log form of the time estimate is highly correlated with the pre-Bhopal variable ($\rho = -0.81$) and thus it reduces the significance of this measure in some models. Neither variable provided significant additional explanatory power.

Throughout our analysis, we explain little of the observed variance in stock prices—between 1 and 2 percent. This is not surprising. Our method essentially removes fixed differences in firm stock prices, leaving only noise and the effect of new information about a firm. When we conducted fixed-effects analysis, we further removed two types of industry effects, and we report only our ability to explain the remaining variance within groups. We evaluate the effect of only one type of news; clearly, numerous additional factors play an important role in determining stock prices. However, so long as this other news is not correlated with our events and uncaptured by our variables, our estimates should be unbiased. As discussed earlier, we carefully screened out events that were contemporaneous with other corporate news. Moreover, the robustness of our analysis to multiple specifications and controls suggests that we have significant and stable estimates.

It might seem that the effects found in our analysis are too small to justify the creation of a self-regulatory institution. Indeed, we are agnostic regarding whether or not these effects drove the observed behavior. We do believe that firms were concerned with the potential for larger accidents to have a serious effect on market values, and industry experts confirmed that these fears provided some of the impetus for self-regulation. We also believe that the response of the stock market to each of the smaller accidents analyzed in our study provides a useful test of the functioning of the institution.

In summary, our analysis suggests that Bhopal indeed increased the interdependence of firms with chemical operations in such a way that an accident at one would have a negative effect on another. Our analysis also suggests that Responsible Care reduced this spillover effect, but it did so not by insulating its members from the consequences of accidents at other facilities but by reducing the industrywide consequences of accidents at Responsible Care facilities.

DISCUSSION AND CONCLUSION

In this article, we have explained industry self-regulation occurring when physical commons are absent. We posited that firms in modern industries share in a nonphysical type of commons—what some have termed a "reputation commons" (King et al., 2002)—that stems from the difficulty that stakeholders face in distinguishing the relative performance of individual firms and from the application of arbitrary or industrywide sanctions. We hypothesized that the risks associated with this commons can become particularly acute following a major industry crisis. We further hypothesized that industries create self-regulatory institutions as a means of ameliorating this heightened threat of shared sanctions.

Through a longitudinal analysis, we found that firms in the U.S. chemical industry did face such an industry commons and that the shared sanctions stemming from this commons became more severe after the industry suffered a major crisis caused by an accident in Bhopal, India. Furthermore, we found that this increased risk of shared sanctions preceded the creation of the industry's self-regulatory program, Responsible Care, and that Responsible Care was able to ameliorate industrywide harm from the errors of individual chemical firms. Thus, in finding that an aggravated commons problem led to the formation of a governing institution and that the institution operated to reduce this problem, our study provides a "good functionalism" perspective on the role of self-regulation in modern industry.

We also explored the mechanism through which Responsible Care functioned. We found that it reduced industrywide harm resulting from the errors of Responsible Care members, but we found no evidence that it provided members more protection from spillovers than nonmembers. Thus, member firms appear to have provided a public benefit to the industry, and the need to coordinate this benefit may have provided a key motivation for the institution's creation.

In *Mending Wall*, the poet Robert Frost wrote of a type of self-regulation of a physical commons, in the form of a tradition that caused neighbors to cooperate in the creation of stone walls between their properties. Each winter, storms and hunters knocked down some stones in these walls, and every spring Frost would "let [his] neighbor know beyond the hill" that they need to "meet to walk the line, and set the wall between us once again." But, as he worked on the wall one year, he wondered why they were remaking it and asked his neighbor:

> He only says, "Good fences make good neighbors."
> Spring is the mischief in me, and I wonder
> if I could put a notion in his head:
> "Why do they make good neighbors? Isn't it
> where there are cows?"
> But here there are no cows.
> Before I built a wall I'd ask to know
> what I was walling in or walling out, . . .

Our analysis suggests that firms in the chemical industry, like Frost and his neighbor, share in the construction of a wall between them. We found that they "wall in" the effects of their own accidents rather than "wall out" the effects of others'. Responsible Care appears to serve the function of ensuring that each firm maintains its walls and so protects its neighbors from the harm its accidents could otherwise cause the broader industry.

Though skepticism about cooperative solutions to commons problems has a lengthy history in scholarship (Hardin, 1968; Lloyd, 1833/1968), as illustrated in Frost's poem, traditions of mending fences to prevent spillover harm have a lengthy history in practice. Societies all over the world have developed norms to ensure that each member acts to protect his neighbor. Indeed, the very normalcy of such traditions represents the culmination of Frost's poem. Speaking of his neighbor, Frost writes, "He will not go behind his father's saying/ And he likes having thought of it so well/ He says again, 'Good fences make good neighbors.' "

Our analysis suggests that analogs to such traditional responses can be found in modern industries. Firms unite with rivals to ensure that each protects the other from a future problem. Because they are "walling in" their own effect on their neighbors, firms cannot achieve such results independently. Rather, at-risk firms must come together to create an institution that helps ensure that each protects its neighbor, so that, in the aggregate, all are subject to less harm.

Implications

Our study suggests a revised interpretation of recent research on industry self-regulation. As discussed earlier, many of these studies show that self-regulatory programs have not measurably improved firm performance (Howard et al., 2000; King & Lenox, 2000; Rivera & de Leon, 2004; Rivera, de Leon, & Koerber, 2006). As a result, scholars have tended to conclude that such programs are a failure and have blamed such failure on the inability of industry associations to control the behavior of member firms. Our analysis suggests that this skepticism may be based on an incorrect assumption about the institutions' function. Rather than acting as a means of improving firm performance or of signaling unobserved attributes, these institutions may be acting to directly reduce the probability of stakeholder sanctions by encouraging firms to engage in greater outreach and communication. From contemporaneous accounts, we know that such outreach occurred following the formation of Responsible Care. Using quantitative data over a number of years, we found evidence consistent with a hypothesis that such outreach and communication may have a positive effect on stakeholder relations, regardless of the performance of the member firms, and so can aid in reducing spillover harm.

Our research also suggests that an industry can maintain a self-regulatory institution, even when it provides benefit to nonmembers. Our findings suggest that the institution examined here protected all firms from the errors of its members. Thus, participants in the program provided a public good to the industry. Despite the incentive of a free ride, however, firms agreed to participate and (over the years of our analysis, at least) the program provided a benefit to the industry. Thus, in accordance with Ostrom's (1990) work demonstrating that actors can self-regulate to avoid destruction of physical commons, we have demonstrated that firms can voluntarily come together to protect an intangible industry commons, despite the risk of free riding.

For policy makers, our research reveals that private institutions may substitute in part for public regulation on information disclosure. The need to prevent spillover harm can help drive the creation of institutions that require the disclosure of information to stakeholders. Thus, government programs on information disclosure should be analyzed by considering both their direct effect on firm behavior and their indirect effect on the formation and function of self-regulatory institutions.

Limitations and Future Research

Although our study addresses several long-standing issues, it also raises several new ones. We used stock price movements to measure changes in stakeholder expectations about firms over time, following specific industry events. This methodology did not allow us to observe the mechanisms that created changes in stakeholders' expectations of a firm's future performance. We did not directly observe, for example, the provision of information from the firm to these stakeholders. In our particular empirical setting, we noted that the CAER program, which is at the core of Responsible Care, requires members to engage in significant communication with stakeholders, but we did not actually measure the degree to which members abided by these requirements. In future research, we hope to directly evaluate differences in communication rates and styles among participants and nonparticipants. We encourage others to further investigate how outreach and communication reduce spillovers rather than focusing on performance differences between members and nonmembers of self-regulatory industry institutions.

In our study, we described industry self-regulation as a private decentralized institution, but it typically involves some central authority. In examples such as Responsible Care, there exists a governing body that oversees compliance with the program's codes. However, compliance is often gauged through self-reporting, and punishment tends to be limited or nonexistent, given antitrust concerns, as well as the institution's desire to retain as many members as possible. Thus, even in exemplary and robust instances such as Responsible Care, industry self-regulation tends toward a decentralized model, relying on peer pressure for compliance. Nonetheless, we could also have categorized Responsible Care as a hybrid form of private institution, since it contains both centralized and decentralized aspects.

This argument suggests that Ingram and Clay's (2000) centralized-decentralized dichotomy for institutions might better be treated as a continuum, and it raises the question of how institutions choose to position themselves along this continuum, both initially and over time. Our study addresses temporal changes, but it does not address changes within the ACC program itself. Responsible Care started as a primarily decentralized institution, but over time it has shifted toward more centralized authority. The program evolved over the 1990s as new codes were hammered out and

1166   *Academy of Management Journal*   December

promulgated to members. After our study time frame ended, Responsible Care's leadership changed—in part because of several articles that suggested the program had not reduced the pollution generated by its members—and reportedly, with the new leadership, the "velvet glove came off" and some members were disciplined for their lax behavior (Reisch, 1998). Future research should investigate how self-regulatory programs balance centralization and decentralization and the stringency of enforcement in order to attract members without diminishing the legitimacy of the institution, as well as how this balance changes over time. The drivers of such changes are poorly understood. Weak enforcement may be necessary to attract members, yet the appearance that standards are enforced may be essential to maintaining the legitimacy of a program in the eyes of observers. In future research, we hope to explore the drivers and mechanisms of these changes.

Finally, our study does not resolve the issue of why firms choose to participate in self-regulatory programs. If participating firms essentially "wall in" their spillovers, safeguarding the rest of the industry, then an institution provides a pure public good. Given the dominating incentive to free ride on pure public goods (Olson, 1965), how then does the institution hold together? Scholars have suggested that the incestuous nature of the chemical industry allows bilateral sanctions that enforce participation. According to Rees, "The chemical industry is its own best customer" (1997: 489), and large firms use their power over subordinate suppliers as "leverage" (Gunningham, 1995: 85) to obtain their compliance. Yet, aside from a few anecdotes, such sanctions remain unobserved. In future research, we hope to further explore the centripetal forces that hold this and similar institutions together.

Despite these limitations, our research makes a significant contribution to emerging scholarship on self-regulatory institutions and broadens understanding of what constitutes a commons problem and how such problems may be resolved. It shows that exchange problems caused by shared reputation and risk of sanction exist in modern industries. It shows that a major crisis can intensify problems associated with this industry commons. Finally, it shows that when faced with exchange problems caused by these commons, the choice is not between "Leviathan or oblivion" (Ophuls, 1973: 215). Industry members can take matters into their own hands and repair shared problems by forging a new institution.

REFERENCES

Acheson, J. M. 1988. *The lobster gangs of Maine.* Hanover, NH: Dartmouth University Press.

Acheson, J. M., & Knight, J. 2000. Distribution fights, coordination games, and lobster management. *Comparative Studies in Society and History,* 42(1): 209–238.

Barnett, M. L. 2006. Finding a working balance between competitive and communal strategy. *Journal of Management Studies,* 43: 1753–1773.

Barnett, M. L., & Hoffman, A. J. 2008. Beyond corporate reputation: Managing reputational interdependence. *Corporate Reputation Review,* 11: 1–9.

Baron, D. P. 1995. The nonmarket strategy system. *Sloan Management Review,* 37(1): 73–85.

Barret, S. 2000. International environmental agreements: Feasibility, efficiency, stability. In H. Siebert (Ed.), *The economics of international environmental problems:* 111–124. Tübingen: Mohr Siebeck.

Begley, R. 1994. After Bhopal: A CMA "war room," new programs, and changed habits. *Chemical Week,* December 7: 32.

Berkes, F. 1989. *Common property resources: Ecology and community-based sustainable development.* London, U.K.: Belhaven Press.

Blacconiere, W., & Patten, D. 1994. Environmental disclosures, regulatory costs, and changes in firm value. *Journal of Accounting and Economics,* 18: 357–377.

Blackman, A., & Boyd, J. 2002. Tailored regulation: Will voluntary site-specific environmental performance standards improve welfare? *Southern Economic Journal,* 69: 309–326.

Brown, S., & Warner, J. 1980. Measuring security price performance. *Journal of Financial Economics,* 8: 205–258.

Brown, S., & Warner, J. 1985. Using daily stock returns: The case of event studies. *Journal of Financial Economics,* 14: 3–31.

CCPA. 2007. *http://www.ccpa.ca/ResponsibleCare/,* accessed July 1.

Coombes, P. 1991. Union Carbide. *Chemical Week,* July 17: 44.

Corbett, C. J., Montes-Sancho, M. J., & Kirsch, D. A. 2005. The financial impact of ISO 9000 certification in the United States: An empirical analysis. *Management Science,* 51: 1046–1059.

Dawson, N. L., & Segerson, K. 2005. *Voluntary environmental agreements with industries: Participation incentives with industry-wide targets.* Working paper, University of Connecticut.

Ember, L. R. 1995. Responsible Care: Chemical makers still counting on it to improve image. *Chemical and Engineering News,* May 29: 10–18.

EPA. 1999. *Introduction to the National Pretreatment Program* (EPA-833-B-98-002). Washington, DC: U.S. Government Printing Office.

Fama, E., & French, K. 1992. The cross-section of expected stock returns. *Journal of Finance,* 47: 427–465.

Fombrun, C. 1996. *Reputation: Realizing value from the corporate image.* Boston: Harvard Business School Press.

Furger, F. 1997. Accountability and systems of self-governance: The case of the maritime industry. *Law and Policy,* 19: 445–476.

Furman, J., & Stern, S. 2006. *Climbing atop the shoulders of giants: The impact of institutions on cumulative research.* National Bureau of Economic Research working paper no.12523, Cambridge, MA.

Galvin, L. 2007. Outbreak linked to spinach forces reassessment of food safety practices. *Amber Waves: The Economics of Food, Farming, Natural Resources and Rural America,* 5(3): 25–31.

Gibson, W. D. 1985a. After Bhopal: First aid for chemicals' public image. *Chemical Week,* February 20: 21–22.

Gibson, W. D. 1985b. Olive branch activity prevails after Institute. *Chemical Week,* October 16: 90–91.

Granovetter, M. 1985. Economic action and social structure: The problem of embeddedness. *American Journal of Sociology,* 91: 481–510.

Greening, D., & Johnson, R. 1997. Managing industrial and environmental crises: The role of heterogeneous top management teams. *Business & Society,* 36: 334–361.

Greenwood, R., Suddaby, R., & Hinings, C. 2002. Theorizing change: The role of professional associations in the transformation of institutionalized fields. *Academy of Management Journal,* 45: 58–80.

Gunderson, L. H., Holling, C. S., & Light, S. S. 1995. Barriers broken and bridges built. In L. H. Gunderson, C. S. Holling, & S. S. Light (Eds.), *Barriers and bridges to the renewal of ecosystems and institutions:* 489–533. New York: Columbia University Press.

Gunningham, N. 1995. Environment, self-regulation, and the chemical industry: Assessing Responsible Care. *Law & Policy,* 17: 57–108.

Gunningham, N., & Rees, J. 1997. Industry self-regulation: An institutional perspective. *Law & Policy,* 19: 363–414.

Gupta, A., & Lad, L. 1983. Industry self-regulation: An economic, organizational, and political analysis. *Academy of Management Review,* 8: 416–425.

Hamilton, J. 1995. Pollution as news: Media and stock market reactions to the TRI data. *Journal of Environmental Economics and Management,* 28: 98–113.

Hannan, M., & Carroll, G. 1992. *Dynamics of organizational populations: Density, legitimation, and competition.* New York: Oxford University Press.

Hardin, G. 1968. The tragedy of the commons. *Science,* 162: 1243–1248.

Heller, K. 1991. Public outreach: The stakes are high. *Chemical Week,* July 17: 81–84.

Heller, K., & Hunter, D. 1994. Responsible Care. *Chemical Week,* July 6: 31.

Hill, J., & Schneeweis, T. 1983. The effect of Three Mile Island on electric utility stock prices: A note. *Journal of Finance,* 38: 1285–1292.

Hoffman, A. 1997. *From heresy to dogma: An institutional history of corporate environmentalism.* San Francisco: New Lexington Press.

Hoffman, A. 1999. Institutional evolution and change: Environmentalism and the U.S. chemical industry. *Academy of Management Journal,* 42: 351–371.

Hoffman, A., & Ocasio, W. 2001. Not all events are attended equally: Toward a middle-range theory of industry attention to external events. *Organization Science:* 414–434.

Hornblower, M. 2000. Wake up and smell the protest. *Time,* 155(15): 58.

Howard, J., Nash, J., & Ehrenfeld, J. 2000. Standard or smokescreen? Implementation of a voluntary environmental code. *California Management Review,* 42(2): 63–82.

Ingram, P., & Clay, K. 2000. The choice-within-constraints new institutionalism and implications for sociology. In K. S. Cook & J. Hagan (Eds.), *Annual review of sociology,* vol. 26: 525–546. Palo Alto, CA: Annual Reviews.

Ingram, P., & Inman, C. 1996. Institutions, intergroup rivalry, and the evolution of hotel populations around Niagara Falls. *Administrative Science Quarterly,* 41: 629–658.

Jarrell, G., & Peltzman, S. 1985. The impact of product recalls on the wealth of sellers. *Journal of Political Economy,* 93: 512–536.

Jiang, R. H. J., & Bansal, P. 2003. Seeing the need for ISO 14001. *Journal of Management Studies,* 40: 1047–1067.

Katzenberg, D. 1985. Liability insurance: The added burden of Bhopal. *Chemical Week,* February 13: 30.

King, A., & Lenox, M. 2000. Industry self-regulation without sanctions: The chemical industry's Responsible Care program. *Academy of Management Journal,* 43: 698–716.

King, A., Lenox, M., & Barnett, M. 2002. Strategic responses to the reputation commons problem. In A. Hoffman & M. Ventresca (Eds.), *Organizations, policy and the natural environment: Institutional and strategic perspectives:* 393–406. Stanford, CA: Stanford University Press.

Lenox, M. J. 2006. The role of private decentralized institutions in sustaining industry self-regulation. *Organization Science*, 17: 677–690.

Lloyd, W. F. 1833/1968. *Two lectures on the checks to population.* Oxford, U.K.: Augustus M. Kelley.

Maitland, I. 1985. The limits of business self-regulation. *California Management Review*, 27(3): 132–147.

Malkin, E. 1996. Pangs of conscience. *BusinessWeek*, July 29: 46–47.

McWilliams, A., & Siegel, D. 1997. Event studies in management research: Theoretical and empirical issues. *Academy of Management Journal*, 40: 626–657.

Meyer, A. 1982. Adapting to environmental jolts. *Administrative Science Quarterly*, 27: 515–537.

Meyer, A., Brooks, G., & Goes, J. 1990. Environmental jolts and industry revolutions: Organizational responses to discontinuous change. *Strategic Management Journal* (special issue): 93–110.

Mitchell, M. 1989. The impact of external parties on brandname capital: The 1982 Tylenol poisonings and subsequent cases. *Economic Inquiry*, 27: 601–618.

North, D. C. 1981. *Structure and change in economic history.* New York: Norton.

North, D. C. 1990. *Institutions, institutional change and economic performance.* Cambridge, U.K.: Cambridge University Press.

Olson, M. 1965. *The logic of collective action: Public goods and the theory of groups.* Cambridge, MA: Harvard University Press.

Ophuls, W. 1973. Leviathan or oblivion? In H. E. Daly (Ed.), *Toward a steady state economy:* 215–230. San Francisco: Freeman.

Ostrom, E. 1990. *Governing the commons: The evolution of institutions for collective action.* Cambridge, U.K.: Cambridge University Press.

Ostrom, E. 2000. Collective action and the evolution of social norms. *Journal of Economic Perspectives*, 14: 137–158.

Patten, D., & Nance, J. 1998. Regulatory cost effects in a good news environment: The intra-industry reaction to the Alaskan oil spill. *Journal of Accounting and Public Policy*, 17: 409–429.

Prakash, A., & Potoski, M. 2006. *The voluntary environmentalist: Green clubs, ISO 14001, and voluntary environmental regulations.* Cambridge, U.K.: Cambridge University Press.

Rees, J. 1994. *Hostages of each other: The transformation of nuclear safety since Three Mile Island.* Chicago: University of Chicago Press.

Rees, J. 1997. The development of communitarian regu-

lation in the chemical industry. *Law and Policy*, 19: 477–528.

Reisch, M. 1998. Industry ponders future of Responsible Care. *Chemical and Engineering News*, May 5: 13.

Rivera, J., & deLeon, P. 2004. Is greener whiter? The sustainable slopes program and voluntary environmental performance of western ski areas. *Policy Studies Journal*, 32: 417–437.

Rivera, J., de Leon, P., & Koerber, C. 2006. Is greener whiter yet? The sustainable slopes program after five years. *Policy Studies Journal*, 34: 195–221.

Schotter, A. 1981. *The economic theory of social institutions.* New York: Cambridge University Press.

Shrivastava, P. 1987. *Bhopal: Anatomy of a crisis.* Cambridge, MA: Ballinger.

Shrivastava, P., & Siomkos, G. 1989. Disaster containment strategies. *Journal of Business Strategy*, 10(5): 26–31.

Slovic, P., & Weber, E. U. 2002. *Perception of risk posed by extreme events.* Paper presented at the Risk Management Strategies in an Uncertain World Conference, Palisades, NY, April 12–13.

Spar, D. L., & La Mure, L. T. 2003. The power of activism: Assessing the impact of NGOs on global business. *California Management Review*, 45(3): 78–102.

Spence, A. M. 1973. Job market signaling. *Quarterly Journal of Economics*, 87: 355–374.

Stefanadis C. 2003. Self-regulation, innovation, and the financial industry. *Journal of Regulatory Economics*, 23: 5–25.

Terlaak, A., & King, A. 2006. The effect of certification with the ISO 9000 quality management standard: A signaling approach. *Journal of Economic Behavior and Organization*, 60: 579–602.

Tirole, J. 1996. A theory of collective reputations. *Review of Economic Studies*, 63: 1–22.

Vasi, I. B., & Macy, M. 2003. The mobilizer's dilemma: Crisis, empowerment, and collective action. *Social Forces*, 81: 979–998.

Wade, R. 1988. *Village republics: Economic conditions for collective action in South India.* Oakland, CA: ICS Press.

Weber, J. M., Kopelman, S., & Messick, D. 2004. A conceptual review of decision making in social dilemmas: Applying a logic of appropriateness. *Personality and Social Psychology Review*, 8(3): 281–307.

Williamson, O. E. 1985. *The economic institutions of capitalism: Firms, markets, and relational contracting.* New York: Free Press.

Yu, T., Sengul, M., & Lester, R. 2008. Misery loves company: The spread of negative impacts resulting from an organizational crisis. *Academy of Management Review*, 33: 452–472.

APPENDIX A

Calculation of Cumulative Abnormal Return (CAR)

To calculate CAR, we first calculated the relationship between the value of each company's stock and the market as a whole (measured by the CRSP value-weighted index with dividends for the entire market):

$$R_{it} = a_i + B_i R_{mt} + e_{it},$$

where R_{it} represents the value of the security i on day t, a_i is a constant, R_{mt} represents the value of the market portfolio for day t, B_i represents the beta of security i, and e_{it} represents the error term. Beta is computed over the period $t = -254$ to $t = -1$, where $t = 0$ is the day of the event.

The abnormal return of a stock is the difference between the actual return of that stock and its expected return. The abnormal return of security i at time t, $AR_{it,}$ is:

$$AR_{it} = R_{it} - (a_i + B_i R_{mt}).$$

The cumulative abnormal return for a firm, CAR_i, is the sum of abnormal returns over the event window:

$$CAR_i = \sum AR_{it}.$$

To allow for continuous compounding when aggregating the abnormal returns, $\ln(1 + R)$ is used in place of R. Thus,

$$CAR_i = \sum [\ln(1 + R_{it}) - (a + B_{im}\ln(1 + R_{mt}))].$$

Key to computation of CAR is determination of the event window, the period of time over which to cumulate abnormal returns. Event studies commonly begin the event window prior to the actual event announcement in order to account for information leakage, but dangerous accidents are, by nature, unanticipated events. Therefore, in this study, if the event occurred during trading hours on a trading day, the window begins that day; if not, the window begins with the next trading day.

While it is straightforward to choose the beginning of the event window for this study, it is less clear when to close the window. The occurrence and magnitude of events sometimes take several days to become apparent to the market. News travels fast and markets update their values nearly instantaneously, yet many characteristics of major accidents take time to establish. For example, the enormous toll of Bhopal took many days to unfold, and the magnitude of the Exxon Valdez oil spill was not immediately evident. Whereas a long event window increases the likelihood of capturing the full impact of unfolding events, a long event window also increases the opportunity for intervening events to confound results (McWilliams & Siegel, 1997). Therefore, researchers should use the shortest possible window that captures the fullest extent of an event. The bulk of the effects tended to occur within five days after the events. Thus, our dependent variable in this study is the cumulative abnormal return on the fifth day after an event.

APPENDIX B

TABLE B1
Direct Effect of Accidents on At-Fault Firms[a]

Variable	Model 1	Model 2	Model 3
Employee killed		−2.60** (1.06)	−2.25** (1.10)
Employee injured		−1.72 (1.15)	−1.50 (1.15)
Assets of perpetrator			0.73* (0.38)
ACC member			−1.69[†] (1.20)
Pre-Bhopal			−1.33 (1.95)
Post–Responsible Care			0.29 (1.17)
Constant	−1.01* (0.51)	1.13 (1.06)	−4.86 (3.92)
R^2		.08	.16

[a] $n = 92$.
[†] $p < .10$
[*] $p < .05$
[**] $p < .01$

APPENDIX C

Probit Analysis of ACC Participation

TABLE C1
Descriptive Statistics for All Years (1980–2000)[a]

Variable	Mean	s.d.	1	2
1. Industry emissions	9.58	2.52		
2. Chemical focus	0.54	0.48	.10	
3. Assets	4.49	2.37	.20	−.15

[a] $n = 5,073$.

TABLE C2
Results of Probit Analysis of ACC Membership[a]

Variable	Membership in 1990
Industry emissions	0.15** (0.05)
Chemical focus	0.61* (0.30)
Assets	0.40** (0.06)
Constant	−5.45** (0.64)
n	276
χ^2	74.24
Pseudo-R^2	.38

[a] We estimated separate probit models for each year from 1980 to 2000 to obtain the Mills ratio and included it in the second-stage regression estimation to reduce the effect of non-random treatment. Inclusion of this term accounts for changes in the expectation of the treatment coefficient but does not correct for heteroskedastic changes in the error terms that result from nonrandom treatment. We used a standard White's method to help correct for these effects.
[*] $p < .05$
[**] $p < .01$

————————ᴧᴧ————————

Michael L. Barnett (mbarnett@coba.usf.edu) is an associate professor of strategic management and Exide Professor of Sustainable Enterprise at the University of South Florida. He received his Ph.D. in management and organizational behavior from New York University. In his research he tries to "enlighten" the notion of self-interest by investigating how, when, and if firms can use forecasting, real options, corporate social responsibility, industry self-regulation, trade associations, Zen teachings, and other perspectives, techniques, and individual and collective forms of organizing to their long-term strategic advantage.

Andrew A. King (aking@hbs.edu) is a visiting associate professor in the Technology and Operations Management Unit at the Harvard Business School and an associate professor at the Tuck School of Business at Dartmouth. He received his Ph.D. from the Sloan School of Management at the Massachusetts Institute of Technology. He holds degrees in engineering from the University of California, Berkeley, and Brown University.

————————ᴧᴧ————————

[8]

Journal of Management Studies 43:8 December 2006
0022-2380

▰▰▰▰▰▰

Finding a Working Balance Between Competitive and Communal Strategies*

Michael L. Barnett

University of South Florida

ABSTRACT This paper presents a dynamic framework that describes how firms allocate limited resources between improving their competitive position relative to rivals and their communal position shared with rivals. This dynamic framework outlines how organizational field-level dynamics influence industry attractiveness and thereby alter a firm's incentive to engage in communal strategy relative to competitive strategy. Communal strategy, in turn, can influence the institutions governing an organizational field and thereby shape industry attractiveness. Overall, the interplay between factors exogenous and endogenous to an industry cause change in an organizational field and so determine the nature of the communal environment shared by a firm and its rivals over time. Analysis of this interplay provides insight into the micro-level drivers of macro-level change and furthers understanding of the conditions under which rivalrous firms voluntarily contribute to collective betterment of their industry despite collective rationality.

INTRODUCTION

Rivals are also roommates. Though they compete against each other, rival firms share an industry. The structure of this industry significantly influences the performance and survival of each of the firms that reside within it (Bain, 1956; Mason, 1939; Porter, 1980). Because both firm and industry characteristics 'matter' (Rumelt, 1991, p. 167; McGahan and Porter, 1997, p. 15), firms should manage *both* in order to maximize performance and survival. Management scholars have intensively studied the strategies that firms use to compete against their rivals, and management scholars have given considerable attention to the strategies that groups of firms use to jointly manage some shared aspects of their environments. However, the management literature has given little attention to the strategies that firms use to influence industry characteristics (Aldrich, 1999; Barnett et al., 2000; Barringer and Harrison, 2000), and it has effectively ignored the dynamic tension that firms necessarily face in allocating limited resources between independently managing their competitive characteristics and collectively managing their industry

Address for reprints: Michael L. Barnett, University of South Florida, College of Business Administration, BSN 3213, Department of Management & Organization, 4202 E. Fowler Avenue, Tampa, FL 33620-5500, USA (mbarnett@coba.usf.edu).

characteristics. Tension exists because resources expended on managing industry characteristics are resources diverted from managing competitive positioning, and vice versa. An adequate understanding of how firms safeguard their survival and maximize performance necessarily entails an understanding of how firms dynamically manage this tension. More boldly stated by Astley and Fombrun (1983, p. 585), 'The most basic operational requirement in the formulation and implementation of strategy, therefore, is to establish a working balance between these opposing pressures.'

In this paper, I develop a dynamic framework that explains how firms strategically allocate their limited resources between independent efforts to improve their competitive position and cooperative efforts to improve their industry's position. This framework is premised on the notion that a firm's strategic interests fluctuate in accordance with changes in the broader organizational field in which it is embedded. Organizational fields are contentious 'arenas of power relations' (Brint and Karabel, 1991, p. 355) with differing groups – firms that produce similar products or services (i.e. an industry), as well as their key suppliers, resource and product consumers, and regulatory agencies (DiMaggio and Powell, 1983, p. 143) – vying to gain the power to alter the institutions or 'rules of the game' (North, 1990, p. 3) governing the field in their favour (see also Hoffman, 1999; Ingram, 1998; Scott, 1995; Vaara et al., 2004). Institutional change can be brought about by cooperation across an industry or among other groups in an organization field (DiMaggio, 1988). When institutions change, an industry can become more or less attractive for the firms within it (Hirsch, 1975; Ingram and Inman, 1996; Miles, 1982).

As institutional change alters industry attractiveness, the working balance of those firms within it will change, as revealed by the ratio of each firm's resources allocated to competitive positioning versus allocated to industry positioning. For example, a consumer group lobbying for regulatory change that threatens the autonomy of an industry increases the likelihood that firms in the industry will shift resources to a cooperative effort to mitigate or overturn this threatened regulatory change. As industry-wide cooperation succeeds in protecting or improving industry attractiveness, the working balance of those firms within the industry will again change.

Based on this dynamic framework, I develop a set of propositions that describe how, even in the face of rivalry and the collective action problem (Olson, 1965), firm-level self-interest aggregates into patterns of industry-level cooperation, and how this cooperation, in turn, produces institutional change that affects the performance of the members of an organizational field. Overall, the framework and propositions developed herein advance our understanding of how 'strategically interdependent organizations navigate between the Scylla of cutthroat competition and the Charybdis of group marriages of reason' (Pennings, 1981, p. 434).

SHARED FATE AND COMMUNAL STRATEGY

More than two decades ago, Astley and Fombrun (1983) criticized strategic management's traditional emphasis on the firm as the sole unit of analysis. Noting that strategic management concerns itself with how organizations adapt to their changing environments, they argued that organizational adaptation, analogous to biological adaptation, is both individual and communal. Strategy, in focusing on individual (i.e. firm) adaptation,

Competitive and Communal Strategies   1755

was overlooking the fact that environmental change can cause the maladaption or extinction of entire industries, not merely individual firms: 'Like the dinosaur, the buggy-whip manufacturer went out of business because it was adapted to a domain that no longer existed' (Astley and Fombrun, 1983, p. 579). Therefore, though they need to manage their individual characteristics to stand apart from rivals, firms must also concern themselves with the fate they share with rivals.

Astley and Fombrun (1983) called for strategy research to account for communal adaptation. They argued that firms manage communal adaptation through 'collective strategy: the joint mobilization of resources and formulation of action within collectivities of organizations' (Astley and Fombrun, 1983, p. 578), and so collective strategy should be a topic of extensive research. Over the past few decades, researchers have heeded their call, and the calls of others, to study collective strategy (see Oliver, 1990, and Barringer and Harrison, 2000, for reviews). However, the resulting literature has generally stopped short of addressing collective strategy as a means of managing the communal adaptation of entire industries.

The literature on collective strategy has largely focused on cooperation within dyads or small groups of firms through joint ventures and alliances (e.g. Contractor and Lorange, 1988; Hennart, 1988; Kogut, 1988; Pfeffer and Nowak, 1976; Porter, 1985; Powell, 1990). These small groups may include a firm and some of its rivals, suppliers, buyers, or even 'complementors' (Brandenburger and Nalebuff, 1996, p. 16). Cooperation up and down a firm's value chain, as well as joint ventures, alliances, networks and other cooperative relations among a subset of firms within an industry or across complementary industries are now deeply entrenched in the literature. Researchers have found such cooperative relationships to be an effective way to share knowledge and improve competitive position. As Lado et al. (1997, p. 111) surmised, '. . . cooperation can enhance the competitive position of a firm. For example, Toyota's cooperation with its suppliers enhances its competitive position in the global automobile industry (Hill, 1995). Similarly, the cooperation between Ford and Mazda on design issues makes each firm a more capable competitor in the product market.'

These types of collective strategy – group versus group network rivalry (Gomes-Casseres, 1994), competitive collaboration (Hamel et al., 1989), collaborative advantage (Lado et al., 1997), and co-opetition (Brandenburger and Nalebuff, 1996) – are additional means of improving competitive position within an industry, not a means of improving the position of an industry relative to its environment. Cooperation to better the position of an entire industry, not just to gain advantage for a single firm or group of firms within it, has received little attention (Aldrich, 1999; Barnett et al., 2000; Barringer and Harrison, 2000). Nonetheless, such forms of cooperation are ubiquitous in practice.

The primary manifestation of industry-wide cooperation is trade association activity, given its allowance under US antitrust laws (Astley and Fombrun, 1983). There are thousands of trade associations within the USA (Aldrich and Staber, 1988). Almost every industry is represented by at least one, and almost every firm is a member of at least one. Firms in an industry may cooperate in other ways to improve their shared positions, but these other ways either focus on the betterment of industry subgroups, or they are tacit, illegal, or simply subsumed within the scope of trade associations. For

1756   M. L. Barnett

example, Astley and Fombrun (1983, p. 581) listed several structures for coordinating collective strategy other than trade associations, to include cartels, collusion, informal leadership, interlocking directorates, and joint ventures. Cartels and collusion are illegal in the USA. Informal leadership is a tacit form of collusion, and so illegal as well. Except in highly concentrated industries, it is not feasible for a set of directors to interlock across an entire industry, and so interlocking directorates tend to serve only the interests of a subgroup of an industry. Likewise, it is improbable that a joint venture would include all the members of an industry. Bresser (1988) also mentioned collective lobbying as a form of collective strategy. Collective lobbying can serve the interests of entire industries, but such activities are often subsumed within industry trade associations. Thus, trade associations provide the primary legal means of intentional coordination of industry-wide efforts.

It is not only the scope but also the aim of industry-wide cooperation through trade association activity that makes it different from that of the more commonly studied forms of collective strategy. Rather than seek to use cooperation to better compete within the established rules of the game, trade associations seek to influence the rules themselves (cf. Holm, 1995). Prior studies of collective strategy have focused on ways in which firms can increase their technical capabilities through cooperation by gaining access to the resources of other firms (Barringer and Harrison, 2000). For example, Ford and Mazda cooperated to share knowledge about automobile design issues, thereby extending the technical capabilities either would have in isolation (Lado et al., 1997). Trade association activity is aimed primarily at influencing the shared environment in which member firms compete for resources, not at creating resources. According to Aldrich (1999, p. 240), trade associations 'conduct marketing campaigns to enhance the industry's standing in the eyes of the public and promote trade fairs at which customers and suppliers can gain a sense of the industry's stability'. They 'attempt to influence . . . those organizations that define and regulate the context within which all transactions occur' (Scott, 1981, p. 199). Thus, industry-wide cooperation typically is not a strategy that firms use to jointly develop new technology, but instead primarily serves as a form of 'institutional strategy': 'patterns of action that are concerned with managing the institutional structures within which firms compete for resources' (Lawrence, 1999, p. 162).

Through trade associations, firms can legally present a united front and speak with a unified voice. Such collective efforts are critical to shaping the rules of the game in the industry's favour (DiMaggio, 1988), and so industry-wide cooperation can bring about significant improvements in the performance and survival rates of the members of an industry. The coordinated effort of hoteliers around Niagara Falls overcame common problems that threatened their growth and prosperity (Ingram and Inman, 1996). The Tobacco Institute protected cigarette manufacturers from a variety of lawsuits and regulations that likely would have resulted in even greater harm to the industry (Miles, 1982). The coordinated might of the pharmaceutical industry enabled it to co-opt critical resource holders and thereby gain higher average profits and survival rates than the recording industry, despite the similar structural characteristics of these two industries (Hirsch, 1975). Industry-wide cooperation through trade associations is particularly critical to recovery from crises that face entire industries (King and Lenox, 2000). By presenting a united front and speaking with a unified voice, firms may collectively

Competitive and Communal Strategies   1757

'improve the legislative, regulatory, market, and public interest climate for the industry' (CMA, 1993) and so help to realign their industry with the demands of its environment (Hoffman, 1997).

To summarize, Astley and Fombrun (1983) argued that firms exert control over their shared environment through collective strategy to achieve, in ecological terms, communal adaptation, or in strategy terms, strategic fit. Collective strategy, as put forth by Astley and Fombrun (1983), incorporated collective efforts to improve industry position, but its common usage today excludes this. Studies of collective strategy have explored cooperation between a firm and its 'complementors' (Brandenburger and Nalebuff, 1996, p. 17), not rivals, and treated cooperation as a strategic tool to improve intra-industry competitive position (e.g. Dyer and Singh, 1998; Hamel and Prahalad, 1989; Teece, 1992). Studies have also explored cooperation among rivals, but focused on dyads and small groups, such as joint ventures and alliances. Even studies of larger network forms of cooperation pit one group of rivalrous firms against another (Gomes-Casseres, 1994). Cooperation to improve the standing of entire industries, despite its omnipresence and importance to the maintenance of strategic fit, has been largely overlooked.

Given standard usage of the term, it is necessary to distinguish the ubiquitous, unique, and critical activities related to industry positioning from those normally associated with collective strategy. Hereafter, this paper refers to a firm's allocation of resources to collective efforts to influence the institutions governing its industry as *communal strategy*. In contrast, this paper denotes the activities a firm undertakes to better position itself relative to rivals, even when these activities are pursued through collective action, as competitive strategy.

Communal strategy addresses gaps in the literature of not only collective strategy, but also that of institutional strategy (Lawrence, 1999). As with collective strategy, communal strategy could be subsumed within institutional strategy, but scholars of the broader concept have not focused on the domain I ascribe herein to communal strategy. Lawrence (1999, p. 168) focused institutional strategy on the role that individual people and individual organizations play as institutional entrepreneurs (DiMaggio, 1988). Thus, whereas collective strategy has tended to ignore institutions, institutional strategy has tended to ignore collectives. Communal strategy bridges these two broader concepts to address collective action aimed at forging institutional change.

The concept of communal strategy particularly draws out the complexity of the tension between competition and cooperation. The types of cooperation commonly addressed in the literature on collective strategy present fairly tractable problems. Firms that engage in cooperative relationships such as joint ventures and alliances can minimize exposure to free riding, asset hold-up, and other problems common to cooperation through the establishment of explicit, thorough, and legally enforceable contracts (Williamson, 1975). Even absent formal contracting, peer pressure and trust can overcome problems that jeopardize collective action so long as participants are few (Olson, 1965). However, communal strategy contributes to a public good – the betterment of an entire industry – produced through the collective action of a large number of rivalrous firms. Industry trade associations frequently have hundreds of member firms. Benefits are non-excludable in that all members of an industry benefit from the improved environment regardless of their participation, and participation is not enforceable due to antitrust laws. Moreover, communal strategy requires immediate firm-level resources while returning uncertain and largely intangible industry-level public goods in the future. Thus, the free rider problem is more acute in communal strategy than in other forms of collective strategy (cf. Aldrich, 1999, p. 240).

Communal strategy consumes limited resources – financial, such as membership dues in trade associations; physical, such as changes to a firm's property, plant, and equipment to abide by the code of an industry self-regulatory initiative; human, such as sweat equity, whereby firms provide personnel, including top management, to participate in and organize industry-wide initiatives – and returns an uncertain, distant, and public good. Thus, the primary challenge in formulating a working balance is in explaining why a rivalrous firm would ever choose to encumber itself with communal strategy in lieu of free riding. That is, 'There must be an explanation of the functional interdependencies . . . that induce organizations to . . . take on responsibilities as members of a larger social entity' (Astley and Fombrun, 1983, p. 586). The following section describes conditions under which interdependence changes, and how these changes in interdependence affect the degree to which firms engage in communal strategy.

TOWARDS A WORKING BALANCE

Industry Effects and Firm Performance

This paper assumes that firms engage in those activities that they believe to be instrumental to increasing their financial performance. When a firm allocates resources to communal strategy, it is not engaging in an act of altruism. Rather, a firm engages in communal strategy because its decision makers believe that such activity is the best way to use its limited resources to achieve the greatest financial returns. Therefore, in order to understand how a firm allocates its resources over time, one must first specify the determinants of firm performance.

Traditional strategic rationale notes that a firm seeks to capture the maximum amount of rent throughout its value chain (Porter, 1980). That is, a firm seeks to obtain its necessary inputs for the lowest possible price, transform these inputs into outputs by the most efficient means, and sell these outputs at the highest possible price at the largest feasible quantity, all subject to some strategically chosen level of quality, and all occurring under rivalry. To do so, a firm may strategically invest in research and development and other capital projects in order to build unique capabilities that allow it to sell more output at a higher price or produce more efficiently than rivals. A firm may negotiate with suppliers to obtain inputs at a lower price or higher quality than can rivals. A firm may diversify upstream, downstream, geographically, or even into unrelated markets in order to obtain greater market power. A firm may seek first mover advantage and launch new products in order to charge premium prices and capture market share, or a firm may produce existing products more efficiently. In sum, a firm has a variety of strategic options that it may pursue to position itself relative to rivals and so capture more profits.

However, a firm's ability to stand apart from its rivals only partially determines its performance. As the structuralist approach to strategy (Bain, 1956; Mason, 1939) has long argued, industry 'matters' (Rumelt, 1991). The characteristics that a firm shares

Competitive and Communal Strategies   1759

with its rivals – the nature of the industry itself – significantly influence financial performance. Schmalensee (1985) found that the industry of which a manufacturing firm was a member explained about 20 per cent of variance in profitability in 1975. Rumelt (1991, p. 167) looked at a four-year period and found that these 'industry effects' explained 9–16 per cent of the variance in profitability. More recently, with a much more extensive data set, McGahan and Porter (1997) found industry effects to be much closer to Schmalensee's original estimate. Sociological approaches to firm performance, likewise, confirm the relevance of industry effects, such as Hirsch's (1975) study of differing profit ranges for the pharmaceutical and recording industries.

Firm performance, then, 'can be decomposed into an industry effect and a positioning effect' (Porter, 1991, p. 100). The structural characteristics of some industries contribute to high profits for the firms within them, whereas others do not (Porter, 1980). As a result, the dominant firm in one industry may be unable to achieve the same level of profitability as a subordinate firm in another industry, no matter the effectiveness of its competitive strategy.

Though strategy scholars have shown that industry also matters to firms' performance, they have primarily modelled industry conditions as exogenous. The only role for strategy relative to industry effects has been in assessing the attractiveness of an industry at a point in time, and then choosing whether to enter or leave it. This is not surprising, given traditional emphasis on the firm as the sole unit of analysis. However, industry conditions are not entirely exogenous, and are particularly controllable when rivals cooperate. Through communal strategy, firms can and do strategically influence industry conditions, as discussed previously.

Stylistically, let us assume that a firm has two strategic levers, broadly classified, through which it can attempt to influence its performance. The commonly studied lever is that of competitive strategy, through which the firm may influence its positioning effect. The uncommonly studied lever is that of communal strategy, through which the firm may participate in efforts to influence its industry effect. As discussed later in this paper, there are other levers available to a firm (e.g. strategies to attempt to influence country or global effects on firm performance), but they offer less likelihood of collective influence over more remote determinants of performance. Thus, since positioning and industry effects determine a large portion of firm performance, such a stylistic assumption seems reasonable.

This paper assumes that a rational profit-maximizing firm will allocate its next unit of resources to whichever of these two broad categories of activity it expects to provide greater marginal returns. All else equal, a firm is likely to favour competitive strategy and shun communal strategy because collective action can 'limit discretion, control, and profit potential while demanding managerial attention and other resources of the firm' (Lifton, 1989, p. 4). On the other hand, it can be marginally more valuable to a firm to participate in collective efforts to stave off an industry's decline than to compete for better position within a declining industry. When industry matters more, communal strategy becomes more valuable, and so becomes a higher priority for firms.

There are points in time at which the expected marginal return to communal strategy increases and can sometimes even entirely overshadow competitive concerns (Barnett, 2002). An extreme example is the nuclear power industry following Three

Mile Island: 'It was a traumatic shock that transformed the industry's traditional habits of thought in fundamental ways by highlighting, as never before, the nuclear utilities' common interests and mutual interdependence . . . the industry was "pulled together" in trying to cope with "a common problem" ' (Rees, 1994, p. 43). The chemical and petroleum industries relay similar accounts following their respective shocks of Bhopal and *Exxon Valdez* (Hoffman, 1997). There are many less extreme examples. For example, protests and proposed legislation concerning the labour practices of apparel and footwear manufacturers brought these firms together to participate in an industry-wide effort called the Worldwide Responsible Apparel Production principles (WRAP, 2003). Industries commonly intensify their collective efforts when threatened by government regulation or loss of public approval (Gupta and Lad, 1983; King and Lenox, 2000; Maitland, 1985).

As industry effects constrain a firm's profitability, that firm is increasingly likely to take on the burden of communal strategy in order to attempt to increase its profitability. A firm may also choose to exit a declining industry, as addressed below in the section preceding Proposition 6, but conditioned on its decision to remain, one expects the following relationship to hold:

> *Proposition 1*: As a firm perceives industry effects to be an increasing constraint on its profitability, it will shift more of its resources away from competitive strategy and into communal strategy.

If the degree to which industry matters drives a firm's working balance, then what makes industry matter more or less? Industry effects are not static. McGahan and Porter (1997) found not only that industry matters, but also that industry mattered more in some economic sectors than in others, and more in some years than in others. However, this and similar other studies have provided no rationale for the underlying processes driving variation in an industry's influence on firm performance (McGahan and Porter, 1997, p. 15). The next section discusses why industry matters and proposes what drives it to matter more or less.

Organizational Field Dynamics, Collective Action, and Industry Effects

A firm is nested within an industry, and this has significant implications for its performance. However, a firm is also nested within an organization field, and this has significant implications for how much industry matters to its performance (cf. Holm, 1995). An organizational field encompasses 'those organizations that, in the aggregate, constitute a recognized area of institutional life: key suppliers, resource and product consumers, regulatory agencies, and other organizations that produce similar services or products' (DiMaggio and Powell, 1983, p. 143). In other words, an organizational field is an industry plus those constituents outside the industry that can influence the performance of the firms inside the industry (Scott, 1995, p. 83).

An organizational field arises as its members interact with each other and, over time, establish shared expectations that become institutionalized (Meyer and Rowan, 1977; Zucker, 1977). Once formed, an institutionalized structure is stable, but not permanent.

Institutionalized norms change over time. For example, acceptable practices in regard to industrial pollution (Hoffman, 1997), corporate philanthropy (Fombrun, 1996), stakeholder voice (Freeman, 1984), and stockholder control (Davis and Thompson, 1994) have changed significantly over time.

The literature on institutional theory has tended to view institutional change as the incidental evolutionary outcome of unguided interactions (Brint and Karabel, 1991; Greenwood and Hinings, 1996; Hirsch and Lounsbury, 1997). However, because 'institutions define the opportunities and incentives that determine outcomes for actors' (Ingram, 1998, p. 258), different actors have a large stake in the characteristics of institutions, and so strive to guide the course of institutional change. Firms and constituents tend to have differing preferences for institutional order, with constituents seeking to place more constraints on a firm's behaviour and firm's seeking greater autonomy (Pfeffer and Salancik, 1978). As a result, struggles to shape institutions ensue (Hoffman, 1999; Ingram, 1998). According to Miles (1982, p. 23), '. . . organizations and elements of society may be found constantly engaged in efforts to insert their interests into the mainstream of societal value and, hence, to create or safeguard the legitimacy of their definition of the "right" social order' (Miles, 1982, p. 23). Thus, organizational fields are characterized as contentious 'arenas of power relations' (Brint and Karabel, 1991, p. 355).

Power in these arenas stems from collective might. The outcome of the 'supergame' (Ingram, 1998, p. 258) of setting the rules of the game for a particular organizational field favours those actors that can mobilize and coordinate their efforts (DiMaggio, 1988; Vogel, 1989; Zald and McCarthy, 1977). As a particular group is able to mobilize and energize its members to pursue a particular goal, the likelihood of achieving that goal increases. For example, activist stockholders garnered control over corporate governance by mobilizing (Davis and Thompson, 1994), and the mobilized efforts of environmentalists helped transform corporate attitudes about investment in protection of the natural environment (Hoffman, 1997). In short, there is strength in numbers.

In light of collective rationality, however, mobilization is problematic (Olson, 1965). The various actors within an organizational field always prefer to change institutional norms in their favour. However, these actors are seldom motivated to exert the effort necessary to pursue such change, given that each could free ride (refer to the discussion prior to Proposition 5 for further explanation of collective rationality and the free rider problem). Thus, desires for change normally remain latent. Sometimes, though, the bad actions of a single firm can serve as a jolt that sparks a mobilization that creates an institutional shift (Fligstein, 1991; Hoffman and Ocasio, 2001; Meyer, 1982). When institutions change, the competitive conditions facing entire industries can change. They may become more or less attractive. Changing industry effects may then spark firms to mobilize across an industry, as noted in the first proposition. Overall, a struggle for control ensues as mobilized constituents pursue institutional change in one direction, and the industry attempts to retard or reverse any change (cf. Hoffman, 1999, p. 352).

Proposition 2: The better mobilized the constituents challenging an industry, the more resources will a firm in the challenged industry allocate to communal strategy.

1762   M. L. Barnett

Though the interests of actors within an organizational field persistently differ, periods of intense conflict between opposing groups are not persistent. Conflict is costly to all participants, and collectives are difficult to maintain over extended periods of time. The salience of a triggering event decreases over time, while the self-interested activities delayed in favour of pursuing collective agendas eventually push to the fore. Given the imperative for a firm to distinguish itself from rivals in order to achieve competitive advantage, periods of strong industry-wide unity are inherently unsustainable (Barnett, 2002; Deephouse, 1999). Over time, opportunities to improve performance through competitive strategy arise. As a result, firms become decreasingly likely to divert resources to communal strategy that otherwise could be expended on competitive strategy. Trade associations are 'minimalist organizations' (Halliday et al., 1987, p. 456) designed to survive such retrenchments.

> *Proposition 3*: As the perceived influence of industry effects on a firm's performance subsides, that firm will decrease the resources it allocates to communal strategy.

The propositions developed above have broadly outlined the dynamics that determine a firm's working balance. Combining them, the resulting general framework proposes that, when mobilized, constituent groups can gain control over the institutions governing an organizational field. Institutional change can alter industry effects and so constrain a firm's profitability. As a firm's profitability is constrained by industry effects, it shifts resources into communal strategy because it can earn higher returns by improving the standing of its industry than it can by improving its competitive position within a diminishing industry. As rival firms effectively mobilize, they can regain control. Once a constituent challenge is countered, industry effects become less constraining, and so firms shift back toward rivalry. As new constituent mobilizations arise, the process begins anew.

   This broad framework provides a general sense of how organizational field-level dynamics influence a firm's working balance. The remainder of this paper outlines some of the contingencies that operate within this broad framework. The next section provides insight into how differences in the ability of constituents to mobilize can cause industry effects to vary.

The Reputation Commons Problem

The rules of the game in an organizational field are normally stable; that is, institutionalized. It is improbable that any individual or firm acting alone could intentionally change them in its favour. Instead, individuals and organizations must act as institutional entrepreneurs to begin movements that, through collective might, change institutions (DiMaggio, 1988). The initial spark that mobilizes a movement, though, can also be unintentional and lead to undesired institutional change (Holm, 1995). That is, a firm can be a reluctant sort of *de*institutional entrepreneur. A single act by a single firm can spark a constituent mobilization that destabilizes the taken-for-granted status of an entire industry. Consider the petroleum industry. Following the massive oil spill from the *Exxon Valdez* in 1989, the entire petroleum industry came under attack from environmental activists groups, organized consumer groups, and regulators (Hoffman, 1997). Following

Competitive and Communal Strategies 1763

Exxon's oil spill, an Amoco executive noted, 'We are still an oil company, and we still have to live with the sins of our brothers. We were doing fine until Exxon spilled all that oil. Then we were painted with the same brush as them' (Hoffman, 1997, p. 189). The response to such a galvanizing event is indeed a broad brush, forging institutional change that alters the performance of all the firms within an industry. King et al. (2002, p. 393) termed this phenomenon a 'reputation commons problem'. If one firm's error can cause its rivals' reputations to diminish, then the industry effectively shares a common reputation and experiences the challenges of managing such a commons (Olson, 1965; Ostrom, 1990).

Certain characteristics render some industries more susceptible to reputation commons problems than others. In particular, the more numerous, distant, and heterogeneous are the members of an organizational field, the less intense is any reputation commons problem likely to be (King et al., 2002). Given collective rationality, mobilization is difficult. These factors create additional barriers to mobilization. As the number of constituents increases, the ability to rely on social pressure to overcome collective rationality decreases (Olson, 1965). Geographical dispersion, especially dispersion across countries, cultures, and languages, creates additional barriers to unity amongst constituents. Finally, heterogeneity in interests, values, and other characteristics of constituents further decreases their ability to unite in an effort to challenge an industry. Moreover, even if constituent groups are able to mobilize, differing constituent groups may work in opposing directions. King et al. (2002, pp. 397–8) cite the fact that, on the same day, one constituent group rated Ford as the cleanest automobile manufacturer and another rated it as the dirtiest. Thus, even though one or more firm's actions may upset constituents, certain characteristics of and differences in constituent groups may render them unable to muster a response that is likely to create institutional change unfavourable to the industry.

Proposition 4: The stronger the ties between constituents in its organizational field, the greater the amount of its resources a firm will allocate to communal strategy.

Characteristics of the firms, too, affect the potential severity of a reputation commons problem. If firms are very similar or provide little information by which constituents may distinguish their relative performance, then the act of any individual firm is more likely to be judged characteristic of the potential of all such firms. For example, to most constituents, one nuclear power plant, oil tanker, or chemical plant is similar to another. Thus, when one suffers a catastrophic incident, constituents are likely to judge similar others to be equally hazardous, and so seek changes to the rules of the game that govern each of the industries. Several empirical studies have shown that rival firms did indeed suffer significant losses in market value following the incidents at Three Mile Island, *Exxon Valdez*, and Bhopal (Blacconiere and Patten, 1994; Hill and Schneeweis, 1983; Patten and Nance, 1998). On the other hand, if firms are easily differentiated, then one firm's mistake may not reflect on its rivals. Constituents, instead, may focus their attacks specifically on the responsible firm, causing damage to its reputation, but not seek changes to the rules of the game. Thus, differentiation among firms allows constituents to better distinguish when the rules of the game are fine, but an individual firm is not abiding by them, versus when the rules themselves need to be altered.

Proposition 5: The more similar is a firm to its rivals, the greater the amount of its resources that firm will allocate to communal strategy.

The most difficult issue facing any rational approach to collective action is the perverse nature of collective rationality (Olson, 1965). While all the members of an industry may have economic incentive to engage in cooperation, collective action frequently fails to emerge: 'Collective interests do not necessarily produce collective action' (Heckathorn, 1986, p. 25). Major events can increase the incentive for constituents to mobilize, and an organized attack by constituents on an industry can increase the incentive for rival firms to mobilize. However, the micro-level driver remains unexplained in light of collective rationality:

> Why should I contribute when there is only a trivial chance that my contribution will make a critical difference and when the only other possibilities are that the group effort will be realized without my contribution (in which case I can 'free ride') and that it will not be realized if I do contribute (in which case I will be 'suckered')? . . . If individuals follow their self-interest, groups confronting such incentives will not attain objectives that members want. (Dawes et al., 1986, pp. 1171–2).

An industry-wide threat provides common incentive for rivals to engage in communal strategy, yet firm-level responses to this incentive vary. Some firm must assume the initial burden of mobilizing for collective action and others must decide to take the risk of participating despite the perverse logic of collective rationality. The remaining propositions address factors which differentially affect the likelihood that particular firms within the same industry will initiate and participate in such collective efforts.

Resource Mobilization and Communal Strategy

Scholars commonly use social movement theory to study the activities of citizens as they collectivize in an attempt to produce societal change, such as the civil rights movement, peace movements, nuclear protests, and the like (Benford and Snow, 2000; Killian, 1984). However, a growing number of organization scholars are applying social movement theory to business activities. According to Berg and Zald, (1978, p. 138), 'Business now behaves more like a visible social movement'. More recently, Davis and McAdam (2000, pp. 216–17) argued: 'We see . . . a strong analogy between the processes of mobilization for collective action in social movements and in contemporary business organizations . . . To the extent that economic action comes to look like contentious politics, we expect that theory about social movements will be applicable to the traditional domain of organizational theory.'

The fields of sociology, economics, and political science have long struggled with the difficult task of explaining why rational individuals would voluntarily participate in collective efforts to produce public goods. Much of the social movement literature has dealt with this difficult problem by explaining away rationality, and instead arguing that participation is non-rational (Morris, 1981), arational (Jenkins, 1983), or irrational (Oliver, 1993). However, the approach taken in this paper is that such actions are rational. A firm takes on the burden of communal strategy because it believes that such efforts are likely to produce greater marginal returns than would similar efforts expended on competitive strategy. This rational approach to collective action is consistent with the social movement literature's resource mobilization theory, which asserts that 'collective action is . . . carried out by rational actors attempting to realize their ends' (Morris, 1981, p. 746). As Jenkins (1983, p. 530) noted, '. . . resource mobilization theory has been posed in terms of collective actors struggling for power in an institutional context' – clearly a perspective that is germane to the notion of struggles for control over the rules of the game outlined previously.

More specifically, resource mobilization theory posits that individual participation in collective activities is based on rational calculation (Wood and Jackson, 1982). Individuals determine a sort of risk–reward ratio (Oberschall, 1973) by comparing the estimated costs versus benefits of participation (Klandermans, 1984). From an organizational perspective, initial action by a large and powerful firm is often essential to shift the risk–reward ratio in favour of collective action for other members of the industry. Participants do not want to be suckered (Dawes et al., 1986) by participating, only to have others not participate and the entire mobilization to fail. The participation of a dominant firm increases the likelihood that the mobilization will succeed, and so improves the risk–reward ratio. Consider the chemical industry of the late 1980s. On the heels of the Bhopal disaster, the industry faced a serious crisis. Most firms recognized the dilemma, but the industry was unable to mobilize until Dow Chemical, a dominant firm in the industry, pushed for a specific collective response (Hoffman, 1997).

Of course, the problem then reduces to explaining why Dow volunteered to serve as an institutional entrepreneur (DiMaggio, 1988). Why did Dow take on the burden and risk? If we suppose that the cost of initiating an industry-wide mobilization is nearly constant across firms, or even decreasing with size given the fixed capital and human resources present in a large firm, while the return to favourable industry conditions increases with size, it is straightforward to conclude that dominant firms have a dominant strategy of institutional entrepreneurship. Dow has an inordinate stake in the fate of its industry, and so its cost–benefit calculus favours communal strategy more than does that of its rivals. In general, then:

Proposition 6: The larger a firm's market share, the more of its resources it will allocate to communal strategy and the more likely it is to be an institutional entrepreneur.

Size matters to a firm's working balance but so, too, does scope. This paper has defined communal strategy as a firm's allocation of resources towards improving the position of its industry. However, many firms operate in multiple industries. Diversified firms must determine a working balance for each line of business and its associated industry. These are not independent decisions.

The fate of a firm with a single business line varies considerably with that of its industry. However, the fate of a diversified firm is not as reliant on a single industry. A diversified firm may manage its businesses across industries as if they were real options (Amram and Kulatilaka, 1999; Barnett, 2003; Luehrman, 1998). Should one industry decline or fail, a diversified firm may exercise its option to decrease or eliminate its investments in that industry and shift its resources to its businesses in other more promising industries. A firm with a single line of business has no such option and so will fight more fiercely to ensure its sole industry remains viable. Thus, all else equal, the more diversified a firm, the less is the need for that firm to assume the burden of communal strategy within any particular industry.

> *Proposition 7*: All else being equal, a diversified firm will allocate fewer resources to communal strategy in a given industry than will an undiversified firm in the same industry.

This does not mean, though, that the more diversified a firm, the fewer *total* resources it will allocate to communal strategy. In fact, a diversified firm may expend considerably more total resources on communal strategy than does an undiversified firm, given that it is likely to be larger and have interests in the fates of more industries. However, if one controls for size and other relevant factors in order to isolate the effects of diversification on communal strategy expenditures, then one should expect to find the relationship specified in Proposition 7. Simply put, increasing diversification allows a firm to concern itself less about the fate of any individual line of business within its portfolio, since the failure of any one line of business is less likely to threaten the survival of the entire firm.

For ease of analysis, the prior propositions have assumed a firm to be monolithic, acting as a coordinated unit to single-mindedly pursue profit maximization. The final proposition relaxes this assumption by accounting for agency issues. A firm may voluntarily devote significant resources to communal strategy because of the personal interests of the agents who manage it. One such personal interest that is particularly influential over top management decision-making is the desire to be respected among peers. Peer pressure creates a strong incentive for managers to devote some of their firms' resources toward industry-wide betterment, where legal obligations cannot due to antitrust laws (Gunningham, 1995, p. 69) and even when it may not be instrumental to profit maximization. In his study of the nuclear power industry, Rees (1994) concluded that peer pressure was the driving force behind the industry's uniquely strong collective efforts. According to one industry CEO, '. . . there's nothing more compelling than to be identified as a laggard among your peers' (Rees, 1994, p. 104). Increased participation in communal efforts not only protects top managers from embarrassment by peers, but can also help top managers build relationships that may further their personal and career prospects, particularly for moves within their industry. Thus, managerial interests can influence a firm's working balance in favour of communal strategy.

> *Proposition 8*: The stronger the intra-industry ties of the top managers of a firm, the greater the amount of its resources that firm will allocate to communal strategy.

DISCUSSION AND CONCLUSION

'Because any organization can act as either an independent actor or an involved part of a larger collectivity, it must inevitably deal with the tensions generated when these two forces conflict' (Astley and Fombrun, 1983, p. 585). One may group these conflicting forces into competitive strategy and communal strategy, which conflict in resource allocation decisions. Organization scholars bear the burden of explaining how a firm should allocate its limited resources amongst conflicting demands so as to maximize performance. Yet prior research has largely overlooked the conflicting demands implicit in these two levels of strategy. To address this gap, this paper proposed a set of dynamic factors at the organizational field, industry, and firm levels that influence a firm's resource allocations, and so determine its working balance over time.

The general framework presented herein notes how periods of collective activity unfold as industry social movements undertaken to counteract constituent social movements. Prior social movement research has focused primarily on constituent mobilization, and has not characterized the dynamics of the ongoing struggle for institutional control as a struggle between social movements and countermovements. Zald and Berger (1978) transformed the notion of social movements from that of a large-scale citizen uprising to include struggles for control of an organization. Davis and Thompson (1994) have, likewise, employed a social movement perspective to illustrate changes in external control of corporations. More recently, Davis and McAdam (2000) have made use of social movement theory to describe the fluid dynamics of the new economy. This paper extended the concept of social movements to the industry level, describing not how individuals mobilize to gain control of a firm, but how firms mobilize to exert influence over the 'rules of the game' (North, 1990, p. 3). Enlargement to an organizational field-level perspective, with consideration of how constituent mobilization triggers industry mobilization and how the ongoing pressure to compete destroys collective action over time, adds dynamism to traditionally static models of industry effects.

The notion of struggles to influence the rules of the game as addressed in this paper adds an important layer to the conceptualization of competitive advantage as the socially constructed outcome of firm-constituent interactions (Rindova and Fombrun, 1999). This perspective highlights the role of individual firm behaviour in building a favourable dialogue, and thus a favourable reputation, with constituents. However, it has overlooked the interdependence between a firm's reputation and that of its rivals. It is important to acknowledge that a firm must act to enhance and protect its individual reputation, but it may also need to participate in collective efforts to manage its industry's reputation in order to achieve competitive advantage. Collective interactions with mobilized constituents are strategically important for 'reasoning with the resource' (King et al., 2002, p. 399) to improve the reputation commons. Moreover, this paper furthers burgeoning research that seeks to extend the notion of a commons beyond the traditional domain of common pool resources (Ostrom, 1990). King et al. (2002) described how prevailing research tends to regard commons problems in terms of physical resources – grazing land, fisheries, wells – but because firms compete for social approval, it is also worthwhile to treat an industry's reputation as a common resource and to further explore ways in which communal strategy can help protect this commons.

This paper's characterization of competitive advantage as the outcome of collective struggles for control of the institutional environment enriches institutional perspectives on strategy. Many scholars have criticized the lack of agency in institutional theory (Brint and Karabel, 1991; Greenwood and Hinings, 1996; Hirsch and Lounsbury, 1997). Powell and DiMaggio (1991, p. 27) argued that scholars need 'to place interests and

1768 M. L. Barnett

power on the institutional agenda, and to clarify and deepen the conversation about the form that a theory of institutional change might take'. Lawrence (1999, p. 162) lamented that 'relatively little attention has been paid to the organizational work of sponsoring new practices or transforming existing institutions'. According to Ingram and Silverman (2002, p. 18), 'an understanding of institutional change, and the ways that firms can influence such change [is] central to the study and practice of strategy'. This paper described how both firms and constituents, as competing collectives, exert control over their institutional environment and produce institutional change.

Such a perspective, wherein rivalrous firms embrace collective action in order to influence external opinion and therein favourably shape competitive dynamics, marks an interesting contrast to classic economic rationale for cooperation amongst rivals. Like the framework developed in this paper, cartel theory addresses the conditions that drive a firm to cooperate with rivals in order to achieve collective gains, or to defect and increase individual benefit. However, cartel theory and communal strategy have very different mechanisms. Cartels achieve gains for their participants by restricting output. As output is restricted, the price of the industry's goods rises for a given level of demand. Once the price rises, firms face the tension of defecting by releasing more supply at the higher price, which brings price down, or remaining within the cartel.

Communal strategy, however, points out that cooperation can shift demand, not merely move a good's price along a given demand curve by restricting supply. The aim of collective action under this approach is to expand, not shrink, the total market for a particular industry. In part because collusion is illegal within the USA, but primarily because constituents are active market participants, not passive recipients of industrial output and institutional conditions, the communal strategy perspective has greater applicability to modern American industry. Recognizing its potential to improve industry behaviour, many governments now condone and actively facilitate industry-wide cooperation, and many industries have heeded this call. Because industry bears the costs of such an approach, though, communal strategy transforms the topic of cooperation amongst rivals into a struggle to justify its existence, not to ban it. This paper outlined a set of conditions under which it is more or less likely to occur.

The contributions of this paper, though, lie at a broad and somewhat abstract level. Collective action ultimately reduces to individual decisions to participate. This paper characterized such decisions as primarily stemming from a rational cost–benefit calculus. However, individuals and the firms they compose are boundedly rational, and so often make decisions that deviate from perfect rationality (Cyert and March, 1963). Bounded rationality leads individuals to make use of heuristics (Tversky and Kahneman, 1973). These heuristics may cause firms to make not fine-grained calibrations to their participation in communal strategy, but coarse decisions coinciding with thresholds (Granovetter, 1978). Future research should seek to clarify the degree and type of constituent mobilizations that exceed certain thresholds and so trigger firms' attention and action toward communal strategy. What factors increase the likelihood that a firm will notice that industry effects have increased or decreased? How widely do these perceptions vary across firms and industries? Do some groups of constituents sway industry effects more than others? The framework presented herein offers only broad strokes.

Competitive and Communal Strategies   1769

This paper characterized institutional dynamics as being forged through collective action, and collective action as being triggered by a firm's misdeeds. Certainly not all changes to industry conditions are brought about by social movements, and not all social movements are sparked by the misdeeds of one or more members of an industry. Firms may collectivize proactively, not just in response to perceived constituent attacks, and constituents may attack an industry prior to a crisis. Given the rationality constraints noted above, it is reasonable to proceed from the base assumption that the limited attention of individuals, managers and constituents alike, must first be triggered and then their efforts intentionally shifted from individual gain and toward collective causes before they take on such burdens. However, future research should further address the situations in which collective action may occur within and against an industry without the trigger of a crisis. Analysis from a network perspective could be particularly insightful here, as the likelihood of firms coming together and staying together varies with prior networking relationships (Fichman and Leventhal, 1991; Gulati, 1995). Also, individuals and firms likely vary in their capacity to simultaneously pursue individual and collective action. Further investigation of these differences in capacity might help better explain the many patterns of cooperation and competition.

Moreover, this paper characterizes all changes in industry conditions as being driven by institutional dynamics. Economic and technological changes, of course, also significantly alter industry conditions (D'Aveni, 1994; Schumpeter, 1942). Nonetheless, economic and technological changes are embedded within a broader social environment (Granovetter, 1985), such that their influences on industry conditions are intertwined with that of institutional change (Garud and Karnoe, 2001; Holm, 1995). No matter the economic or technological merit of an industry's activities and outputs, social dynamics shape the ability of that industry to attract resources and so profit and survive.

Finally, for ease of analysis, this paper makes the stylistic assumption that firm performance, and firm control over performance, can be approximated with two 'levers' – one controlling resource allocations to competitive strategy to influence firm effects, and the other controlling resource allocations to communal strategy to influence industry effects. Of course, more than firm effects and industry effects matter, and firms may allocate resources to activities that influence these other effects; in short, there are additional levers. For example, a firm's performance varies to some degree with the health of the national economy in which it is embedded, with the state of national security, with the health of the public education system, with the status of trade relations amongst countries, and even with the health of the natural environment. Firms may individually attempt to improve these problems through acts of corporate social responsibility, but they are more likely to have an impact through large-scale cooperative efforts such as those of business meta-associations like the Business Roundtable or the World Business Council for Sustainable Development. Though influence over firm and industry characteristics offers the most direct means for firms to control their fates, many firms employ these additional levers. For example, DuPont is a participating member in the chemical industry's primary trade association, the American Chemistry Council, and in the World Business Council for Sustainable Development. Thus, a complete picture of a firm's strategy must take account of the multiple communities of which it is a part, even beyond the industry.

1770   M. L. Barnett

In conclusion, to varying degrees firms are 'hostages' (Rees, 1994, p. 1) of their industries. From a sociological perspective, the legitimacy of a population influences the survival chances of each of its members (Aldrich and Fiol, 1994; Dowling and Pfeffer, 1975; Meyer and Rowan, 1977). In blunter economic terms, industry matters to firm performance (McGahan and Porter, 1997; Rumelt, 1991; Schmalensee, 1985). However, this constraint is not static or entirely exogenous. One firm's actions can alter the institutional environment and decrease the attractiveness of an industry. The collective efforts of rivals can alter the institutional environment and increase the attractiveness of an industry. Because such collective efforts are costly and constraining, though, firms face an ongoing tension. This paper has presented a framework to further understanding of how firms manage this tension.

NOTE

*I thank the editor, Mike Wright, and three anonymous reviewers for helpful suggestions. This paper is based on my dissertation, and so I owe a debt of gratitude to my committee: Bill Starbuck, Andy King, and Brian Uzzi. I also appreciate the editing insights of Gary Gebhardt.

REFERENCES

Aldrich, H. (1999). *Organizations Evolving*. San Francisco, CA: Sage.
Aldrich, H. and Fiol, C. M. (1994). 'Fools rush in? The institutional context of industry creation'. *Academy of Management Review*, **19**, 645–71.
Aldrich, H. and Staber, U. H. (1988). 'Organizing business interests: patterns of trade association foundings, transformations, and deaths'. In Carroll, G. R. (Ed.), *Ecological Models of Organizations*. Cambridge, MA: Ballinger, 111–26.
Amram, M. and Kulatilaka, N. (1999). *Real Options: Managing Strategic Investment in an Uncertain World*. Boston, MA: Harvard Business School Press.
Astley, W. G. and Fombrun, C. J. (1983). 'Collective strategy: social ecology of organizational environments'. *Academy of Management Review*, **8**, 576–87.
Bain, J. S. (1956). *Barriers to New Competition*. Cambridge, MA: Harvard University Press.
Barnett, M. L. (2002). 'From me to we . . . and back again: returning to business as usual'. *Journal of Management Inquiry*, **11**, 249–52.
Barnett, M. L. (2003). 'Falling off the fence? A realistic appraisal of a real options approach to corporate strategy'. *Journal of Management Inquiry*, **12**, 185–96.
Barnett, W. P., Mischke, G. and Ocasio, W. (2000). 'The evolution of collective strategies among organizations'. *Organization Studies*, **21**, 325–54.
Barringer, B. R. and Harrison, J. S. (2000). 'Walking a tightrope: creating value through interorganizational relationships'. *Journal of Management*, **26**, 367–403.
Benford, R. D. and Snow, D. A. (2000). 'Framing processes and social movements: an overview and sassessment'. *Annual Review of Sociology*, **26**, 611–39.
Berg, I. and Zald, M. N. (1978). 'Business and society'. *Annual Review of Sociology*, **4**, 115–43.
Blacconiere, W. and Patten, D. (1994). 'Environmental disclosures, regulatory costs, and changes in firm value'. *Journal of Accounting and Economics*, **18**, 357–77.
Brandenburger, A. and Nalebuff, B. (1996). *Co-opetition*. New York: Doubleday.
Bresser, R. K. F. (1988). 'Matching collective and competitive strategies'. *Strategic Management Journal*, **9**, 375–85.
Brint, S. and Karabel, J. (1991). 'Institutional origins and transformations: the case of American community colleges'. In Powell, W. and DiMaggio, P. (Eds), *The New Institutionalism in Organizational Analysis*. Chicago, IL: University of Chicago Press, 337–60.
CMA (Chemical Manufacturers Association) (1993). *On the Road to Success* (Responsible Care Progress Report). Washington, DC: CMA.

Contractor, F. and Lorange, P. (Eds) (1988). *Cooperative Strategies in International Business*. Lexington, MA: Lexington Books.

Cyert, R. M. and March, J. G. (1963). *A Behavioral Theory of the Firm*. Englewood Cliffs, NJ: Prentice-Hall.

D'Aveni, R. A. (1994). *Hypercompetition: Managing the Dynamics of Strategic Maneuvering*. New York: Free Press.

Davis, G. F. and McAdam, D. (2000). 'Corporations, classes, and social movements after managerialism'. *Research in Organizational Behaviour*, **22**, 239–82.

Davis, G. F. and Thompson, T. A. (1994). 'A social movement perspective on corporate control'. *Administrative Science Quarterly*, **39**, 141–73.

Dawes, R. M., Orbell, J. M., Simmons, R. T. and Van De Kragt, A. J. C. (1986). 'Organizing groups for collective action'. *American Political Science Review*, **80**, 1171–85.

Deephouse, D. L. (1999). 'To be different, or to be the same? It's a question (and theory) of strategic balance'. *Strategic Management Journal*, **20**, 147–66.

DiMaggio, P. J. (1988). 'Interest and agency in institutional theory'. In Zucker, L. G. (Ed.), *Institutional Patterns and Organizations*. Cambridge, MA: Ballinger, 3–22.

DiMaggio, P. J. and Powell, W. W. (1983). 'The iron cage revisited: institutional isomorphism and collective rationality in organizational fields'. *American Sociological Review*, **48**, 147–60.

Dowling, J. and Pfeffer, J. (1975). 'Organizational legitimacy: social values and organizational behavior'. *Pacific Sociological Review*, **18**, 122–36.

Dyer, J. H and Singh, H. (1998). 'The relational view: cooperative strategy and sources of interorganizational competitive advantage'. *Academy of Management Review*, **23**, 660–79.

Fichman, M. and Leventhal, D. A. (1991). 'Honeymoons and the liability of adolescence: a new perspective on duration dependence in social and organizational relationships'. *Academy of Management Review*, **16**, 442–68.

Fligstein, N. (1991). 'The structural transformation of American industry: an institutional account of the causes of diversification in the largest firms: 1919–1979'. In Powell, W. and DiMaggio, P. (Eds), *The New Institutionalism in Organizational Analysis*. Chicago, IL: University of Chicago Press.

Fombrun, C. J. (1996). *Reputation: Realizing Value from the Corporate Image*. Cambridge, MA: Harvard Business School Press.

Freeman, R. E. (1984). *Strategic Management: A Stakeholder Approach*. Boston, MA: Pitman.

Garud, R. and Karnoe, P. (Eds) (2001). *Path Dependence and Creation*. Mahwah, NJ: Lawrence Erlbaum Associates.

Gomes-Casseres, B. (1994). 'Group versus group: how alliance networks compete'. *Harvard Business Review*, July–August, 62–70.

Granovetter, M. (1978). 'Threshold models of collective behavior'. *American Journal of Sociology*, **83**, 1420–43.

Granovetter, M. (1985). 'Economic action and social structure: the problem of embeddedness'. *American Journal of Sociology*, **91**, 481–510.

Greenwood, R. and Hinings, C. (1996). 'Understanding radical organizational change: bringing together the old and the new institutionalism'. *Academy of Management Review*, **21**, 1022–54.

Gulati, R. (1995). 'Does familiarity breed trust? The implications of repeated ties for contractual choice in alliances'. *Academy of Management Journal*, **38**, 85–112.

Gunningham, N. (1995). 'Environment, self-regulation, and the chemical industry: assessing responsible care'. *Law & Policy*, **17**, 57–108.

Gupta, A. and Lad, L. (1983). 'Industry self-regulation: an economic, organizational, and political analysis'. *Academy of Management Review*, **8**, 416–25.

Halliday, T., Powell, M. and Granfors, M. (1987). 'Minimalist organizations: vital events in state bar associations, 1870–1930'. *American Sociological Review*, **52**, 456–71.

Hamel, G. and Prahalad, C. K. (1989). 'Strategic intent'. *Harvard Business Review*, May–June, 63–76.

Hamel, G., Doz, Y. L. and Prahalad, C. K. (1989). 'Collaborate with your competitors – and win'. *Harvard Business Review*, January–February, 133–9.

Heckathorn, D. D. (1986). 'The dynamics and dilemmas of collective action'. *American Sociological Review*, **61**, 250–77.

Hennart, J. F. (1988). 'A transactions cost theory of equity joint ventures'. *Strategic Management Journal*, **9**, 361–74.

Hill, C. W. L. (1995). 'The Toyota Corporation in 1994'. In Hill, C. W. and Jones, G. R. (Eds), *Strategic Management: An Integrated Approach*. Boston, MA: Houghton-Mifflin, C249–63.

Hill, J. and Schneeweis, T. (1983). 'The effect of Three Mile Island on electric utility stock prices: a note'. *Journal of Finance*, **38**, 1285–92.

Hirsch, P. (1975). 'Organizational effectiveness and the institutional environment'. *Administrative Science Quarterly*, **20**, 327–44.

Hirsch, P. and Lounsbury, M. (1997). 'Ending the family quarrel: toward a reconciliation of "old" and "new" institutionalisms'. *American Behavioral Scientist*, **40**, 406–18.

Hoffman, A. (1997). *From Heresy to Dogma: An Institutional History of Corporate Environmentalism*. San Francisco, CA: The New Lexington Press.

Hoffman, A. (1999). 'Institutional evolution and change: environmentalism and the U.S. chemical industry'. *Academy of Management Journal*, **42**, 351–71.

Hoffman, A. and Ocasio, W. (2001). 'Not all events are attended equally: toward a middle-range theory of industry attention to external events'. *Organization Science*, **12**, 414–34.

Holm, P. (1995). 'The dynamics of institutionalization: transformation processes in Norwegian fisheries'. *Administrative Science Quarterly*, **40**, 398–422.

Ingram, P. (1998). 'Changing the rules: interests, organizations, and institutional change in the U.S. hospitality industry'. In Brinton, M. C. and Nee, V. (Eds), *The New Institutionalism in Sociology*. New York: Russell Sage, 258–76.

Ingram, P. and Inman, C. (1996). 'Institutions, intergroup rivalry, and the evolution of hotel populations around Niagara Falls'. *Administrative Science Quarterly*, **41**, 629–58.

Ingram, P. and Silverman, B. (2002). 'The new institutionalism in strategic management'. *Advances in Strategic Management*, **19**, 1–30.

Jenkins, J. C. (1983). 'Resource mobilization theory and the study of social movements'. *Annual Review of Sociology*, **9**, 527–53.

Killian, L. M. (1984). 'Organization, rationality and spontaneity in the civil rights movement'. *American Sociological Review*, **49**, 770–83.

King, A. and Lenox, M. (2000). 'Industry self-regulation without sanctions: the chemical industry's Responsible Care program'. *Academy of Management Journal*, **43**, 698–716.

King, A., Lenox, M. and Barnett, M. L. (2002). 'Strategic responses to the reputation commons problem'. In Hoffman, A. and Ventresca, M. (Eds), *Organizations, Policy and the Natural Environment: Institutional and Strategic Perspectives*. Stanford, CA: Stanford University Press, 393–406.

Klandermans, B. (1984). 'Mobilization and participation: social-psychological expansions of resource mobilization theory'. *American Sociological Review*, **49**, 583–600.

Kogut, B. (1988). 'Joint ventures: theoretical and empirical perspectives'. *Strategic Management Journal*, **9**, 319–22.

Lado, A. A., Boyd, N. G. and Hanlonm, S. C. (1997). 'Competition, cooperation, and the search for economic rents: a syncretic model'. *Academy of Management Review*, **22**, 110–41.

Lawrence, T. B. (1999). 'Institutional strategy'. *Journal of Management*, **25**, 161–88.

Lifton, L. R. (1989). 'Rational Firm Behavior in Response to Environmental Uncertainty: Collective Marketing Activities in the New York State Wine Grape Industry'. Unpublished doctoral dissertation, Marketing Department, Cornell University.

Luehrman, T. A. (1998). 'Strategy as a portfolio of real options'. *Harvard Business Review*, **76**, 89–99.

Maitland, I. (1985). 'The limits of business self-regulation'. *California Management Review*, **27**, 132–47.

Mason, E. S. (1939). 'Price and production policies of large scale enterprises'. *American Economic Review*, **29**, 61–74.

McGahan, A. M. and Porter, M. E. (1997). 'How much does industry matter, really?'. *Strategic Management Journal*, **18**, 15–30.

Meyer, A. (1982). 'Adapting to environmental jolts'. *Administrative Science Quarterly*, **27**, 515–37.

Meyer, J. and Rowan, B. (1977). 'Institutionalized organizations: formal structure as myth and ceremony'. *American Journal of Sociology*, **83**, 340–63.

Miles, R. H. (1982). *Coffin Nails and Corporate Strategies*. Englewood Cliffs, NJ: Prentice-Hall.

Morris, A. (1981). 'Black southern sit-in movement: an analysis of internal organization'. *American Sociological Review*, **46**, 744–67.

North, D. C. (1990). *Institutions, Institutional Change and Economic Performance*. Cambridge: Cambridge University Press.

Oberschall, A. (1973). *Social Conflict and Social Movements*. Englewood Cliffs, NJ: Prentice Hall.

Oliver, C. (1990). 'Determinants of interorganizational relationships: integration and future directions'. *Academy of Management Review*, **15**, 241–65.

Oliver, P. E. (1993). 'Formal models of collective action'. *Annual Review of Sociology*, **19**, 271–300.

Olson, M. (1965). *The Logic of Collective Action: Public Goods and the Theory of Groups*. Cambridge, MA: Harvard University Press.

Competitive and Communal Strategies   1773

Ostrom, E. (1990). *Governing the Commons: The Evolution of Institutions for Collective Action*. Cambridge: Cambridge University Press.

Patten, D. and Nance, J. (1998). 'Regulatory cost effects in a good news environment: the intra-industry reaction to the Alaskan oil spill'. *Journal of Accounting and Public Policy*, **17**, 409–29.

Pennings, J. M. (1981). 'Strategically interdependent organizations'. In Nystrom, P. C. and Starbuck, W. H. (Eds), *Handbook of Organizational Design*. New York: Oxford University Press, 433–55.

Pfeffer, J. and Nowak, P. (1976). 'Joint ventures and interorganizational interdependence'. *Administrative Science Quarterly*, **21**, 398–418.

Pfeffer, J. and Salancik, G. (1978). *The External Control of Organizations: A Resource Dependence Perspective*. New York: Harper & Row.

Porter, M. E. (1980). *Competitive Strategy*. New York: Free Press.

Porter, M. E. (1985). *Competitive Advantage*. New York: Free Press.

Porter, M. E. (1991). 'Towards a dynamic theory of strategy'. *Strategic Management Journal*, **12**, 95–117.

Powell, W. W. (1990). 'Neither market nor hierarchy: network forms of organization'. In Cummings, L. L. and Staw, B. M. (Eds), *Research in Organizational Behavior*. Greenwich, CT: JAI Press, 295–336.

Powell, W. and DiMaggio, P. (1991). *The New Institutionalism in Organizational Analysis*. Chicago, IL: University of Chicago Press.

Rees, J. (1994). *Hostages of Each Other: The Transformation of Nuclear Safety Since Three Mile Island*. Chicago, IL: University of Chicago Press.

Rindova, V. P. and Fombrun, C. J. (1999). 'Constructing competitive advantage: the role of firm-constituent interactions'. *Strategic Management Journal*, **20**, 691–710.

Rumelt, R. (1991). 'How much does industry matter?'. *Strategic Management Journal*, **12**, 167–85.

Schmalensee, R. (1985). 'Do markets differ much?'. *American Economic Review*, **75**, 341–51.

Schumpeter, J. (1942). *Capitalism, Socialism, and Democracy*. New York: Harper & Row.

Scott, W. R. (1981). *Organizations: Rational, Natural, and Open Systems*. Englewood Cliffs, NJ: Prentice-Hall.

Scott, W. R. (1995). *Institutions and Organizations*. Thousand Oaks, CA: Sage.

Teece, D. J. (1992). 'Competition, cooperation, and innovation: organizational arrangements for regimes of rapid technological progress'. *Journal of Economic Behavior and Organization*, **18**, 1–25.

Tversky, A. and Kahneman, D. (1973). 'Availability: a heuristic for judging frequency and probability'. *Cognitive Psychology*, **5**, 207–32.

Vaara, E., Kleymann, B. and Seristö, H. (2004). 'Strategies as Discursive Constructions: The Case of Airline Alliances'. *Journal of Management Studies*, **41**, 1–35.

Vogel, D. (1989). *Fluctuating Fortunes: The Political Power of Business in America*. New York: Basic Books.

Williamson, O. E. (1975). *Markets and Hierarchies: Analysis and Antitrust Implications*. New York: Free Press.

Wood, J. L. and Jackson, M. (1982). *Social Movements*. Belmont, CA: Wadsworth.

WRAP (Worldwide Responsible Apparel Production) (2003). http://www.wrapapparel.org/.

Zald, M. N. and Berger, M. A. (1978). 'Social movements in organizations: coup d'etat, insurgency, and mass movements'. *American Journal of Sociology*, **83**, 823–61.

Zald, M. N. and McCarthy, J. D. (Eds) (1977). *The Dynamics of Social Movements: Resource Mobilization, Social Control, and Tactics*. Cambridge, MA: Winthrop.

Zucker, L. G. (1977). 'The role of institutionalization in cultural persistence'. *American Sociological Review*, **42**, 726–43.

9

Article

One Voice, But Whose Voice? Exploring What Drives Trade Association Activity

Business & Society
52(2) 213–244
© 2012 SAGE Publications
Reprints and permission:
sagepub.com/journalsPermissions.nav
DOI: 10.1177/0007650309350211
bas.sagepub.com

Michael L. Barnett[1]

Abstract

Trade associations operate under the premise of advancing the shared interests of their member firms. How well do they fulfill this role? This article measures the activity of 148 major industry trade associations over time and relates this activity to the performance of the relevant industries and dominant firms within them. Findings suggest that trade association spending increases when the profitability of the four largest firms in an industry decreases, but spending is unrelated to the profitability of the industry overall. This implies that large firms exert control over trade association agendas and may use these communal organizations to advance their own interests rather than the shared interests of the entire industry. Moreover, it points to the need for further development of the currently anemic management literature on the activities of trade associations.

Keywords:

trade associations; collective action; cooperative strategy; industry effects

Trade associations are a pervasive part of our economic landscape. Most firms hold membership in at least one trade association. Nearly every industry, across all sectors of the economy, has organized at least one and often several trade associations. From the American Apparel Manufacturers Association to

[1]Rutgers University

Corresponding Author:
Michael L. Barnett, Rutgers Business School, 1 Washington Park, 11th Floor, Room 1110, Newark, NJ 07102, USA.
Email: mbarnett@business.rutgers.edu

the American Wind Energy Association, there are thousands of trade associations in the United States alone and thousands more in countries throughout the developed world (Aldrich & Staber, 1988; Bailey & Rupp, 2006; Collins & Roper, 2005; Lane & Bachmann, 1997). Yet "[v]ery little academic research has focused on trade associations" (Barringer & Harrison, 2000, p. 393). As a result, we have little systematic understanding of what these ubiquitous organizations actually do.

The lack of research on trade associations is lamentable. These organizations can amass budgets of millions of dollars and employ staffs of hundreds, and their lobbying activities can significantly influence the competitive environment, shaping regulations in ways that affect industry survival rates, growth, and profitability (Hirsch, 1975; Ingram & Inman, 1996; Miles, 1982). Many trade associations not only influence government regulation but even assume the role of government through industry self-regulation (Barnett & King, 2008; Gupta & Lad, 1983; Lenox & Nash, 2003; Maitland, 1985). Thus, if we are to understand the competitive environment, we cannot ignore the role of trade associations.

In this article, I examine the conditions that drive trade associations to action. Trade associations are organizations through which a group of interdependent firms, typically in the same industry, pool their resources and coordinate their efforts so that they may "speak with one voice"[1] on matters of shared interest. However, member firms are typically rivals and so they may not always share the same interests. Some firms may seek to direct the amassed resources of their trade associations in ways that maximize their individual interests and not necessarily the memberships' shared interests. Empirically discerning what actually drives trade associations to "speak up"—be it the interests of a few powerful firms or the shared interests of the industry—is a critical step in better understanding these ubiquitous and influential organizations.

I conduct a longitudinal study of the activity of 148 major U.S. industry trade associations. Findings suggest that industry-wide downturns may not drive trade association activity. Rather, it is downturns in the performance of the dominant firms within an industry that are strongly associated with increased trade association activity. These findings thus imply that when trade associations speak with "one voice," the most powerful firms may be writing the script.

What Do We Know About Trade Associations?

Trade associations are commonly defined as "organizations created to represent business interests within specific domains, mobilizing firms within their domain so that collective action can be taken on common problems" (Aldrich &

Staber, 1988, p. 111). There are several thousand trade associations within the United States that represent the interests of almost every industry and thousands more across the industrialized world. Many are highly active, with large staffs, a wide range of active committees, and generous budgets. For example, the American Chemistry Council,[2] the primary trade association for nearly 200 chemical manufacturers, has a paid staff of approximately 300 personnel overseeing the association and its more than one dozen major subgroups, operating on an annual budget of around US$110 million (Swartout, 2008).

Not only the level but also the type of activity varies across trade associations. Hemphill (1992, p. 916) described the range of trade association activities as "data collection, educational programs, facilitating technical standards and specifications, insurance programs, legal assistance and government relations." Oliver (1990, p. 249) listed trade association activities to include lobbying state regulators, promoting collective good through events such as trade shows, seeking to obtain economic advantages, reducing legislative uncertainty through activities such as product standardization, and enhancing members' image. Staber and Aldrich (1983) distinguished four trade association "activity areas: commercial, public, political, and solidaristic" (p. 168). These encompass the organization of trade shows and conventions, product standardization, and the collection of industry statistics (commercial); compilation of statistics for regulatory compliance (public); lobbying the government (political); and building consensus and shared purpose within the industry (solidaristic).

Others have made a blunter distinction, wherein trade associations serve as the bodies through which firms pursue collective strategy in the political (Hillman & Hitt, 1999) or nonmarket (Baron, 1995) environments. This is an important distinction to make because colluding in market activities constitutes a violation of antitrust laws.[3] Thus, legally, trade associations operate entirely within the nonmarket environment, which consists of "the social, political, and legal arrangements that structure interactions among companies and their public" (Baron, 1995, p. 73).

Though they cannot coordinate market activities, trade associations can enhance the performance and survival rates of their member firms by exerting influence on nonmarket forces. For example, the coordinated might of the pharmaceutical industry enabled it to co-opt critical resource holders and thereby gain higher average profits and survival rates than the recording industry, despite the similar structural characteristics of these two industries (Hirsch, 1975). The Tobacco Institute protected cigarette manufacturers from a variety of lawsuits and regulations that likely would have resulted in even greater harm to the industry (Miles, 1982). The coordinated effort of hoteliers around

Niagara Falls led to regulation that overcame common problems that threatened their growth and prosperity (Ingram & Inman, 1996). Industry-wide cooperation through trade associations is particularly critical to recovery from crises that face entire industries (Barnett, 2006a, 2006b). By presenting a united front and speaking with a unified voice, firms may collectively "improve the legislative, regulatory, market, and public interest climate for the industry" (Chemical Manufacturers Association Report, 1993) and so help to realign their industry with the demands of its environment.

Yet despite their prevalence and potential impact, trade associations have received relatively little attention from organizational scholars (Barnett, Mischke, & Ocasio, 2000; Barringer & Harrison, 2000). The studies mentioned above focused on the effects that trade associations can have on parties external to an industry. The few other studies of trade associations have focused on population dynamics. Howard Aldrich, Udo Staber, and colleagues put forth several articles that explored variations in the rates of founding, transformation, and death of trade associations (Aldrich & Staber, 1988; Aldrich, Staber, Zimmer, & Beggs, 1990; Aldrich, Zimmer, Staber, & Beggs, 1994; Staber & Aldrich, 1983). They found that trade associations are very robust organizational forms due to their minimalist nature. Minimalist organizations are a special class of organizations that require few resources for founding and sustenance (Halliday, Powell, & Granfors, 1987). Trade associations require little overhead to initiate and, if necessary, can survive for extended periods of time with relatively little financial support. Members may withhold resources from a trade association in difficult times without causing the trade association to collapse. Thus, trade associations are relatively easy to found and likely to survive once founded.

Because of the minimalist nature of trade associations, population studies offer limited insight into key dynamics of these important organizations. Population studies are not sensitive to variation in organizational activity short of the disbanding of an existing organization or the establishment of a new one. An industry's trade association is often founded early in the industry's life because such collective action aids in gaining legitimacy for new types of organizations (Aldrich & Fiol, 1994; DiMaggio, 1988; Oliver, 1990). Yet once legitimacy is established, and so this shared problem is resolved, trade associations rarely disband. Rather, these robust organizations tend to survive for long periods of time. For example, though its name has changed several times, the American Chemistry Council has represented the evolving collective interests of chemical manufacturers since 1872. Thus, when an established industry faces a shared problem, its members are more likely to address this problem within the framework of an existing trade association than to create an entirely new one. As Aldrich and Staber (1988) acknowledged, population-level studies are not sensitive to this activity: "New positions might have been created, new committees formed, dues raised, lobbyists hired, and other actions taken . . . Such developments would not show up at the level of the analysis reported here" (p. 125).

What Do We Need To Know About Trade Associations?

To better understand the nature of trade associations, one must look beyond a few blunt milestones such as creation, reorganization, and eventual abandonment. Much happens in the intervening years. Some trade associations dominate their industries' affairs, controlling large budgets and employing large staffs; others assume a minimalist posture and play a largely ceremonial role. Within a given trade association, activity waxes and wanes over time. Depending on the level of activity, trade associations can shape the competitive landscape, or they can be relatively inert. We need to look inside this black box and assess what drives variation in a trade association's activity throughout its typically long life.

Collective Responses to Shared Problems

A trade association draws resources from its member firms. Firms often incur significant financial and human resource commitments as a condition of participation. For example, American Chemistry Council member firms pay annual dues ranging well into the hundreds of thousands of dollars.[4] Furthermore, they provide "sweat equity" in the form of skilled personnel who participate in the thousands of meetings held at the Council's headquarters each year (Rees, 1997). Yet membership and, accordingly, the associated resource commitments are voluntary. When will firms be willing to commit resources to their trade associations?

Profit-seeking firms, of course, prefer to limit their expenses, all else equal. In the case of trade association spending, this tendency would seem to be exacerbated because firms may engage in free riding. The benefits of trade association activity, such as an improved political and regulatory environment and a better industry reputation, are nonexcludable. When a trade association's efforts leads to a reduction in the regulatory burden on an entire industry, all the firms in the industry benefit, including those who did not contribute to the trade association. Thus, as Olson's (1965) influential work argued, the logic of collective action dictates that so long as participation in an initiative is voluntary and the fruits of the effort are nonexcludable, the rational choice is to free ride. In aggregate, this suggests that the "tragedy of the commons" (Hardin, 1968) prevails in these situations, producing not a voluntary organization that resolves shared problems but inaction that exacerbates these problems.

Despite the logic of collective action, a burgeoning body of research has shown that the tragedy of the commons is often averted in practice. Ostrom (1990) demonstrated that individuals did not succumb to the temptation to free ride under a number of circumstances relating to the preservation of shared natural resources. For example, individuals voluntarily created and participated in organizations that governed the use of fisheries and water sources. Others have extended these ideas on cooperation in the protection of natural resources to industrial settings. Rees (1994) found that the nuclear power industry, facing intense public criticism and rigid government oversight following a nuclear accident at Three Mile Island in 1979, quickly banded together through a trade association, the Institute of Nuclear Power Operations, to increase the industry's prospects for survival. Barnett and King (2008) found that when the chemical industry was under threat following a deadly chemical spill, chemical firms came together to create a new industry self-regulatory program that significantly increased their voluntary commitments to their trade association.

In light of this growing body of research demonstrating that, when confronted by shared problems, firms can avert the tragedy of the commons and come together to create new institutional structures, I hypothesize that firms will increase their activity within existing trade associations when confronted by shared problems. The existing relationships between firms forged over time within a trade association facilitates mobilization by creating a common culture that unifies members (Abrahamson & Fombrun, 1994) and engenders peer pressure to cooperate (Gunningham, 1995), thereby helping overcome the collective action problem (Olson, 1965). In short, it is easier to respond to a shared problem through the action of an existing trade association than it is to create a new organization, and so if firms can create new organizations to manage shared problems, it seems only logical that they can take the less burdensome action of expanding activity within existing organizations to manage shared problems.

> *Hypothesis 1:* A shared problem facing the members of an industry precipitates an increase in the activity of that industry's trade association.

Collective Responses to the Problems of a Few

Though firms may overcome the collective action problem and voluntarily contribute to trade association efforts to manage shared problems facing their industry, how do they recognize a shared problem? The problems faced by a firm are often ambiguous (March & Olsen, 1976). The shared problems faced by an entire industry are yet more ambiguous. For example, how does a firm surmise that its industry's legitimacy is under threat or that the regulatory climate has become problematic?

Hoffman and Ocasio (2001) found that the objective characteristics of a critical event confronting an industry often had little to do with the likelihood that the industry would attend to the event. Lacking objective guidelines on what constitutes a shared problem, firms may rely on social cues (DiMaggio & Powell, 1983). Firms tend to follow the actions of market leaders, presuming that if dominant firms are taking certain actions, then these actions must be appropriate (Ferrier, Smith, & Grimm, 1999). Thus, firms may be alerted to an issue and gauge its importance by the involvement of dominant firms.

In fact, without the leadership of large firms, the collective action problem inherent in trade association activity might never be surmounted (Olson, 1965). Large firms often put forth the initial effort and resources essential for beginning new collective endeavors (Hoffman, 1997; Rees, 1994). Moreover, the involvement of dominant firms increases the perceived feasibility of resolution, thereby increasing the likelihood that firms will participate and a coalition will arise. Faced with an array of potential issues vying for their limited attention, firms tend to participate in those issues that they perceive as most likely to be resolved because involvement with failed issues provides no rewards to offset the costs of participation (Bacharach & Lawler, 1981; Dutton & Webster, 1988).

The associated "follow the leader" behavior provides dominant firms the opportunity to set the agendas of their trade associations. Participation in a collaborative group such as a trade association is a mixed motive game involving simultaneous incentives to compete and cooperate (Phillips, Lawrence, & Hardy, 2000). Although member firms may share some common interests, they are ultimately rivals. There is no reason to believe that rivalry is set aside at the doorstep of a trade association. In fact, it seems more reasonable to believe that those firms with the power to sway trade association agendas actively seek to do so in their favor. Enterprising individuals and organizations have been shown to define, create, and manipulate issues to spur collective action toward some desired end (Davis & Thompson, 1994;

McCarthy & Zald, 1977). Dominant firms in an industry are in a particularly opportune setting to define, create, and manipulate the problems that their trade association pursues.

The strategic intent behind some agenda setting efforts may be hidden. For example, a firm may champion a trade association program that mandates improvements in the social or environmental performance of an industry under the premise that the increased standards will improve the industry's standing with regulators, customers, and other stakeholder groups. But if the championing firm can abide by these higher industry standards at a lower cost or in a superior way than can its rivals, then it gains competitive advantage. Large firms can have a strong hand in establishing these sorts of self-regulatory programs and so can shape these intraindustry policies in ways that play to their scale advantage. For example, Gunningham (1995) discussed the role of Dow Chemical in guiding the development of the chemical industry's self-regulatory program, Responsible Care, and how Dow was able to benefit from this program more easily than were smaller firms who could not spread their costs over such a large asset base. A variety of studies have documented that firms may strategically pursue changes in government policy and regulation that actually increase their regulatory burden as a means of raising rivals' costs even more and deterring new entrance (McWilliams, Van Fleet, & Cory, 2002; Salop & Scheffman, 1983; Williamson, 1968).

It is logical for large firms to initiate collective action on those issues for which they may receive private benefits more than ample to offset their costs of participation (Olson, 1965). But this logic does not suggest that smaller members of a trade association will knowingly subjugate their interests and willingly join efforts that disproportionately advantage their rivals. Especially in light of antitrust laws that limit the scope of coordination among rivals, it is not feasible for the dominant firms in an industry to force their trade association to pursue ventures that clearly disadvantage a substantial portion of the membership, no matter their relative power. However, many of the issues that trade associations face have subjective goals and largely intangible or distant measures of progress (e.g., choosing an ad campaign to improve public opinion, engaging a lobbyist to enhance the regulatory climate). Moreover, dominant firms hold considerable sway over smaller firms. They may use peer pressure or the threat of exclusion from business subcultures to forge cooperation (Galaskiewicz, 1985; Useem, 1984). This makes trade associations a fertile ground for enterprising firms to put forth their favored projects. In fact, a trade association provides the opportunity to engage in these practices more efficiently and effectively. By engaging a trade association instead of going it alone, a firm spreads the costs of its political and regulatory influence efforts.

In sum, the nature of the shared problems facing an industry is often sub-jective, which leaves the agenda of a trade association open to manipulation. Dominant firms have both the incentive and the ability to take the lead in mobilizing trade association activity. Other firms take their cue from domi-nant firms in deciding what constitutes a shared problem and whether or not collective action is likely to resolve it. Thus, dominant firms may seize the opportunity to mobilize trade associations to action to solve their particular problems rather than the problems of the industry as a whole. Therefore, I hypothesize the following:

> *Hypothesis 2:* A problem facing the dominant members of an industry pre-cipitates an increase in the activity of that industry's trade association.

Data and Method

The lack of prior empirical research on activity within trade associations over time may be due, in part, to the difficulty of finding useful longitudinal data. The *Encyclopedia of Associations* (Swartout, 2008) is the primary source of data on trade associations. It annually reports activity figures such as member-ship, budget, and staffing for all trade associations. However, the *Encyclopedia of Associations* relies on self-reporting. Whether out of desire to disguise true spending or lack of desire to report annually, many trade associations report no figures, similar figures, or very round figures each year. Thus, it serves as a poor source of analysis of variability in spending.

Given these limitations, I turned instead to a source of compulsory reporting. Trade associations, as 501(c) nonprofit organizations, are required to file the Internal Revenue Service Form 990 every year. The Form 990 requires detailed reporting of a trade association's income and expenses. A check of this data, made available by The Urban Institute,[5] revealed that, indeed, trade asso-ciation activity is not stagnant. For example, although the *Encyclopedia of Associations* reported an unchanging budget of US$3 million for the National Petroleum Refiners Association from 1990 to 2000, Form 990 data showed that this trade association's total expenses ranged from US$3,610,483 to US$7,266,164, its gross income varied from US$2,969,870 to US$5,091,364, and its gross receipts changed from US$4,825,223 to US$7,838,843 over this same period. Thus, the Form 990 data provide several precise measures of a trade association's annual activity.

Though the *Encyclopedia of Associations* data are of limited use in assessing variability in a trade association's activity over time, they help in choosing a sam-ple from among the large population of trade associations. The *Encyclopedia of Associations* lists more than 22,000 associations. From this list, I selected a sample of 148 major industry trade associations based on several criteria. The electronic version of the *Encyclopedia of Associations*, "Associations Unlimited," provides several options for selecting a sample. I chose only those trade associations that were national in scope so as to avoid double-counting regional associations. Furthermore, I limited the sample to mature trade associations to factor out volatility in activity based on early industry growth. To do this, I included only those trade associations founded in 1980 or earlier—a full decade prior to the beginning of the study period. In addition, I excluded any trade association with more than 1,000 members because such large associations were likely to be professional associations representing the interests of individuals (e.g., lawyers, doctors, actors), not firms. Finally, I restricted the sample to those associations with significant annual budgets, defined as greater than US$1 million, to increase the likelihood that each trade association had more than just a symbolic role in furthering the interests of its members.

This search produced 255 trade associations. I then reviewed on-line documentation for each of these associations to screen out those trade associations that met the above search criteria but did not actually represent the interests of for-profit member firms within a particular industry. For example, the search returned trade associations such as the International Cotton Advisory Committee (countries, not firms as members), the Society of Professional Benefit Administrators (individuals, not firms as members), and the International Trade Council (peak or meta-association serving no single industry). Moreover, I excluded those associations that were not fully discretionary but were partially or fully overseen by a government agency (e.g., U.S. Wheat Associates). Finally, I excluded those trade associations for which I could not find a valid employer identification number (EIN), which serves as a link to the Form 990 database, as well as those trade associations that did not have Form 990 data for at least 8 years of the total 11-year period of this study (1990 to 2000). This resulted in a final sample of 148 major and mature industry trade associations and 1,589 trade association / year observations. The appendix provides a list of these trade associations along with some descriptive characteristics.

For the dependent variable in this study, I chose "annual total expenditures" (totexp). The Form 990 data provided annual figures for a variety of measures of trade association activity, such as the total dues paid, gross receipts, and gross income. I chose total expenditures because a trade association may accumulate assets and so has discretion as to when it may choose to add to or deplete these accumulated assets. Thus, a measure of total expenditures in a given year provides a more direct assessment of activity than does membership dues, gross receipts, or gross income. In other words, totexp assumes that trade associations will "put their money where their mouth is" and so will reveal their true agendas in the ways that they expend their resources over time.

There are two independent variables in this study—one measuring the annual performance of a given industry and the other measuring the annual performance of the dominant firms in that industry. Associations Unlimited provides one or more four-digit standard industrial classification (SIC) code for most trade associations. To augment this data where no SIC code was listed, to judge a primary SIC code where more than one SIC code was listed, and more generally, to serve as an additional check on what I have described above as often questionable data, an independent coder and I examined on-line documentation for each of the 148 trade associations. We independently determined the primary four-digit SIC code for each trade association. In any cases in which we had conflicting judgments, we discussed the cases and then came to a final mutual decision. In those cases in which our final choice of SIC conflicted with that of Associations Unlimited, we deferred to our judgment.

I measure the annual financial performance of a given industry with the variable "% profit for industry." I computed % profit for industry as the total value of shipments for an industry in a particular year, less labor, material, and energy costs, all divided by total value of shipments. I obtained these figures from the U.S. Census Bureau's *Annual Survey of Manufacturers* (ASM). Because of a change of classification system in 1997 (from SIC to NAICS), I could not obtain this measure after 1997. Thus, though the dependent variable spans 1990 to 2000, the time period over which the hypotheses can be tested is effectively restricted to the years 1990 to 1997.

To measure the annual financial performance of the dominant firms in a given industry (a test of Hypothesis 2), I turned to the Combined Compustat/CRSP Business Segment Database. ASM data are not available at the firm level. I computed the variable "% profit for top4" as the net operating profit (or loss) for the four largest firms (in terms of sales) in an industry as a percentage of that industry's total assets. Compustat computes operating profit as operating revenue minus operating expense.

In addition to the above variables, I assembled several control variables. Trade associations with more members, all else equal, should have greater expenditures. Thus, I control for size through the variable "TA members." Industries with high market concentration, wherein the bulk of market share is held by one or a few large firms, should have an easier time mobilizing for collective action than will industries with low market concentration, populated by a broad swath of small firms. I control for market concentration with the variable "HH index," which is the Herfindahl–Hirschman index for each industry. The HH index takes account of the relative size and distribution of firms in an industry in forming an overarching measure of concentration. As noted above in my explanation of the chosen dependent variable, trade associations have discretion. I control for this discretion with the variables "age of TA" and "% rcpts not from dues." As a trade association ages, it becomes more institutionalized and thus potentially more inertial. It may be difficult to disband the myriad projects and committees that arise over time. In addition, the more of a trade association's receipts that are garnered through sources other than direct member dues, such as outside consulting, the more discretion the trade association maintains.

A major expense of trade associations is political lobbying. Therefore, I include a control for whether or not a trade association is headquartered in the Washington, D.C., area (DC office), as such positioning may be indicative of higher lobbying costs.[6] Finally, to control for any effects on the dependent variable caused by variation in the overall economy over time, I include "year dummies."

Table 1 provides descriptive statistics and correlation coefficients for these variables. Many of the correlations are significant. Therefore, I calculated variance inflation factors (VIFs) for each of the independent variables. These VIFs are well within the acceptable range, varying from 1.10 to 1.26, and so multicollinearity does not appear to be a problem.

Results

Table 2 provides the results for several regression models predicting totexp. The odd-numbered models show the results of regressions that did not include % profit for top4, whereas the even-numbered models include this variable. Adding % profit for top4 into the regression separately allows one to more clearly distinguish the effects on the dependent variable attributed to the performance of the dominant firms (Hypothesis 2) from that of the overall industry (Hypothesis 1).

Model 1 is an ordinary least squares regression model. The results of Model 1 show that % profit for industry is not a significant predictor of totexp, thus providing no support for Hypothesis 1. When % profit for top4 was added to the regression in Model 2, % profit for industry remained insignificant, but % profit for top4 was significant and negative at the $p < .01$ level. These results indicate support for Hypothesis 2, wherein trade association expenditures are high when the profitability of dominant firms in an industry is low.

Across both models, several control variables produced significant results. TA members was positively related to totexp, suggesting that, as expected, trade associations with more members tend to have higher expenditures. HH index was also positive and significant, indicating that industries with greater concen-

Table 1. Descriptive Statistics and Correlation Coefficients.

Variable	1	2	3	4	5	6	7	8
1. ln (totexp)								
2. % profit for industry	-.028							
3. % profit for top4	-.194**	.348**						
4. ln (TA members)	.154**	.035	.048					
5. ln (HH index)	.208**	-.104	.067	-.204**				
6. Age of TA	.334**	.082	.024**	.144**	.162**			
7. % rcpts not from dues	0*	-.139	.133**	.338**	.014	-.064		
8. DC office	.368**	.04	.036	.04	.169**	.226**	-.12**	
n	1,583	624	1,246	1,589	970	1,589	1,567	1,589
M		14.8	0.3	0.08	5.3	6 60	0.44	0.66
SD		1.2	0.13	0.07	1.2	1.226	0.26	0.48
Minimum	11	-0.17	-0.15	1.8	2.6	20	0	0
Maximum	18.6	0.65	0.46	7.5	7.9	128	0.99	1

*p < .05. **p < .01.

225

tration have higher trade association spending. Age of TA was also positive and significant, pointing to a somewhat slight tendency for older trade associations to have higher expenditures. Moreover, trade associations headquartered in the Washington, D.C., area, as expected, tended to outspend those headquartered elsewhere. The percentage of receipts of a trade association generated from sources other than member dues appeared to have no significant effect on trade association expenditures.

Models 3 and 4 show the output of a robust regression (rreg method in Stata). Robust regression limits the effects of outliers through weighting (Rousseeuw & Leroy, 1987). I ran robust regression to ensure that none of the larger trade associations had undue influence on the results. Again, the results support Hypothesis 2 and provide no support for Hypothesis 1. In fact, Model 4 shows some slight support for the notion that trade association activity is low when the profitability of the overall industry is low. This may be due to the difficulty of garnering resources from member firms when they face resource constraints. All control variables follow a very similar pattern to that found in Models 1 and 2.

Across this panel, all observations are not independent. The total expenditures of a given trade association are generally not independent of its expenditures in prior years. To account for this, in Models 5 and 6, I ran a robust cluster model. This model relaxes the assumption of independent observations within clusters; in this case, each cluster represents a single trade association. The results again appear to support Hypothesis 2 and provide results quite similar to the prior models, though several of the control variable effects become weaker.

As a stronger control for the lack of independence of observations within a trade association, Models 7 and 8 show the results of a between-effects regression model. This model effectively treats each trade association as a single observation and instead focuses on measuring variation across trade associations. The results are quite consistent with prior models, again lending support to Hypothesis 2, but further highlighting a constraint inherent in this study: The effects found within this panel are cross-sectional, not longitudinal.

Because of data constraints, the portion of the panel included in these regressions encompasses only the period from 1990 to 1997. The total expenditures within a given trade association often do not vary greatly over this time period. As a result, the data reveal little about differences in performance within a given trade association over the time period and instead serve as a test of differences across trade associations. Models 9 and 10, which are fixed effects regressions, confirm this. The fixed effects model factors out the average total expenditures for each trade association and seeks to explain differences within each trade association that deviate from this average factor or fixed effect. Both independent variables are insignificant in the fixed effects models. Moreover, the year dummies, though not listed independently in Table 2, become highly significant ($p < .01$) in these models yet were generally not significant in the prior models.

The variables were assembled from differing sources, so not all variables were available for all trade associations for all years, leading to a significant decrease in the number of trade association / year observations included in the regression models. For example, some of the variables were available only for trade associations with manufacturing SIC codes, from 1990 to 1997. Other variables were available for all years and nonmanufacturing SIC codes but often not all of the same SIC codes as the other variables. Thus, there are 617 observations in the odd-numbered models and 489 in the even-numbered models. Because these two samples may have differing characteristics, I also ran each odd-numbered model on only those 489 observations in the even-numbered model sample. The results were nearly identical and produced identical directionality.

Some of the effects of the independent variables on the dependent variable may be lagged, as it may take some time to mobilize the trade association to increase spending in response to a decline in performance. I ran all 10 models with 1- and 2-year lags. This lagging further reduced the data set, providing somewhat weaker fit but overall similar results in terms of significance and directionality. These results are again consistent with the problem of limited variability in spending across years producing effectively a cross-sectional study.

Discussion

The lack of research on trade associations has left a large and important part of the competitive landscape uncharted. The findings of this study are limited in significant ways, so they cannot provide a detailed map of the uncharted territory of trade associations, but they do suggest some basic points of interest that are worthy of more detailed mapping. This study was unable to explain variations in the activity of a given trade association over time. Nonetheless, in a robust manner and controlling for a variety of variables, this study found that across trade associations, low performance of their primary industry's four largest firms was associated with high trade association expenditures, yet low performance of their primary industry was not associated with high trade association expenditures. This suggests that trade

Table 2. Regression Results Predicting Trade Association Total Expenditures.

Variable	OLS		Robust		Cluster		Between Effects		Fixed Effects	
	1	2	3	4	5	6	7	8	9	10
Constant	12.1***	12.1***	12.3***	12.1***	12.4***	12.1***	9.8***	8.8**	14.5***	14.6***
% profit for industry	-.306	.374	.005	.731*	-.306	-.374	-.255	.569	-.142	-.37
% profit for top4		-3.98***		-3.82***		-3.98***		-5.98***		-0.037
ln (TA members)	.108**	.147***	.129***	.148***	.108	.147	.091	.158	D	D
ln (HH index)	.143***	.182***	.158***	.194***	.143**	.182**	.145	.183	D	D
Age of TA	.01***	.01***	.007***	.007***	.01*	.01*	.011*	.01**	D	D
% rcpts not from dues	-.03	.205	-.184	.135	-.03	.205	-.097	.122	.71***	.801***
DC office	.664***	.726***	.624***	.699***	.664***	.726***	.604**	.716***	D	D
Year dummies	Incl.	Incl.	Incl.	Incl.	Incl.	Incl.	Ircl.	Incl.	Incl.	Incl
No. of observations	617	489	617	489	617	489	617	489	617	489
No. of clusters/groups					90	78	90	78	90	78
Adjusted R^2	.20	.28			.22	.30	.26[a]	.39[a]	.33[b]	.39[b]
F			11.3***	12.3***						

Note: OLS = ordinary least squares; D = dropped from model.
a. Between groups (trade associations) R^2.
b. Within groups (trade associations) R^2.
*$p < .1$. **$p < .05$. ***$p < .01$.

228

associations may speak for and serve the interests of the dominant firms in an industry more so than the interests of the industry as a whole.

Some of the findings across the models offer more nuance. Model 4 found that the performance of the industry was positively, though weakly, associated with the total expenditures of its trade association. Though inferences must be made with caution given the limits of the data, this finding suggests that not only may the industry's voice be primarily that of the dominant firms, but these dominant firms may have an easier time pushing their agendas when the members firms have slack resources, as contrasted with the difficulty they would face in garnering additional funds to pursue their agendas during lean times.

The findings of the fixed effects analyses offer a bit more insight. Models 9 and 10 show a strong positive relationship between the percentage of a trade association's receipts derived from sources other than membership dues and trade association spending. This suggests that as trade associations secure more funding independent of direct dues payments, they tend to make use of this discretion in spending rather than by contributing to reserves. The average nondues income in the sample is 44%, and it can rise to as high as 99%. Thus, it appears that trade associations are fairly independent bodies, able to survive, and spend, in the near term without necessarily having to directly raise member dues. Instead, a significant portion of receipts may come from interest on investments or the sale of assets, or from trade association activities such as program service revenues and meetings and seminars. With such a high level of financial discretion, it seems all the more important to understand how trade associations choose to spend their funds.

Trade associations occupy a tricky legal space that sometimes borders on violation of antitrust laws (Luria, 2005). Though trade associations explicitly involve coordination among rivals, trade associations are allowed to exist under the premise that they serve as a means of resolving shared problems in a way that advances competition while avoiding collusion. If, indeed, trade associations tend to be tools of domination by powerful firms, their antitrust exemption becomes questionable. The findings in this article are not adequate to draw such a conclusion, but they do point to the need for further investigation of just how trade associations work.

For firms that do not dominate their industries—that is, most firms—these findings should give pause for reflection on the benefits they receive relative to the contributions they make to their trade associations. Paying trade association dues may be more or less a rote exercise for most firms, and managers may have no more an expectation of measurable financial returns from these investments than they have from, say, sponsorship of a local little league team. However, when member firms are called on to increase their involvement or support particular trade association initiatives, they should not simply assume that these efforts are in their best interests and so worth pursuing. Instead, they should give consideration to the possibility that they may be using their limited resources in a way that contributes more to the advancement of their rivals' interests than to their industry's shared interests.

The management research on trade associations is limited, but it does recognize that these organizations face an ongoing tension associated with size (Aldrich, 1999; Schmitter & Streeck, 1981; Van Waarden, 1992). Each trade association, as an organization pursuing its own interests, wishes to gain membership and grow larger. Member firms can benefit from increased size because it can bring with it increased influence. However, as a trade association gets larger and its membership grows more diverse, it becomes less able to fully satisfy the unique needs of its individual members, and so this leads to pressure to splinter into subgroups. The findings of this study cannot conclude when a firm no longer fits with its trade association, but it does provide some suggestion that smaller firms may be remaining in large associations longer than they should and might better be served by splintering into smaller specialized trade associations with less heterogeneity in size and power. A smaller trade association means less influence, but it may be that this lessened influence is of greater benefit to its members than is being part of a larger organization that predominantly serves the interests of larger rivals.

Overall, this study helps bring the field a little closer to understanding the drivers of trade association activity, but obviously much more needs to be done. For one, future studies would benefit greatly from lengthier windows. Prior studies in the ecological tradition had very lengthy windows but did not focus on variations in activity within trade associations. The combination of long windows and performance data would be ideal. Trade association activity appears to be fairly constant in the short run. Longer time periods are necessary to evince any measurable disruptions. However, given the underdeveloped state of this literature, it may be necessary to first proceed with smaller scale studies. Qualitative studies may be necessary to observe and understand the actual mechanisms. Although motives can be inferred from spending patterns and other such outcome measures over time, it would be particularly insightful to directly observe trade association activity through field studies. Such work would be laborious, of course, and it could be difficult to gain access to trade associations, but where feasible, such studies offer great promise of rich insight into the workings of these important organizations.

Future studies should also look at the ways in which factors other than changes in profit affect changes in trade association activity. I operationalized a shared problem as a decline in the industry's profitability. Collective action can be difficult to organize (Olson, 1965) especially in the face of ill-defined threats. A decline in profitability would seem to be a tangible and significant threat and so a conservative measure of what might spur firms to take collective action through their trade associations. However, trade associations may not be spurred to action when profit declines if they perceive the decline in profit as relating to factors outside of their control. The inclusion of year effects in this study helped alleviate some concern that exogenous macroeconomic factors such as a general market downturn in any given year might be responsible for trade association activity. However, this study could not determine whether firms perceived any change in industry profitability as something they could influence through trade association activity. Moreover, it is possible that firms may perceive other actions as shared threats, to cope with through trade association activity, before they cause any decline in industry profitability. For example, firms may recognize negative press coverage, looming lawsuits, or a general decline in reputation scores as signaling problems and take action in advance. Future studies should further explore how firms come to recognize shared threats and just how serious the threat must be perceived to be before it spurs collective action (cf. Hoffman & Ocasio, 2001).

In this study, I stepped down from the population level of analysis at which the few prior studies in the organizations literature resided (e.g., Aldrich & Staber, 1988) to look inside trade associations. Nonetheless, the level of insight I was able to garner with the data available was still too abstract to enable strong inference about the inner workings of trade associations. To develop richer insights, future studies will need to gather data that likely will only be feasible to collect through smaller sample sizes. For example, with 148 trade associations, each with membership bases ranging into the hundreds and spanning many years, I was unable to verify that the largest firms in each industry were always members of the trade association affiliated with that industry in this study. Firms may come and go from a trade association over time for any of a number of reasons. Thus, it is possible that even though a firm is a dominant firm in an industry, in any given year it may not be a member of that industry's major trade association.

Trade associations generally do not provide direct access to their membership archives over time. In this study, I checked a sample of five trade associations to confirm that the current membership rosters contained the "top four" firms in their industry during the study period. Of the 20 firms, I could not account for 2. Because I do not have the membership rosters over time and instead am relying on a current membership roster, it is possible that these two firms were members during the study period, but I cannot say with certainty.

However, Staber's (1987) interviews of trade associations in the manufacturing sector add confidence that this is unlikely to be a significant problem:

> Most associations are highly representative of the domain they cover, regardless of their size. Ninety-three per cent cover more than half of their members' industry share, and 74 per cent represent more than three-quarters of their domain . . . all but one represent the four largest producers in their industry. (p. 284)

Another limitation of the large sample study I conducted is that I was unable to account for the performance of private firms. I relied on Compustat/ CRSP for firm-level performance data. As a result, though I tested for whether or not trade association activity was reliant on changes in the performance of dominant firms, I was unable to contrast changes in large firm performance with changes in the profitability of smaller firms, or even many medium-sized firms in the same industry, since these tend not to be publicly listed. Smaller sample studies might be able to obtain useful performance measures for the entirety of their member firms and so contrast large firm effects with those of medium and small firms to better specify the true drivers of trade association activity.

Finally, it is important to note that the broad view of trade associations taken in this study did not allow me to determine the fit between the mission of any particular trade association and the performance of the particular four-digit SIC industry to which I assigned it. As noted previously, I did follow a systematic process for determining the appropriate industry for a given trade association. But this process cannot ensure that the firms within a given SIC rely on that particular trade association exclusively to manage their shared problems. Future smaller scale studies might be able to determine performance of the relevant population of a given trade association at a finer-grained level than that of the four-digit SIC code.

Conclusion

Because firms face many critical interdependencies, strategy researchers have broadly concluded that competition alone is insufficient for the success and survival of most firms. Environmental conditions often affect the likelihood of survival not of individual firms but of groups of firms and entire industries (Astley & Fombrun, 1983). Firms may find that their reputations and performance are intertwined such that the acts of one firm can harm similar other firms (Barnett & Hoffman, 2008; King, Lenox, & Barnett, 2002). To cope with these interdependencies, rival-rous firms often must cooperate (Barnett, 2006a). Especially, in recent years, as many industries have come under attack from increasingly powerful constituent groups (Davis & Thompson, 1994; Freeman, 1984) and government has relaxed many relevant antitrust concerns, firms have coordinated more of their efforts through trade associations. Many indus-try trade associations now go so far as to stringently regulate and stan-dardize the behavior of member firms through industry self-regulation (Barnett & King, 2008; Prakash & Potoski, 2006). Thus, it is all the more important to understand what goes on within trade associations over time.

It is important to note that firms do not rely exclusively on trade associa-tions to deal with problems in their competitive environments. "Communal strategies" (Barnett, 2006a) may be operationalized through venues other than industry trade associations or through multiple trade associations. In addition, when individual firms, especially dominant firms, experience difficult times, they may engage in a variety of individual strategies, such as lobbying and contributions to political action committees. The literature has tended to describe such activities in terms of a dichotomy—firms either act individually to pursue their own nonmarket or political activi-ties, or they join collective efforts such as those of trade associations (see, for example, Hillman & Hitt, 1999). The costs of individually pursuing these activities are high and often may not be effective at favorably in-fluencing the competitive environment. As Astley and Fombrun (1983) argued, "the very impotence of organizations acting in isolation merely elevates the importance of collective action" (p. 582). As a result, trade associations, wherein the costs are pooled and the influence enhanced, are often the primary means of influencing the competitive environment. The findings of this study suggest a sort of third "hybrid" form whereby large firms might use trade associations to pursue their individual goals, effec-tively leveraging the might of the trade association at a fractional cost of engaging in these efforts alone. Future studies should seek to parse out the degree to which they turn to each of these varying activities. The more refined such work becomes the closer we will come to achieving "the most basic operational requirement in the formulation and implementation of strategy," which is to explain the degree to which rivalrous firms also choose to "take on responsibilities as members of a larger social entity" (Astley & Fombrun, 1983, p. 585).

Appendix

Trade Associations in Sample

Name of Trade Association	Founded	Classification	Standard Industrial Staff	Members
Adhesive and Sealant Council	1957	2891	10	130
Aerospace Industries Association of America	1919	3721	44	56
Air Conditioning and Refrigeration Institute (ARI)	1953	3585	45	207
Aluminum Association	1933	3334	30	54
American Architectural Manufacturers Association	1962	3272	14	280
American Association of Advertising Agencies	1917	7311	80	505
American Crop Protection Association	1933	5191	40	78
American Film Marketing Association	1980	7812	35	180
American Insurance Association	1964	6311	140	350
American Iron and Steel Institute	1908	3325	50	50
American Pet Products Manufacturers Association	1959	5199	14	600
American Petroleum Institute	1919	2911	270	400
American Short Line Railroad Association	1913	4011	9	775
American Warehousemen's Association	1891	4225	10	550
American Waterways Operators	1944	4491	20	375
American Wind Energy Association	1974	3511	13	850
American Bakers Association	1897	2051	14	300
American Council of Life Insurance (ACLI)	1976	6311	184	427
American Feed Industry Association	1909	2048	17	675
American Financial Services Association (AFSA)	1916	6061	30	569
American Gas Association (AGA)	1918	5172	100	185
American Gear Manufacturers Association (AGMA)	1916	3462	13	410
American Wood Preservers Institute (AWPI)	1920	2491	7	120
Asphalt Institute (AI)	1919	2911	42	48

(continued)

Appendix (continued)

Name of Trade Association	Founded	Classification	Standard Industrial Staff	Members
Association of International Automobile Manufacturers	1964	3711	11	17
Association of Oil Pipe Lines	1947	4612	5	56
Association of Rotational Molders	1976	3089	6	460
Association of Air Medical Services (AAMS)	1980	4522	5	400
Association of American Publishers (AAP)	1970	2731	23	310
Association of Directory Publishers (ADP)	1898	2741	6	274
Automotive Warehouse Distributors Association	1947	5013	23	335
Battery Council International	1924	3691	3	175
Bituminous Coal Operators' Association (BCOA)	1950	1221	4	19
Bond Market Association	1977	6211	70	200
Chemical Manufacturers Association	1872	2819	300	195
Chlorine Institute	1924	2812	12	240
Chocolate Manufacturers Association of the USA	1923	2064	7	11
Cigar Association of America (CAA)	1937	2121	5	61
Council For Responsible Nutrition	1973	2834	11	100
Commercial Finance Association	1944	6282	15	290
Composite Panel Association	1960	2493	12	36
Composites Fabricators Association (CFA)	1979	2221	14	800
Compressed Gas Association (CGA)	1913	2813	16	230
Copper Development Association (CDA)	1963	3331	22	70
Cosmetic Toiletry and Fragrance Association	1894	2844	49	600
Council of Insurance Agents and Brokers	1913	6411	18	100
Direct Selling Association	1910	5963	22	200
Edison Electric Institute	1933	4911	260	240
Engine Manufacturers Association	1968	3519	5	29
Envelope Manufacturers Association of America	1933	2677	7	175

(continued)

Appendix (continued)

Name of Trade Association	Founded	Classification	Standard Industrial Staff	Members
Equipment and Tool Institute	1947	3559	4	70
Equipment Leasing Association of America (ELA)	1961	7353	27	850
Flexible Packaging Association	1950	3089	20	150
Forging Industry Association (FIA)	1913	3312	13	230
Glass Packaging Institution	1945	3221	5	43
Grocery Manufacturers of America	1908	5141	40	135
Hardwood Plywood and Veneer Association	1921	2435	11	195
Health Industry Distributors Association (HIDA)	1902	5047	21	850
Health Industry Manufacturers Association	1974	3841	55	800
Health Insurance Association of America	1956	6321	100	290
Health Care Distribution Management Association	1876	5122	41	456
Hearing Industries Association (HIA)	1957	3842	4	32
INDA—Association of the Nonwoven Fabrics Industry	1968	2297	20	220
Independent Liquid Terminals Association	1974	4226	6	70
Industrial Fasteners Institute	1931	3452	8	150
Industrial Truck Association	1924	3537	5	145
Information Technology Industry Council	1916	3571	30	28
International Association of Plastics Distributors	1956	5162	7	450
International Mass Retail Association (IMRA)	1966	5399	25	750
International Sleep Products Association (ISPA)	1915	2515	18	750
International Jelly and Preserve Association	1945	2033	5	75
International Tape-Disc Association	1970	3651	9	450
Juvenile Products Manufacturers Association	1962	2512	10	400
Landscape Nursery Council (LANCO)	1952	0181	2	11
Lead Industries Association (LIA)	1928	1031	2	80
Leather Industries America	1917	3111	6	250

(continued)

Appendix (continued)

Name of Trade Association	Founded	Classification	Standard Industrial Staff	Members
Luggage and Leather Goods Manufacturers of America	1938	3161	9	240
Magazine Publishers of America	1919	2721	37	200
Mailing and Fulfillment Service Association (MFSA)	1920	7331	11	720
Manufactured Housing Institute (MHI)	1936	2452	25	350
Material Handling Industry	1945	5084	30	700
Metal Powder Industries Federation	1944	3399	18	315
Motion Picture Association of America	1922	7812	120	8
Motor and Equipment Manufacturers Association	1904	3711	90	700
Motorcycle Industry Council (MIC)	1914	3751	20	310
Napa Valley Vintners	1943	2084	15	150
National Association of Hosiery Manufacturers, NC	1905	2251	9	425
National Association of Small Business Investment	1958	6159	6	300
National Concrete Masonry Association	1918	3271	29	500
National Confectioners Association	1884	2064	27	700
National Electrical Manufacturers Association	1926	3621	95	550
National Electronic Distributors Association	1937	5065	8	300
National Fluid Power Association	1953	3492	16	250
National Food Processors Association	1909	2099	185	500
National Insulation Association	1953	1742	9	700
National Investment Company Service Association	1962	6211	7	400
National Milk Producers Federation	1916	241	20	25
National Multi Housing Council	1978	6531	31	900
National Oilseed Processors Association	1929	2079	6	13
National Paint and Coatings Association	1933	2851	40	450
National Petroleum Refiners Association	1902	2911	31	480
National Precast Concrete Association	1965	3272	13	700
National Renderers Association	1933	2077	5	300
National Venture Capital Association	1973	6799	10	335

(continued)

Appendix (continued)

Name of Trade Association	Founded	Classification	Standard Industrial Staff	Members
National Asphalt Pavement Association	1955	1611	25	750
National Association of Chemical Distributors (NACD)	1971	5169	7	265
National Association of Independent Insurers (NAII)	1945	6331	190	690
National Association of Recording Merchandisers	1958	5735	14	1,000
National Association of Water Companies (NAWC)	1895	4941	10	340
National Chicken Council (NCC)	1954	0251	12	225
National Coffee Association of USA (NCA)	1911	5149	5	185
National Coil Coating Association (NCCA)	1962	3479	6	167
National Soft Drink Association	1919	2086	36	865
National Wooden Pallet and Container Association	1947	2448	10	525
Nonprescription Drug Manufacturers Association	1881	2834	39	215
North American Insulation Manufacturers Association	1933	3296	8	13
Optical Laboratories Association	1894	3851	8	375
Outdoor Power Equipment Institution	1952	3524	8	78
Paperboard Packaging Council	1967	2652	8	65
Personal Communications Industry Association	1965	4812	75	550
Pharmaceutical Care Management Association	1975	6321	16	147
Physician Insurers Association of America	1977	6324	14	60
Portland Cement Association	1916	3241	90	50
Power Transmission Distributors Association	1960	3566	7	465
Precision Machined Products Association	1933	3451	16	550
Promotion Marketing Association of America	1911	8742	12	700
Real Estate Roundtable	1969	6531	11	200
Recording Industry Association of America	1952	3652	60	250

(continued)

Appendix (continued)

Name of Trade Association	Founded	Classification	Standard Industrial Staff	Members
Recreation Vehicle Industry Association	1973	3711	56	520
Reinsurance Association of America	1969	6331	24	36
Rubber Manufacturers Association	1915	2822	22	97
Semiconductor Industry Association	1977	3674	12	40
Snack Food Association	1937	2096	13	700
Society of Independent Gasoline Marketers of America	1958	5172	10	350
Solar Energy Industries Association (SEIA)	1974	3433	4	500
Steel Tube Institute	1930	3312	3	75
Sugar Association	1949	2062	10	23
Synthetic Organic Chemical Manufacturers Association	1921	2869	45	300
The Sulphur Institute (TSI)	1960	2819	9	30
Toy Manufacturers America	1916	3944	24	300
Truck Renting and Leasing Association (TRALA)	1978	4212	7	700
Trucking Management	1963	4212	7	6
Uniform and Textile Service Association (UTSA)	1933	3582	15	200
Valve Manufacturers Association of America	1938	3491	7	120
Vinegar Institute	1967	2099	3	45
Wheat Foods Council (WFC)	1972	0111	3	50
Wine and Spirits Wholesalers of America (WSWA)	1943	5182	11	530
World Wide Pet Supply Association	1951	2047	6	550

Author's Note

This article stems from work associated with my dissertation. My thanks to mydis-sertation committee members: Bill Starbuck, Andy King, and Brian Uzzi.

Notes

1. "One voice" is a common motto of trade associations of all sizes throughout the world. See, for example, the Georgia Urban Agriculture Council (www .urbanagcouncil.com), whose mission statement is "to address issues of common

interest as "one voice—one industry," or the British Insurance Brokers' Association (www.biba.org.uk), which touts "One voice. Strength in numbers." In his interviews of trade association executives, Staber (1987) found the phrase "speak with one voice" to be a common characterization.

2. The interested reader may find more information about the American Chemistry Council (formerly the Chemical Manufacturers Association) at http://www.aga.org/Legislative/legislative+advocacy/legalmatters/antitrust+issues/antitrust-guidelines.htm.

3. For an example of how trade associations attempt to draw the line between legal coordination and collusion, see the American Gas Association's Antitrust Compliance Guidelines, available at http://www.aga.org/NR/rdonlyres/E955E78D-D41D-4BDA-9B8E-6B7B68A 24178/0/0707ANITGUIDE.PDF.

4. Dues vary by trade association and are often based on firm size. Industry trade associations typically do not make public the amount of dues paid by individual firms. The figures cited here are likely at the upper end of the range, representing the amount of dues paid by the largest firms in the most active trade associations.

5. Form 990 data are publicly available through a variety of sources, such as the Foundation Center, but typically not in aggregate form. The Urban Institute was kind enough to provide aggregated data.

6. The DC office control is a common (see Lenway & Rehbein, 1991; Schuler, 1996) but blunt indicator that an organization has a high level of lobbying expenditures. Lobbying may occur in other ways and at other levels, such as the state. However, it is not feasible to obtain a list of the states in which each trade association has a lobbying office, over time, and moreover, it is not clear how one would weight such information. For example, would a Rhode Island office be comparable to a California office? Thus, I retained the common DC office proxy.

References

Abrahamson, E., & Fombrun, C. (1994). Macrocultures: Determinants and consequences. *Academy of Management Review, 19,* 728-755.

Aldrich, H. (1999). *Organizations evolving.* Thousand Oaks, CA: Sage.

Aldrich, H., & Fiol, C. M. (1994). Fools rush in? The institutional context of industry creation. *Academy of Management Review, 19,* 645-671.

Aldrich, H., & Staber, U. H. (1988). Organizing business interests: Patterns of trade association foundings, transformations, and deaths. In G. R. Carroll (Ed.), *Ecological models of organizations* (pp. 111-126). Cambridge, MA: Ballinger.

Aldrich, H., Staber, U. H., Zimmer, C., & Beggs, J. (1990). Minimalism and organizational mortality: Patterns of disbanding among U.S. trade association, 1900-1983. In J. V. Singh (Ed.), *Organizational evolution: New directions* (pp. 21-52). Beverly Hills, CA: Sage.

Aldrich, H., Zimmer, C., Staber, U. H., & Beggs, J. (1994). Minimalism, mutualism, and maturity: The evolution of American trade associations in the 20th century. In J. Singh & J. Baum (Eds.), *The evolutionary dynamics of organizations* (pp. 223-239). Oxford, UK: Oxford University Press.

Astley, W., & Fombrun, C. (1983). Collective strategy: Social ecology of organizational environments. *Academy of Management Review, 8*, 576-587.

Bacharach, S., & Lawler, E. (1981). *Power and politics in organizations.* San Francisco: Jossey Bass

Bailey, I., & Rupp, S. (2006). The evolving role of trade associations in negotiated environment agreements: The case of United Kingdom climate change agreements. *Business Strategy and the Environment, 15*, 40-54.

Barnett, M. (2006a). Finding a working balance between competitive and communal strategy. *Journal of Management Studies, 43*, 1753-1773.

Barnett, M. (2006b). Waves of collectivizing: A dynamic model of competition and cooperation over the life of an industry. *Corporate Reputation Review, 8*, 272-292.

Barnett, M., & Hoffman, A. (2008). Beyond corporate reputation: Managing reputational interdependence. *Corporate Reputation Review, 11*, 1-9.

Barnett, M., & King, A. (2008). Good fences make good neighbors: An institutional explanation of industry self-regulation. *Academy of Management Journal, 51*, 1150-1170.

Barnett, W., Mischke, G., & Ocasio, W. (2000). The evolution of collective strategies among organizations. *Organization Studies, 21*, 325-354.

Baron, D. (1995). The nonmarket strategy system. *Sloan Management Review, 37*, 73-85.

Barringer, B. R., & Harrison, J. S. (2000). Walking a tightrope: Creating value through interorganizational relationships. *Journal of Management, 26*, 367-403.

Chemical Manufacturers Association Report. (1993). *On the road to success* (Responsible Care progress report). Washington, DC: Author.

Collins, E., & Roper, J. (2005). Strategic schizophrenia: The strategic use of trade associations in New Zealand. *Journal of Communication Management, 9*, 256-266.

Davis, G., & Thompson, T. (1994). A social movement perspective on corporate control. *Administrative Science Quarterly, 39*, 141-173.

DiMaggio, P. (1988). Interest and agency in institutional theory. In L. Zucker (Ed.), *Institutional patterns and organizations* (pp. 3-22). Cambridge, MA: Ballinger.

DiMaggio, P., & Powell, W. W. (1983). The iron cage revisited: Institutional isomorphism and collective rationality in organizational fields. *American Sociological Review, 48*, 147-160.

Dutton, J., & Webster, J. (1988). Patterns of interest around issues: The role of uncertainty and feasibility. *Academy of Management Journal, 31*, 663-675.

Ferrier, W., Smith, K., & Grimm, C. (1999). The role of competitive actions in market share erosion and industry dethronement: A study of industry leaders and challengers. *Academy of Management Journal, 42*, 372-388.

Freeman, R. (1984). *Strategic management: A stakeholder approach.* Boston: Pitman.

Galaskiewicz, J. (1985). Interorganizational relations. *Annual Review of Sociology, 11*, 281-304.

Gunningham, N. (1995). Environment, self-regulation, and the chemical industry: Assessing Responsible Care. *Law & Policy, 17*, 59-109.

Gupta, A., & Lad, L. (1983). Industry self-regulation: An economic, organizational, and political analysis. *Academy of Management Review, 8*, 416-425.

Halliday, T., Powell, M., & Granfors, M. (1987). Minimalist organizations: Vital events in state bar associations, 1870-1930. *American Sociological Review, 52*, 456-471.

Hardin, G. (1968). The tragedy of the commons. *Science, 162*, 1243-1248.

Hemphill, T. (1992). Self-regulating industry behavior: Antitrust limitations and trade association codes of conduct. *Journal of Business Ethics, 11*, 915-920.

Hillman, A., & Hitt, M. (1999). Corporate political strategy formulation: A model of approach, participation, and strategy decisions. *Academy of Management Review, 24*, 825-842.

Hirsch, P. (1975). Organizational effectiveness and the institutional environment. *Administrative Science Quarterly, 20*, 327-344.

Hoffman, A. (1997). *From heresy to dogma: An institutional history of corporate environmentalism.* San Francisco: New Lexington Press.

Ingram, P., & Inman, C. (1996). Institutions, intergroup rivalry, and the evolution of hotel populations around Niagara Falls. *Administrative Science Quarterly, 41*, 629-658.

Hoffman, A., & Ocasio, W. (2001). Not all events are attended equally: Toward a middle-range
theory of industry attention to external events. *Organization Science, 12*, 414-434.

King, A., Lenox, M., & Barnett, M. (2002). Strategic responses to the reputation commons problem. In A. Hoffman & M. Ventresca (Eds.), *Organizations, policy, and the natural environment: Institutional and strategic perspectives* (pp. 393-406). Stanford, CA: Stanford University Press.

Lane, C., & Bachmann, R. (1997). Cooperation in inter-firm relations in Britain and Germany: The role of social institutions. *British Journal of Sociology, 48*, 226-254.

Lenox, M., & Nash, J. (2003). Industry self-regulation and adverse selection: A comparison across four trade association programs. *Business Strategy and the Environment, 12*, 343-356.

Lenway, S., & Rehbein, K. (1991). Leaders, followers, and free riders: An empirical test of variation in corporate political involvement. *Academy of Management Journal, 34*, 893-905.

Luria, M. (2005). Trade associations face important patent/antitrust issues. *Intellectual Property & Technology Law Journal, 17*, 13-19.

Maitland, I. (1985). The limits of business self-regulation. *California Management Review, 27*, 132-147.

March, J. G., & Olsen, J. P. (1976). *Ambiguity and choice in organizations.* Bergen, Norway: Universitetsforlaget.

McCarthy, J., & Zald, M. (1977). Resource mobilization and social movements: A partial theory. *American Journal of Sociology, 82*, 1212-1241.

McWilliams, A., Van Fleet, D., & Cory, K. (2002). Raising rivals' costs through political strategy: An extension of resource-based theory. *Journal of Management Studies, 39*, 707-723.

Miles, R. H. (1982). *Coffin nails and corporate strategies.* Englewood Cliffs, NJ: Prentice-Hall.

Oliver, C. (1990). Determinants of interorganizational relationships: Integrations and future directions. *Academy of Management Review, 15*, 241-265.

Olson, M. (1965). *The logic of collective action: Public goods and the theory of groups.* Cambridge, MA: Harvard University Press.

Ostrom, E. (1990). *Governing the commons: The evolution of institutions for collective action.* Cambridge, UK: Cambridge University Press.

Phillips, N., Lawrence, T., & Hardy, C. (2000). Inter-organizational collaboration and the dynamics of institutional fields. *Journal of Management Studies, 37*, 23-43.

Prakash, A., & Potoski, M. (2006). *The voluntary environmentalists: Green clubs, ISO 14001, and voluntary environmental regulations.* Cambridge, UK: Cambridge University Press.

Rees, J. (1994). *Hostages of each other: The transformation of nuclear safety since Three Mile Island.* Chicago: University of Chicago Press.

Rees, J. (1997). The development of communitarian regulation in the chemical industry. *Law & Policy, 19*, 477-528.

Rousseeuw, P. J, & Leroy, A. M.(1987). *Robust regression and outlier detection.* New York: Wiley.

Salop, S., & Scheffman, D. (1983). Raising rivals' costs. *American Economic Review, 73*, 267-271

Schmitter, P., & Streeck, W. (1981). *The organization of business interests* (IIM/LMP 81-13). Berlin, Germany: International Institute of Management, Labour Market Policy Group.

Schuler, D. (1996). Corporate political strategy and foreign competition: The case of the steel industry. *Academy of Management Journal, 39*, 720-737.

Staber, U. (1987). Corporatism and the governance structure of American trade associations. *Political Studies, 35*, 278-288.

Staber, U., & Aldrich, H. (1983). Trade association stability and public policy. In R. Hall & R. Quinn (Eds.), *Organizational theory and public policy* (pp. 163-178). Beverly Hills, CA: Sage.

Swartout, K. (Ed.). (2008). *Encyclopedia of associations: National organizations of the U.S.* (46th ed.). Detroit, MI: Gale Research Co.

Useem, M. (1984). *The inner circle: Large corporations and the rise of business political activity in the U.S. and U.K.* New York: Oxford University Press.

Van Waarden, F. (1992). Emergence and development of business interest associations: An example from the Netherlands. *Organization Studies, 13*, 521-562.

Williamson, O. (1968). Wage rates as a barrier to entry: The Pennington case in perspective. *Quarterly Journal of Economics, 85*, 85-116.

Author Biography

Michael L. Barnett is Professor 1 in the Management and Global Business Department and Vice Dean for Academic Programs at Rutgers Business School–Newark and New Brunswick. Mike's research focuses on the firm-stakeholder interface. In particular, he studies how firms individually and collectively manage their relationships with stakeholders, and how their efforts at stakeholder management, through acts of corporate social responsibility and via communal institutions such as industry trade associations, influence their reputations and financial performance.

10

Journal of Management
Vol. 40 No. 3, March 2014 676–702
DOI: 10.1177/0149206311433854
© The Author(s) 2012
Reprints and permissions:
sagepub.com/journalsPermissions.nav

Why Stakeholders Ignore Firm Misconduct: A Cognitive View

Michael L. Barnett

University of Oxford

This article explains inconsistency in stakeholder punishment for firm misconduct. It does so by developing a cognitive view of the process by which stakeholders allocate their limited attention. This cognitive view outlines individual and situational factors that produce variation in a stakeholder's likelihood of noticing that an act of misconduct has occurred, in how the stakeholder will assess misconduct if he or she does notice it, and in the stakeholder's decision to punish a firm if he or she judges it to have engaged in misconduct. In sum, this process suggests that as stakeholder attention varies across each step of this process, misconduct often will not result in punishment. This suggests limits on the ability to deter firm misconduct through social control.

Keywords: *business case; corporate misconduct; social cognition; social control; stakeholder theory*

Firms sometimes do bad things. Stakeholders can punish firms for doing bad things. Customers can stop purchasing firms' outputs, suppliers can stop providing inputs, employees can withhold their labor, and investors can withdraw their capital, for example. Sometimes stakeholders do this, and sometimes they do not. Why this inconsistency?

To explain inconsistency in stakeholder punishment of firm misconduct, this article develops a cognitive view of the process stakeholders undertake in attending to misconduct.

Acknowledgments: My sincere thanks to the editor and the anonymous reviewers for their insights and prodding throughout a rather lengthy review process. Along the way, I had the benefit of feedback provided by participants in many seminars, to include those at Oxford University, Erasmus University (a few times), Cambridge University, University of Granada, University of Reading, University of St. Andrews, University of Bath, INSEAD, and the Academy of Management conference (a time or two).

Corresponding author: Michael L. Barnett, University of Oxford, Said Business School, Park End Street, Oxford OX1 1HP, UK.

E-mail: michael.barnett@sbs.ox.ac.uk

A cognitive view recognizes that people cannot attend to all the stimuli competing for their limited attention (James, 1890/1983; Simon, 1947). Moreover, a cognitive view recognizes that factors particular to the person and the situation influence how one allocates his or her attention and responds to stimuli (Fiske & Taylor, 1991). Variation in these factors, then, produces variation in a stakeholder's likelihood of punishing any given act of misconduct. A stakeholder may fail to punish a firm because he or she does not notice that it engaged in any misconduct, whereas at other times he or she will be vigilant. Sometimes a stakeholder may notice a firm's misconduct yet give the firm the benefit of the doubt, but under other circumstances he or she will judge the firm harshly. Despite taking a harsh view of the firm and its misconduct, a stakeholder may decide that engaging in punishment is too burdensome, yet at other times he or she will allocate significant effort to punishment.

It is necessary to explain variation in how stakeholders respond to firm misconduct in order to better align the interests of business and society. Drawing from stakeholder theory (Freeman, 1984), scholars have widely advanced a "business case" that argues that stakeholder rewards and punishments condition firms to become good corporate citizens (Fombrun, Gardberg, & Barnett, 2000). However, this literature has largely assumed that stakeholders consistently police firm behavior. If stakeholders sometimes ignore misconduct, the business case may sometimes be ineffective at driving improvements in corporate social responsibility (CSR). Thus, addressing stakeholder cognition, and the inconsistency in punishment for firm misconduct it may bring, helps elicit bounds on the effectiveness of the business case.

This article next reviews the business case literature and highlights assumptions regarding stakeholder attentiveness. Thereafter, it outlines the complex process required of a stakeholder to be attentive to firm misconduct. It then develops a process model that proposes the influence of individual and situational factors on stakeholder attentiveness to misconduct. It concludes with a discussion of the implications of stakeholder cognition for macro- and microlevel research on the business case for CSR and for public policy regarding the balance of formal and informal regulation of business.

Assessing the Business Case

Myriad laws ban specific types of firm misconduct, and criminal and civil courts provide a formal means of punishing violators. However, there are many acts of misconduct[1] that, though they may impose harm on society, are not illegal or are impractical to control through legal proceedings. To fill this void, a few decades ago scholars in the burgeoning field of business and society began to study informal means by which society might control firm behavior. As Jones put it, "The notion of 'social control of business,' defined as the means by which society directs business activity to useful ends . . . is the core of the business and society field" (1982: 560).

Freeman's (1984) stakeholder approach outlined the mechanisms that make business amenable to social control. He highlighted the relationships that exist between a firm and its various stakeholders,[2] beyond just those who own shares of its stock, and argued that the strategic management of these relationships underpins firm performance. If its stakeholder relationships are weak, a firm will have difficulty attracting essential inputs and selling its outputs on favorable terms. Simply, if they are unhappy with a firm, "Customers stop buying products, shareholders sell their stock, employees withhold loyalty and best efforts" (Wood, 1991: 697), and so forth. But if these relationships are strong, the firm can gain competitive advantage (Jones, 1995). For example, firms that have developed strong stakeholder relationships through socially responsible behaviors can better attract quality employees (Turban & Greening, 1997) and may have easier access to foreign markets (Gardberg & Fombrun, 2006). Thus, the benefits to be reaped by courting stakeholder favor and the costs to be suffered by engendering their anger combine to form a profit motive—a "business case"—that logically drives firms to voluntarily seek to behave responsibly and to eschew misconduct (Burke & Logsdon, 1996; Vogel, 2005).

Scholars have widely touted the "win-win" promise of the business case for both business and society (cf. Margolis & Walsh, 2003), and firms have widely proclaimed their support of its clear logic of enlightened self-interest (Hockerts, 2007). For example, Starbucks took out a full-page advertisement in *The New York Times* to proclaim, "High ideals don't have to conflict with the bottom line. . . . When we reached out through community programs, people bought more of our coffee. Values can actually enhance value, as revolutionary as that may sound. . . . Our shareholders think so, too." Walmart, though initially hesitant to engage, in recent years has come around to an appreciation of the business case, noting on its website: "At Walmart, we know that being an efficient and profitable business and being a good steward of the environment are goals that can work together."

Despite its deep entrenchment in business and academia, however, the business case is not consistently effective at deterring misconduct. Though firms now broadly recognize the importance of maintaining favorable stakeholder relations, examples of misconduct continue, and those firms that engage in it may not always have reason to conclude that more misconduct would be detrimental to their self-interest. Consider banks. Irresponsible banking practices recently contributed to a severe downturn and near collapse of the world's economic system. Yet banks seem to have failed to "understand the huge and devastating impact they have had on the economy and society" and within a short amount of time thought it "OK to return to business as usual" (Lord Davies, U.K. Minister for Trade, Investment and Business, as quoted in Armitstead, 2009). Overall, investment bankers may have profited from the state bailout (Aldrick, 2009). Likewise, oil firms have caused great destruction yet profited greatly. Though BP recently suffered severe punishment for its oil leak in the Gulf of Mexico, other oil firms have been leaking oil for decades without punishment. "The Niger Delta . . . has endured the equivalent of the Exxon Valdez spill every year for 50 years by some estimates. The oil pours out nearly every week, and some swamps are long since lifeless" (Nossiter, 2010). Exxon Mobil and Royal Dutch Shell, whose pipes were said to have leaked (Nossiter, 2010), recently set a string of record profits. Thus, the business case may be ineffective at deterring some significant and recurring forms of misconduct.

How can examples of misconduct such as these persist in the face of widespread acceptance of the business case? By its own logic, the business case is a deterrent only to the degree that stakeholders present a credible threat of punishing those firms that engage in misconduct, thereby leading firms to conclude that misconduct would be too costly were it pursued. For example, when a firm decides to lower its costs of production through the socially irresponsible practice of exploiting child labor in its factories, if stakeholders react by boycotting, leaving the employ of the firm, terminating supply or distribution relationships, and so forth, then the firm should conclude that the use of child labor is too costly and, on the basis of self-interest alone, stop engaging in such practices. But if banks, oil firms, or others may sometimes engage in misconduct without engendering costly stakeholder punishment, then these firms may not learn to extinguish their bad behaviors.

In sum, the business case is only as effective a means of social control as those agents who underpin it—stakeholders. But how effective are stakeholders? Over the past several decades, the many studies of the business case have primarily sought to discern a correlation between corporate social and financial performance (Margolis & Walsh, 2003). They have largely failed to assess the mechanisms that might drive this relationship. The next section focuses on the critical role of stakeholders and the scope of the challenge they face in serving as agents of social control. The section thereafter proposes factors that cause variation in their likelihood of fulfilling this role.

The Complexity of Stakeholder Punishment

Stakeholders undertake a complex and cognitively demanding task when deciding to punish firms for their misconduct. To determine a punishment, a stakeholder must assess not only the characteristics of the act but also the character of the actor. As Godfrey (2005: 788) noted, firms accrue positive moral capital through philanthropy, and stakeholders account for this positive moral capital when weighing punishment:

> When bad acts occur, it is reasonable to assume that stakeholders invoke the cognitive template suggested by the mens rea doctrine to help determine appropriate sanctions. As stakeholders consider possible punishments and sanctions, positive moral capital acts as character evidence on behalf of the firm. Positive moral capital provides counterfactual evidence to mitigate assessments of a bad mind; it reduces the probability that the firm possessed the evil state of mind that justifies harsh sanctions. Positive moral capital encourages stakeholders to give the firm the benefit of the doubt regarding intentionality, knowledge, negligence, or recklessness.

Thus, when a firm engages in a bad act, the more positive moral capital it has accrued, the better it is protected from stakeholder sanction, as stakeholders account for this capital when imputing a sort of "culpability score" for the bad act (Godfrey, 2005: 788).

Barnett (2007a) argued that stakeholders account not just for a firm's past philanthropy but for its overall corporate social performance—effectively, its historical record of socially responsible and irresponsible acts—when assessing a firm's character and deciding how to respond to its acts. Wood (1991: 693), who provides the most cited definition of corporate social performance, suggests the following means for assessing it:

> Thus, to assess a company's social performance, the researcher would examine the degree to which principles of social responsibility motivate actions taken on behalf of the company, the degree to which the firm makes use of socially responsive processes, the existence and nature of policies and programs designed to manage the firm's societal relationships, and the social impacts (i.e., observable outcomes) of the firm's actions, programs, and policies. In addition, the researcher would examine all these elements—principles, processes, and outcomes—in conjunction with each other to permit identification of analytically crucial but politically

difficult results such as good outcomes from bad motives, bad outcomes from good motives, good motives but poor translation via processes, good process use but bad motives, and so on.

This is quite a burden to place on a researcher assessing even a single firm at a single point in time and perhaps explains why corporate social performance remains a problematic measure (Margolis & Walsh, 2003). Yet, as the literature acknowledges, stakeholders bear such a burden when deciding how to punish firms for misconduct. In fact, the process stakeholders undertake in punishing firms for misconduct is even more complex than the literature has acknowledged. Before a stakeholder can assess the nature of misconduct and decide an appropriate punishment, that stakeholder must have noticed that the act occurred. That is, events first "must be bracketed from an amorphous stream of experience and be labeled as relevant before ongoing action can be focused on them" (Weick, Sutcliffe, & Obstfeld, 2005: 415).

Is it correct to assume that stakeholders can effectively bear these burdens, and so consistently police firm misconduct? In short, no, it is not. One of the foundational concepts of the modern management literature is that people have limited attention and so are boundedly rational in their decision making (Cyert & March, 1963; March & Simon, 1958; Simon, 1947). Accordingly, stakeholders have limited attention and are boundedly rational. This significantly constrains their ability to notice, assess, and thereafter punish firm misconduct.

A person can focus his or her attention on only a portion of the unbounded environment, creating a limited field of vision (Simon, 1947). Stimuli falling outside this field of vision are unlikely to be noticed (James, 1890/1983; Kahneman, 1973). When a firm engages in an act of misconduct, if a stakeholder is busy attending to other matters, that stakeholder may not notice the misconduct. If noticed, the stakeholder then faces the challenge of making sense of what he or she has noticed (Weick, 1995). For misconduct, this entails judging the act relative to the firm's history of good and bad acts (Barnett, 2007a; Godfrey, 2005) and in consideration of the processes and policies in place (Wood, 1991). It is thus not a certainty but a probability that a stakeholder will even face the decision to punish a firm for its misconduct; the act may go unnoticed, or the firm may be given the benefit of the doubt instead. Yet even if a stakeholder is faced with the decision to punish a firm for an act he or she has deemed to be misconduct, punishment still may not result. The stakeholder may choose to do nothing, not necessarily because the firm has accrued moral capital ample to offset its misconduct, but because he or she perceives that punishment requires too much effort relative to other demands on his or her limited resources.

The literature has relaxed some of its underlying assumptions of unbounded stakeholder rationality. For example, Rowley and Moldoveanu (2003: 205) stated:

> Our model builds on the work of stakeholder researchers dissatisfied with the strict behavioral assumptions underlying economic models of managerial and firm behaviors (Donaldson & Preston, 1995; Jones, 1995; Jones & Wicks, 1999): actors are assumed to have stable preferences based on utility maximization, which guide their behavior.

Instead, they introduced identity as a driver of stakeholder action. But this and other studies still assumed that stakeholders are alert to misconduct and unconstrained in their ability to assess it and take action, whether they decide to act on the basis of economic utility, identity, or something else. The next section relaxes this assumption. Instead, it offers a model of the process required of cognitively constrained stakeholders to attend to misconduct and develops a series of propositions that outline individual and situational influences on each stage of this process.

A Cognitive View of Stakeholder Punishment

Before outlining the process involved in stakeholder punishment of firm misconduct, it is important to first define both stakeholders and misconduct. Given the broad and subjective nature of the term, defining stakeholders tends to be more a matter of clarifying who is not rather than who is. The generally accepted definition, offered by Freeman, is "any group or individual who can affect or is affected by the achievement of the firm's objectives" (1984: 25). Goodpastor (1991) pointed out that the distinction between "can affect" and "affected by" serves as a way of parsing stakeholders into two categories: strategic and moral. The first category is particularly germane to this article, as the focal concern is the stakeholder's decision to punish a firm. Thus, stakeholders herein are confined to strategic stakeholders. Purely moral stakeholders, lacking the ability to affect the firm, are excluded.

For similar reasons, the media are also excluded. The media are intermediaries that do not directly control resource flows to and from firms, as do stakeholders, but instead affect how resource-wielding stakeholders perceive firms (Carroll & Hannan, 2000; Yu, Sengul, & Lester, 2008). This distinction between stakeholders and intermediaries is similar to that between primary and secondary stakeholders (Carroll, 1979). For example, Clarkson defines secondary stakeholders as "those who influence or affect, or are influenced or affected by, the corporation, but they are not engaged in transactions with the corporation and are not essential for its survival" (1995: 107). Thus, given their indirect influence on the firm, the media and other intermediaries or secondary stakeholders are excluded,[3] though their influence on stakeholders will be considered.

This article further narrows Freeman's (1984) definition by focusing on individuals. Several studies have explored group decisions to act. For example, Hendry (2006) investigated when nongovernmental organizations (NGOs), defined as stakeholders, choose to target firms. Membership within a group, such as an NGO, shapes identity and influences focus of attention, as later discussed, but members' perspectives are broader than those of the groups to which they belong. One member of a group may closely attend to a particular act of misconduct that another may completely ignore. Defining stakeholders at the group level masks this individual variation, and so herein, a stakeholder is taken to be an individual, though group-level influences on individual stakeholders will be discussed.

In sum, the definition of stakeholder used herein—*those individuals who can directly affect the achievement of a firm's objectives*—is at the finer grained level of the individual, not consolidated at the group level, and excludes intermediaries. Moreover, it is not limited to individuals of certain types, such as only consumers (e.g., Schuler & Cording, 2006), since limited cognitive capacity is common to all individuals (Miller, 1956). Thus, despite excluding aspects of Freeman's (1984) definition, this definition of stakeholder is broader than that used in much of the literature because it encompasses (individual strategic) stakeholders regardless of group, whether passive consumer or active investor, for example.

Misconduct is yet harder to define. Though statutes define legality, lawyers make careers of arguing what constitutes illegal behavior. What constitutes unethical or socially irresponsible behavior is all the more debatable. Based on an extensive review, Greve, Palmer, and Pozner argue that there is no objective definition of misconduct; rather, those who have the power to impose sanctions on a firm determine what constitutes misconduct: "We define organizational misconduct as behavior in or by an organization that a social-control agent judges to transgress a line separating right from wrong; where such a line can separate legal, ethical, and socially responsible behavior from their antitheses" (2010: 56).

For the purposes of this article, and consistent with Greve et al. (2010), we need not wade into the murky waters of declaring that any given act is, by some objective standard, misconduct. Rather, we need only to assume that, under some set of conditions, a stakeholder *would* notice the act, judge it to be misconduct, and act to punish it. The model developed in this article then assesses the likelihood that this stakeholder *will* do these things as individual and situational factors vary. Thus, we define misconduct here to mean *any publicly disclosed firm action that, under some set of conditions, a stakeholder would deem illegal, unethical, or socially irresponsible and take action to punish.*[4]

Having established the definitions that bound it, Figure 1 illustrates the process by which stakeholders come to punish misconduct. The process is composed of the three stages previously mentioned—noticing, assessing, and acting—with each stage arranged consecutively.[5] As illustrated at the top of Figure 1, it is assumed that among the unbounded environmental stimuli there exists some set of acts of misconduct. The smaller subset at the bottom of the figure denotes that a stakeholder will punish only a portion of these acts. Many instead will be filtered out at the intervening stages along the way.

The primary nature of this filtering process varies across each stage. In the initial noticing stage, it entails recognition, as the stakeholder must discern misconduct amid the broader cacophony of environmental stimuli (Kiesler & Sproull, 1982). In the ensuing assessment stage, the primary cognitive task entails retrospection. To make sense of noticed stimuli, stakeholders compare against preexisting mental maps (Weick, 1995), and to judge the act, stakeholders recall and take into account the firm's history (Barnett, 2007a; Godfrey, 2005; Wood, 1991). In the final stage, calculation comes more to the fore. Here, the stakeholder, having noticed and assessed the misconduct, makes an intendedly rational decision whether or not to allocate his or her limited resources to punishing it. Of course, stakeholders combine elements of recognition, retrospection, and calculation within each stage. For example, a cost–benefit calculation to punish may be swayed by recall of past related situations. As well, recognition may involve calculated decisions about where to allocate one's search efforts.

Figure 1 lists, by stage, individual and situational factors that are proposed to influence the likelihood that a stakeholder will engage in each of these tasks. Individual factors are characteristics particular to a stakeholder, and situational factors are characteristics particular to the context in which the misconduct occurs. As these factors vary, what a stakeholder is likely to attend to and how a stakeholder is likely to behave vary. We next develop the propositions listed in Figure 1, stage by stage.

Figure 1
A Cognitive Process of Stakeholder Punishment for Firm Misconduct

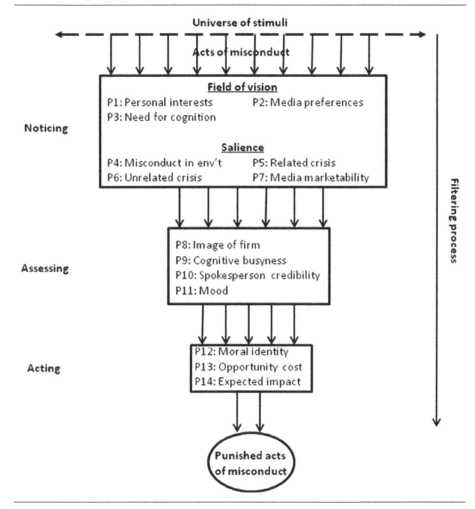

Noticing: The Stakeholder as Selective Observer

Despite its inherent attention-attracting qualities, misconduct can be overlooked. Stakeholders have overlooked even major acts of misconduct (Hoffman, 1997; Hoffman & Ocasio, 2001). Misconduct may fall outside of a stakeholder's limited field of vision or prove indistinctive from the surrounding stimuli and so fail to be noticed (Kiesler & Sproull, 1982; Starbuck & Milliken, 1988). This section first explains how individual characteristics influence the likelihood that a stakeholder's field of vision will encompass areas of the environment where misconduct is likely to be present and, thereafter, how situational factors affect the likelihood that any misconduct that is present will be salient.

Field of vision. Lacking omniscience, we are forced to limit the scope of the unbounded world to which we attend. Much falls outside one's field of vision. So to which limited portion do we pay attention? Often, we look to others for guidance. People are likely to attend to something when directed to do so (Taylor & Fiske, 1975). For example, if someone shouts, "Hey, look over there!" you probably will.

Things that direct our attent need not be surprising or fleeting, though. Organizations formally and informally direct the limited attention of their members through concrete and contextual structures that channel attention to those areas of the environment that support organizational goals (Ocasio, 1997). Thus, if a stakeholder is a member of an organization that seeks to address misconduct, such as a regulatory body or an NGO, then that stakeholder is more likely to be attentive to such misconduct. The more a stakeholder identifies with the organization's goals, the more attentive to such misconduct the stakeholder is likely to be (cf. Rowley & Moldoveanu, 2003). For those in its employ, organizations can formally direct their fields of vision for substantial periods of time through work duties that entail scanning particular areas of the environment.

More generally, through both intentional and unconscious processes, people seek to use their limited attention to maximum benefit by selectively attending to those things that most fit with their goals and consequently ignoring those things that do not (Fiske & Taylor, 1991). Unsurprisingly, for example, people are more likely to direct their attention to others upon whom their success depends, such as their superiors in the workplace (Porter & Roberts, 1976), crowding out attention to those of lesser instrumental value (Berscheid, Graziano, Monson, & Dermer, 1976). Likewise, rivals pay closer attention to each other than to nonrivals (Ruscher & Fiske, 1990). Accordingly, if one's personal or professional interests are likely to be furthered by uncovering particular acts of misconduct, then one is more likely to look for them.

A stakeholder's self-interest need not be conceptualized merely as the opportunity for personal and professional gain, however. It can include protecting oneself and one's community from harm. For example, a stakeholder who lives beside an oil pipeline is more likely to notice that the pipe is leaking oil than is a stakeholder who lives in another country (cf. Nossiter, 2010). In fact, since risk of loss tends to be more salient than opportunity for gain (Tversky & Kahneman, 1974), a stakeholder may be more likely to notice misconduct that threatens his or her self-interest, to include the interests of others he or she wishes to safeguard, than misconduct that might advance these interests. This leads to the following proposition[6]:

> *Proposition 1:* The likelihood that a stakeholder will notice a particular act of firm misconduct varies with his or her personal interests.

Proposition 1 does not imply that stakeholders will ignore all misconduct that does not promise to help or threaten to hinder their interests. In fact, studies have demonstrated that people sometimes behave in self-sacrificial ways (e.g., Fiske, 1991; Kahneman, Knetsch & Thaler, 1986; Turillo, Folger, Lavelle, Emphress, & Gee, 2002). Nonetheless, even self-sacrificial stakeholders have limited fields of vision and so can notice only a portion of the environment wherein those events that they might deem to warrant their sacrifices occur. Proposition 1 argues that the likelihood of a stakeholder's limited field of vision encompassing an act that may draw him or her to action, whether that action is then self-sacrificial, self-interested, or some combination thereof, increases with his or her stake in attending to that portion of the environment that contains it. For example, though a stakeholder may be willing to punish any firm that pollutes a river, even if such actions require self-sacrifice, all else equal, that stakeholder is more likely to notice river pollution occurring in his or her community than that occurring outside of it.

Simply, as one's personal interests change, due to a change in location or employment, for example, one's field of vision changes. But regardless of one's personal interests, or tendencies toward self-sacrifice, most stakeholders do not actively police most firms most of the time. It is impossible for a stakeholder to directly observe all firm actions at all points in time, even were all firms completely transparent. Except for those issues in which they have particularly strong self-interest (or strong desire for self-sacrifice) and are able and willing to take on the burdensome duties of directly monitoring firm activities, most stakeholders become aware of most firm actions through an intermediary, typically the media (Deephouse, 2000).

The media make it easier for stakeholders to notice a firm's activities without having to directly monitor the firm, but the media cannot resolve the problem of stakeholder limited field of vision. There are numerous media outlets pushing numerous stories from myriad perspectives, all vying for an audience. A stakeholder cannot attend to all media. So which media outlets are likely to fall within a stakeholder's field of vision?

People tend to seek out information that confirms their prior beliefs and to ignore disconfirming information (Wason, 1960). This confirmation bias influences which media outlets are likely to fall within a stakeholder's field of vision. Media outlets vary, for example, in their political leanings (Groseclose & Milyo, 2005), and people prefer those media outlets that match their own political leanings (Mullainathan & Shleifer, 2005). Those with conservative political leanings often attend to different news sources than do those with liberal political leanings (Bernhardt, Krasa, & Polborn, 2008; Virag, 2008). For example, former U.S. Vice President Dick Cheney, a political conservative, required that televisions in his hotel rooms be preset to Fox News, a media source with conservative political leanings (Groseclose & Milyo, 2005).

The news stories that one is likely to be exposed to vary with the media outlets to which one attends, as differing media outlets feature differing stories. Coverage choices have been shown to vary, for example, with the political leanings of the media outlet (Baron, 2006; Patterson & Donsbach, 1996). Of particular relevance, Benediktsson (2010) found that the political ideology of newspapers significantly influenced their coverage of corporate scandals. Those with conservative political leanings, as evidenced by their political endorsements, were much less likely to cover incidents of high-profile accounting scandals than were those with liberal political leanings. Corporate ownership can also influence scandal reporting. Studies suggest that media owned by large corporations are prone to less negative coverage of business activity (Bagdikian, 2000). Overall, studies have uncovered a variety of persistent biases in media reporting about firm behavior and beyond (Baron, 2006).

Given the presence of more and more media outlets, the likelihood that any given act of misconduct will be covered by a media source has likely increased. Yet, despite increased access to information in general, the likelihood that any given stakeholder will encounter information that challenges his or her beliefs may have decreased. Stakeholders now have access to so much belief-consistent information that media sources offering contrary evidence have difficulty crowding into a stakeholder's limited field of vision (Sunstein, 2001). With more media outlets customizing their content to compete for a niche in a crowded space, audience polarization and selective exposure to information continues to increase (Bernhardt et al., 2008; Virag, 2008). Thus, the following relationship is expected:

> *Proposition 2:* The likelihood that a stakeholder will notice a particular act of firm misconduct varies with the media sources he or she favors.

Stakeholders vary not only in where they tend to look for news but also in *whether* they tend to look for news. Increased media choices have brought increased access to entertainment as well as to news (Prior, 2005). Whether one seeks out news or entertainment depends upon one's motivations (Rubin, 1981). The personality trait "need for cognition" captures one's motivational tendency toward engaging in effortful cognitive endeavors such as information gathering (Cacioppo & Petty, 1982). People who are high in need for cognition are more likely to take on the burden of searching media sources for information and search more broadly than are people who are low in need for cognition (Cacioppo, Petty, Feinstein, & Jarvis, 1996). Those high in need for cognition also rely more on newspapers and magazines than on television for news (Ferguson, Chung, & Weigold, 1985), but when watching local television news, they favor news items over sports or entertainment, in contrast to those who are low in need for cognition (Perse, 1992). The following is thus expected:

> *Proposition 3:* The likelihood that a stakeholder will notice a particular act of firm misconduct varies with his or her need for cognition.

In sum, the limited portion of the unlimited environment to which a stakeholder attends will vary as his or her personal interests change (Proposition 1), as he or she looks to differing outlets for news (Proposition 2), and as he or she becomes more or less interested in attending to news at all (Proposition 3). As these factors vary, the likelihood that any particular act of misconduct will fall within that stakeholder's field of vision varies. If misconduct falls within a stakeholder's field of vision, however, it still may go unnoticed. People selectively perceive only a subset of the stimuli that fall within their fields of vision (Hambrick & Mason, 1984). The next propositions address influences on the saliency of misconduct.

Salience. Confronted with unbounded stimuli, people act as "cognitive misers" (Taylor, 1981) who tune out common and expected stimuli while conserving their attention for stimuli that differ from expectations (Kiesler & Sproull, 1982). Even misconduct can fade into the background if commonplace. For example, bribery is more common yet less likely to attract attention in countries that are high in corruption (Lee, Oh, & Eden, 2010; Mauro, 1998).

As the severity of misconduct to which a stakeholder has become accustomed increases, the stakeholder's sensitivity to misconduct should decrease. One's ability to detect contrasting stimuli depends upon the base rate of the stimuli; the higher is the base rate, the greater must be the change to be detectible (i.e., Weber-Fechner's law; see Luce & Galanter, 1963). Thus, a stakeholder situated in a country, community, or corporation where corruption is rampant might be well aware that corruption exists but fail to register any particular minor breach. Therefore:

> *Proposition 4:* The likelihood that a stakeholder will notice a particular act of firm misconduct varies with the overall level of misconduct in his or her surroundings.

If an act of misconduct does manage to cross a stakeholder's perceptual threshold, it can cast a wide attentional net. Lacking the cognitive capacity to independently assess all actions, people place actors into broad categories and assume similarity of attributes within these categories (Bruner, 1957). This conserves attention but produces stereotyping (Allport, 1954).

When applied to firm misconduct, King, Lenox, and Barnett (2002) termed this a "reputation commons problem." Unable to observe all the practices of all firms, people presume that similar firms behave similarly. As a result, when a firm engages in misconduct, its entire industry may be "tarred by the same brush" (Barnett, 2007b; Yu et al., 2008). With suspicions raised, stakeholders direct their attention toward the entire industry, and so any new acts of misconduct therein become highly salient. Barnett and King (2008) found this to hold in the chemical industry, for example, where in the aftermath of Union Carbide's disaster in Bhopal, India, a sort of "chemophobia" (Gunningham, 1995: 72) arose in which stakeholders attended more closely to reports of chemical spills that might have received very limited attention previously. Similar patterns of heightened salience of previously ignored practices following crises can be seen in response to nuclear disasters, accounting scandals, and financial institution bankruptcies, for example. Thus, the following relationship is expected:

> *Proposition 5:* The likelihood that a stakeholder will notice a particular act of firm misconduct varies with the recency of a crisis in the same or related industry as that of the misconduct.

Though one firm's misconduct can bring unwelcome attention to the previously overlooked misconduct of similar firms, it may benefit dissimilar firms. If a stakeholder's limited attention is directed toward the activity of one group, that attention is unavailable to focus elsewhere (Kahneman, 1973). As a result, a firm may benefit from a crisis in an unrelated area because stakeholder attention is less available to notice its misconduct.

In the media, where stakeholders tend to garner news of misconduct, there is evidence of the crowding out of rather significant events when more newsworthy events coincide. Eisensee and Stromberg (2007) found that media coverage of the Olympic Games could crowd out coverage of deadly natural disasters. Given limited capacity, even events as extreme as terrorism go uncovered at times (Delli Carpini & Williams, 1987: 60). Thus, the following is expected:

> *Proposition 6:* The likelihood that a stakeholder will notice a particular act of firm misconduct varies with the recency of a crisis that is unrelated to the misconduct.

However, even on a slow news day, some acts of misconduct can receive scant media coverage. The media choose which misconduct to cover not only by comparison to other events that might be covered but also based on the circumstances in which the misconduct occurs. As a result, though two acts of misconduct might be of similar magnitude and cause similar amounts of social, environmental, and economic harm, they may receive different amounts and intensity of media coverage.

King and Baerwald (1998) argue that there are three biases in the type of misconduct that the media choose to cover. The media are more likely to pursue the misconduct of celebrity firms, to overlook misconduct without a clear cause or culprit, and to cover events with a "villain" and straightforward plot. Thus, stakeholder attention is channeled toward stories "with a villain, a hero, and exciting action sequences" and away from stories that are "difficult to measure, difficult to link to a single action, and difficult to communicate" (King & Baerwald, 1998: 310-11). Rindova, Pollock, and Hayward (2006) similarly argue that the media focus their attention on those firm events that can be dramatized and made entertaining to the reader (Bryant & Miron, 2002) and in the process create celebrity firms that draw increased public attention. This suggests the following:

> *Proposition 7:* The likelihood that a stakeholder will notice a particular act of firm misconduct varies with the media's perceived marketability of the circumstances in which it occurs.

In sum, any given act of misconduct can lose salience amid a backdrop of corruption (Proposition 4), yet a recent crisis in a particular area can shine a harsh light on similar types of misconduct (Proposition 5) while drawing the spotlight away from other types of misconduct (Proposition 6). Furthermore, the firm in which it occurs and the stories that can be told about it affect whether misconduct will be highlighted by the media (Proposition 7).

As illustrated in Figure 1, when misconduct does make its way into a stakeholder's field of vision and is salient, the stakeholder next faces the task of assessing it. For example, if a stakeholder notices that a firm has closed its call center in Kansas and outsourced its customer service function to a firm in India, that stakeholder could interpret this as a sensible response to an economic downturn or as an indicator of the firm's lack of concern for its employees. Or, if a stakeholder notices that a firm has suffered a chemical spill that led to an evacuation of the neighborhood surrounding one of its facilities, that stakeholder could interpret this as a minor and well-managed consequence of a complex production process or as a symptom of the firm's underlying disregard for public safety. The next four propositions identify causes of variation in how a stakeholder assesses the misconduct he or she has noticed.

Assessing: The Stakeholder as Biased Judge

People tend to interpret the stimuli that they notice in ways that confirm their prior beliefs (Einhorn & Hogarth, 1986; Fazio & Williams, 1986; Pettigrew, 1979). This confirmation bias creates stickiness and path dependence in a stakeholder's assessment of misconduct; how one assesses it depends upon what one already thinks of the firm. Some scholars have addressed this when theorizing about how stakeholders infer firms' social actions. Barnett (2007a) argued that stakeholders view a firm's actions relative to its history. A firm with a good reputation can improve its stakeholder relations through CSR because its stakeholders believe the act to be genuine, but a firm with a poor reputation may be unable to obtain the same benefits from the same act of CSR because its stakeholders discount or disbelieve the action. Barnett and Salomon (in press) found empirical support that, indeed, firms with different histories of social performance earn different financial returns from CSR. Fombrun et al. (2000) and Godfrey (2005) argued that because of their different histories, firms vary not only in the financial returns they might accrue from CSR but also in the harm they might suffer from misconduct. Fombrun et al. (2000) theorized that by engaging in corporate citizenship activities, firms build reputational capital that improves stakeholder relations in good times and buffers them from stakeholder attacks during crises. Godfrey (2005) framed reputational capital as chits that accrue to a firm from its good deeds and that are cashed in to offset damage during crises. That is, stakeholders interpret misconduct relative to the goodwill the firm has built up and, as Godfrey, Merrill, and Hansen (2009) found empirical support for, this can create a sort of insurance that provides firms that have more socially favorable histories with more protection from stakeholder punishment.

Though this burgeoning literature demonstrates that, indeed, history matters in matters of misconduct, the argument is made at too high a level to adequately explain the influence of the confirmation bias on variation in stakeholder assessment of misconduct. Though a firm may accrue a favorable reputation overall, individual stakeholders may hold negative views of the firm, and vice versa. Thus, to explain how a firm's history affects how a stakeholder makes sense of its misconduct, the firm's overall reputation must be parsed into the views held by individual stakeholders. In parsing the reputation construct, Barnett, Jermier, and Lafferty (2006) term the view of a firm held by a particular stakeholder as "image." As with overall reputation, a stakeholder's image of a firm is based on the firm's history, and so the more favorable this record, the more favorable should be the stakeholder's image of the firm, and vice versa. However, as a stakeholder attends to different aspects of a firm over time, his or her image of the firm will vary. As a result, stakeholders vary in the image of a firm they seek to confirm as they assess an act of misconduct.

> *Proposition 8:* A stakeholder's assessment of a particular act of firm misconduct varies with his or her image of the firm in which it occurs.

Misconduct is itself multidimensional and varying in description as it unfolds over time. As with the firm's activities in general, stakeholders will selectively attend to different aspects of this unfolding process (cf. Olson & Zanna, 1979), causing variation in interpretation. If a firm outsources its call center, a stakeholder may focus on the jobs lost by current employees or on the jobs saved by keeping the firm viable—the gains to shareholders or the jobs created in India. If a firm suffers a chemical spill, a stakeholder may focus on the disruption to the community or on the fact that no one was seriously injured. Stakeholders may also attend to or ignore the process involved; did the firm give timely notice, provide severance pay, or apologize to those affected? As details of an event unfold, depending upon which aspects he or she attends to, a stakeholder may conclude that an act is a minor error or a major catastrophe.

Cognitive busyness affects how one attends to unfolding events (Gilbert, Pelham, & Krull, 1988) and so is likely to shape interpretation of misconduct. People tend to quickly and automatically form an initial impression, which they may later correct through more effortful analysis as new information arises (Quattrone, 1982). However, the initial impression is sticky. When making sense of uncertain situations, information first encountered can create an anchor point from which one makes incremental adjustments as new information arises (Tversky & Kahneman, 1974). Cognitive busyness decreases the likelihood that one will allocate effort to correcting this initial anchor point, and so initial impressions weigh heavily (Gilbert et al., 1988).

As previously noted, misconduct must stand out against a noisy background of other stimuli competing for stakeholder attention and media space if it is to be noticed. Thus, acts of misconduct that capture attention and so become subject to interpretation are likely to appear initially in relatively negative ways (Kiesler & Sproull, 1982). However, follow-up reports can correct the initial story or add context that explains or mitigates the initial negative impression. For example, Thevenot (2005) described how gruesome stories of gunfights, murders, and rapes filled the media in the aftermath of Hurricane Katrina but were later recanted. Further, firms are likely to pursue a communications strategy to deny or deflect blame or explain contextual factors that lessen the perceived severity of the misconduct (Benoit, 1997). As firms attempt to engage in "sensegiving" (Gioia & Chittipeddi, 1991), people who are occupied with other mental tasks—those who are cognitively busy—are less likely to attend to these additional details and correct their initial impressions (Gilbert et al., 1988).[7] Thus:

> *Proposition 9:* A stakeholder's assessment of a particular act of firm misconduct varies with his or her cognitive busyness.

Should a stakeholder attend to a firm's efforts at sensegiving in the aftermath of misconduct, his or her interpretation of the event may be influenced by the communicator. Some communicators are more credible than others, and so their arguments are more persuasive (Eagly, Chaiken, & Wood, 1981). For example, the former CEO of BP, Tony Hayward, was widely perceived to lack credibility with American audiences and so was not effective at mitigating negative perceptions of the severity of the BP oil spill in the Gulf of Mexico. Studies have uncovered a variety of factors that shape perceived credibility, such as the attractiveness of the communicator (Eagly & Chaiken, 1975), the similarity between the communicator and the message recipient (Goethals, 1976), and the perceived self-interest of the communicator (Eagly et al., 1981). The following is thus expected:

> *Proposition 10:* A stakeholder's assessment of a particular act of firm misconduct varies with his or her perception of the credibility of the focal firm's spokesperson.

Finally, permeating all aspects of sensemaking and assessment is mood (Mayer, 1986). Those who are in a good mood prefer to maintain this state and so attend to and interpret information in a way that prolongs the good mood (Isen, 1987). People in a good mood are more likely to recall positive events from memory (Teasdale & Russell, 1983). When making sense of a firm's potential act of misconduct, a stakeholder in a good mood is thus more likely to recall a favorable image of the firm and so less likely to interpret it as misconduct, as contrasted with a stakeholder in a bad mood. People in a good mood also tend to be more considerate of contextual information in decision making (Estrada, Isen, & Young, 1997) and more likely to respond positively to corporate communications (Milberg & Clark, 1988). As a result, they may take mitigating factors into account when assessing potential misconduct. Thus, the following is expected:

> *Proposition 11:* A stakeholder's assessment of a particular act of misconduct varies with his or her mood.

In sum, the image a stakeholder holds of a firm shapes what he or she expects of the firm and so determines the frame applied to make sense of the new information (Proposition 8), and cognitive busyness affects the stakeholder's willingness to attend to additional information that might alter his or her framing (Proposition 9). Further, the success of a firm in altering a stakeholder's perceptions of an act of misconduct depend upon his or her perception of the credibility of the firm's spokespersonal (Proposition 10) and his or her mood (Proposition 11).

Acting: The Stakeholder as Inconsistent Punisher

A stakeholder may remain relatively passive, though cognitively engaged, while noticing and assessing a firm's actions. Punishing a firm, however, can require significant action. As a result, though people may recognize the right thing to do, sometimes they do not take on the burden of doing the right thing (Weber & Gillespie, 1998). This section outlines factors that cause variation in stakeholder ability and willingness to punish a firm for its misconduct.

People vary in their sense of obligation and commitment to taking action to ensure moral outcomes (Eisenberg, 1986; Rest, Narvaez, Bebeau, & Thoma,1999). This variation in what may be termed moral motivation helps explain the loose link between cognition and action when faced with ethical dilemmas (Trevino, Weaver, & Reynolds, 2006). Some describe moral motivation as an unconscious urge or need to act to uphold one's moral standards (Blasi, 2005; Oliner & Oliner, 1988), and others describe it as the result of a deliberative process of moral reasoning (Rest, 1979). The stronger is one's moral motivation, the more one feels emotional discomfort for failing to act (Blasi, 1999). To avoid this discomfort, those with strong moral motivation are driven to take action to resolve ethical dilemmas despite the personal cost.

Whether realized through unconscious or deliberative processing, moral motivation may stem from one's moral identity. Moral identity is "a self-conception organized around a set of moral traits" (Aquino & Reed, 2002: 1424). People vary in the strength and centrality of morality in their self-conceptualizations (Blasi, 1984). People with strong and central moral identities are committed "to lines of action that promote or protect the welfare of others" (Hart, Atkins, & Ford, 1998: 515). But one's moral identity is not fixed. Over time, through exposure to differing life experiences, one's moral maturity (Rest, 1979) and the content of one's moral identity may change (Hart et al., 1998). Further, the centrality of moral identity to one's overall sense of self can vary across contexts (Forehand, Deshpande, & Reed, 2002). Accordingly, a stakeholder's drive to punish a particular act of misconduct will vary with his or her moral identity.

> *Proposition 12:* The likelihood that a stakeholder will act to punish a firm for a particular act of misconduct varies with his or her moral identity.

At any point in time a stakeholder may be aware of a range of acts of misconduct as well as a range of other stimuli that he or she might be motivated to act upon. All stakeholders, even those with the strongest of moral identities, face limits on their abilities to pursue punishment of misconduct. How does a stakeholder ration his or her resources across a set of acts of misconduct that he or she may be motivated to punish, in light of other demands on these resources as well?

Though they may not explicitly calculate it, people may be considered to undertake a sort of cost–reward analysis when deciding which activities to undertake (Dovidio, 1995). That is, people are motivated to minimize costs[8] and maximize rewards (Piliavin, Dovidio, Gaertner, & Clark, 1981), though these costs and rewards may be subjective. Dovidio, Piliavin, Gaertner, Schroeder, and Clark (1991) found, for example, that situations that decreased the net costs of taking action increased prosocial behavior. In a similar vein, but with a less optimistic twist, Vogel (2005) found that the presence of any significant cost could deter action from the vast majority of consumers. After reviewing surveys across multiple countries wherein the majority of respondents reported a willingness to alter purchase behaviors in response to firms' social and environmental actions, yet only a small minority did so (Capron & Quairel-Lanoizelee, 2004; O'Rourke, 2004), Vogel (2005: 49) concluded that customers typically are not willing to bear much of a burden to pursue their ethical concerns:

> Consumers will only buy a greener product [if] it doesn't cost more, comes from a brand they know and trust, can be purchased at stores where they already shop, doesn't require a significant change in habits to use, and has at least the same level of quality, performance, and endurance as the less-green alternative.

Because personal convenience appears to trump ethical concerns in many purchase decisions, some go so far as to describe the ethical consumer as a myth (Carrigan & Attala, 2001; Devinney, Auger, & Eckhardt, 2010). Though it is overreaching to dismiss the ethical consumer as fantasy—certainly some and perhaps many exist (for a review, see Newholm & Shaw, 2007)—it is clear that the willingness of consumers and other stakeholders to take action in concert with their moral identity can be dampened by the burden of doing so.

The action-dampening burden of punishing any particular act of misconduct varies with the stakeholder. A stakeholder wishing to punish BP for its oil spill by boycotting BP gasoline could take action relatively easily if a rival supplier is located nearby, for example. However, a stakeholder located in an area where BP is the only supplier may find it too burdensome to drive to another town to purchase gasoline or to stop driving and so may decide to not punish BP. Likewise, an investor searching for a franchise could punish BP relatively easily by purchasing a different franchise, while a current BP franchisee would face a more significant burden to break an existing contract and reorganize to operate a different franchise.

Moreover, this burden is not an absolute cost but varies with the possible alternative uses of a particular stakeholder's limited resources. A busy senior executive may willingly punish BP by purchasing gasoline from a rival supplier even if it costs several cents more per gallon. However, he or she may feel that driving 10 minutes out of the way to punish BP is a poor use of limited time. A retired senior citizen, by contrast, may be unwilling to punish a firm by financial expenditure but willing to punish by time expenditure. This notion of opportunity cost shaping one's actions is validated by many studies that have found that people's tendencies to engage in a variety of prosocial behaviors, such as volunteering in the community (Schneider, 1975; Strober & Weinberg, 1980) and giving blood (Oborne & Bradley, 1975), are moderated by their level of income and available time (Unger, 1991). It is thus expected:

Proposition 13: The likelihood that a stakeholder will act to punish a firm for a particular act of misconduct varies with his or her perceived opportunity cost.

Though cost can deter action, reward can motivate it. The reward to a stakeholder from undertaking the burden of punishing a firm is that he or she effects some desired change in the target firm. An activist investor may, for example, initiate a proxy fight in hopes of garnering change in a firm's governance practices, or a citizen may attempt to mobilize his or her community in hopes of closing a polluting plant. But the stakeholder cannot be certain his or her punishment will have any effect on the target firm. As the uncertainty of effecting change rises, the stakeholder's likelihood of action is dampened. Lacking belief that their actions will be noticed, some stakeholders will not punish firms for even the most egregious acts of misconduct. This logic is implicit, for example, in the strategic location of industrial plants. Plants tend to be located such that those neighborhoods least inclined to act on their concerns suffer a disproportionate share of industrial pollution (Brooks & Sethi, 1997).

Faced with uncertainty about which issues to pursue, "people gravitate toward issues more easily when they perceive the issues as having a high probability of resolution" (Dutton & Webster, 1988: 671). Accordingly, though some are willing to serve as "gadflys" with no realistic hope of success (Ross, 1983), a stakeholder is more likely to expend his or her limited resources in those pursuits that promise success than in those that he or she believes will fail. Some people have a stronger generalized belief than others that their actions will produce change in the world, measured through traits such as locus of control (Rotter, 1966) and sense of self-efficacy (Bandura, 1986). As well, some people are more confident than others that misconduct begets fair punishment, measured as one's belief in a just world (Rubin & Peplau, 1973). These traits have been positively associated with one's willingness to engage in prosocial behavior (Ball, Trevino, & Sims, 1994; Spector, 1982) and to take on burdensome and risky punishments such as whistle-blowing (Dozier & Miceli, 1985). All else equal, the stronger are such personality traits, the more likely is a stakeholder to act.

Whatever one's set of personality traits, however, the presence of others can affect one's likelihood of taking action to punish a firm. A firm may easily ignore the demands of an individual protestor or a single customer's boycott. But as a protest or boycott grows in size, the target firm becomes increasingly likely to respond. Recognizing the strength in numbers, and the potential futility of solo action, a stakeholder should thus be more likely to act alongside

others than to stand alone. Simply, the likelihood of successful influence on the target firm—
and so reward ensuing from action—grows with the size of the group taking action. As well,
the cost to the individual decreases once a movement infrastructure is in place.

Once success is perceived as likely though, what would stop all stakeholders from piling
onto the rolling bandwagon? Interestingly, the expectation of reward provides a theoretical
braking mechanism as well. As a group targeting a firm grows in size, the likelihood of
success increases, thus increasing any given stakeholder's motivation to act. But as success
appears certain, the marginal difference that any given stakeholder could expect to make by
participating approaches zero. A well-established literature on the bystander effect supports
this notion by demonstrating that large groups deter individual action (Latane & Darley,
1968). Instead, individuals tend to remain passive as they presume that others will resolve the
problem, no matter how drastic the scenario. This then suggests a curvilinear relationship
between the size of a movement and individual willingness to contribute: as group size
increases, the likelihood of success increases but the marginal contribution of any individual
decreases. More generally:

Proposition 14: The likelihood that a stakeholder will act to punish a firm for a particular
act of misconduct varies with the impact he or she expects to have on the firm.

Discussion

By consistently rewarding firms for good acts and, conversely, punishing them for bad
acts, stakeholders can push firms toward greater social responsibility (and so lesser
misconduct). But do stakeholders have the ability to do so? After considering the underlying
cognitive processes, the picture that emerges is one not of consistent stakeholder action and
resulting widespread social control. Rather, stakeholders' attention is directed in certain
ways that bound where they look, limit what they notice, bias their assessment, and constrain
their willingness to act. As a result, firms' bad behaviors may not be consistently extinguished
through social control. Thus, firms may continue to "supply" bad behavior because the
market does not effectively signal its "demand" for good behavior (cf. McWilliams & Siegel,
2001). Stated differently, there appear to be failures in what Vogel (2005) characterized as
"the market for virtue" due to stakeholders' limited ability to patrol, perceive, and punish
firm misconduct.

Cognitive constraints do not simply leave stakeholders unable to see past firms'
"smokescreens" or "greenwashing" efforts (Howard, Nash, & Ehrenfeld, 2000), as is often
the focus of management studies on firm misconduct. Even in the presence of perfect and
costless information about all aspects of firm performance, cognitive constraints pose a
problem. In fact, with more information comes more problems. As firms increase transparency,
stakeholders have no greater prospects for processing this flood of information. Apart from
those stakeholders whose livelihoods and identities depend upon their relationships, or
antagonisms, with specific firms, more information may not lead to more stakeholder action.
Perversely, as more information abounds, the likelihood that any given stakeholder will
notice any particular act of misconduct decreases.

As more and more information is disclosed about firm practices and consequences, the uncertainty stakeholders face in deciding what to attend to has only increased. Regarding stakeholder decisions about supporting "green businesses," for example, Williams (2008) describes the problem of "green noise" whereby a torrent of information by myriad agencies serves only to confuse well-intentioned activists who want to make purchases that further a green agenda. Some blame this information overload for survey results that indicate a substantial decline from 2006 to 2007 in the number of consumers who intended to buy green products (Williams, 2008). Thus, attentional constraints appear to be increasingly at play in consumer behavior and stakeholder action in general.

In light of information overload, attentiveness may be a better way to classify stakeholders. Scholars have long debated which stakeholders "really count" for firms (Mitchell, Agle, & Wood, 1997). Rather than continuing to refine stakeholder classification systems based upon stakeholders' "salience to managers of the firm" (Mitchell et al., 1997: 853), we should consider the salience of the firm to stakeholders. If a stakeholder is not observing a firm's actions or is otherwise occupied and so does not have the desire or ability to respond, then even if powerful and legitimate, the stakeholder has no instrumental relevance to the firm (though ethics may dictate otherwise). Whether primary or secondary, legitimate or illegitimate, powerful or weak, a stakeholder is constrained by limited attention. It is important for firms, themselves with limited resources, to make distinctions regarding the relative importance of stakeholders. Further clarification of the conditions that shape what firm actions stakeholders attend to will help firms in making decisions about where they should focus their attention and how they should behave. That said, business and society scholars should bear in mind that the dark side of developing such insights is increasing firms' abilities to strategically target distribution of negative externalities toward those stakeholders least likely to notice, infer, or act on misconduct. In the pursuit of profits, firms may be prone to, for example, strategic placement of polluting plants (Brooks & Sethi, 1997), and so as the business case becomes more explicit, the ethical concerns do not fade away but may become more pronounced.

More broadly, this suggests a need for reconsideration of the notion of social control of business through stakeholder action. Waddock (2008: 105) recently lamented that even though CSR initiatives are garnering more attention, participation is still limited:

> Admittedly, the proportion of companies actively engaged with this infrastructure is still rather small compared to the total population; many leaders are companies with brand reputations to protect or are otherwise highly visible and subject to pressure tactics. . . . Most of the attention to date has been on large companies, largely ignoring the millions of small and medium-sized enterprises.

The cognitive view proffered in this article suggests that social control mechanisms are unlikely to change this dynamic. For large and highly visible firms, social control may work. Analysts and the media cover such firms with consistency, and so stakeholder attention may be drawn toward the actions of large firms. But the vast majority of firms are not large and highly visible. Without consistent visibility, do the mechanisms of social control hold for small and medium-sized enterprises? The literature on social control has been based on the study of large firms; case examples of Nike, Walmart, and Starbucks abound. A cognitive view suggests that these findings may not be generalizable. Since stakeholders lack the capacity to attend to the actions of all firms, small and medium-sized firms may be playing by different rules than are highly visible large firms. Future research on social control needs to look beyond the domain of large firms and investigate whether other firms receive stakeholder attention.

In addition to investigating small and medium-sized firms, future research needs to better investigate the process of stakeholder attention to misconduct. The literature's core question is not simply when do stakeholders choose to act, but preceding that, when do stakeholders even get to the point of facing a decision to act. This article presented noticing as primarily a reactive process, based upon reflexively discerning stimuli from background noise; assessment primarily as a retrospective process, based upon a stakeholder's prior expectations; and finally, acting to punish as primarily a rational process, based upon a cost–benefit calculation of opportunity cost and efficacy. However, reactive, retrospective, and rational factors may be present in all three parts of this process, the extent to which may be better identified in deeper empirical treatment of this topic.

Moreover, the characteristics of the acts of misconduct remained unspecified in this model. Certainly these characteristics are not irrelevant to stakeholder punishment decisions. On the contrary, the most obvious reason why a stakeholder would attend to one act of misconduct and not another is the nature of the act. Simply, a major catastrophe is more likely to be salient than is a minor mess. Nonetheless, given the aims of the model, it is problematic to specify misconduct. Rather, to focus on differences in the individual and the situation, misconduct itself was effectively held constant. Future studies could sort out how variations in misconduct—for example, whether it be an act of omission or commission, internal or externally driven, or the fault of the firm or a single employee—affect stakeholder noticing, assessment, and action.

It is hoped that this article will spur research on both the macro- and microconditions that shape how stakeholders attend to—or ignore—firm misconduct. The individual and situational characteristics brought forth herein are neither exhaustive nor definitive. Rather, empirical testing is needed to test these propositions, as the evidence motivating them largely has not been applied to this particular setting. As more is known about how this diverse group of people responds to a diverse set of firm actions under a litany of conditions, the more we will be able to understand when social control can and cannot work and how it might be better balanced with formal regulation.

Conclusion

Business and society scholars have set up a research paradigm that assumes that business makes decisions that account for the concerns of society because society makes decisions about business based on business's concerns for society. Research in this paradigm of social control has focused on outcomes and found mixed results—business still does things that harm society, and society still allows harmful businesses to survive and even prosper. This article looked at the underlying decision-making processes inherent in social control to advance understanding of how society attends to business activity. Stakeholders are the agents of social control. They face cognitive constraints that bound their rationality and so bound their ability to consistently reward and punish firms for their actions. This article provides a theoretical basis for future empirical work that may better define the limits to social control.

Notes

1. This article defines misconduct as any publicly disclosed firm action that, under some set of conditions, a stakeholder would deem illegal, unethical, or socially irresponsible and take action to punish. For further explanation, please refer to the section headed "A Cognitive View of Stakeholder Punishment."

2. This article defines stakeholders as those individuals who can directly affect the achievement of a firm's objectives. For further explanation, please refer to the section headed "A Cognitive View of Stakeholder Punishment."

3. The exclusion of moral and secondary stakeholders from the definition of stakeholder used in this article does not imply their exclusion from any protection that may come from social control. Strategic stakeholders may represent moral and secondary stakeholders' interests and seek to influence firms on their behalf.

4. This definition is admittedly rather broad. But it is beyond the scope of this article and perhaps implausible to place tighter bounds on something so subjective. Further, this article is interested in inconsistency in stakeholder attention to misconduct as caused by differing conditions, not in determining whether or not a stakeholder is "correct" in his or her assessment that an act is misconduct. Thus, though broad, the definition used herein is suited to its purpose.

5. Portraying the process as linear and multistage forces somewhat artificial breaks. For example, noticing and assessing can occur simultaneously or iteratively (Weick, 1995). Nonetheless, each stage represents a meaningful and distinct cognitive action (Kiesler & Sproull, 1982; Starbuck & Milliken, 1988), and the linear flow is common to models of the "filtering process" by which unbounded environmental stimuli are honed down to a set of individual responses (e.g., Barnett, 2008; Hambrick & Mason, 1984).

6. All propositions in this article assume that all other conditions are held equal (i.e., ceteris paribus).

7. This helps distinguish noticing from sensemaking. These interdependent concepts are difficult to untangle (Weick, 1995). The above logic suggests that noticing refers to awareness that a firm has engaged in a particular act, whereas sensemaking occurs as some aspects of the noticed act are attended to and others ignored. Thus, noticing occurs at the level of the event—a stakeholder notices the firm's act or does not—and sensemaking occurs at the intraevent level, as a stakeholder selectively attends to aspects of a given act, leading to the event's enactment as an act of a particular nature and magnitude in that stakeholder's mind.

8. Perception of the cost of punishment can include expected retaliation, such as a whistle-blower may suffer.

References

Aldrick, P. 2009. Investment bankers profit from state bail-out. *Telegraph,* March 26. Retrieved from http://www.telegraph.co.uk/finance/newsbysector/banksandfinance/5056251/Investment-bankers-profit-from-state-bail-out.html.

Allport, G. 1954. *The nature of prejudice.* Reading, MA: Addison-Wesley.

Aquino, K., & Reed, A., II. 2002. The self-importance of moral identity. *Journal of Personality and Social Psychology,* 83: 1423-1440.

Armitstead, L. 2009. Lord Davies says banks must wake up to financial reform. *Telegraph,* July 11. Retrieved from http://www.telegraph.co.uk/finance/newsbysector/banksandfinance/5802743/Lord-Davies-says-banks-must-wake-up-to-financial-reform.html.

Bagdikian, B. 2000. *The media monopoly* (6th ed.). Boston: Beacon Press.

Ball, G., Trevino, L., & Sims, H., Jr. 1994. Just and unjust punishment: Influences on subordinate performance and citizenship. *Academy of Management Journal,* 37: 299-322.

Bandura, A. 1986. *Social foundations of thought and action: A social cognitive theory*. Englewood Cliffs, NJ: Prentice-Hall.

Barnett, M. 2007a. Stakeholder influence capacity and the variability of financial returns to corporate social responsibility. *Academy of Management Review,* 32: 794-816.

Barnett, M. 2007b. Tarred and untarred by the same brush: Exploring interdependence in the volatility of stock returns. *Corporate Reputation Review,* 10: 3-21.

Barnett, M. 2008. An attention-based view of real options reasoning. *Academy of Management Review,* 33: 606-628.

Barnett, M., Jermier, J., & Lafferty, B. 2006. Corporate reputation: The definitional landscape. *Corporate Reputation Review,* 9: 26-38.

Barnett, M., & King, A. 2008. Good fences make good neighbors: A longitudinal analysis of an industry self-regulatory institution. *Academy of Management Journal,* 51: 1150-1170.

Barnett, M., & Salomon, R. in press. Does it pay to be *really* good? Addressing the shape of the relationship between social and financial performance. *Strategic Management Journal.*

Baron, D. 2006. Persistent media bias. *Journal of Public Economics,* 90: 1-36.

Benediktsson, M. 2010. The deviant organization and the bad apple CEO: Ideology and accountability in media coverage of corporate scandals. *Social Forces,* 88: 2189-2216.

Benoit, W. 1997. Image repair discourse and crisis communication. *Public Relations Review,* 23: 177-186.

Bernhardt, D., Krasa, S., & Polborn, M. 2008. Political polarization and the electoral effects of media bias. *Journal of Public Economics,* 92: 1092-1104.

Berscheid, E., Graziano, W., Monson, T., & Dermer, M. 1976. Outcome dependency: Attention, attribution, and attraction. *Journal of Personality and Social Psychology,* 34: 978-989.

Blasi, A. 1984. Moral identity: Its role in moral functioning. In W. Kurtines & J. Gewirtz (Eds.), *Morality, moral behavior and moral development:* 128-139. New York: Wiley.

Blasi, A. 1999. Emotions and moral motivation. *Journal for the Theory of Social Behavior,* 29: 1-19.

Blasi, A. 2005. Moral character: A psychological approach. In D. K. Lapsley & F. C. Power (Eds.), *Character psychology and character education:* 67-100. Notre Dame, IN: University of Notre Dame Press.

Brooks, N., & Sethi, R. 1997. The distribution of pollution: Community characteristics and exposure to air toxics. *Journal of Environmental Economics and Management,* 32: 233-250.

Bruner, J. 1957. On perceptual readiness. *Psychological Review,* 64: 123-152.

Bryant, J., & Miron, D. 2002. Entertainment as media effects. In J. Bryant & D. Zillmann (Eds.), *Media effects: Advances in theory and research:* 437-463. Mahwah, NJ: Lawrence Erlbaum.

Burke, L., & Logsdon, J. 1996. How corporate social responsibility pays off. *Long Range Planning,* 29: 495-502.

Cacioppo, J., & Petty, R. 1982. The need for cognition. *Journal of Personality and Social Psychology,* 42: 116-131.

Cacioppo, J., Petty, R., Feinstein, J., & Jarvis, W. 1996. Dispositional differences in cognitive motivation: The life and times of individuals varying in need for cognition. *Psychological Bulletin,* 199: 197-253.

Capron, M., & Qauirel-Lanoizelee, F. 2004. *Mythes et realities de l'entreprise responsable*. Paris: La Decouverte.

Carrigan, M., & Attala, A. 2001. The myth of the ethical consumer: Do ethics matter in purchase behaviour? *Journal of Consumer Marketing,* 18: 560-577.

Carroll, A. 1979. A three-dimensional conceptual model of corporate performance. *Academy of Management Review,* 4: 497-505.

Carroll, G., & Hannan, M. 2000. *The demography of corporations and industries*. Princeton, NJ: Princeton University Press.

Clarkson, M. 1995. A stakeholder framework for analyzing and evaluating corporate social performance. *Academy of Management Review,* 20: 92-117.

Cyert, R., & March, J. 1963. *A behavioral theory of the firm*. Englewood Cliffs, NJ: Prentice-Hall.

Deephouse, D. 2000. Media reputation as a strategic resource: An integration of mass communication and resource-based theories. *Journal of Management,* 26: 1091-1112.

Delli Carpini, M., & Williams, B. 1987. Television and terrorism: Patterns of presentation and occurrence, 1969 to 1980. *Western Political Quarterly,* 40: 45-64.

Devinney, T., Auger, P., & Eckhardt, G. 2010. *The myth of the ethical consumer*. Cambridge, UK: Cambridge University Press.

Donaldson, T., & Preston, L. 1995. The stakeholder theory of the corporation: Concepts, evidence, and implications. *Academy of Management Review,* 20: 65-91.

Dovidio, J. 1995. Helping behavior. In A. Manstead & M. Hewtone (Eds.), *The Blackwell encyclopedia of social psychology:* 290-295. Malden, MA: Blackwell.

Dovidio, J., Piliavin, J., Gaertner, S., Schroeder, D., & Clark, R., III. 1991. The arousal: Cost–reward model and the process of intervention: A review of the evidence. In M. S. Clark (Ed.), *Review of personality and social psychology: Vol. 12. Prosocial behavior:* 86-118. Newbury Park, CA: Sage.

Dozier, J., & Miceli, M. 1985. Potential predictors of whistle-blowing: A prosocial behavior perspective. *Academy of Management Review,* 10: 823-836.

Dutton, J., & Webster, J. 1988. Patterns of interest around issues: The role of uncertainty and feasibility. *Academy of Management Journal,* 31: 663-675.

Eagly, A., & Chaiken, S. 1975. An attribution analysis of the effect of communication characteristics on opinion change: The case of communicator attractiveness. *Journal of Personality and Social Psychology,* 32: 136-144.

Eagly, A., Chaiken, S., & Wood, W. 1981. An attribution analysis of persuasion. In J. Harvey, W. Ickes, & R. Kidd (Eds.), *New directions in attribution research* (Vol. 3): 37-62. Hillsdale, NJ: Lawrence Erlbaum.

Einhorn, H., & Hogarth, R. 1986. Judging probable cause. *Psychological Bulletin,* 99: 3-19.

Eisenberg, N. 1986. *Altruistic emotion, cognition and behavior.* Hillsdale, NJ: Lawrence Erlbaum

Eisensee, T., & Stromberg, D. 2007. News droughts, news floods, and U.S. disaster relief. *Quarterly Journal of Economics,* 122: 693-728.

Estrada, C., Isen, A., & Young, M. 1997. Positive affect improves creative problem solving and influences reported source of practice satisfaction in physicians. *Motivation and Emotion,* 18: 285-299.

Fazio, R., & Williams, C. 1986. Attitude accessibility as a moderator of the attitude–perception and attitude–behavior relations: An investigation of the 1984 presidential election. *Journal of Personality and Social Psychology,* 51: 505-514.

Ferguson, M., Chung, M., & Weigold, M. 1985. *Need for cognition and the medium dependency components of reliance and exposure.* Paper presented at the International Communication Association Convention, Honolulu, HI.

Fiske, A. 1991. *Structures of social life: The four elementary forms of human relations.* New York: Free Press.

Fiske, S., & Taylor, S. 1991. *Social cognition* (2nd ed.). New York: Random House.

Fombrun, C., Gardberg, N., & Barnett, M. 2000. Opportunity platforms and safety nets: Corporate citizenship and reputational risk. *Business and Society Review,* 105: 85-106.

Forehand, M., Deshpande, R., & Reed, A., II. 2002. Identity salience and the influence of differential activation of the social self-schema on advertising response. *Journal of Applied Psychology,* 87: 1086-1099.

Freeman, R. 1984. *Strategic management: A stakeholder approach.* Marshfield, MA: Pitman.

Gardberg, N., & Fombrun, C. 2006. Corporate citizenship: Creating intangible organizational assets across institutional environments. *Academy of Management Review,* 31: 329.

Gilbert, D., Pelham, B., & Krull, D. 1988. On cognitive busyness: When person perceivers meet persons perceived. *Journal of Personality and Social Psychology,* 54: 733-739.

Gioia, D., & Chittipeddi, K. 1991. Sensemaking and sensegiving in strategic change initiation. *Strategic Management Journal,* 12: 433-448.

Godfrey, P. 2005. The relationship between corporate philanthropy and shareholder wealth: A risk management perspective. *Academy of Management Review,* 30: 777-798.

Godfrey, P., Merrill, C., & Hansen, J. 2009. The relationship between corporate social responsibility and shareholder value: An empirical test of the risk management hypothesis. *Strategic Management Journal,* 30: 425-445.

Goethals, G. 1976. An attributional analysis of some social influence phenomena. In J. Harvey, W. Ickes, & R. Kidd (Eds.), *New directions in attribution research* (Vol. 1): 291-310. Hillsdale, NJ: Lawrence Erlbaum.

Goodpastor, K. 1991. Business ethics and stakeholder theory. *Business Ethics Quarterly,* 1: 53.

Greve, H., Palmer, D, & Pozner, J. 2010. Organizations gone wild: The causes, processes, and consequences of organizational misconduct. *Academy of Management Annals,* 4: 53-107.

Groseclose, T., & Milyo, J. 2005. A measure of media bias. *Quarterly Journal of Economics,* 120: 1191-1237.

Gunningham, N. 1995. Environment, self-regulation, and the chemical industry: Assessing responsible care. *Law and Policy,* 17: 57-108.

Hambrick, D., & Mason, P. 1984. Upper echelons: The organization as a reflection of its top managers. *Academy of Management Review,* 9: 193-206.

Hart, D., Atkins, R., & Ford, D. 1998. Urban America as a context for development of moral identity in adolescence. *Journal of Social Issues,* 54: 513-530.

Hendry, J. 2006. Taking aim at business: What factors lead environmental non-governmental organizations to target particular firms? *Business and Society,* 45: 47-86.

Hockerts, K. 2007. *Managerial perceptions of the business case for corporate social responsibility.* Working paper no. 03-2007, Copenhagen Business School, Copenhagen, Denmark.

Hoffman, A. 1997. *From heresy to dogma: An institutional history of corporate environmentalism*. San Francisco: New Lexington Press.

Hoffman, A., & Ocasio, W. 2001. Not all events are attended equally: Toward a middle-range theory of industry attention to external events. *Organization Science,* 12: 414-434.

Howard, J., Nash, J., & Ehrenfeld, J. 2000. Standard or smokescreen? Implementation of a voluntary environmental code. *California Management Review,* 42: 63-82.

Isen, A. 1987. Positive affect, cognitive processes, and social behavior. In L. Berkowitz (Ed.), *Advances in experimental social psychology* (Vol. 20): 203-253. New York: Academic Press.

James, W. 1890/1983. *The principles of psychology*. Cambridge, MA: Harvard University Press.

Jones, T. 1982. An integrating framework for research in business and society: A step toward the elusive paradigm? *Academy of Management Review,* 8: 559-564.

Jones, T. 1995. Instrumental stakeholder theory: A synthesis of ethics and economics. *Academy of Management Review,* 20: 404-437.

Jones, T., & Wicks, A. 1999. Convergent stakeholder theory. *Academy of Management Review,* 24: 206-221.

Kahneman, D. 1973. *Attention and effort*. Englewood Cliffs, NJ: Prentice-Hall.

Kahneman, D., Knetsch, J., & Thaler, R. 1986. Fairness and the assumptions of economics. *Journal of Business,* 59: 285-300.

Kiesler, S., & Sproull, L. 1982. Managerial response to changing environments: Perspectives on problem sensing from social cognition. *Administrative Science Quarterly,* 27: 548-570.

King, A., & Baerwald, S. 1998. Using the court of public opinion to encourage better business decisions. In K. Sexton et al. (Eds.), *Better environmental decisions: Strategies for governments, businesses and communities:* 309-330. Washington, DC: Island Press.

King, A., Lenox, M., & Barnett, M. 2002. Strategic responses to the reputation commons problem. In A. Hoffman & M. Ventresca (Eds.), *Organizations, policy and the natural environment: Institutional and strategic perspectives:* 393-406. Stanford, CA: Stanford University Press.

Latane, B., & Darley, J. 1968. Group inhibition of bystander intervention in emergencies. *Journal of Personality and Social Psychology,* 10: 215-221.

Lee, S., Oh, K., & Eden, L. 2010. Why do firms bribe? Insights from residual control theory into firms' exposure and vulnerability to corruption. *Management International Review,* 50: 775-796.

Luce, R., & Galanter, E. 1963. Discrimination. In R. Lute, R. Bush, & E. Galanter (Eds.), *Handbook of mathematical psychology* (Vol. 1): 191-244. New York: Wiley.

March, J., & Simon, H. 1958. *Organizations*. New York: Wiley.

Margolis, J., & Walsh, J. 2003. Misery loves company: Rethinking social initiatives by business. *Administrative Science Quarterly,* 48: 268-305.

Mauro, P. 1998. Corruption causes, consequences, and agenda for further research. *Finance Development,* 35: 11-14.

Mayer, J. 1986. How mood influences cognition. In N. Sharkley (Ed.), *Advances in cognitive science:* 290-314. Chichester, UK: Ellis Horwood.

McWilliams, A., & Siegel, D. 2001. Corporate social responsibility: A theory of the firm perspective. *Academy of Management Review,* 26: 117-127.

Milberg, S., & Clark, M. 1988. Moods and compliance. *British Journal of Social Psychology,* 27: 79-90.

Miller, G. 1956. The magical number seven, plus or minus two: Some limits on our capacity for processing information. *Psychological Review,* 63: 81-97.

Mitchell, R., Agle, B., & Wood, D. 1997. Toward a theory of stakeholder identification and salience: Defining the principle of who and what really counts. *Academy of Management Review,* 22: 853-886.

Mullainathan, S., & Shleifer, A. 2005. The market for news. *American Economic Review,* 95: 1031-1053.

Newholm, T., & Shaw, D. 2007. Studying the ethical consumer: A review of research. *Journal of Consumer Behavior,* 6: 253-270.

Nossiter, A. 2010. Far from Gulf, a spill scourge 5 decades old. *New York Times,* June 16. Retrieved from http://www.nytimes.com/2010/06/17/world/africa/17nigeria.html

Oborne, D., & Bradley, S. 1975. Blood donor and nondonor motivation: A transnational replication. *Journal of Applied Psychology,* 60: 409-410.

Ocasio, W. 1997. Towards an attention-based view of the firm. *Strategic Management Journal,* 18: 187-206.

Oliner, S., & Oliner, P. 1988. *The altruistic personality*. New York: Free Press

Olson, J., & Zanna, M. 1979. A new look at selective exposure. *Journal of Experimental Social Psychology,* 15: 1-15.

O'Rourke, D. 2004. *Opportunities and obstacles for corporate social reporting in developing countries*. Washington, DC: World Bank/International Finance Corporation.

Patterson, T., & Donsbach, W. 1996. News decisions: Journalists as partisan actors. *Political Communication,* 13: 453-468.

Perse, E. 1992. Predicting attention to local television news: Need for cognition and motives for viewing. *Communication Reports,* 5: 40-49.

Pettigrew, T. 1979. The ultimate attribution error: Extending Allport's cognitive analysis of prejudice. *Personality and Social Psychology Bulletin,* 5: 461-476.

Piliavin, J., Dovidio, J., Gaertner, F., & Clark, R., III. 1981. *Emergency intervention.* New York: Academic Press.

Porter, L., & Roberts, K. 1976. Organizational communication. In M. Dunnette (Ed.), *Handbook of industrial and organizational psychology:* 1553-1589. Chicago: Rand McNally.

Prior, M. 2005. News vs. entertainment: How increasing media choice widens gaps in political knowledge and turnout. *American Journal of Political Science,* 49: 577-592.

Quattrone, G. 1982. Overattribution and unit formation: When behavior engulfs the person. *Journal of Personality and Social Psychology,* 42: 593-607.

Rest, J. 1979. *Revised manual for the Defined Issues Test: An objective test of moral judgment development.* Minneapolis: Minnesota Moral Research Projects.

Rest, J., Narvaez, M., Bebeau, J., & Thoma, S. 1999. *Postconventional moral thinking: A neo-Kohlbergian approach.* Mahwah, NJ: Lawrence Erlbaum.

Rindova, V., Pollock, T., & Hayward, M. 2006. Celebrity firms: The social construction of market popularity. *Academy of Management Review,* 31: 50-71.

Ross, N. 1983. Gadflies set to buzz shareholders' meetings. *Washington Post,* April 17: G1.

Rotter, J. 1966. Generalized expectancies for internal versus external control of reinforcement. *Psychological Monographs,* 80: 1-28.

Rowley, T., & Moldoveanu, M. 2003. When will stakeholder groups act? An interest- and identity-based model of stakeholder group mobilization. *Academy of Management Review,* 28: 204-219.

Rubin, A. 1981. An examination of television viewing motivations. *Communication Research,* 8: 141-165.

Rubin, Z., & Peplau, L. 1973. Who believes in a just world? *Journal of Social Issues,* 31: 65-89.

Ruscher, J., & Fiske, S. 1990. Interpersonal competition can cause individuating impression formation. *Journal of Personality and Social Psychology,* 58: 832-842.

Schneider, K. 1975. *Altruistic behavior: The effects of two experimental conditions on helping behavior and personality correlates of this behavior.* Unpublished doctoral dissertation, Purdue University.

Schuler, D., & Cording, M. 2006. A corporate social performance–corporate financial performance behavioral model for consumers. *Academy of Management Review,* 31: 540-558.

Simon, H. 1947. *Administrative behavior.* New York: The Free Press.

Spector, P. 1982. Behavior in organizations as a function of employee's locus of control. *Psychological Bulletin,* 91: 482-497.

Starbuck, W., & Milliken, F. 1988. Executive perceptual filters: What they notice and how they make sense. In D. Hambrick (Ed.), *The executive effect: Concepts and methods for studying top managers:* 35-65. Greenwich, CT: JAI Press.

Strober, M., & Weinberg, C. 1980. Strategies used by working and nonworking wives to reduce time pressures. *Journal of Consumer Research,* 6: 338-348.

Sunstein, C. 2001. *Republic.com.* Princeton, NJ: Princeton University Press.

Taylor, S. 1981. A categorization approach to stereotyping. In D. Hamilton (Ed.), *Cognitive processes in stereotyping and intergroup behavior:* 88-114. Hillsdale, NJ: Lawrence Erlbaum.

Taylor, S., & Fiske, S. 1975. Point-of-view and perceptions of causality. *Journal of Personality and Social Psychology,* 32: 439-445.

Teasdale, J., & Russell, M. 1983. Differential effects of induced mood on the recall of positive, negative, and neutral words. *British Journal of Clinical Psychology,* 22: 163-171.

Thevenot, B. 2005. Myth-making in New Orleans. *American Journalism Review,* 27: 30-37.

Trevino, L., Weaver, G., & Reynolds, S. 2006. Behavioral ethics in organizations: A review. *Journal of Management,* 32: 951-990.

Turban, D., & Greening, D. 1997. Corporate social performance and organizational attractiveness to prospective employees. *Academy of Management Journal,* 40: 658-672.

Turillo, C., Folger, J., Lavelle, J., Emphress, E., & Gee, J. 2002. Is virtue its own reward? Self-sacrificial decisions for the sake of fairness. *Organizational Behavior and Human Decision Processes,* 89: 839-865.

Tversky, A., & Kahneman, D. 1974. Judgment under uncertainty: Heuristics and biases. *Science,* 185: 1124-1131.

Unger, L. 1991. Altruism as a motivation to volunteer. *Journal of Economic Psychology,* 12: 71-100.

Virag, G. 2008. Playing for your own audience: Extremism in two-party elections. *Journal of Public Economic Theory,* 10: 891-922.

Vogel, D. 2005. *The market for virtue: The potential and limits of corporate social responsibility.* Washington, DC: Brookings Institution Press.

Waddock, S. 2008. Building a new institutional infrastructure for corporate responsibility. *Academy of Management Perspectives,* 22: 87-108.

Wason, P. 1960. On the failure to eliminate hypotheses in a conceptual task. *Quarterly Journal of Experimental Psychology,* 12: 129-140.

Weber, J., & Gillespie, J. 1998. Differences in ethical beliefs, intentions, and behaviors. *Business and Society,* 37: 447-467.

Weick, K. 1995. *Sensemaking in organizations.* Thousand Oaks, SA: Sage.

Weick, K., Sutcliffe, K., & Obstfeld, D. 2005. Organizing and the process of sensemaking. *Organization Science,* 16: 409-421.

Williams, A. 2008. That buzz in your ear may be green noise. *New York Times,* June 15. Retrieved from http://www .nytimes.com/2008/06/15/fashion/15green.html?pagewanted=all.

Wood, D. 1991. Corporate social performance revisited. *Academy of Management Review,* 16: 691-718.

Yu, T., Sengul, M., & Lester, R. 2008. Misery loves company: The spread of negative impacts resulting from an organizational crisis. *Academy of Management Review,* 33: 452-472.

11

Article

Sorry to (Not) Burst Your Bubble: The Influence of Reputation Rankings on Perceptions of Firms

Business & Society
1–17
© The Author(s) 2016
Reprints and permissions:
sagepub.com/journalsPermissions.nav
DOI: 10.1177/0007650316643919
bas.sagepub.com

Michael L. Barnett[1] and Sohvi Leih[2]

Abstract
We measure the influence of reputation rankings on individuals' perceptions of firms. Through experimental design, we vary whether and how participants are exposed to a reputation ranking alongside other information about a firm. We find that rankings influence perceptions when they are negative and congruent with other information about the firm. These findings help explain how a firm's reputation can change even if its characteristics remain constant and why change in a firm's characteristics can be slow to produce change in its reputation.

Keywords
cognition, corporate reputation, experiment, reputation rankings

What do you think of Walmart? How did you form this view? The corporate reputation literature assumes that what one thinks of a given firm is based on the actions of that firm. For example, Barnett, Jermier, and Lafferty's (2006) review of the literature produced the following definition of corporate reputation: "observers' collective judgments of a corporation based on assessments

[1]Rutgers, The State University of New Jersey, Newark, USA
[2]University of California, Berkeley, USA

Corresponding Author:
Michael L. Barnett, Rutgers Business School, Rutgers, The State University of New Jersey, 1 Washington Park, #1054, Newark, NJ 07102, USA.
Email: mbarnett@business.rutgers.edu

of the financial, social, and environmental impacts attributed to the corporation over time" (p. 34). However, given limited cognitive capacity (March & Simon, 1958), most people are unaware of the ongoing financial, social, and environmental impacts of Walmart or most any other firm. So what information do people rely on to form their views?

To cope with their bounded ability to constantly observe myriad firm characteristics, people often rely on intermediaries to help understand and assess firms. Reputation rankings[1] from *Businessweek*, the *Financial Times, Fortune, US News & World Report*, and other such sources have proliferated. Researchers have voiced concerns about reputation rankings; particularly the methodologies used to determine them (see Gardberg & Dowling, 2012). In this article, though, we are concerned not with the methods but with the influence of reputation rankings. How do people use rankings when forming their views of a firm? Do rankings affect or overshadow other information that one may have about a firm?

Herein, we report the results of an experiment in which we isolate the effects of reputation rankings on individuals' perceptions of a firm. Indeed, we find that perceptions are influenced by reputation rankings, particularly when these rankings are negative and congruent with other information about the firm. These findings suggest the need to develop a richer perspective on reputation. Corporate reputation has long been conceptualized as an aggregation of individual perceptions (cf. Fombrun, 1996), but it also needs to be understood as a driver of individual perceptions. Greater focus on this latter aspect may help to explain loose linkages between a firm's characteristics and its reputation. As a result of the influence of reputation rankings, a firm's reputation may change even if its characteristics remain constant and, conversely, changes in a firm's characteristics may be slow to produce change in its reputation. Additional insights into the information that individuals do and do not attend to in revising their perceptions of a firm can help better explain the connection between a firm's behavior and its reputation and thus deepen understanding of how to effectively manage reputation (Barnett, 2014; Mishina, Block, & Mannor, 2012).

We begin by briefly reviewing the corporate reputation literature. We then develop two hypotheses that outline ways in which reputation rankings sway stakeholder perceptions. Thereafter, we describe our experimental study and detail the results. We conclude with a discussion of the implications of these findings for reputation theory and practice.

Corporate Reputation: A Brief Overview

Reputation is a valuable firm resource (Barney, 1991). It may underpin the majority of a firm's market value (Fombrun, 1996). Firms with a good reputation can gain the favor of their stakeholders, whereas those with a bad reputation may endure stakeholder attacks (Fombrun, Gardberg, & Barnett, 2000). Given these benefits and risks, firms seek to manage their reputations. However, what are they actually managing? What is a reputation?

Conceptually and empirically, a firm's reputation traditionally has been treated as a collective assessment of the firm by its many stakeholders (Barnett et al., 2006; Fombrun, 1996). That is, a firm's reputation at any point in time is understood and measured as an average, perhaps weighted, of what various constituencies think of the firm. Many have pointed out the problems of treating reputation as a collective assessment (Bromley, 2002; Wartick, 2002). Stakeholders may vary considerably in their view of a firm. Aggregating these varying viewpoints into a collective assessment muddles meaningful differences and does not accurately reflect the overall state of the firm. Some stakeholders are more influential than others. However, schemes for weighting the views of one set of stakeholders more heavily than those of others have proven problematic (Wartick, 2002). As a result, existing measures of corporate reputation may do little to help managers understand the status of their firms' stakeholder relationships at a given point in time or to help investors understand how a firm is likely to behave in the future (Chatterji, Levine, & Toffel, 2009).

Nonetheless, aggregated measures of reputation are influential. An overall reputation score, measured by whatever imperfect method, can influence how those inside and outside a firm think about the firm and behave toward it. Looking inside, Elsbach and Kramer (1996) showed that school rankings influence how students, staff, and faculty members of rated schools think and behave, and Martins (2005) showed how these rankings influence top managers and the direction in which they guide their organizations. Looking outside, Sauder and Lancaster (2006) found that changes in law school rankings influenced prospective students' behavior and subsequently affected the number and quality of applicants these schools received. Others have found that consumer decisions about which books to buy (Sorensen, 2007), which songs to download (Salganik & Watts, 2008), and even from which hospitals to seek treatment (Pope, 2009) are affected by rankings.

Reputation measures can be so influential as to become self-fulfilling prophecies (Merton, 1948). A reputation measure is intended to be an aggregate representation of the perceptions of a firm's various audiences (Fombrun, 1996), but once revealed, the resulting measure shapes the individual perceptions that compose it, thereby reifying the reputational measure (Espeland & Sauder, 2007). Consider Walmart once again. If you have a highly favorable view of Walmart but then become aware that it has received a highly unfavorable rating from a popular magazine, you may reconsider and perhaps downgrade your view of this firm. As individuals downgrade their views, future reputation measures that aggregate these views will report yet lower ratings for Walmart. All the while, Walmart's characteristics may remain constant or even improve.

Extant studies have shown that reputation measures produce such a self-fulfilling effect (Deephouse, 2000; Gioia & Corley, 2002) but have identified few of the factors influencing the degree to which it occurs. In the next section, we hypothesize about the influence of two characteristics of a reputation ranking—its congruency with other information about the firm and its negativity—on individual perceptions of firms.

Assessing the Influence of Reputation Rankings

People make decisions about favoring, avoiding, or even attacking a firm based on the firm's reputation (Fombrun et al., 2000). However, it can be difficult to determine a firm's reputation. A reputation constitutes a multi-faceted assessment of a firm's performance across a variety of dimensions over time (Barnett et al., 2006). Yet people have limited attention and are selective in where they allocate it (March & Simon, 1958). As a result, most people are unaware of most actions of most firms (Barnett, 2014).

Lacking the ability or will to evaluate firms' entire historical behaviors, people often look to others for insights. Numerous organizations and media outlets promote reputational rankings that draw a large readership and affect important decisions such as where to attend college or work and what to buy (Sauder & Lancaster, 2006). Many bemoan the methods behind such rankings (Wartick, 2002), but their influence is significant. One's views and perceptions are subject to social influence, and knowing what others think can cause one to question and alter one's prior views, bringing them more in line with those of the referent other (Espeland & Sauder, 2007). Whether driven by lack of other information or out of a desire to avoid punishment from the majority group (Deutsch & Gerard, 1955), this influence has been found in a variety of settings, to include not just consumer goods (Salganik & Watts, 2008) and universities (Bowman & Bastedo, 2011), but even extending to the ballot box (Laponce, 1966).

However, when informed of a reputation ranking, one may not accept it at face value. New information is subject to interpretation (Weick, 1995). People have a tendency to interpret new information in a way that supports their existing beliefs, because this alleviates the psychological discomfort that cognitive dissonance brings (Festinger, 1962). For example, scientists rate research that reports findings consistent with their prior beliefs more positively than studies that present results inconsistent with their prior beliefs (Koehler, 1993).

We therefore expect that the degree of influence of a reputation ranking on an individual's perception of a firm will vary according to its fit with existing information that the individual has about that firm. If a reputation ranking contradicts one's established view, the cognitive dissonance it may evoke can lead one to ignore, discount, or reinterpret the new information. In contrast, if the reputation ranking is consonant with one's prior beliefs, then it is more likely to be noticed and accepted and so more likely to strengthen the established view. Thus, we hypothesize the following:

Hypothesis 1: The influence of a reputation ranking on one's perception of a firm is moderated by the ranking's congruency with other information one has about the firm

People are loathe to break with their existing views of organizations. As Garud, Dunbar, and Raghuram (1996) put it, "the human brain . . . makes Procrustean transformations and then justifies them . . . Confronted with contrary evidence, we can come up with more powerful explanations that incorporate or dismiss such evidence . . ." (p. 170). This tendency is especially strong for those whose identities are based on their affiliation with an organization (Elsbach & Kramer, 1996).

However, given their limited cognitive capacity, many people are unfamiliar with many firms. In these cases, there will be no frame to break and no identity to be protected at any cognitive cost when they are faced with new information about these firms. Where prior information and attachment are less pervasive or even absent, reputation rankings may have a particularly strong influence on perceptions, especially when negative. Negative information is more salient. People are more likely to react and remember negative information than neutral or positive information (Taylor, 1991). Even in the presence of prior information, negative information is more diagnostic than positive information when updating one's views. As Carter and Ruefli (2006) found, improvements in firms' reputations tend to come in relative small increments, whereas losses in reputation are more precipitous. Thus, a negative ranking revealed for a positively reputed firm may destroy its reputation, whereas a positive ranking may not change it significantly. We therefore expect the following to hold:

Hypothesis 2: The more unfavorable a firm's reputation ranking, the greater is the influence of that ranking on one's perceptions of that firm

Data and Method

To isolate the effects of reputation measures on individual perceptions under various conditions, we use an experimental method. We recruited 68 participants from a major city in the United Kingdom with the assistance of academic researchers at a university lab. Participants were paid £10 per hour. Almost half were students. About half were female, and half were younger than 30. The majority had work experience.

The participants were randomly assigned to one of two groups: experimental ($n = 34$) or control ($n = 34$). Because we are interested in discerning the influence of reputation rankings, the scenarios provided to the participants in the experimental group included a reputation score, whereas the scenarios for those in the control group did not disclose a reputation score. As shown in Table 1, the random assignments produced great similarity across the two groups.

The experiment was conducted through a written instrument in an experimental lab under the supervision of the authors. Each participant received a questionnaire booklet that contained 15 scenarios. Participants were instructed to play the role of an analyst on behalf of a wide range of stakeholder groups and to rate the firm described in each scenario. The names of the firms were kept generic so that prior knowledge of the firms could not influence participants' perceptions.

Each scenario provided a description of the firm that included the following characteristics: (a) quality of management; (b) quality of goods or services; (c) innovativeness; (d) long-term investment value; (e) financial soundness; (f) ability to attract, develop, and keep talented people; (g) wise use of corporate assets; and (h) community and environmental responsibility. These are the same characteristics that *Fortune* uses for its reputation surveys. Each characteristic was described in such a way as to convey that it was negative or positive (see the appendix for sample scenarios).[2]

The dependent variable is each participant's assessment of each firm in each scenario. In consonance with *Fortune*'s rating scale, we asked participants to assess each firm on a 7-point scale, ranging from *very poor* (1) to *excellent* (7). We sought to explain the influence of two variables—*Congruence* (Hypothesis 1) and *Negativity* (Hypothesis 2)—on our dependent variable. *Congruence* refers to the match between the type of ranking (positive or negative) and the type of description (positive or negative) provided in each scenario. *Negativity* refers to the unfavorability of the ranking. Ratings disclosed in the scenarios were on a scale of 1 (*very poor*) to 7 (*excellent*), consistent with *Fortune*'s scale. Ratings of 1 (*very poor*), 2 (*poor*), and 3 (*below average*) were considered negative; 5 (*good*), 6 (*very good*), and 7 (*excellent*)

Table I. Participant Characteristics.

Variable	Experimental (34 in total)		Control (34 in total)	
	n	%	*n*	%
Gender				
Male	15	38	16	47
Female	19	56	18	53
Nationality				
The United Kingdom	19	56	20	59
Other	15	44	14	41
Profession				
Student	14	41	12	35
Other	20	59	21	62
Years worked				
<1 year	7	21	11	32
1-4 years	6	18	8	24
5-10	6	18	7	21
11+	14	41	8	24
Age				
18-25	12	35	16	47
26-30	7	21	7	21
31-40	10	29	6	18
41+	3	9	5	15

were considered positive. Moreover, the variable *Group* accounted for exposure to the reputation rating. Half of the participants (experiment group) were provided with a *Fortune* rating in each scenario, and half were not (control group). Finally, to control for other factors that might influence assessment, we established control variables for gender, nationality, profession, and age of each participant.[3]

We seek to capture the influence of contextual factors on individual assessments that the individual may be unaware of, so we use a "policy capturing" approach (cf. Webster & Trevino, 1995). We used a $2 \times 2 \times 2$ mixed design that used *Group* as a between-participants variable and *Negativity* and *Congruence* as within-participants variables. When judgments are used as a dependent variable, such as assessments of task importance and job choice decisions (Rynes & Lawler, 1983; Zedeck, 1977), a within-participants design is called for (Aguinis & Bradley, 2014). In a within-participants design, each participant reviews a set of scenarios and comparisons are made between scenarios by the same person, thus investigating the effects of a manipulation on one individual (Atzmuller & Steiner, 2010). In our mixed design, two groups of participants received different sets of scenarios, but within each group, participants viewed the same scenarios. This design allowed us to control for individual-specific effects in the statistical analysis. With this design, we were able to collect more information from each participant than if we had used a between-participants design, thereby allowing us to proceed with a smaller group of participants.

Although it has many advantages, a challenge of within-participants design is "carryover effects" (Myers & Hansen, 2011). One condition might affect performance in other conditions. We addressed this by carefully constructing the experimental procedures and conducting the appropriate statistical analyses. Each scenario consisted of a different combination of treatments based on a $2 \times 2 \times 2$ factorial, with each scenario represented by one firm. We randomized the order of scenario presentation to avoid a potential confound between the order of scenarios and the manipulations. We pilot tested the complete questionnaire on a sample of four participants to ensure that participants could process the scenarios without any fatigue effects.

We performed three-factor mixed ANOVAs on overall ratings, with *Group* as the between-participant factor and *Congruence* and *Negativity* as within-participant factors. The individual participant was the unit of analysis. Participants remained in their assigned groups. Results were corrected by the Greenhouse–Geisser procedure (Greenhouse & Geisser, 1959) where appropriate. We also tested the data for normal distribution and homogeneity of variance using a Kolmogorov–Smirnov test and Levene's test, respectively, before statistical procedures were applied. We observed no gross departures from the assumptions.

Using the statistical software G-Power (Version 3.1, G* Power), we conducted a priori power analysis to determine the study's sensitivity. As suggested in the literature (Sawyer & Ball, 1981), the power of all tests was set at 0.80 for the conventional Type I error rate of 5%. A power analysis using estimated variables and a medium effect size (0.3) as suggested in previous studies[4] determined that a total sample size of 40 was needed to detect differences between conditions ($\alpha = .05$; $1 - \beta = .80$). After using listwise deletion[5] to eliminate participants with missing data on any predictor, our total sample size is 52, and so exceeds the 40 required (see Table 2 for additional details).

Results

As shown in Table 3, *Congruence* did not exert a significant main effect on the dependent variable ($F = 0.143$, $p > .05$). This indicates that differences in overall ratings between the experimental and control groups were not driven by whether or not a given rating was consistent with the other information

Table 2. Power Analysis Results.

F tests—ANOVA: Repeated measures, within–between interaction
Analysis: A priori: Compute required sample size
Input:
  Effect size *f* = 0.3
  α err prob = .05
  Power (1 − β err prob) = .8
  Number of groups = 8
  Number of measurements = 4
  Corr among rep measures = 0.5
  Nonsphericity correction ε = 1
Output:
  Noncentrality parameter λ = 28.8
  Critical *F* = 1.67
  Numerator *df* = 21
  Denominator *df* = 96
  Total sample size = 40
  Actual power = 0.868

Table 3. Analysis of Variance.

Source of variance	*df*	Sum of Squares	*F*	*p*
Congruence	1	0.146	0.143	.707
Negativity***	1	26.28	22.49	.00
Congruence × Group	1	0.836	0.825	.37
Negativity × Group	1	3.28	2.81	.10
Congruence × Negativity***	1	778.5	546.9	.00
Congruence × Negativity × Group*	1	9.50	6.68	.01

*$p < .05$. **$p < .01$. ***$p < .001$.

given in a scenario. Thus, counter to Hypothesis 1, the congruence between a reputation ranking and other information that one has about a firm does not appear to directly affect how one rates that firm. In contrast, there is a significant main effect for *Negativity* ($F = 22.49$, $p < .001$). As expected, when rating firms, the participants were more influenced by a *Fortune* score if it was negative than if it was positive. Thus, Hypothesis 2 is supported.

Table 3 also lists results for several interactions. The interaction between *Negativity, Congruence*, and *Group* is significant ($F = 6.68$, $p < .01$). To interpret this three-way interaction, we performed tests of each of the underlying two-way interactions (see Aiken & West, 1991). The only two-way interaction term to reach statistical significance is *Negativity* by *Congruence* ($F = 546.9, p < .01$), and so this appears to be the main driver of the overall three-way interaction. Thus, we find additional support for Hypothesis 2 and partial support for Hypothesis 1: Although there is no direct effect for *Congruence*, when the other information provided about the firm (the scenario) is negative, a congruent (negative) ranking has a significant effect on the participant's rating of the firm.

Discussion

Do reputation rankings influence perceptions of firms? Our findings suggest that they do, under certain conditions. In particular, a negative ranking tends to make one's assessment of a firm more negative, especially when the negative ranking is consistent with other information one has about the firm. Thus, rankings are influential, but cognitive dissonance (Festinger, 1954) and the salience of negative information (Taylor, 1991) render this influence strongest when a ranking reinforces one's unfavorable view of a firm.

Our study answers recent calls to delve more deeply into the cognitive underpinnings of corporate reputation (Barnett, 2014; Love & Kraatz, 2009; Mishina et al., 2012). People face cognitive constraints that limit their ability to assess the actions of firms. They turn to reputation rankings to help fill this void. In support of Mishina et al. (2012)'s conceptual model of reputational assessment, we find that the effect of a focal cue (herein, a *Fortune* score) on one's assessment of the reputation of a firm is path-dependent, varying with prior information one has about the firm (herein, the additional scenario details). Moreover, adding to Barnett's (2014) conceptual model of stakeholder punishment of firm misconduct, negative information about firms is processed differently than is positive information. Combining all this suggests that a firm with an unfavorable history may be tipped into a downward reputational spiral by a negative ranking, but given its incongruence, a positive ranking of the same firm may go unnoticed and so is unlikely to tip the firm into an upward spiral. Thus, from the firm's perspective, reputation rankings may be more accurately perceived as threats than as opportunities, particularly for those firms without favorable prior reputations.

Herein, we also extend the broader corporate reputation literature by noting that reputation rankings, of which there are now many, do not merely reflect the views of various observers but also influence these views. Because of this, a firm's actual characteristics and qualities can become disconnected from the perceptions that individuals hold of it, and the firm can lose or gain reputation without ever having changed its qualities. The results herein indicate that stakeholders focus on the features that the firm and its ranking hold in common. For example, stakeholders might overlook negative news about a firm and highlight the positive if that firm has a history of good behavior (Barnett, 2007). As a result, favorable reputations may be sticky, due to observers contorting new information to fit their existing beliefs. In contrast, unfavorable reputations may be quite fragile, quickly shattering in the face of a negative event. By further exploring the use of heuristic processing, more insights can be gained regarding the fragility and durability of reputations and the mechanisms by which corporate rankings influence the perceptions of stakeholders.

Our study also contributes to the large literature on the "business case" for corporate social responsibility, which seeks to determine the relationship between corporate social and financial performance (Barnett & Salomon, 2012). To determine the conditions under which it "pays to be good," it is necessary to account for how stakeholders actually assess the social performance of a firm. The assumption typically used in the business case literature—that stakeholders are aware of the social performance of firms—often does not hold (Barnett, 2014). Instead, stakeholders fill in gaps in their knowledge of firm performance with other information, and these shortcuts create biased perceptions. We need more studies that demonstrate how stakeholders process new information about firms.

Our findings also have implications for practice. Managers are keenly interested in what people think of their firms because one's feelings about a firm influence how one behaves toward that firm—whether one chooses to buy its output, become an employee, or otherwise transact with the firm—and these behaviors, in turn, affect the success and survival of that firm (Fombrun et al., 2000). How can managers shape what people think about their firm? Clearly, the link between a firm's behavior and its reputation is a loose one, and so firms may be unable to change their reputations solely by changing their behaviors. Although a firm may significantly improve its social or financial performance, the changes the firm makes may go unnoticed or be misinterpreted by the firm's stakeholders.

That is not to say that, because of this loose link, firms need not concern themselves with their behaviors. However, it does imply that firms ought to also concern themselves with the context in which their behaviors are perceived. The way in which information is presented and even who presents the information is of relevance to how stakeholders notice and interpret it. Firms should exploit the presence of positive aspects of their reputation and make them more congruent with other information they present so as to make the positive aspects of reputation stickier. In the face of a negative ranking, a firm can increase the salience of other positive rankings. Marketing scholars have proposed various strategies for how companies can capitalize on existing brands that are already favorable to customers when launching new products or entering new markets (Aaker & Keller, 1990).

Although our experimental methods allowed for isolating and documenting the effects of reputation rankings on individual perceptions, the results are based on an artificial situation. Participants in the lab might have behaved differently than they would have had they been outside the lab, because they were aware that they were being observed. Experimental investigations tend to produce larger effects of information on perception than do non-experimental investigations into the same phenomenon (Hovland, 1959). Thus, future studies may seek to uncover the influence of reputation rankings on firm reputation in real-world settings.

Although our experiments are reasonable abstractions, issues in the real world such as the reputation of the CEO and the organization's detailed history were excluded. However, by isolating these issues, we have established that the excluded factors did not cause the outcomes we observed herein. In addition, the process that participants followed in this study closely resembles the processes needed to evaluate firms: processing information about the firms, developing perceptions of them, and expressing perceptions by providing rankings, often under time pressure. As K. J. Cohen and Cyert (1965) wrote,

> Even though the assumptions of a model may not literally be exact and complete representations of reality, if they are realistic enough for the purposes of our analysis, we may be able to draw conclusions which can be shown to apply to the world. (p. 306)

This study focused on the influence of a single overall ranking on perception. An obvious question to consider is whether our results hold in a more complex condition in which more than a single overall ranking is known. Reputation is a multidimensional construct, and so the effects of exposure to various individual ratings dimensions, as well as multiple and perhaps conflicting rankings, are worthy of further study. For example, how do potential college students make sense of conflicts between *Business Week* and *US News & World Report* college rankings when formulating a perception of a given college? Are they able to parse variation in the dimensions on which each rates a college? Do they weight one more heavily than another? How does exposure to the first ranking shape interpretation of the subsequent ranking? Although this article offers insights into the general case, the influence of multidimensional and multiple reputations on perception remains an open question.

Appendix

Sample Scenario for Experimental Group

Company B operates in many different industries and works with customers in different countries. Its financial results were excellent, with revenues and profits up last year. Its prudent risk management as well as its good practice in stakeholder engagement contributed to the company's strong performance. Company B usually makes wise use of corporate assets; it earns a higher return using the same amount of assets as other competitors. This in part makes investors believe that Company B is considered a good long-term investment. The quality of its managers and their integrity are good. Company B provides quality products and services. According to a recent customer satisfaction survey, 85% of the customers said they would use the service again. Company B is known for attracting talent. The employee retention rate was also in the high 90% range last year. The company displays above-average concern for its community and is known as responsive to environmental concerns. Last year, some of its employees collaborated with an NGO, and a large amount of money was raised for cancer research. Employee innovativeness at Company B is high. Company B's investment in innovation research and development was increased by 34% last year. According to *Fortune* magazine, Company B is assessed favorably as 7 (*excellent*) in the "World's Most Admired Companies" list.

What rating will you give Company B for this year? (1 = *very poor*; 2 = *poor*; 3 = *below average*; 4 = *satisfactory*; 5 = *good*; 6 = *very good*; 7 = *excellent*)

Sample Scenario for Control Group

Company G recorded mixed financial results last year. They made zero profit; the stock price dropped marginally; the long-term value of the company was slightly adjusted upward. Company G follows industry standards that outline appropriate use of corporate assets. The quality of management at Company G is neither good nor bad. There were two appointments, former CEOs of information technology (IT) companies, to the board. The new directors maintained the current budget allocation for research and development (R&D) last year. Innovativeness at Company G is average. Concerns are raised occasionally that the level of investment in R&D is too low. The quality of products and services is mid-range as are prices. The foundation, a corporate arm for corporate social responsibility, is left independent and has several initiatives for the community where the company is located. The company displays some concern for its community and is relatively responsive to environmental issues. Company G was partially successful for keeping talented people. Some highly competent managers left the company last year.

What rating will you give Company G for this year? (1 = *very poor*; 2 = *poor*; 3 = *below average*; 4 = *satisfactory*; 5 = *good*; 6 = *very good*; 7 = *excellent*)

Acknowledgments

Our sincere thanks to the Oxford University Centre for Corporate Reputation for its financial support of this project and to the editor and anonymous reviewers for their help in refining the article.

Declaration of Conflicting Interests

The author(s) declared no potential conflicts of interest with respect to the research, authorship, and/or publication of this article.

Funding

The author(s) disclosed receipt of the following financial support for the research, authorship, and/or publication of this article: Financial support for this project was provided by the Oxford University Centre for Corporate Reputation.

Notes

1. *Ranking* and *rating* are terms often used interchangeably in the reputation literature. Although the measure we later use is technically a rating because it is a numerical score, for consistency, we use the term *ranking* throughout the article. This seems the more common term in the business and society literature.
2. Results of a manipulation check indicated the participants interpreted our descriptions as intended. For example, as expected, positive descriptions were rated as more positive than negative descriptions. To determine differences across descriptions, we performed paired analyses of the group, two at a time: positive versus negative. The two-tailed t statistic was 25.25, and the p value was less than .05. Thus, we reject the null hypotheses of equal means between positive and negative conditions.
3. We dropped "work experience" from the set of control variables because of its strong correlation with the "student" control variable ($r = .58$).
4. It is often acceptable to use a medium effect size (0.3) as suggested in J. Cohen (1988), but to obtain a more realistic effect, we used the effect size (0.35) reported in previous relevant studies on judgment and encoding (Block & Zakay, 1997; Storbeck & Clore, 2011).
5. This method is often the default option in statistical software packages (Little & Rubin, 1987).

References

Aaker, D., & Keller, K. L. (1990). Consumer evaluations of brand extensions. *Journal of Marketing, 54*, 27-41.

Aguinis, H., & Bradley, K. J. (2014). Best practice recommendations for designing and implementing experimental vignette methodology studies. *Organizational Research Methods, 17*, 351-371.

Aiken, L. S., & West, S. G. (1991). *Multiple regression: Testing and interpreting interactions*. Newbury Park, CA: Sage.

Atzmuller, C., & Steiner, P. M. (2010). Experimental vignette studies in survey research. *Methodology, 6*, 128-138.

Barnett, M. L. (2007). Stakeholder influence capacity and the variability of financial returns to corporate social responsibility. *Academy of Management Review, 32*, 794-816.

Barnett, M. L. (2014). Why stakeholders ignore firm misconduct: A cognitive view. *Journal of Management, 40*, 676-702.

Barnett, M. L., Jermier, J. M., & Lafferty, B. A. (2006). Corporate reputation: The definitional landscape. *Corporate Reputation Review, 9*, 26-38.

Barnett, M. L., & Salomon, R. M. (2012). Does it pay to be really good? Addressing the shape of the relationship between social and financial performance. *Strategic Management Journal, 33*, 1304-1320.

Barney, J. B. (1991). Firm resources and sustained competitive advantage. *Journal of Management, 17*, 99-120.

Block, R. A., & Zakay, D. (1997). Prospective and retrospective duration judgments: A meta analytic review. *Psychonomic Bulletin & Review, 4*, 184-197.

Bowman, N. A., & Bastedo, M. N. (2011). Anchoring effects on world university rankings: Exploring biases in reputation scores. *Higher Education, 61*, 431-444.

Bromley, D. (2002). Comparing corporate reputations: League tables, quotients, benchmarks, or case studies? *Corporate Reputation Review, 5*, 35-51.

Carter, S. M., & Ruefli, T. W. (2006). Intra-industry reputation dynamics under a resource-based framework: Assessing the durability factor. *Corporate Reputation Review, 9*, 3-25.

Chatterji, A. K., Levine, D. I., & Toffel, M. W. (2009). How well do social ratings actually measure corporate social responsibility? *Journal of Economics & Management Strategy, 18*, 125-169.

Cohen, J. (1988). *Statistical power analysis for the behavioral sciences* (2nd ed.). Hillsdale, NJ: Lawrence Erlbaum.

Cohen, K. J., & Cyert, R. M. (1965). Simulation and organizational behavior. In J. G. March (Ed.), *Handbook of organizations* (pp. 305-334). Chicago, IL: Rand McNally.

Deephouse, D. L. (2000). Media reputation as a strategic resource: An integration of mass communication and resource-based theories. *Journal of Management, 26*, 1091-1112.

Deutsch, M., & Gerard, H. (1955). A study of normative and informational influence upon individual judgment. *Journal of Abnormal and Social Psychology, 51*, 629-636.

Elsbach, K. D., & Kramer, R. M. (1996). Members' responses to organizational identity threats: Encountering and countering the *Business Week* rankings. *Administrative Science Quarterly, 41*, 442-476.

Espeland, W. N., & Sauder, M. (2007). The reactivity of rankings: How public measures recreate social worlds. *American Journal of Sociology, 113*, 1-40.

Festinger, L. (1954). A theory of social comparison processes. *Human Relations, 7,* 117-140.

Festinger, L. (1962). *A theory of cognitive dissonance.* Stanford, CA: Stanford University Press.

Fombrun, C. J. (1996). *Reputation: Realizing value from the corporate image.* Boston, MA: Harvard Business School Press.

Fombrun, C. J., Gardberg, N. A., & Barnett, M. L. (2000). Opportunity platforms and safety nets: Corporate citizenship and reputational risk. *Business and Society Review, 105,* 85-106.

Gardberg, N., & Dowling, G. (2012). Keeping score: The challenges of measuring corporate reputation. In M. Barnett & T. Pollock (Eds.), *The Oxford handbook of corporate reputation* (pp. 34-68). Oxford, UK: Oxford University Press.

Garud, R., Dunbar, R. L. M., & Raghuram, S. (1996). Run, rabbit, run! But can you survive? *Journal of Management Inquiry, 5,* 168-175.

Gioia, D. A., & Corley, K. G. (2002). Being good vs. looking good: Business school rankings and the Circian transformation from substance to image. *Academy of Management Learning & Education, 1,* 107-120.

Greenhouse, S. W., & Geisser, S. (1959). On methods in the analysis of profile data. *Psychometrika, 24,* 95-112.

Hovland, C. L. (1959). Reconciling conflicting results derived from experimental and survey studies of attitude change. *American Psychologist, 14,* 8-17.

Koehler, J. J. (1993). The influence of prior beliefs on scientific judgments of evidence quality. *Organizational Behavior and Human Decision Processes, 56,* 28-55.

Laponce, J. (1966). An experimental method to measure the tendency to equibalance in a political system. *American Political Science Review, 60,* 982-993.

Little, R. J. A., & Rubin, D. B. (1987). *Statistical analysis with missing data.* New York, NY: Willey.

Love, E. G., & Kraatz, M. (2009). Character, conformity, or the bottom line? How and why downsizing affected corporate reputation. *Academy of Management Journal, 52,* 314-335.

March, J. G., & Simon, H. A. (1958). *Organizations.* Oxford, UK: John Wiley.

Martins, L. L. (2005). A model of the effects of reputational rankings on organizational change. *Organization Science, 16,* 701-720.

Merton, R. K. (1948). The self-fulfilling prophecy. *Antioch Review, 8,* 193-210.

Mishina, Y., Block, E. S., & Mannor, M. J. (2012). The path dependence of organizational reputation: How social judgment influences assessments of capability and character. *Strategic Management Journal, 33,* 459-477.

Myers, A., & Hansen, C. (2011). *Experimental psychology.* Belmont, CA: Cengage Learning.

Pope, D. G. (2009). Reacting to rankings: Evidence from "America's best hospitals." *Journal of Health Economics, 28,* 1154-1165.

Rynes, S. L., & Lawler, J. (1983). A policy-capturing investigation of the role of expectancies in decisions to pursue job alternatives. *Journal of Applied Psychology, 68,* 620-631.

Salganik, M. J., & Watts, D. J. (2008). Leading the herd astray: An experimental study of self- fulfilling prophecies in an artificial cultural market. *Social Psychology Quarterly, 71*, 338-355.

Sauder, M., & Lancaster, R. (2006). Do rankings matter? The effects of *U.S. News & World Report* rankings on the admission process of law schools. *Law & Society Review, 40*, 105-134.

Sawyer, A., & Ball, D. (1981). Statistical power and effect size in marketing research. *Journal of Marketing Research, 18*, 275-290.

Sorensen, A. T. (2007). Bestseller lists and product variety. *Journal of Industrial Economics, 55*, 715-738.

Storbeck, J., & Clore, G. L. (2011). Affect influences false memories at encoding: Evidence from recognition data. *Emotion, 11*, 981-989.

Taylor, S. E. (1991). Asymmetrical effects of positive and negative events: The mobilization-minimization hypothesis. *Psychological Bulletin, 110*, 67-85.

Wartick, S. L. (2002). Measuring corporate reputation: Definition and data. *Business & Society, 41*, 371-393.

Webster, J., & Trevino, L. (1995). Rational and social theories as complementary explanations of communication media choices: Two policy-capturing studies. *Academy of Management Journal, 38*, 1544-1572.

Weick, K. E. (1995). *Sensemaking in organizations*. Thousand Oaks, CA: Sage.

Zedeck, S. (1977). An information processing model and approach to the study of motivation. *Organizational Behavior and Human Performance, 18*, 47-77.

Author Biographies

Michael L. Barnett (PhD, New York University) is professor of management and global business at Rutgers Business School—Newark and New Brunswick. His research focuses on how firms individually and collectively manage their relationships with stakeholders, and how their efforts at stakeholder management, through acts of corporate social responsibility and via communal institutions such as industry trade associations, influence their reputations and financial performance, as well as affect society. His articles have appeared in such journals as *Academy of Management Journal; Academy of Management Review; Business & Politics, Business & Society; Journal of Management; Journal of Management Studies; Long Range Planning*; and *Strategic Management Journal*.

Sohvi Leih (PhD, University of Oxford) is a visiting scholar at the University of California, Berkeley, where she was previously a postdoctoral scholar. Her work has appeared, or is forthcoming, in management journals to include *California Management Review, Global Strategy Journal*, and *Strategic Organization*, and from publishers such as Oxford University Press.

12

Original Manuscript

The Business Case for Corporate Social Responsibility: A Critique and an Indirect Path Forward

Business & Society
1–24
© The Author(s) 2016
Reprints and permissions:
sagepub.com/journalsPermissions.nav
DOI: 10.1177/0007650316660044
bas.sagepub.com

Michael L. Barnett[1]

Abstract

Do firms benefit from their voluntary efforts to alleviate the many problems confronting society? A vast literature establishing a "business case" for corporate social responsibility (CSR) appears to find that usually they do. However, as argued herein, the business case literature has established only that firms usually benefit from responding to the demands of their primary stakeholders. The nature of the relationship between the interests of business and those of broader society, beyond a subset of powerful primary stakeholders, remains an open question despite this vast literature. This article develops a set of propositions that highlight constraints on firms' ability to profit from CSR and outlines a set of managerial challenges on which researchers must focus their attention to truly determine whether and when firms can profit by responding to the needs of society.

Keywords

business case, corporate social responsibility (CSR), social welfare, stakeholder theory

[1]Rutgers, The State University of New Jersey, NJ, USA

Corresponding Author:
Michael L. Barnett, Rutgers Business School–Newark & New Brunswick, Rutgers, The State University of New Jersey, 1 Washington Park, #1054, Newark, NJ, USA.
Email: mbarnett@business.rutgers.edu

You know, we're living in a society!

> —George Costanza, Seinfeld (Episode 16; May 23, 1991)

The world cries out for repair. While some people in the world are well off, many more live in misery . . . In the face of these broad and deep problems, calls go out for companies to help.

> —Margolis and Walsh (2003, pp. 268-69)

We now have the opportunity to eradicate poverty and deal with the issue of climate change. What bigger opportunity do you want to see? . . . Companies make up 60 percent of the global economy. If they don't play an active part, how can we solve [these crises]?

> —Paul Polman, CEO of Unilever, quoted in Burn-Callander (2015)

Why don't more firms take a more active role in resolving more of society's problems? After all, firms gain myriad benefits from being socially responsible (Fombrun, Gardberg, & Barnett, 2000). In this article, I argue that the voluminous literature supporting firms' ability to profit from corporate social responsibility (CSR)—the "business case" for CSR—has had the perverse effect of limiting firms' efforts to resolve critical issues facing society. These studies have enacted CSR to entail strategically responding to primary stakeholder demands rather than as a matter of resolving society's problems (Walsh, 2005). The resulting literature has shown that "it pays to be good" but only to firms' most powerful stakeholders (cf. Mitchell, Agle, & Wood, 1997). As firms have taken an increasingly strategic view of CSR (McWilliams, Siegel, & Wright, 2006), those without the power to directly affect firms—that is, most of those suffering the worst of society's ills—have become less likely to find a place on corporate agendas. Thus, despite hundreds of studies linking corporate social and financial performance, the gap between the interests of business and society may be widening, not shrinking.

Herein, I seek to redirect scholarship on the business case for CSR toward investigating the conditions under which firms may profit from engaging in practices that go beyond "managing for stakeholders" (Freeman, Harrison, & Wicks, 2007), to entail truly managing for society. I first review the literature underlying the established business case. Extant literature has pushed management scholarship and practice beyond exclusive concern for shareholder interests. However, it has settled into a focus on firms triaging the issues brought to bear on them by powerful stakeholders rather than, and often to the exclusion of, alleviating society's problems. As a result, hundreds of studies have largely validated a business case for critical stakeholder responsiveness while largely leaving untested a business case for engagement in broader societal problems. Thereafter, I clarify the nature of CSR and explain how, by benefitting society rather than by selectively responding to the demands of their most powerful stakeholders, firms can improve relationships with their primary stakeholders. Furthermore, I develop a set of propositions that explain how the increasingly strategic use of CSR hampers a firm's ability to build stakeholder relationships. I conclude with a revised agenda for research on the business case for society.

The Weak Link Between CSR and Society

Our society faces many serious problems: poverty, disease, and environmental destruction, to name a few. We often look to corporations to help alleviate these problems (Margolis & Walsh, 2003). They are not legally bound to address social problems, but the resources at their disposal place corporations in a position of unique strength to do so (Walsh, 2005). For problems that cross borders and so are difficult or intractable for sovereign governments to address, corporations may be the only viable means of ameliorating causes of great human misery (Scherer, Palazzo, & Matten, 2014).

When will corporations address society's problems? With limited resources and operating in competitive environments, corporations are more likely to take on social problems and more able to sustain their efforts if they profit from doing so (Aguilera, Rupp, Williams, & Ganapathi, 2007). Fortunately, studies have demonstrated that firms can "do well by doing good." Under a variety of conditions, firms gain financial (Barnett & Salomon, 2012), reputational (Fombrun et al., 2000), and insurance-like benefits (Godfrey, 2005) from their acts of CSR. At minimum, socially responsible firms rarely suffer financial harm (Margolis & Walsh, 2003). Overall, there is a well-established "business case" showing how firms benefit from engaging in acts of CSR (Fombrun et al., 2000).

The business case for CSR is well established not just in the academic literature but also in practice. It is now commonplace for firms to file annual social responsibility reports alongside their financial reports and, therein, to declare a positive relationship between the firm's success and its contributions to society. For example, the 2014 CSR Report from Cisco states,

> We are committed to being a responsible company and making a positive contribution to society and the environment. This helps us inspire trust in our brand, develop strong relationships with our stakeholders, and create long-term value for society and our business. (p. A5)

Within this report, Cisco's Chairman and CEO, John T. Chambers, states,

> Our focus is not only on our customers and partners, but also on society and the environment. . . CSR has always been one of the pillars of our culture, and I'm extremely proud of the global impact of our programs. (p. A3)

Yet, despite so many major firms espousing the centrality of society to their missions and declaring the many benefits their firms gain by focusing on society, social problems still abound and many are worsening. For example, economic inequality is rising, as is the planet's temperature, and with it, the oceans. Ecological disasters are commonplace. Women and children continue to be sold into slavery. Diseases still kill thousands for want of a vaccine or clean water. How can this be?

The literature and along with it, firms, have confused CSR with critical stakeholder responsiveness. The two, though, are far from synonymous. As firms have honed their stakeholder management strategies, they have largely ignored many of society's problems. Rather, powerful stakeholders have benefitted over social problems from the extensive and, perhaps, sincere corporate interest in social responsibility.

Aided by the clarity of purpose it provides managers (cf. Jensen, 2000), the notion that a firm should be operated solely for the benefit of its shareholders has held sway with many for many decades. This position is famously represented by Friedman (1970), who decreed that the business of business is business and not to meddle in society's problems. Freeman (1984) later noted, though, in now nearly as famous a fashion that the firm's strategic imperative is to attend to the concerns of "any group or individual who can affect or is affected by the achievement of the organization's objectives" (p. 46). This stakeholder approach, or what is now generally deemed stakeholder theory, has "infiltrated the academic dialogue in management" (Harrison & Wicks, 2013, p. 97) and helped to spur legions of scholars as well as titans of industry to broadly discredit the shareholder model as "wrong," "a tragically flawed premise," "dreary and demeaning," "totally idiotic," and even "the dumbest idea in the world" (Denning, 2015).

Although they are commonly depicted as diametrically opposed, the shareholder and stakeholder perspectives both seek to maximize the profitability of the firm and differ only in the path prescribed to do so. Whereas Friedman (1970) was quick to dismiss spending on non-compulsory benefits to employees, suppliers, customers, and the like as tantamount to theft from the firm's owners, Freeman (1984) shines a favorable light on the benefits that can accrue to the firm from investing in its relationships with its various stakeholder groups. In any situation where it is demonstrated that attending to stakeholder concerns helps the firm to improve its financial performance, the "Friedman-Freeman debate" (Freeman, 2008) comes to an amicable close. Under such conditions, the only difference between the two is that Friedman would portray any stakeholder who favors a firm due to its CSR as misguided, whereas Freeman is pleased by the prospect of stakeholders making social demands of firms. Yet, even Friedman would encourage rather than begrudge managers for seeking to capture any profit that CSR can bring the firm through gaining the favor of its stakeholders, misguided or not.

Note that neither perspective is concerned with alleviating the broader ills of society. Friedman was quite clear about his exclusive focus on firm profitability. But Freeman and his colleagues have not hidden the fact that the primary concern of stakeholder theory is also the welfare of the firm, not of society. For example, Freeman and Phillips (2002) declared, "first and foremost, stakeholder theory is about business and capitalism" (p. 340). Walsh (2005) thoroughly reviewed Freeman (1984) and two other books core to stakeholder theory (Phillips, 2003; Post, Preston, & Sachs, 2002) and honed in on their lack of concern for social or even stakeholder welfare:

> . . . make no mistake, he [Freeman] is not interested in serving stakeholders to satisfy their needs in any altruistic sense. (p. 428)

> . . . stakeholder management ideas complement the neoclassical theory of the firm; they do not challenge it . . . If we want to browbeat infidels and supplant the stockholder theory of the firm, then we must look elsewhere for relief. (p. 437)

Nevertheless, stakeholder theory underpins the management literature on the social responsibilities of corporations. In fact, stakeholder theory is so consonant with the CSR literature that, as Laplume, Sonpar, and Litz's (2008) systematic review noted, many have argued that stakeholder theory obviates and even supersedes the CSR construct (p. 1168). Wood (1991) framed stakeholder theory as a means of helping firms to think more concretely about their responsibilities to society, whereas Waddock and Graves (1997) described CSR as being composed of the firm's interactions with its various stakeholders. Argandoña (1998) combined the two perspectives into a single term, "the stakeholder theory of the social responsibility of business" (p. 1093). Freeman (2005) characterized CSR as superfluous, given stakeholder theory and its associated focus on the firm's responsibilities to a broad set of stakeholders, and Rowley and Berman (2000), a fortiori, suggested replacing the CSR construct with stakeholder theory.

Conflating or replacing the concept of CSR with that of stakeholder management has led to a rather narrow interpretation of the firm's obligations to society, one that rarely reaches beyond the interests of those stakeholders who have direct power over the firm. Some corporations have more resources than some countries, but even the largest cannot attend to all the demands of all its stakeholders, let alone all of society's problems. Stakeholder management, thus, entails sorting out which stakeholder demands to address. This sorting process tends to exclude many social issues from the firm's agenda.

Scholars have written extensively about how managers should decide which stakeholder demands to fulfill and which to ignore. Freeman's (1984) guidance was blunt, advising firms to focus on stakeholders who could jeopardize the firm's survival and to not "give in" (p. 149) to those who lack such power (see Walsh, 2005, p. 428). Phillips (2003) argued for a graduated approach: A firm ought to concern itself with a stakeholder issue only to the degree that the stakeholder affects the firm, and those stakeholders without amply strong influence over the firm "should look elsewhere for relief" (p. 142). The most dominant perspective specified three factors that underpin the triage process that managers use to determine whether or not a stakeholder "really counts": power, legitimacy, and urgency (Mitchell et al., 1997).

But what about those problems that lack the urgent push of a powerful and legitimate stakeholder? Such problems fall to the wayside under the stakeholder model. Walsh (2005) concluded that when managers are guided by stakeholder theory, the call of the Secretary-General of the United Nations for corporations to help in the fight against AIDS goes unheeded. Disasters in the natural environment are ignored (Starik, 1995). The suffering of the impoverished, diseased, starving . . . if lacking power over firms, they "should look elsewhere for relief" (Phillips, 2003, p. 142). Granted, acting at the behest of those without power, stakeholders with power can push the firm to address animal welfare, global warming, rainforest destruction, or any other social problems (Frooman, 1999). But even for social problems that powerful stakeholders push firms to address, the same problematic logic holds: Only the concerns of the powerful, whether self-serving or in selective support of those without power, will gain managerial attention and perhaps firm resources. As prescribed by stakeholder theory, there is no direct access to the firm for those in society without power; the interface is via amply powerful stakeholders.

Given the nature of stakeholder management, is there a way to bring more of society's problems to the attention of more firms? The key to broadening a firm's concerns is to show that addressing these additional issues benefits the firm (Aguilera et al., 2007). For example, firms moved beyond managing for shareholders in response to a business case that demonstrated the returns to serving stakeholder interests. I next explain how addressing society's problems can improve a firm's relationships with its primary stakeholders and thereby benefit the firm.

Resocializing CSR

Motivated by a desire to bring business interests into alignment with those of society (Preston, 1975) and augmented by a zeal to legitimize the field of study (Rowley & Berman, 2000), business and society scholars have actually established what is tantamount to a business case for serving powerful stakeholders. After decades of research, it is evident and perhaps obvious that firms' interests are well aligned with those of their most powerful stakeholders and so firms do better by ensuring that the concerns of these stakeholders are addressed. However, we still have few insights about the alignment between broader societal interests and those of the firm (Margolis & Walsh, 2003).

Do firms do better by ensuring that society does well? Extant literature answers part of this question in the affirmative but suggests that, overall, the relationship may be negative. Powerful stakeholders are members of society, just as shareholders are a subset of a firm's stakeholders. Therefore, advancing powerful stakeholder interests advances society, in part.[1] However, society is composed of much more than just powerful stakeholders. The amorphous nature of the stakeholder concept (cf. Orts & Strudler, 2002) has blurred the distinction between responding to stakeholder demands and acting responsibly toward broader society. Whenever the literature has unpacked the stakeholder concept, though, the resulting contingent view (Rowley & Berman, 2000) suggests that the business case may not hold for much of society.

The Primacy of the Primary Stakeholder

Since its inception, the stakeholder concept has been bemoaned as vague. Freeman's (1984) initial definition of a stakeholder as "any group or individual who can affect or is affected by the achievement of the firm's objectives" ruled little out (p. 46), as mostly anyone or anything has the potential to affect or be affected by any firm by at least some stretch of the imagination (Orts & Strudler, 2002). Others have since parsed stakeholders many ways, particularly along the dimension of whether they can affect the firm or are affected by the firm. For example, Goodpaster (1991) categorized those who can affect the firm as strategic stakeholders, whereas those who are affected by the firm, he deemed to be moral stakeholders. Given interest in establishing a business case, though, most scholars have focused on strategic stakeholders and parsed them according to the degree to which they could affect the firm (Mitchell et al., 1997). Those with direct influence on the firm are often characterized as primary stakeholders, whereas those with only indirect influence are typically relegated to secondary stakeholder status (Carroll,

1979; Clarkson, 1995). Those who lack power, legitimacy, and urgency entirely are considered "nonstakeholders" (Mitchell et al., 1997, p. 873).

Empirical studies isolating the financial returns from serving different stakeholder groups have found the business case to hold for primary stakeholders—those without whose support the firm would cease to exist—but the more secondary are stakeholders, the less likely is the firm to profit from serving them. Berman, Wicks, Kotha, and Jones (1999) found a positive relationship between return on assets and the level of support the firm provides its employees, as well as its level of concern for customers through the production of safer and higher quality goods. In contrast, the firm's support of diversity, safeguarding of the natural environment, and contributions to the broader community had no significant relationship with its return on assets. Hillman and Keim (2001) contrasted firm support for primary stakeholders with support of social issues and found the former to be positively related to financial performance but the latter negatively related. Although hypothesizing the opposite, Van der Laan, Van Ees, and Van Witteloostuijn (2008) also found empirical support for a positive relationship with financial performance for primary stakeholders and a negative relationship for secondary stakeholders. Thus, there is empirical validation that serving those who can directly affect the firm pays, but extending the firm's actions beyond this powerful core group does not.

These findings seem to refute the validity of a business case for tackling social issues, as they appear to show that the interests of firms and the welfare of broader society, beyond primary stakeholders, do not coincide and often may conflict. However, such a conclusion is premature. Should there be a valid business case for society at large, the same empirical results would prevail. By definition, secondary stakeholders and nonstakeholders lack an exchange relationship with the firm (Clarkson, 1995). Therefore, they are unable to directly reciprocate for the firm's good deeds. Prior studies isolated firms' efforts to advance social issues from their efforts to satisfy primary stakeholder interests and found that the pursuit of social issues was not positively associated with firm profitability and often reduced it. But when studies isolate the firm's efforts to aid non-primary stakeholders, all else equal, they will necessarily find that as firms do more, they lose more because non-primary stakeholders are unable to provide compensating revenues for the firm. Only primary stakeholders transact with the firm, so any returns to the firm must occur via these relationships. Simply, a business case can only be made by focusing on those with whom the firm does business—its primary stakeholders.[2]

The relationships between the firm and its non-primary stakeholders are akin to cost centers. Firms benefit from cost centers to the degree that they improve the firm's primary functions. Viewed independent of the performance of these primary functions, though, investing more in a cost center generates only more losses. For example, as a firm spends more on R&D or advertising, it may benefit from new product development and sales. But if R&D and advertising are assessed alone, then greater spending on each will appear to lead to greater losses for the firm. To understand their true value, their effects on the firm's primary functions must be assessed. Does investing more in R&D and advertising help to build and sell more innovative and marketable products? If so, then a business case may be established. Likewise, one cannot conclude that firms do not benefit from their efforts to alleviate social problems unless the effects of these initiatives on primary stakeholder relationships are accounted for.

Despite frequent operationalization otherwise, prior conceptual studies have framed the business case in this indirect way, arguing that a firm's contributions to society can increase the degree to which its primary stakeholders view the firm as a trustworthy, and so favored, party with which to transact. Although primary stakeholders do not receive the direct benefit of these acts of CSR, they still may respond in ways that benefit the firm:

> The business case for CSR implies that as stakeholders observe a firm's socially responsible behaviors, they will deem the firm a more favorable party with which to conduct their own transactions . . . Trust arises and relationships improve as stakeholders observe a firm's CSR activities, not as a consequence of a firm's use of direct influence tactics to capture their favor. (Barnett, 2007, p. 800)

Barnett (2007) argued that when firms respond to demands from their stakeholders, they are engaging in "direct influence tactics," not acts of social responsibility. Direct influence tactics are reciprocal, intended to maintain and improve relationships with powerful stakeholders through direct exchange. Such acts "are not necessarily focused on improving social welfare" and can even "be instrumental in reducing a firm's contributions to social welfare" (p. 799). In contrast, CSR aims to improve social welfare rather than directly satisfy a stakeholder demand.

Empirical studies evince that CSR, as distinguished from direct influence tactics, can help firms gain better access to key resources held by their primary stakeholders. Being a good corporate citizen has been shown to increase the desirability of firms to potential employees (Turban & Greening, 1997) and decrease constraints on firms' ability to acquire capital (Cheng, Ioannou, & Serafeim, 2014), for example. Thus, there exist both theoretical rationale and empirical support for the possibility of a business case for managing societal problems that is distinct from the extant business case that focuses on responding to primary stakeholder demands. But under what conditions will it hold?

Giving, Not Giving In: Distinguishing CSR From Critical Stakeholder Responsiveness

When a firm seeks to benefit society, its stakeholders may infer that the firm is trustworthy and so favor the firm. For example, a firm's donation of goods and services to local food pantries might help the firm to improve its employee relations. Because of this donation, the firm's employees may view it as more trustworthy and so a more desirable place to work, and then reward the firm with greater loyalty (Fombrun et al., 2000). If the gains to the firm from employee loyalty exceed the costs of the donations, then the firm profits from its efforts to improve its local community; that is, there is a business case. However, a firm might also improve its employee relations by acquiescing to labor union demands to increase wages. If gains to the firm from improved employee relations exceed the costs of the wage increase, then the firm profits by increasing wages; thus, there is also a business case for this.

Both the wage raise and the donation to local food pantries seek the same means of benefitting the firm—via improved relations with a primary stakeholder group—but the way each pursues this outcome differs. A firm's acts of CSR build trust by signaling to its primary stakeholders that the firm is "other-considering," not purely self-interested (Godfrey, Merrill, & Hansen, 2009). Actions taken at the behest of stakeholders, by contrast, rely on power rather than trust and so "precisely because these actions can be viewed through a power-exchange lens they may be seen as wholly consistent with the firm's profit-making interest and viewed as merely self-serving, rather than other-regarding, behaviors" (Godfrey et al., 2009, p. 429).

A significant body of literature has explored the varying conditions under which it pays to respond to the demands of powerful stakeholders. But under what conditions will it pay to address social problems? We cannot expect every "other-serving" CSR act to produce a positive return for every firm, else we would see firms earning infinite returns by investing in infinite amounts of CSR (Barnett, 2007). Rather, there are a variety of contingencies that influence whether or not it pays to be good (Rowley & Berman, 2000).

Barnett (2007) identified the importance of firm characteristics to stakeholder inferences about CSR (p. 803). A firm with a weak record of social performance lacks the "stakeholder influence capacity" that is needed to transform an act of social responsibility into an increase in stakeholder favor.

That firm will gain no benefit from an isolated act of kindness because this act alone is not ample to convince stakeholders that the firm is truly "other-considering." In contrast, a firm with a strong record of social involvement may profit from engaging in the same act of CSR because stakeholders may interpret the act as sincere and, therefore, favor the firm. Thus, under differing conditions, stakeholders may respond very differently, even negatively, to a particular effort to tackle a social problem. In the remainder of this section, I develop a set of propositions that detail how the characteristics of an act of CSR, not just the characteristics of the firm engaging in the CSR act, affect a firm's relationships with its primary stakeholders.

Giving or taking? The core premise of a business case for society is that stakeholders have greater trust in firms that engage in altruistic actions and so favor them as exchange partners. Stakeholders still expect firms to pursue profit but firms do not accrue goodwill from such self-serving pursuits (Godfrey et al., 2009). In fact, firms' actions that are perceived as self-serving can destroy trust (Varadarajan & Menon, 1988). However, it may not be feasible for a stakeholder to categorize any particular action of a firm as entirely self- or other-serving. Even the most altruistic actions may have self-serving aspects to them (Glazer & Konrad, 1996). Because they have opposing influences, with other-serving actions building trust but self-serving actions destroying it, these mixed motives thus need to be accounted for when trying to understand how a particular CSR act affects stakeholder relationships.

CSR can take many forms, and these varying forms affect stakeholder perceptions of the degree of altruism present in a given act of CSR. Some acts of CSR are perceived as more altruistic than others, not as merely altruistic or not (Ellen, Webb, & Mohr, 2006). For example, firms often engage in cause-related marketing, through which they may tie their contributions to a social cause to product sales, such as donating to a charity a certain percentage or flat amount for each item purchased (Varadarajan & Menon, 1988). This approach to CSR benefits both a social cause and the firm. However, firms may also directly donate to a charity independent of firm sales. This latter approach is less transparently self-serving. Accordingly, the following general relationship is expected:

Proposition 1: The more that a firm's initiative to help society also directly benefits the firm, the less likely will that initiative improve the firm's relationships with its primary stakeholders.

Giving 'til it hurts? In his 2014 Lenten message, Pope Francis declared, "I distrust a charity that costs nothing and does not hurt" (Vatican, 2014). His comments suggest that there must be sacrifice involved in an action for it to convey altruism and so earn trust. Symbolic adoption of a social cause does not signal a firm's concern for others as effectively as does substantively participating in an effort to resolve that same social problem. For example, a firm that issues a press release in support of marriage equality is likely to be perceived as less supportive of that social cause than is a firm that provides full benefits to same-sex couples and lobbies legislators for new laws supporting equality. The more difficult and costly is the firm's effort to support the social cause, the more altruistic the firm is likely to be perceived to be, and so the more stakeholder trust it may generate. Du, Bhattacharya, and Sen (2011) demonstrated the effects of having more "skin in the game" from a different perspective, showing that when consumers went beyond mere awareness of a firm's CSR effort and physically participated in it, they developed a more positive attitude toward the firm. More generally, the following is proposed:

> **Proposition 2:** The less burdensome to a firm is its initiative to help society, the less likely will that initiative improve the firm's relationships with its primary stakeholders.

Giving early? When a firm increases employee pay or benefits, it is generally considered to be behaving in a socially responsible way. However, the context in which the action occurs can alter stakeholder perceptions about the degree to which the act may instead be self-serving. For example, in February 2015, Walmart announced that it would raise its minimum wage to US$1.75 above the federal minimum wage and then by another US$1 the following year. Whereas some saw this as an act of good corporate citizenship, others pointed out that Walmart did so under pressure. As a result, this socially responsible action engendered more skepticism than it likely would have had Walmart acted earlier:

> . . . you cannot deny the role of the United Food and Commercial Workers' campaign to organize Wal-Mart workers. "This is not an act of corporate benevolence," said Marc Perrone, president of UFCW, in a statement on the Wal-Mart announcement. "Walmart is responding directly to calls from workers and their allies to pay a living wage." In fact, the last time Wal-Mart faced significant labor unrest in 2006, it raised wages as a direct result, according to Federal Reserve minutes. It, like most businesses, makes changes that benefit workers only when its reputation is threatened and poor publicity ensues. That means that worker voices play a powerful role in wage growth. (Dayen, 2015)

More generally, the more time that a firm takes to respond to a social problem, particularly in the face of mounting pressure to act, the less likely is a stakeholder to perceive the eventual response to be indicative that the firm is altruistic. Thus, the following is proposed:

> **Proposition 3:** The less proactive is a firm's initiative to help society, the less likely will that initiative improve the firm's relationships with its primary stakeholders.

Giving consistently? Barnett (2007) theorized that firms that suddenly engage in CSR are not believable. Stakeholders treat an unexpected act of CSR with suspicion. A good act by a bad firm can even backfire, harming trust between the firm and its stakeholders (Varadarajan & Menon, 1988). Barnett and Salomon (2012) empirically validated the importance of firm history, demonstrating that firms need an extensive record of social responsibility before they are able to profit from it.

The need to establish a consistent record of social involvement before being able to profit from it may apply not just at the firm level but also to specific social initiatives. Although two firms may allocate the same overall level of funding and other resource commitments to addressing social issues, these firms may assemble very different CSR portfolios. One firm might support a large number of ad hoc social projects, whereas the other might focus deeply on one or a few specific issues. For example, Google doles out a variety of grants to address various social issues each year, whereas McDonald's is closely associated with one particular charity, that of the Ronald McDonald House. A firm's consistency in addressing a particular social issue in depth over time should provide its stakeholders a greater indication that the firm is other-considering than would another firm's new or intermittent support of that same issue. Thus, the following is proposed:

> **Proposition 4:** The less sustained is a firm's involvement in an initiative to help society, the less likely will that initiative improve the firm's relationships with its primary stakeholders.

Giving and gabbing? Firms face a conundrum in publicizing their good deeds. A firm needs its primary stakeholders to be aware of its socially responsible actions if it is to gain increased trust as a result. Thus, it needs to publicize these acts. Yet, when a firm publicizes its good deeds, stakeholders may perceive the firm to be behaving in a self-serving way, and this may cause stakeholders to limit or even decrease their trust in the firm. As Du, Bhattacharya, and Sen (2010) noted, "While stakeholders claim they want to know about . . . good deeds . . . they also quickly become leery of the CSR motives when companies aggressively promote their CSR efforts" (p. 9). The following relationship is thus expected to hold:

> **Proposition 5:** The more that a firm promotes its initiative to help society, the less likely will that initiative improve the firm's relationships with its primary stakeholders.

These propositions highlight the difficulty that firms face when attempting to simultaneously serve themselves and society. An act of CSR is more likely to improve primary stakeholder relationships and so benefit the firm if it entails self-sacrifice (Proposition 1), is costly to the firm (Proposition 2), occurs in advance of calls for such action (Proposition 3), is a sustained effort (Proposition 4), and is not self-promoted (Proposition 5). Perversely, it thus seems that the better aligned is an act of CSR with a firm's self-interest, be that because it is cheaper, easier, or less risky to undertake, then the less that act may be capable of advancing the firm's self-interest. That is, for CSR initiatives, the pursuit of self-interest can be self-defeating. How effectively can firms balance these competing pressures so that they gain private benefits from serving the public good? The next section outlines a research agenda for determining this.

Business and/or Society? Uncovering (Mis) Alignment

Figure 1 illustrates how the pathways to profit differ across firms when they are managed for shareholders, or for stakeholders, or for society. The dotted line in the lower part of the figure that links a firm's actions directly to its financial returns represents the traditional view that firms are managed solely for the benefit of their shareholders and so are obligated to take actions that maximize the firm's financial returns, unfettered by concern for others (cf. Friedman, 1970). The bold arrows through the center of the figure complicate this direct path to financial returns by introducing stakeholders as mediator. The positive signs reflect the findings of the literature on stakeholder theory that a firm's financial returns are enhanced through actions that improve its relationships with its primary stakeholders (cf. Freeman, 1984).

The dashed arrows at the top of Figure 1 illustrate the yet-more-complicated link between a firm's actions and its financial returns that is the focus of this article. Many studies have shown that a firm's efforts to benefit anyone other than its primary stakeholders tend to be to the financial detriment of the firm (e.g., Hillman & Keim, 2001). Therefore, the figure portrays firm actions to better society as leading to a decrease in firm's financial returns. However, as

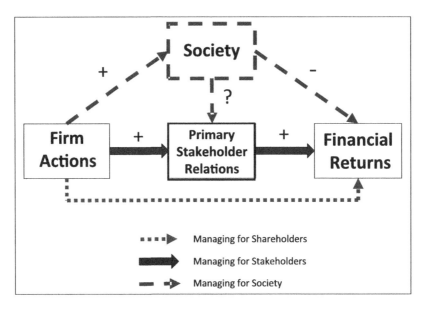

Figure 1. Mapping the business cases.

previously argued, a firm's actions to better society can improve its financial returns indirectly, via its effects on primary stakeholder relations. The established business case literature has provided few insights into the validity of this indirect path to financial returns, so Figure 1 labels this pathway with a question mark. This is the open question that we seek to answer in refocusing business case research. As suggested in the propositions developed in the prior section, this complex third path to profit may often be difficult for firms to traverse. To determine the conditions under which firms can, in fact, serve their own interests by serving the interests of society, researchers will need to move past their ongoing efforts to correlate "various mishmashes" (Rowley & Berman, 2000, p. 405) of variables with financial performance and instead focus on developing an understanding of how well firms can manage conflicting pressures, as next discussed.

When Do Stakeholders Begin to View Selfless Acts as Selfish?

Figure 1 depicts alternative pathways to profitability, but any given act of CSR can traverse all three. For example, if a firm decreases its waste production, it may directly improve its financial returns through savings on material costs and waste disposal; thus, there is a shareholder business case to support it. Moreover, the firm may have acted to reduce its pollution at the behest of a powerful stakeholder group and so the firm may improve stakeholder relations by taking this action. And, of course, society may benefit from the resulting decrease in pollution.

Proposition 1 suggests that perceptions that a firm is profiting via the first (shareholder) and second (stakeholder) paths may crowd out its ability to profit via the third, focal (society) path. Firms build trust with their primary stakeholders by demonstrating that they are concerned with the plight of others (Godfrey et al., 2009). The resulting improved relationships with these key resource holders benefit the firm. Such "win–win" outcomes are the defining characteristic of the business case (cf. Porter & Van der Linde, 1995). Yet, a firm's wins have the potential to be self-defeating. The more that a stakeholder perceives that a firm's actions are self-serving, the less likely will the firm be able to gain the trust of the stakeholder (Varadarajan & Menon, 1988). Therefore, as firms publicize the ways that they have benefited from their CSR initiatives, they may harm their ability to continue to gain such benefits.

This co-mingling of social and corporate benefit is common in CSR reporting. Consider the 2014 CSR Report from Cisco mentioned at the start of this article. Cisco's CEO states that the firm is proud of its contributions to improving society and the environment, but the report also notes that these contributions benefit the firm by improving its stakeholder relationships and generating long-term value. CEO Howard Schultz similarly introduces Starbucks' (2014) Global Responsibility Report by writing, "I am proud that Starbucks not only achieved another year of record financial performance, but we did so while doing more for our people and the communities we serve than at any time in our history" (p. 1).

Firms' returns from CSR initiatives are likely to be affected by the way they publicize these efforts. Because other-serving and self-serving actions have offsetting effects on stakeholder trust, firms may be able to improve their returns by downplaying the private benefits and focusing their messaging instead on the gains these initiatives create for society. For example, describing CSR as an investment rather than as an act of goodwill may harm a firm's ability to build stakeholder trust. However, the degree to which mention of gains to the firm harms the ability of the firm to realize these gains is likely to vary by stakeholder group. In particular, investors may view a firm's declaration that it profits from its social investments as further assurance that the firm is fulfilling its fiduciary responsibility and, therefore, increase trust in the firm.

Proposition 5 suggests that not only the way in which firms publicize their CSR initiatives but also the degree to which they do so can limit their ability to profit from them. Firms must publicize their CSR acts to create awareness, yet "tooting one's own horn" can appear self-serving to the stakeholders that it is intended to impress. Thus, even advertising that focuses on the benefits that a CSR initiative brings to society, not just to the firm, can become problematic.

Scholars need to conduct additional research on the way in which messaging about CSR affects various stakeholders. How does variation in the wording of a press release or an annual report on CSR affect stakeholder perceptions of a firm's trustworthiness? Are there guerilla marketing techniques that allow firms to bring their good deeds to the attention of their primary stakeholders without risking the backlash that a traditional marketing campaign might trigger? We need to determine how and when firms may gain the most benefit from their acts of CSR, given their potential to build stakeholder trust, without tipping over into the downside by instead causing stakeholders to question the firm's sincerity. Rather than seek linear correlations, scholars ought to test for U-shaped relationships between key variables (cf. Barnett & Salomon, 2012) to uncover when seemingly beneficial things, such as publicity, turn negative.

When Are the Powerful Better Served by Not Serving Them?

Figure 1 also illustrates that both the established business case, which has focused on how firms may profit by managing in the interests of stakeholders, and the revised business case, which as outlined herein is focused on how firms may profit by managing in the interests of society, are premised on gaining favor with primary stakeholders. Where they differ is in how the firm gains this favor. The established business case argues that firms maintain the most stakeholder favor by prioritizing the needs of their most powerful, legitimate, and urgent stakeholders (Mitchell et al., 1997). But in a business case for society, the reverse may hold true. Proposition 3 suggests that by responding to social issues for which the firm is not under immediate pressure, the firm is better able to demonstrate to its primary stakeholders that it is other-serving and so gain their favor. If the firm faces urgent pressure from its powerful stakeholders to deal with a social issue, then the response, though still to the benefit of society, may be perceived as self-serving and so produce no gain and, perhaps, a loss of favor with primary stakeholders.

Power and trust thus interact in determining the degree to which a firm's social initiatives affect stakeholder favor, but exactly how remains unclear. A firm's relationships with its primary stakeholders is a function of how it deals with the demands these stakeholders make of the firm to take on specific issues, as well as how these stakeholders react to its decisions to take on or ignore other social issues absent such pressure. Given limited time, attention, and resources, firms must be selective in their pursuits of social causes. The calculus involved in rationing the firm's resources must include more than just power, legitimacy, and urgency if it is to determine the most optimal way to manage primary stakeholder relations. Perhaps the firm best advances its own interests by dealing with any particular social problem before rather than after it becomes a stakeholder demand. However, any given firm is likely to face a mix of social issues vying for its limited resources, to include many that are championed by powerful stakeholders. How do primary stakeholders weigh a firm's decision to acquiesce to their demands relative to a firm's proactive effort to take on a social issue? How do stakeholders process conflicting firm actions, such as denying one direct demand but pursuing another social issue? Our lack of understanding of how these issues are weighed in the minds of stakeholders and how they affect their trust in and favor toward a given firm highlights the need for more work on stakeholder cognition, as it is the core determinant of whether or not it pays to be good (Barnett, 2014).

When Do the Costs of Being Good Start to Outweigh the Benefits?

A firm can increase its financial returns not only by increasing its revenues but also by decreasing its costs. The literature has typically focused on the ability of CSR to bring about increased revenues but it has also recognized that CSR helps to buffer firms from losses (Fombrun et al., 2000). The actual costs of CSR—the resources a firm expends in pursuing a given social initiative—typically have not been considered.

Proposition 2 suggests that costs both benefit and harm firms' ability to profit from CSR and so must be carefully studied when assessing the viability of a business case. Perceptions that a firm has willingly taken on a significant burden in its efforts to better society are helpful in convincing stakeholders of the firm's trustworthiness. Thus, firms may gain valuable stakeholder favor as a result of committing more resources to CSR initiatives. However, greater spending, all else equal, simply means greater difficulty in turning a profit. Therefore, to profit, firms must manage CSR spending in a way that allows them to gain the most benefit at the lowest cost.

Barnett and Salomon (2012) acknowledged the countervailing force of costs on returns to CSR and called for research on the efficiency by which firms are able to produce stakeholder favor through CSR. Some firms may have to spend considerably more than others, and perhaps more than they can recover through improved stakeholder favor, to convince their primary stakeholders that their firm is other-considering. More generally, the efficiency of firms in running social initiatives has not been well accounted for. Some firms may be able to mount a campaign to, say, end homelessness in their local community or increase high school graduation rates, at lower cost than others. Overall, business case research must better measure the costs of engaging in CSR if it is to understand when firms can and cannot profit from these actions.

Conclusion

By helping others, do firms help themselves? An extensive literature has found that typically they do (Orlitzky, Schmidt, & Rynes, 2003), at least when we define helping others to mean meeting the demands of firms' primary stakeholders (cf. Walsh, 2005). However, finding that it pays to maintain favorable relationships with those whose support is essential for firm survival—primary stakeholders—is a validation of resource dependence theory (Pfeffer & Salancik, 1978), not a test of the returns to social responsibility. Such findings are effectively tautological, establishing only a business case for taking actions that are necessary to remain in business. When helping others is instead defined as voluntarily tackling the many problems of society at large, as firms are often called upon to do, the business case remains largely untested.

Given the challenges facing society and the important role that firms could play in resolving them, it is important that we seek to fill this research gap. Management theories can become self-fulfilling prophecies (Ghoshal, 2005), and so getting the theories right can help in getting practice right. If firms expect that addressing social problems comes at a cost, firms rationally are unlikely to do so, especially repeatedly or in significant numbers, and so societal problems are unlikely to be resolved through this means. However, if firms expect that they can profit from alleviating social ills, then knowledge of such win–win scenarios ought to spur widespread and ongoing corporate action to better society.

Because of its indirect, complex nature and in light of its costs, many of the conditions necessary for firms to profit from social responsibility may prove invalid when scholars refocus their efforts on validating a business case for society. This is not particularly surprising, as a business case for society requires firms to find a way to simultaneously be other-serving and self-serving, and these aims are fundamentally at odds. As a field, we may have successfully fooled ourselves into believing that these opposing states can be brought consistently into alignment through market mechanisms. But as argued above, we have brought them into alignment by artifice, having minimized the requirement that firms serve society and instead measured how effectively they serve themselves by satisfying the demands of their primary resource holders. After we reorient, will it still work? Rather than finding win–win outcomes as the rule, we may instead find that there are many trade-offs (Hahn, Figge, Pinkse, & Preuss, 2010). Where the business case falls short, we will need to consider the appropriateness and desirability of formal regulation as a means of managing any misalignments.

This call to reorient business case research is not a call to supplant or replace stakeholder theory. Rather, such a reorientation would advance and enrich stakeholder theory by further clarifying what stakeholder theory is and is not, and more clearly distinguishing it from, rather than muddling it with or substituting it for, CSR. Although it seems rather obvious now, it was indeed a contribution to establish that building and maintaining trusting relations with one's stakeholders can be a better way to manage long-run firm performance. But it is now time to recognize that stakeholder theory may not be effective at managing many of society's pressing problems and, in fact, could be driving firms away from deeper involvement with society. Perhaps stakeholder theory could be enriched so as deal with social welfare directly. But as it has become more instrumental and we have further clarified the contingencies of the business case, the non-instrumental, social welfare aspects of stakeholder theory have only fallen away. By highlighting the ways in which it may be profitable to manage for society, not just for stakeholders, we can begin to assess when and if business and society can align via market mechanisms and, where they cannot, we may spur much-needed conversation about the role of formal government intervention in bringing about the desired level of alignment.

Acknowledgment
The author sincerely thanks the editors and Rob Phillips for their constructive feedback.

Declaration of Conflicting Interests
The author declared no potential conflicts of interest with respect to the research, authorship, and/or publication of this article.

Funding
The author received no financial support for the research, authorship, and/or publication of this article.

Notes

1. Consider the notion of "too big to fail" as popularly applied to certain corporations in recent years, as well as the famous paraphrase of former General Motors president Charles Wilson, "As GM goes, so goes the nation."
2. Hart and Sharma (2004) argued that firms that directly engage their "fringe"

stakeholders gain "competitive imagination" from the resulting market intelligence and limit the likelihood that "smart mobs" will attack the firm. Although these are potential benefits that could accrue directly from non-primary stakeholders, they are connected to firm performance via primary stakeholder relationships, either by creating future customers who come in from the fringe when market intelligence uncovers new ways to serve them, or by offsetting future regulations through relationship building that proves ample to hold off the pressure that would otherwise accrue from smart mobs.

References

Aguilera, R. V., Rupp, D. E., Williams, C. A., & Ganapathi, J. (2007). Putting the S back in corporate social responsibility: A multilevel theory of social change in organizations. *Academy of Management Review, 32*, 836-863.

Argandoña, A. (1998). The stakeholder theory and the common good. *Journal of Business Ethics, 17*, 1093-1102.

Barnett, M. L. (2007). Stakeholder influence capacity and the variability of financial returns to corporate social responsibility. *Academy of Management Review, 32*, 794-816.

Barnett, M. L. (2014). Why stakeholders ignore firm misconduct: A cognitive view. *Journal of Management, 40*, 676-702.

Barnett, M. L., & Salomon, R. M. (2012). Does it pay to be really good? Addressing the shape of the relationship between social and financial performance. *Strategic Management Journal, 33*, 1304-1320.

Berman, S. L., Wicks, A. C., Kotha, S., & Jones, T. M. (1999). Does stakeholder orientation matter? The relationship between stakeholder management models and firm financial performance. *Academy of Management Journal, 42*, 488-506.

Burn-Callander, R. (2015, January 28). Unilever boss Paul Polman slams capitalist obsession with profit. *The Telegraph*. Retrieved from http://www.telegraph.co.uk/finance/newsbysector/epic/ulvr/11372550/Unilever-boss-Paul-Polmanslams-capitalist-obsession-with-profit.html

Carroll, A. B. (1979). A three-dimensional conceptual model of corporate performance. *Academy of Management Review, 4*, 497-505.

Cheng, B., Ioannou, I., & Serafeim, G. (2014). Corporate social responsibility and access to finance. *Strategic Management Journal, 35*, 1-23.

Cisco. (2014). *Social responsibility report*. Retrieved from http://www.cisco.com/assets/csr/pdf/CSR_Report_2014.pdf

Clarkson, M. E. (1995). A stakeholder framework for analyzing and evaluating corporate social performance. *Academy of Management Review, 20*, 92-117.

Dayen, D. (2015, February 24). Scott Walker's economic mess: How worker wages were gutted in Wisconsin. *Slate.com*. Retrieved from http://www.salon.com/2015/02/24/scott_walkers_economic_mess_how_worker_wages_were_gutted_in_wisconsin/

Denning, S. (2015, February 5). Salesforce CEO slams world's' dumbest idea. *Forbes.com*. Retrieved from http://www.forbes.com/sites/stevedenning/2015/02/05/

salesforce-ceo-slams-the-worlds-dumbest-idea-maximizing-shareholder-value/#333d65525255

Du, S., Bhattacharya, C. B., & Sen, S. (2010). Maximizing business returns to corporate social responsibility (CSR): The role of CSR communication. *International Journal of Management Reviews, 12*, 8-19.

Du, S., Bhattacharya, C. B., & Sen, S. (2011). Corporate social responsibility and competitive advantage: Overcoming the trust barrier. *Management Science, 57*, 1528-1545.

Ellen, P. S., Webb, D. J., & Mohr, L. A. (2006). Building corporate associations: Consumer attributions for corporate socially responsible programs. *Journal of the Academy of Marketing Science, 34*, 147-157.

Fombrun, C. J., Gardberg, N. A., & Barnett, M. L. (2000). Opportunity platforms and safety nets: Corporate citizenship and reputational risk. *Business and Society Review, 105*, 85-106.

Freeman, R. E. (1984). *Strategic management: A stakeholder perspective*. Boston, MA: Pitman.

Freeman, R. E. (2005). The development of stakeholder theory: An idiosyncratic approach. In K. G. Smith & M. A. Hitt (Eds.), *Great minds in management: The process of theory development* (pp. 417-435). Oxford, UK: Oxford University Press.

Freeman, R. E. (2008). Ending the so-called "Friedman-Freeman" debate. *Business Ethics Quarterly, 18*, 153-190.

Freeman, R. E., Harrison, J. S., & Wicks, A. C. (2007). *Managing for stakeholders: Survival, reputation, and success*. New Haven, CT: Yale University Press.

Freeman, R. E., & Phillips, R. A. (2002). Stakeholder theory: A libertarian defense. *Business Ethics Quarterly, 12*, 331-349.

Friedman, M. (1970). The social responsibility of business is to increase its profits. *New York Times Magazine, 13*, 32-33.

Frooman, J. (1999). Stakeholder influence strategies. *Academy of Management Review, 24*, 191-205.

Ghoshal, S. (2005). Bad management theories are destroying good management practices. *Academy of Management Learning & Education, 4*, 75-91.

Glazer, A., & Konrad, K. A. (1996). A signaling explanation for charity. *The American Economic Review*, 1019-1028.

Godfrey, P. C. (2005). The relationship between corporate philanthropy and shareholder wealth: A risk management perspective. *Academy of Management Review, 30*, 777-798.

Godfrey, P. C., Merrill, C. B., & Hansen, J. M. (2009). The relationship between corporate social responsibility and shareholder value: An empirical test of the risk management hypothesis. *Strategic Management Journal, 30*, 425-445.

Goodpaster, K. E. (1991). Business ethics and stakeholder analysis. *Business Ethics Quarterly, 1*, 53-73.

Hahn, T., Figge, F., Pinkse, J., & Preuss, L. (2010). Trade-offs in corporate sustainability: You can't have your cake and eat it. *Business Strategy and the Environment*, *19*, 217-229.

Harrison, J. S., & Wicks, A. C. (2013). Stakeholder theory, value, and firm performance. *Business Ethics Quarterly*, *23*, 97-124.

Hart, S. L., & Sharma, S. (2004). Engaging fringe stakeholders for competitive imagination. *The Academy of Management Executive*, *18*, 7-18.

Hillman, A. J., & Keim, G. D. (2001). Shareholder value, stakeholder management, and social issues: What's the bottom line? *Strategic Management Journal*, *22*, 125-139.

Jensen, M. C. (2000). Value maximization and the corporate objective function. In M. Beer & N. Nohria (Eds.), *Breaking the code of change* (pp. 37-57). Boston, MA: Harvard Business School Press.

Laplume, A. O., Sonpar, K., & Litz, R. A. (2008). Stakeholder theory: Reviewing a theory that moves us. *Journal of Management*, *34*, 1152-1189.

Margolis, J. D., & Walsh, J. P. (2003). Misery loves companies: Rethinking social initiatives by business. *Administrative Science Quarterly*, *48*, 268-305.

McWilliams, A., Siegel, D. S., & Wright, P. M. (2006). Corporate social responsibility: Strategic implications. *Journal of Management Studies*, *43*, 1-18.

Mitchell, R. K., Agle, B. R., & Wood, D. J. (1997). Toward a theory of stakeholder identification and salience: Defining the principle of who and what really counts. *Academy of Management Review*, *22*, 853-886.

Orlitzky, M., Schmidt, F., & Rynes, S. (2003). Corporate social and financial performance: A meta-analysis. *Organization Studies*, *24*, 403-441.

Orts, E. W., & Strudler, A. (2002). The ethical and environmental limits of stakeholder theory. *Business Ethics Quarterly*, *12*, 215-233.

Pfeffer, J., & Salancik, G. R. (1978). *The external control of organizations: A resource dependence approach*. New York, NY: Harper & Row.

Phillips, R. (2003). *Stakeholder theory and organizational ethics*. San Francisco, CA: Berrett-Koehler.

Porter, M. E., & Van der Linde, C. (1995). Green and competitive: Ending the stalemate. *Harvard Business Review*, *73*, 120-134.

Post, J. E., Preston, L. E., & Sachs, S. (2002). *Redefining the corporation: Stakeholder management and organizational wealth*. Stanford, CA: Stanford University Press.

Preston, L. E. (1975). Corporation and society: The search for a paradigm. *Journal of Economic Literature*, *13*, 434-453.

Rowley, T., & Berman, S. (2000). A brand new brand of corporate social performance. *Business & Society*, *39*, 397-418.

Scherer, A. G., Palazzo, G., & Matten, D. (2014). The business firm as a political actor a new theory of the firm for a globalized world. *Business & Society*, *53*, 143-156.

Starbucks. (2014). *Global responsibility report*. Retrieved from http://www.starbucks.com/responsibility/global-report

Starik, M. (1995). Should trees have managerial standing? Toward stakeholder status for non-human nature. *Journal of Business Ethics*, *14*, 207-217.

Turban, D. B., & Greening, D. W. (1997). Corporate social performance and organizational attractiveness to prospective employees. *Academy of Management Journal, 40*, 658-672.

Van der Laan, G., Van Ees, H., & Van Witteloostuijn, A. (2008). Corporate social and financial performance: An extended stakeholder theory, and empirical test with accounting measures. *Journal of Business Ethics, 79*, 299-310.

Varadarajan, P. R., & Menon, A. (1988). Cause-related marketing: A coalignment of marketing strategy and corporate philanthropy. *The Journal of Marketing, 52*, 58-74.

Vatican. (2014). *Lenten message of our Holy Father Francis.* Retrieved from https://w2.vatican.va/content/francesco/en/messages/lent/documents/papa-francesco_20131226_messaggio-quaresima2014.html

Waddock, S. A., & Graves, S. B. (1997). The corporate social performance-financial performance link. *Strategic Management Journal, 18*, 303-319.

Walsh, J. P. (2005). Book review essay: Taking stock of stakeholder management. *Academy of Management Review, 30*, 426-438.

Wood, D. J. (1991). Corporate social performance revisited. *Academy of Management Review, 16*, 691-718.

Author Biography

Michael L. Barnett (PhD, New York University) is professor of management and global business at Rutgers Business School–Newark & New Brunswick. His research focuses on how firms individually and collectively manage their relationships with stakeholders, and how their efforts at stakeholder management, through acts of corporate social responsibility and via communal institutions such as industry trade associations, influence their reputations and financial performance, as well as affect society. His articles have appeared in such journals as *Academy of Management Journal, Academy of Management Review, Business & Politics, Business & Society, Journal of Management, Journal of Management Studies, Long Range Planning*, and *Strategic Management Journal*.

13

Building a better business case: where do we go from here?

When discussing the business case for corporate social responsibility in the classroom, I often start by showing contrasting clips from the movie *Other People's Money*, which is about a hostile takeover of a struggling firm called New England Wire and Cable. I first show a speech by the firm's chairman, 'Jorgy' Jorgeson. Played by Gregory Peck, Jorgy is quite adept at making an impassioned plea to stockholders, imploring them to stick with the company rather than sell to 'Larry the Liquidator' Garfield who, true to his nickname, seeks to liquidate the firm. Then it's Larry's turn, wherein Danny DeVito channels his inner (not so much outer) Gordon Gecko in arguing that shareholders should embrace their good ol' greed: '*And lest we forget, that's the only reason any of you became stockholders in the first place. You want to make money! You don't care if they manufacture wire and cable, fried chicken, or grow tangerines! You want to make money!*'

Jorgy makes clear the human toll of closing the firm, while Larry clarifies the central mechanism of any business case: firms do whatever makes money. If there is a change in where the big bucks abound, a change in firm behavior eventually follows, propelled at minimum by the threat of someone like Larry liquidating those firms that fail to follow the money. In 1802, DuPont made black powder. Around 1902, DuPont recognized that chemicals made more money than black powder and so became a chemical company. By 2002, DuPont was also manufacturing food products, fibers, and more. A firm will grow fruit or shift to manufacturing toilet brushes shaped like fruit (it's a real thing somehow; just look it up on the ever-evolving Amazon website) if there's more money to be made in the latter.

Accordingly, if firms believe that being good makes more money than being bad, then firms will become good. That's the essence of the business case for CSR. On the other hand, if firms realize that being bad makes more money than being good, then firms will become bad. That, we must acknowledge, is also the essence of the business case. Therefore, if we want to understand whether a firm will serve the best interests of society or take self-serving actions that harm society, then we must follow the money.

The studies republished in this book explain why following the money does not consistently lead firms down a path of doing good things. Stakeholders are the means of transforming corporate good into gold, as well as bad into bubkis, yet they have limited abilities to fulfill their critical role. As a result, firm behavior is imperfectly tied to financial performance. For the business case to work better, stakeholders must be more alert and responsive to firm behaviors, rewarding good acts and punishing bad acts as they arise. However, it's not evident that most stakeholders have the ambition and ability to do so. Thus, the link between doing good (bad) and doing well (poorly) remains uncomfortably loose.

While it is important to point out that stakeholders are imperfect and, moreover, to recognize that these imperfections bound the business case for CSR, this is just a first step. What are the next steps? This concluding chapter outlines three steps forward that can help to bring the interests of business more firmly and consistently into alignment with the welfare of society. First, we must revise our empirical models to ensure that they actually test the relationship between business and society, so that we can figure out when it really does pay to be good to society, not just to powerful stakeholders. Second, we need to bring government back into the relationship between business and society, so that we can address situations in which it does not pay to be good. Finally, we need to account for the realities of the digital age, wherein stakeholder influence practices and outcomes may differ significantly from established literature and expectations. There are many strong and insightful scholars eagerly engaging in CSR research, as the mountain of publications evidences. If we can focus this contagious energy in the right directions (cf. Barnett, 2016a), then maybe we can fine-tune, if not outright fix the problematic relationship between business and society.

Follow a crooked path

There's no shortage of publications that explore the relationship between doing good and doing well. Typically they begin by bemoaning the sheer number of prior publications that have sought to study this same link, then they take a crack at it themselves, and ultimately they conclude that yes, it pays to be good. Great! So we're done here, right? Not so fast . . .

The key subject of the central research question in this ever-expanding literature is rarely made explicit: does it pay to be good *to whom*? The immediately prior chapter argued that although society is the presumed beneficiary of this good corporate behavior, the benefits to society have not been taken into consideration in most of these studies. Intended to validate a business case for corporate social responsibility, these voluminous studies have instead been designed in ways that validate a business case for critical stakeholder responsiveness. Yet, the things that appease powerful stakeholders are not necessarily the same things that are good for society and can be quite the opposite. As a result, we now know a great deal about whether or not it pays to respond to the demands of powerful stakeholders (spoiler alert: it does!), but we know little about whether or not it pays to be good to society.

The little that we do know about whether or not it pays to be good to society suggests that it does not. On a daily basis we can observe profitable firms doing things that harm society. Following business case logic (that is, following the money), we therefore must conclude that at least sometimes it does not pay to be good, and sometimes it may even pay to be bad to society; else, logically, firms wouldn't do these bad things. If we venture beyond simple observation and logic, and dig into the bountiful empirical literature, the picture comes into finer-grained focus and, fair warning, gets even uglier. We're talking black velvet Elvis art genre ugly here. Again referencing the immediately prior chapter: 'Empirical studies isolating the financial returns from serving different stakeholder groups have found the business case to hold for primary stakeholders – those without whom the firm would cease to exist – but the more secondary are stakeholders, the less likely is the firm to profit from serving them' (p.235). So what we see once we flip on the ol' black light is that attending to the needs of those with little or no power over the firm – most of society – does not pay. As firms follow the money, they chart a path leading to only a small portion of society, and a powerful and privileged portion at that.

But don't fret just yet. Nothing looks good under black light. Despite these findings, it's still possible that it pays to be good to society, beyond just a subset of powerful stakeholders therein. To really find out, we need to view the business case in a different light. We need to view it as akin to the classic job interview test at a restaurant. Perhaps you're familiar with the premise. As part of a job interview, you are taken to a restaurant. However, you are not really brought there to chat with the interviewer about the job. Instead, the interviewer is trying to assess your character. Obviously you're going to be nice to the interviewer because you know where your bread is buttered. But the interviewer wants to see how you relate to others. Will you be nice to the waiter and other restaurant staff? That's the test. The inference is that if you are nice to those who lack power over you, you are trustworthy and so a more suitable candidate for the job.

Likewise, powerful stakeholders may use observations about how a firm treats those without power to assess the firm's true character. Any non-suicidal firm will of course be responsive to the demands of those who can withhold critical resources and so bring about its demise. But these stakeholders want to know not just that the firm is sane and business savvy, but also that it is trustworthy and so safe to transact with. Stakeholders' decisions about whether or not to work for a particular firm, invest in it, allow it to build a new plant in their community, buy goods and services from it, and so on, are risky. Stakeholders must decide whether or not to take such risks with any given firm. By observing whether or not the firm voluntarily takes actions that benefit others in society, stakeholders gain insights about the firm's trustworthiness, and these insights influence their willingness to transact with the firm.

But we know this already, right? It's old news that acts of CSR may signal a firm's trustworthiness to its stakeholders and thereby help the firm to gain and maintain favorable access to critical resources. This instrumental logic of how it pays to be good has long underpinned the business case. Nonetheless, we still need to thoroughly test our working model in order to understand if and when it holds, because the data and methods we've come to rely on haven't really done so. And, to do this, we first must untangle two muddled paths to gaining and maintaining stakeholder favor: direct versus indirect.

As argued in Chapter 4, when firms are nice to their primary stakeholders, they are using direct influence tactics, not engaging in CSR. They aren't bettering society and thereby building trust with those who hold critical resources; instead, they're directly engaging these resource holders. Our frequent tests of the direct relationship between actions that benefit primary stakeholders and firm financial performance have largely found positive results, because obviously it's better for the bottom line to pander to rather than piss off the powerful. What remains under-researched though, and frankly the only thing that makes the business case for CSR interesting, is the indirect path to stakeholder favor.

Financial returns only come from those who can transact with the firm. Whether they are elated or angered, helped or harmed by the firm, those without resources to provide or withhold cannot be directly accounted for in the business case because, simply, they cannot pay. There's no money to follow. However, those who can pay might be affected by how the firm behaves toward those who cannot, much as the interviewer in the earlier example was moved by how the interviewee behaved toward the waiter. This is the indirect path. To follow it, we must focus on when being good to those *without* power over the firm helps the firm to gain favor from those *with* power over the firm. That is, apart from any favor generated through direct influence tactics, we need to assess the degree to which a firm's good acts toward society curry the favor of its powerful stakeholders. The converse is also relevant: to what degree do a firm's bad acts toward society destroy this favor?

A research agenda that really tests whether or not it pays to be good (and hurts to be bad) thus entails getting inside stakeholders' minds (Barnett, 2016b). When does a good or bad act toward society catch their attention? To what degree does it please or anger them? And, ultimately, how does it alter their degree of trust in and desire to transact with the firm? The literature has not been completely blind to these sorts of questions, but often empirical studies have aggregated data and used methods that don't allow us to distinguish how specific acts influence various stakeholders. For example, in the study presented in Chapter 5, we found a curvilinear relationship between corporate social and financial performance, from which we concluded that it pays to be good, but it also pays to be bad, depending upon the firm's history. To find this, we used annualized measures of social and financial performance, which is standard practice. But this means that we have no way of distinguishing the specific acts that built a firm's overall social performance in any given year, nor can we link individual acts directly to changes in annual financial performance.

Because the measures are aggregated, we don't know if there were good things that went unrewarded or bad things that went unpunished in any given year. Moreover, we can't untangle the effects of those acts that benefited society from those that directly benefited primary stakeholders. On the other hand, in the study presented in Chapter 7, we used an event study, which isolates the financial effects of individual good and bad acts. Using this method, we gained confidence that a particular event was associated with a particular change in a firm's market value. However, market value itself is an aggregated measure that masks variation in individual stakeholder responses. A firm may gain market value immediately following a given act even if it loses favor with some of its primary stakeholders, and vice versa. Moreover, a firm's market value 'corrects' over time, leading to further confusion about the full and final financial effects of any given act. Overall, the data and methods commonly used in the business case literature just don't reveal what is going on inside a given stakeholder's mind in response to a particular act of CSR.

Our data and methods will always have limits; we can devise no perfect test, especially when seeking to look inside stakeholders' minds. Fine. But whatever the imperfect test used, we must at least follow the right path. In the indirect path outlined here, stakeholder perceptions mediate the relationship between doing good (bad) and doing well (poorly). Our empirical studies ought to be designed to match. Setting aside the very real challenge of disaggregating available measures, this means that we must at least measure the financial returns to a firm's actions via their effects on their primary stakeholders. If we don't test along this mediated pathway, then we are measuring something other than the business case for CSR. For example, a study that finds a positive correlation between, say, a firm's decision to install pollution reducing equipment in its plants and that firm's financial performance, finds only that process improvement pays, as shown in Figure 1 of Chapter 4. To determine if this effort to dampen harm to the natural environment is good for both business and society, we must traverse the crooked path, testing for returns to this investment via its influence on the firm's primary stakeholders.

Because we are seeking to understand when it pays to be good to (and hurts to harm) society, it seems essential to also include society in our mediated model of the business case for CSR, as shown in Figure 1 of Chapter 12. Revisiting the example of the job interview over dinner, was it necessary to help the waiter clear the table and even help him move into a new apartment over the weekend, or was a forced smile enough to demonstrate concern for others and thereby gain the interviewer's favor? What if you were just a little snappy with the waiter? Would that be enough for the interviewer to toss you out of the candidate pool, or would you need to dump your cold, non-al dente pasta over the waiter's head to really make a difference? To help understand the limits of this indirect path to job placement, we need a measure of how nice you were to the waiter. Likewise, if we are to understand how stakeholder perceptions of a firm are shaped by the good (bad) acts of the firm toward society, then we need to know just how good (bad) these acts were.

This isn't a call for measuring the magnitude of the good and bad acts, such as how much a firm spent on a philanthropic initiative or how many tons of toxic pollutant it emitted in an accidental release. Many studies already do this. Rather, it's a call for measuring the impacts of these actions on society. Extant business case literature rarely measures societal outcomes, instead focusing on what the firm does. But there may be a sizeable gap between, say, funding an initiative to save the whales and actually saving the whales. If we don't measure societal outcomes, then at best we may validate a business case for CSR efforts, leaving us well short of our aim to better align the interest of business and society. Said another way, we want to know when it pays to be good to society, not just when it pays to appear to try to be good to society. Measuring outcomes instead of inputs pushes us in this desired direction.

But wait, there's more! As if our model weren't getting complicated enough, we also need to peek inside managerial minds. Were stakeholders to become perfectly responsive to firm actions, the business case for CSR would still be problematic if there are significant constraints on managerial sensemaking and firm responsiveness to stakeholder feedback. For the business case to work, firms must be alert and responsive to stakeholder rewards and punishments, maintaining those actions that are rewarded and stopping those actions that are punished. But we don't yet have a thorough understanding of when managers and their firms learn the right lessons and take the right actions at the right magnitude and speed in response to the feedback that stakeholders send them. Firms and the managers they employ vary in how effectively they notice, process, and act on both subtle and substantive signals from their stakeholders. Thus, we need to pursue research that mirrors the stakeholder cognition issues proposed in Chapter 10, sorting out how well different firms process varying stakeholder feedback across a variety of settings.

As we comprehensively chart this indirect path of the business case, we may come upon some interesting forks in the road. Returning to the restaurant interview example one last time (I promise!), suppose you were very nice to the waiter but kind of a jerk to the interviewer. Would you still receive the job offer? The rewards and punishments that powerful stakeholders dole out in response to how firms treat others are unlikely to be independent of how the firms treat these stakeholders. But how these factors interact is unclear. Can a firm disavow the direct demand of a powerful stakeholder yet make up for this transgression with good CSR? Or the reverse: can a firm get away with poor CSR so long as it maintains strong direct influence tactics? Think of Apple or Amazon, two firms with strong customer loyalty and huge profits despite poor CSR records. Stakeholders prefer to transact with firms that are both responsive to their demands and nice to society, but stakeholders do not always have the option to transact with only the nicest firms. How these tradeoffs play out is worthy of further study.

Ultimately, managers decide how to invest the firm's limited time and resources, and they favor investments that, as they make society better off, make a firm's powerful stakeholders more favorably inclined toward the firm, thereby making the firm better off. As we take the steps mentioned above to more accurately model and test the complex indirect relationship between business and society, there is good reason to believe that we will validate a variety of such 'win–win' scenarios, and so help managers to identify these favored investment opportunities. However, it is also entirely possible that we will find that in many instances, it costs more than it pays to be good. Clearly delineating these boundaries will be a huge step forward that will force a reckoning with the reality rather than the rhetoric of the business case for CSR. When we can clearly distinguish acts of CSR that are rewarded in the marketplace from those that are not, business can make better decisions about how to invest limited resources, and society can make better decisions about what to do when it doesn't pay to be good. The next section addresses the role of government in instances of the latter.

(Re)embrace the holy trinity
In 1992, I graduated from the School of Business and Public Administration at the University of Missouri-Columbia. In 2007, my undergraduate school was renamed the Trulaske School of Business. I note this not as an excuse to give a shout out to my alma mater (Go Tigers!), or to highlight the pervasive influence of multi-million-dollar naming gifts on universities, but to point out that somewhere along the way, business has become disconnected from public administration in many universities, and this reflects a broader trend across society. In the 1980s, Reagan and Thatcher were successful in framing public oversight of the private sector as a hindrance rather than a help. Reagan famously quipped, 'The most terrifying words in the English language are: I'm from the government and I'm here to help.' In the decades since, government has become a third wheel in the relationship between business and society, often treated as a burden by both. Yet, if we are to bring business and society into alignment, we need to get the trio back together.

Government has been a willing participant in its separation from the business and society relationship, and business case scholars have been enablers of this conscious uncoupling. Formal regulation is a blunt tool, often producing unintended consequences. If firms, alone or united across industries (see Chapters 7 and 9), can self-regulate, then this reduces the burden on government while increasing the effectiveness of governance – yet another 'win–win'! When the market punishes bad behavior, there's no need for the heavy hand of government; instead, firms have ample private incentive to be good corporate citizens. Studies supporting the business case for CSR have thus bolstered the willing retreat of government.

Yet, as we've discussed throughout, stakeholders have limited abilities to monitor, make sense of, and police firms, so the good and bad acts of firms are not firmly tied to their financial performance. As a result, delegating corporate oversight to the machinations of the market leaves gaps in governance. As conservative and libertarian politicians such as Grover Norquist strive to 'shrink government to the size where we can drown it in a bathtub,' we must be careful not to throw the baby out with the bathwater. OK, so I've mixed bathing metaphors here, but the point is, government serves an essential role in making the business case work, and in protecting society when it does not.

Sure, government can be a hindrance if it interferes in a smoothly working relationship between firms and stakeholders. But without government facilitating this relationship, the business case cannot work. For example, absent regulations requiring information disclosure, stakeholders would have little sense of how firms are behaving. Firms would have no incentive to voluntarily disclose bad behaviors, and stakeholders would have little confidence in the veracity of voluntary reports of good behaviors. Thus, to make the business case feasible in its absence, the presence of government must still cast a strong shadow.

As outlined in Chapter 10, even with perfect information flows, facilitated by strong regulations about corporate disclosure, stakeholders will ignore a sizeable portion of corporate misconduct. Given their cognitive limitations, stakeholders cannot keep track of all of the things that firms are doing, good or bad. And that's a good thing. Stakeholders have better things to do with their limited time and attention than police firms. Come on, isn't it better to spend your precious time reading this great book thoroughly, rather than spending these same few days monitoring ExxonMobil closely? Besides, government shouldn't be offloading their regulatory duties to stakeholders. It's actually supposed to work in the reverse. When startups get too complex, firms hire decision-making specialists – managers – to oversee their firms. When it becomes too unwieldly to hold a town hall meeting about every municipal decision, towns elect decision-making specialists – mayors, councilpersons, and so on – to oversee their towns. Yet, as firms have become more omnipresent, impactful, and complex, rather than turning to decision-making specialists – regulators – to oversee them, we have farmed out much oversight to stakeholders. But stakeholders can't be expected to attend to or even understand the myriad complex transactions of multitudinous firms. Regulators, though, can be. Regulators play a critical role in the specialized task of corporate governance. Through centralized and professionalized management, and with its ability to compel information, government can be more efficient and effective at regulating corporate behavior than can decentralized stakeholders in many instances.

Government is necessary to make the business case work, but all the more so, to intervene when it doesn't work. When it doesn't pay to be good, only government can force firms to be good. In such situations, if there is no cop on the beat, society takes a beating. For example, air pollution in some cities has reached debilitating and deadly levels, and greenhouse gas emissions have contributed to catastrophic climate change. For the welfare of society and perhaps our collective survival, firms must pollute less. In pursuit of this aim, governments have required firms to report on how much of various pollutants they release annually. This requirement has been ample to bring about decreases in some forms of pollution. Expecting that disclosures of their high levels of pollution will lead to punishment from powerful stakeholders, and that stakeholders will respond favorably to news of decreases in pollution, some firms have cut pollution. But this has gotten us only so far. Disclosure laws have been around for decades, yet we are far from retarding or reversing climate change. It is evident that, in many cases, firms do not believe that it pays to decrease pollution. If we seek further pollution reductions, then we need government intervention. Environmental problems can be too 'wicked' for the actions of individual stakeholders to add up to ample collective betterment (Barnett, Henriques, and Husted, 2018). We simply can't get to a sustainable future by relying on stakeholders to motivate firms by shifting their transactions to green firms, and most firms won't do it voluntarily if it doesn't pay this way. Instead, where air pollution has decreased considerably, government has mandated specific pollution reductions, rather than left it to the machinations of the market.

Effective corporate governance is a three-legged stool that includes government, not a tipsy two-legged one that excludes it. To align business and society, and especially to deal with situations in which market mechanisms fail to produce such an alignment, we need to embrace, not expel, government. Society shouldn't be so reliant on stakeholders to prod firms to engage in socially responsible behaviors and to police them when they fall short. Stakeholders are often at an informational disadvantage and their power is typically fragmented. Greater inclusion of government in corporate governance is all the more important as we face major social issues that span countries, while firms forum shop for locations offering the least governance. Sure, government brings with it its own set of problems, but there are certain strengths associated with a strong government that are essential in our complex business environment.

Our charge now is to first figure out when the business case really works, and to use government judiciously to ensure that business and society continue to communicate well enough to keep things in balance. But where the business case doesn't work, let's weigh the costs and benefits of bringing government back in to steady things. It may not be worth its heavy footprint in some circumstances, but government is not wholly bad for business, despite Reagan's whimsical quotes otherwise. In many cases, it may indeed 'pay to be governed.' Perhaps Thomas Jefferson's quote provides a fair boundary condition: 'The care of human life and happiness, and not their destruction, is the first and only object of good government.' Let's at least start there with bringing government back in.

Cross the digital divide
As the constant audible pings and mental tugs of our email and social media accounts confirm, for better or worse we are now firmly entrenched in the digital age. But the literature on stakeholder influence is not. And that's a problem. The digital age has changed how stakeholders exert influence over firms. YouTube clips, Yelp reviews, Facebook rants, and Twitter tirades abound. Yet, much of what we know about stakeholder influence fails to take account of digital age advances (Barnett, Henriques, and Husted, in press).

The stakeholder influence literature is currently based in a world where stakeholder actions tend to be slow and burdensome, often requiring structures to be built to organize social movements over time. However, the digital age has made it virtually costless and instantaneous for anyone to publicly praise or condemn any firm's actions. Just post a clip or write a statement online. These social media postings can 'go viral' in a few hours, quickly gathering the support of thousands or millions, sometimes causing firms to alter their practices overnight.

Because nearly everyone has access to social media megaphones nowadays, it seems reasonable to expect that stakeholders have gained greater influence over firms. After all, if a firm doesn't do right by a stakeholder nowadays, whether that stakeholder is powerful or not, they can quickly subject that firm to a 'Twitterstorm.' Knowing the consequences, firms should acquiesce more readily to stakeholder demands.

That's not what Irene Henriques, Bryan Husted, and I found, though, when we recently explored the effects of the digital age on stakeholder influence. Instead, we concluded that because of (surprise!) cognitive limitations, stakeholder influence over firm behavior has stalled, and probably even declined, with the rise of social media in the digital age: 'Overall, our analysis suggests that the methods that boundedly rational stakeholders use to cope with the overwhelming cognitive complexity of the digital age have retarded rather than reinforced and redoubled their influence over firm behavior' (Barnett, Henriques, and Husted, in press).

It seems counterintuitive to claim that, despite having access to the megaphone of social media, stakeholders have not gained influence until you realize that when everyone's voices are amplified, it becomes harder to hear what anyone is saying. The collective result is a lot of shouting, and not so much action. In the digital age, 'liking' a social media post or 'retweeting' it can make stakeholders feel as if they have acted. Thus stakeholder activism now entails considerable 'slacktivism.' Such actions may have very little or no lingering influence on firm behavior. Moreover, under digital cover, firms can now more easily disguise themselves in order to engage in fake grassroots movements. That is, they may portray themselves as stakeholders on social media platforms and use these outlets to shape the narrative around their good and bad deeds, pushing back against authentic stakeholder criticisms of the firm. Perhaps the biggest challenge of the digital age to stakeholder influence, though, is the fragmentation of media channels, which now enable most everyone to isolate themselves in their own media 'bubbles' and face little exposure to critical or disconfirming information. As a result, once an opinion is formed or an identity shaped, it is very difficult to challenge it. Thus, few online postings and pleas do anything other than preach to the choir.

In the US, we currently have a president who communicates national policy via Twitter. Across the globe, secondary stakeholders can now exert direct and urgent influence over firms. However, extant literature has thus far done little to acknowledge these shifts in the dynamics of stakeholder influence. We need to explore the realities of how business, government, and society interact now that the digital age provides virtually costless and instantaneous communication.

In closing

'The business of business is business,' Milton Friedman famously decreed. And that's fine, so long as there really is a business case for society. If there is, then in a sort of mirrored Adam Smithian fashion, it's not just that in serving their private interests, firms will advance the public good by providing valuable products and services, jobs, and economic advancement; it's also the case that as they pursue the public interest through acts of CSR, they advance their private interests. It's a win–win world, where business and society can peacefully co-exist, prosper, and comfortably grow old together.

Problem is, we don't know exactly when it pays to be good to society. In testing what we presumed was the business case over the last few decades, we couldn't stop ourselves from falling back through the looking glass to search directly for private gains from stakeholder favor, rather than follow the crooked path of advancing society in order to get these private gains. This book is a call to examine the business case for CSR the right way and, in doing so, to find and acknowledge the bounds of the business and society relationship. It's also a call for government to reassert its important role between and over business and society.

References

M.L. Barnett. 2016a. Strategist, organize thyself. *Strategic Organization*, 14(2): 146–55.

M.L. Barnett. 2016b. Mind: the gap – To advance CSR research, think about stakeholder cognition. *Annals in Social Responsibility*, 2(1): 4–17.

M.L. Barnett, I. Henriques, and B. Husted. 2018. Governing the void between stakeholder management and sustainability. *Advances in Strategic Management*, 38: 121–43.

M.L. Barnett, I. Henriques, and B. Husted (in press). The rise and stall of stakeholder influence: How the digital age limits social control. *Academy of Management Perspectives*.

Index

Printed and bound by CPI Group (UK) Ltd, Croydon, CR0 4YY

23/04/2025